Managing Service Delivery Processes

Also available from ASQ Quality Press:

5S for Service Organizations and Offices: A Lean Look at Improvements
Debashis Sarkar

Transactional Six Sigma for Green Belts: Maximizing Service and Manufacturing Processes
Samuel E. Windsor

Everyday Excellence: Creating a Better Workplace through Attitude, Action, and Appreciation
Clive Shearer

Office Kaizen: Transforming Office Operations into a Strategic Competitive Advantage
William Lareau

Cracking the Case of ISO 9001:2000 for Service
Charles A. Cianfrani and John E. (Jack) West

SPC for Right-Brain Thinkers: Process Control for Non-Statisticians
Lon Roberts

Enterprise Process Mapping: Integrating Systems for Compliance and Business Excellence
Charles G. Cobb

The Path to Profitable Measures: 10 Steps to Feedback That Fuels Performance
Mark W. Morgan

The Quality Toolbox, Second Edition
Nancy R. Tague

The Quality Improvement Handbook
ASQ Quality Management Division and John E. Bauer, Grace L. Duffy, Russell T. Westcott, editors

To request a complimentary catalog of ASQ Quality Press publications,
call 800-248-1946, or visit our Web site at http://qualitypress.asq.org.

Managing Service Delivery Processes

Linking Strategy to Operations

Jean Harvey, Ph.D.

ASQ Quality Press
Milwaukee, Wisconsin

American Society for Quality, Quality Press, Milwaukee 53203
© 2006 by American Society for Quality
All rights reserved. Published 2006
Printed in the United States of America

12 11 10 09 08 07 06   5 4 3 2 1

Library of Congress Cataloging-in-Publication Data
Harvey, Jean, 1950–
  Managing service delivery processes : linking strategy to operations / Jean Harvey.
    p. cm.
  Includes bibliographical references and index.
  ISBN 0-87389-675-0 (pbk. : alk. paper)
  1. Business planning. 2. Organizational learning. 3. Management. I. Title.

  HD30.28.H3814 2006
  658—dc22   2005027833
  ISBN-13: 978-0-87389-675-7
  ISBN-10: 0-87389-675-0

Publisher: William A. Tony
Acquisitions Editor: Annemieke Hytinen
Project Editor: Paul O'Mara
Production Administrator: Randall Benson

ASQ Mission: The American Society for Quality advances individual, organizational, and community excellence worldwide through learning, quality improvement, and knowledge exchange.

Attention Bookstores, Wholesalers, Schools, and Corporations: ASQ Quality Press books, videotapes, audiotapes, and software are available at quantity discounts with bulk purchases for business, educational, or instructional use. For information, please contact ASQ Quality Press at 800-248-1946, or write to ASQ Quality Press, P.O. Box 3005, Milwaukee, WI 53201-3005.

To place orders or to request a free copy of the ASQ Quality Press Publications Catalog, including ASQ membership information, call 800-248-1946. Visit our Web site at www.asq.org or http://qualitypress.asq.org.

♾ Printed on acid-free paper

Quality Press
600 N. Plankinton Avenue
Milwaukee, Wisconsin 53203
Call toll free 800-248-1946
Fax 414-272-1734
www.asq.org
http://qualitypress.asq.org
http://standardsgroup.asq.org
E-mail: authors@asq.org

To my wife Carole, for her unrelenting support,
understanding, and courage in the face of adversity.

Contents

Major Abbreviations

PSO	Professional service organization
P2P	Positioning to processes. Refers to the model presented in Figure 5.11.
SDP	Service delivery process
PSDP	Professional service delivery process
CTP	Critical to process
CTS	Critical to satisfaction
CTQ-CTD-CTC	Critical to quality, Critical to delivery, Critical to cost
SIPOC	Supplier, input, Transformation, Output, Customer
PFD	Process flow diagram
FAST	Functional analysis system technique
SMART	Specific, measurable, ambitious, realistic, and timely
VAA	Value-added analysis
FMEA	Failure mode and effect analysis
QFD	Quality functions deployment
IT	Information technology
DMAIC	Define, Measure, Analyze, Improve, and Control
DCDV	Define, Characterize, Design, and Verify

Preface

Professionals are some of the most rigorous and structured people in our advanced economies. They are trained to understand the relationships in a system of complex notions (such as the human body, the legal system, or the laws of physics) and to use different techniques and procedures to intervene and effect desirable changes for the benefit of a client. Yet, a single individual, no matter how competent, cannot single-handedly bring about the solutions that people and organizations need. For all their strengths, and probably because of that training, professionals are staunch individualists and often do not function well in teams, especially multidisciplinary ones. This situation is largely attributable to their lack of understanding of how organizations work. Ironically, they are unable to transfer to the discipline of management the systems' notions that have become second nature to them in their discipline. This book means to facilitate such a transfer.

A process is a system of activities (together with the associated resources) that takes an input and transforms it into an output of greater value for a customer, and it is processes that create value, not individual departments (or centers of expertise) in an organization. Functions contribute to value creation through the part they play (that is, the tasks they perform) in processes. Processes create the benefits customers want by delivering the service, or by making this delivery possible in one way or another. Treating a cancer, for instance, is a process. The input is the patient with an active cancer. The desired output is the patient with a cancer in remission. The transformation (treating the cancer) involves many centers of expertise, such as family medicine, radiology, medical oncology, surgical oncology, and radiation oncology, and value comes from the synergistic interaction of all these departments. Antagonism, or simply a lack of coordination, denies that value, in whole or in part.

Processes embody the know-how of an organization. Understanding the DNA of processes is the key to becoming a learning organization. The classical image of an organization, conveyed by the ubiquitous organizational chart, as a set of functions linked at the top is very convenient for professionals, as it reinforces their paradigm. It does not, however, reflect the reality of value creation. The reader will come to view an organization as a complex system of processes, criss-crossing the organizational chart as if there were no boundaries between functions. Nevertheless, boundaries do exist and are sometimes very hard to cross, thus producing the interference that can be so detrimental to the smooth operation of processes, and thereby to value creation.

The process view of organizations is far from prevalent in organizations today. Professional service organizations may be the ones experiencing the most difficulties in managing processes, as professional *bubbles* create a multitude of rigid boundaries. Professionals focus on their body of knowledge and on accepted practices in their fields. All too often, they pay little or no attention to the way their actions mesh with those of others in the generation of an overall result for a client.

Compounded by the substantial power wielded by professionals–individually and as a group–this narrow perspective results in poor performance.

SERVICES AND PROFESSIONAL SERVICES

People need help, either because they lack the knowledge or skills required to achieve, by themselves, the result they want or because they do not have the right tools, facilities, or equipment. Perhaps they do not have access to the required network or they would simply rather have help than do it alone. Help may take the form of providing information or advice, performing some of the required actions on the customer's behalf, performing some actions jointly with the customer, or assuming full responsibility for delivering the desired results (that is, providing a *solution*).

The book focuses on complex services, that is, services sought because of a lack of knowledge or skills. Complex services fall into three categories: professional services, semi-professional services, and technical services. Strictly speaking, we use the word *professional* to designate a university graduate in an applied field such as law, engineering, or architecture (that is, excluding theoretical fields such as mathematics or philosophy). Professionals often belong to a professional regulating body such as the American Board of Medical Specialties or a state Board of Public Accountancy. Such bodies are needed because these services address very important needs and because the knowledge gap between the client and the professional makes the former vulnerable to malpractice. A constantly evolving body of knowledge, generally requiring compulsory continuing education, and a code of ethics guide professionals in their practice. They are subject to sanctions by the regulating body for any malpractice, including suspension or the withdrawal of practice privileges.

Semi-professional services are similar in many ways to professional services, except that the service providers receive much less training. Insurance brokers, real estate agents, radiology technologists, and electricians, for example, do not need a college education. They do need a permit, however, which can be revoked if they are caught breaking important rules. Their training is not at university level and may typically last between six months and two years. The knowledge and skills they acquire, linked as they are to specific legislation or technologies, is typically shorter lived than that of professionals. In addition, the stakes when they perform their procedures are often lower than is the case for professionals.

Finally, technical services involve helping the customer to use complex products or technology-based services. Computers, telecommunications systems, software, camcorders, Internet access, and satellite dishes are examples of such products, and they are all critical to self-service. I exclude from this category the direct repair of complex products such as cars, aircraft, or home appliances, which are quasi-manufacturing activities, but do include customer support activities (such as training car dealership technicians to service a new model, for example). Technicians providing such services are generally not responsible to a regulating body, but solely to their employers. People use these services in order to be able to perform complex tasks themselves (such as using a computer or a camcorder). Even though the knowledge gap may be very substantial here as well, the consequences of the service are often more immediate and easier to verify than would be the case for professional and semi-professional services.

Why do these three categories of service deserve special attention?

- Professional services[1] are centered on the most important human needs, and it is very hard for the client to assess their quality and thus to make sure of being in competent hands. As mentioned above, the knowledge gap between provider and client gives the former power over the latter, and, like any power, entails the potential for abuse.

---

[1] A term used loosely throughout the book to refer to the three categories of complex services, unless otherwise specified.

- As a class of workers, professionals share a number of characteristics, such as autonomy and independence, which separate them from other categories of workers, and require a different management approach.

- Professionals represent an increasingly high proportion of the workforce in industrialized countries, as machines perform many tasks which add less value (such as many manufacturing tasks) and the tasks that remain are rapidly moving to developing countries. Using these machines, however, requires assistance, a sector of the economy that is growing very fast (and, incidentally, one that is not immune to international outsourcing, as information technology (IT) and telecommunications increasingly facilitate delocation).

- Finally, the management literature has focussed excessively on the process of making a hamburger, for example, to the detriment of processes which create more value, such as the counselling of a dysfunctional couple or helping someone fend off a liability suit. Professional services in general, and professional service delivery processes in particular, remain to this day a blur in the literature—a shortfall that needs to be remedied.

This book is also concerned with the many organizations that provide services requiring a mixture of professional and other services to produce the results that customers or clients want. Hospitals and banks, for instance, cover the spectrum of types of services. These organizations face the added challenge of managing the often turbulent interface between professional services, technical services, and other services. I include internal services as well, such as those offered by the legal or engineering department within an organization.

TARGET AUDIENCE

I have written this book for professionals, semi-professionals, and technical workers, laboring in all spheres of human endeavor, from law to medicine, from accounting to engineering, who are involved or are interested in taking part in managing their businesses. Most professionals, however, even those who do not care about management, could benefit from the book. Indeed, most do assume some level of management responsibility through such activities as:

- Giving instructions to semi-professionals, technicians, or clerical workers, or coordinating the activities of service providers of all kinds

- Assuming a responsibility for practice development, their take-home income depending on how good they are at it

- Managing their own one-person business

- Managing what customers do (customers are very much a part of the service delivery process)

Processes play a vital role in all these activities. The notions, methods, and tools presented in this book present the reader with a perspective on his work that was most likely never envisaged, and which could lead to a marked improvement in their effectiveness.

STYLE

For professionals or managers interested in learning more about how the process view applies to their own environments, I provide hands-on, end-of-chapter exercises. Your own organization and environment constitute the proving ground for the material presented in each chapter. The exercises are structured in such a way that the new theory added by each chapter can be immediately applied to work done in earlier chapters, giving you an opportunity to apply the theories just learned, and so transform knowledge into know-how. Thus, a global picture gradually emerges, as early chapters paint a broad-brush picture of the connection between strategy and processes, and later chapters delve into the specifics of designing and improving processes in a professional service environment.

This book does not shy away from theory, but illustrates it abundantly with examples. All case studies presented here are fictitious and draw on the author's general experience. While the book broadly assumes the context of a for-profit organization, much of the discussion is readily transferable to non-profit organizations. Indeed, the latter also have customers to satisfy, employees to keep happy, and shareholders looking for the *biggest bang for the buck*, whatever the socially desirable *bang* (healthy population, low crime rate, socially healthy families, safe kids, and so on) may be. Such organizations, as illustrated by the health and social services examples used extensively in this book, are also competing for funds with other service providers, and achieving superior performance is just as important to them as it is for private sector organizations.

The book also draws on a broad spectrum of complex services such as legal, financial planning and management, consulting, and real estate services. Complex notions are first illustrated with simple examples, often drawn from the personal sphere (processes occur in the home as well) or simple services (such as restaurants or airports), before adapting them to the more intricate reality of professional services.

Professionals evolving in organizations of all sizes, ranging from the one-person firm to the huge professional bureaucracies that constitute large hospitals, will discover that the process view of the organization is universal and all can benefit from it.

Senior executives who want to explore the potential of a process-based strategic initiative in their organization will find it worthwhile to share the book with their associates and compare notes on the end-of-chapter exercises. While this is not a *cookbook*, it is detailed enough and specific enough to allow experimentation to take place, as well as vetting of the principles and tools of process-based management in an individual's own environment and shaping of an operational change initiative. Of course, large organizations should use a consultant to guide them through such an undertaking. Having experienced the book, however, they will be in a better position to select suitable consultants and stay in the driver's seat throughout the initiative.

ACKNOWLEDGMENTS

I have tested all the methodologies and techniques presented in this book. I have invented some of them, and have adapted and improved many of them. I have combined them in creative ways to suit the specific circumstances of complex services. I cannot, however, claim them all as my own. The content of this book has evolved over more than 25 years of research, teaching, and consulting after obtaining a doctorate in management science. It has been influenced—one way or another—by every business with which I interacted during those years, as a consultant or researcher, by every executive that has attended an in-house seminar or Executive MBA program (thousands, in more than ten countries around the globe), every book and article that I have read during these years of practice. This is what is generally called experience. I cannot possibly give credit to all of them, nor name them all. However, I do most sincerely thank them all. The result, however, is my own paradigm, and any limitations or error that it may still contain are my own.

1

Toward Value and Strategic Advantage through Rigorous Execution

Execution matters. The devil is in the details. Rigor is required to excel in execution.

Strategists can produce a great recipe for making the best pudding. Salespersons can vaunt the pudding until you can almost taste it. Financiers, bringing salespersons along, can raise the money to make the pudding. Human resource persons can recruit the best cook. The proof of the pudding, however, is in the eating. In final analysis, two action verbs are of the essence of value creation here: making and eating. Where there is an action verb, there is a process. This is our topic.

In this chapter, we first make the point that execution matters. We then proceed directly to the heart of the matter, presenting the secret ingredient in the recipe of the learning organization, and illustrating it with a few *short stories*. After presenting, using an intriguing example, a preview of the process design methodology, we conclude the chapter with a discussion of the structure of the book.

1.1 EXECUTION MATTERS

On November 7, 2000, Americans voted to elect the 43rd president of the United States. As one of the oldest standing democracies, the United States has had more time than any other nation to consolidate its deeply rooted democratic foundations. Yet, something went wrong on that day. Punching machines left chads on many voting cards in Florida, raising questions about the validity of the vote. As George W. Bush was proclaimed president, at the end of a prolonged politico-legal drama, doubt remained about his legitimacy—a troubling outcome in any democracy. Was the intent of each Florida voter correctly interpreted and counted? The world might well be a very different place today had the voting process flawlessly produced the output that it was meant to produce.

Early in the morning of September 11, 2001, busy travelers lined up at several New England airports to clear security before boarding their flights. The security clearing process is meant to block anything or anyone that could represent a risk to the safety of the flight from boarding the aircraft. That morning, there were at least four defects in that process. Had the process performed flawlessly, the world would be a different place today.

At 7 a.m. on the morning of December 26, 2004, tsunami waves hit the coast of Indonesia, killing upwards of a quarter million people. While there had been much discussion and efforts

1

dedicated to installing a tsunami detection system, none had come to fruition. However, the Indonesian town of Banda Aceh, the town nearest to the epicenter, had an earthquake monitoring station. Over 10,000 cell phones were operating in *international roaming* mode in Sri Lanka (death toll upwards of 30,000), some 1600 km (about two hours, at tsunami speed) away. Unfortunately, the Banda Aceh monitoring station could not send a message, because the tsunami destroyed the phone network before they could make a call requesting that a message be sent to each one of those phones. That a tsunami would destroy the power grid and phone system in the event of a tsunami was a probability. Had a satellite phone been included as part of the process, thousands more would be alive today.

Think globally, act locally. The value of a great plan occurs when flawless execution takes place. In any sphere of human endeavor (political, social, economical, technological, or environmental), flawed execution of a good plan, just like flawless execution of a bad plan, deny the results you seek, and is a waste of time and resources. Some are better at strategic thinking, that is, viewing the forest as a whole. Others are more comfortable in the realms of execution, focusing on trees, branches, and leaves. Few people, however, are equally versed in both aspects of performance. Thus, the risk of a disconnection between strategy and action is very real. Establishing and maintaining this connection as environments evolve cannot be left to chance: it has to occur by design.

Whereas the consequences of the flawed voting process in Florida were global, the problem was strictly one of local execution. Better card punching would have eliminated the problem. They did the right thing wrong. A combination of design and execution issues, on the other hand, is at the root of the flaws in the safety inspection process at airports. The terrorists knew that the various blades they brought on board were not formally prohibited, since those who designed the process did not think that a plane could be hijacked the way these four planes were. As well, the inspectors, who are trained to be suspicious of anything unusual, did not notice anything untoward in the behavior or luggage of the four terrorists. They did the wrong thing wrong.

The international organizations involved in exploring the technical and financial feasibility of a tsunami detection system were looking for the *integrated system* that would solve the problem. Not a misguided pursuit by itself, of course, but one that can be counterproductive if it drags on and prevents fixes to the current process. "All my life," once said French director and actor Sacha Guitry, "I looked for the ideal woman. When at last I met her, I did not marry her: she was looking for the ideal man." In other words, the search for the best can easily become the enemy of the good. In many organizations, such searches often become red herrings and reflect the organization's lack of rigor in analyzing and fixing existing processes.

All three examples reflect a failure to explore what could happen, what the consequences would be if it did, and how it could be prevented. Monday morning quarterbacking is easy, but not very useful. Prevention is tough, requiring much rigorous analysis, but it creates much more value. Failure mode and effect analysis (see Chapter 10), for instance, is a well-known technique that would have allowed the organizations involved to identify and assess these risks and guide them towards a solution. The fundamental problem is not that we do not know how to design and operate processes that deliver, but rather that many organizations lack the rigor required to do it right.

1.2 THE DNA OF THE LEARNING ORGANIZATION

In this section, the book focuses on how organizations learn, fail to do so, or worse, acquire superstitions. We show that rigor lies at the root of all learning and explore the linkage between processes, rigor, and organizational learning.

1.2.1 Learning and Superstition

The example in Box 1.1 illustrates how superstition drives much of what we do. Helen is disciplined and proud of her cooking skills. She probably has much success with her ham. She may attribute part of that success to cutting the tips off of the ham. She may even keep it a secret that she only tells her best friends. We call this attribution error. The cutting of the tips does not cause her success. Her success stems from other things (or variables) that she does. Because of this attribution error, she puts much discipline in perpetuating a wasteful action (or non-value-added action), while the truly critical aspects of what she does are repeated mindlessly, and may be lost one day, much to her dismay, because she is not aware of their importance.

Box 1.1: Why do you do it that way?

Issue: *Knowledge vs. superstition—take one: family life*

A few months into their marriage, a man watches his wife preparing a ham for dinner. She unwraps the football-size piece of meat, places it on a butcher's block, carefully cuts both ends off of the ham, throws away the tips, and places the ham in a slow cooker.

"Why do you that honey? Ham is very expensive, why throw away the tips?" asks the man.

"You're not going to question the way I cook dear, are you? I've been doing that for years. Daddy taught me. As you know, when it comes to cooking, he is world class."

"Yeah, I know he says that a lot . . . No, no, I'm not questioning, just curious. Still, I don't understand. Why is it better to do it that way?"

"I think it has something to do with all the fat ending up there, or was it that this part is really tough . . . Honestly, I'm not sure. You know, there are so many things you have to do carefully in cooking, you can't remember the reason for every single one."

"But why would the fat end up at the tips? Or why would the tips be harder? It does not make sense to me."

"You ask too many questions. Why don't you prepare the salad and set up the table, or we'll never be ready on time."

"Sure, I was just about to do that."

The following weekend, Daddy is having the kids over for a barbecue. As the man watches daddy put on his world-class performance, the man thinks back on the ham discussion.

"Dad, Helen and I had this discussion the other day . . . " and he goes on to tell the story. "So why is it better to cut the tips off of the ham?"

"Oh that! Well, I learned cooking the hard way. My mother was so busy, she did not have time to teach me anything. But I have a keen eye. Everybody said she was the best, so I did not have to look any further. I watched carefully as my mother performed this procedure. You know, son, I've learned it from the best, that's why I'm the best now. But if you want to know why, you'd have to ask her. Me, I don't know, and if truth be known, I don't care."

"Ignorance, indifference, and mindless repetition," the man thought, "the key to world class cooking! Now, here's a lesson I better keep to myself." Soon after, during a family reunion to celebrate Granny's 80th birthday, the man takes the opportunity to pursue his enquiry.

"Granny, why is it that you have to cut the tips off a ham before cooking?"

Continued

Continued

> "What are you talking about son? Why, I have not done that for forty years! Funny you'd know this. We were very poor you see, and I only had one small cooking pot. On those rare occasions when we bought a ham, I had to cut the tips so that it would fit!"

The origin of this superstition is Helen's blind faith in her father's cooking skills and in what he taught her. Implicit transmission of knowledge, such as the father observing his mother, or explicit transmission, such as the father teaching Helen how to cook a ham, is a double-edged sword. It can perpetuate and reinforce knowledge or superstition. In other words, when it comes to training, garbage in, gospel out. The father created the superstition and reinforced it by building a rationale around it after the fact and teaching it to his daughter. Then it became part of the family culture (albeit a tiny part . . .): "that's the way we do things around here." It is easy to lose touch with the *why of things* when a process is repeated very often. Whether in a family or business setting, you are the same person, subject to the same limitations. Businesses, like families, are social organizations. Once a belief is engrained in the culture, it is very hard to change.

How are beliefs created? Through a mixture of faith (learning it, explicitly or implicitly, from someone you trust), logic, and experience. Science is a self-correcting process of discovery. You observe a phenomenon, correlate what you saw with what you know (your knowledge base), formulate a hypothesis, test it, and learn something. If the experiment fails, you reject the hypothesis and formulate a new one. Science progresses toward truth from one failure to the next. As Thomas Edison once said, after numerous failed attempts at creating the light bulb, "No, I haven't failed a hundred times. On the contrary, I have successfully proven that these hundred ways do not work!" This is indeed worthwhile knowledge. Such progress, however, only works if a number of factors are present: inquisitive observation with intent to learn; thorough understanding and analysis of the facts and current knowledge base to formulate a hypothesis; and careful design of experiment, analysis, and interpretation of results. Lack of rigor denies the progress and lets a failure be just a failure, rather than a step forward on a learning path.

1.2.2 Processes and Learning

A defect or failure in a repetitive process, from which we do not learn, is one that we are condemned to repeat from time to time. As Box 1.2 shows, a defect from which we draw the wrong conclusion (superstition) is one that we are condemned to relive for a long time (one is reminded of the movie Groundhog Day, where a character played by Bill Murray gets many chances to get a personal process just right . . .) until (if ever) we succeed in unlearning it. An unexpectedly good result, from which we do not learn, is unlikely to be repeated very often.

Box 1.2: A consultant improves his performance

Issue: *Knowledge vs. superstition—take two: a professional service*

Many years ago, as a young consultant with one of the then *big eight* consulting firms, I was going through my first experience with international executive training. It was a two-week course, with the first week taking place in France and the second week in the United States, a month later. The first week went very well. On the last day, I asked the participants to fill out an

Continued

Continued

anonymous feedback form. On the flight back, while enjoying what I thought was a well-deserved glass of French wine (can't go wrong with that), I started reading the forms.

"They liked it," I thought to myself, as the flight attendant was kindly offering to refill my glass. "Yes ma'am, I deserve it today," I replied. In the section on "suggestions for improvement," most had minor points or had left it blank completely, that is, until I got to an executive who had filled it completely . . . and continued on the other side of the page. Her comments (she had signed the form) were very incisive. The course was okay, but many improvements were required. She had obviously given this considerable thought. I read it thoroughly, several times over. I put aside the other 30 odd forms and kept that one on my table, as I took out my notepad to start planning how I would go about reengineering my course.

I now cut to the chase. The second week was a total flop. One feedback form was laudatory, however, praising me on my openness and willingness to change . . . Most of the other forms though, showed that the class was wondering what happened to me in that month since we had last met in France.

To say that one topic I was addressing in that course was statistical process control goes a long way in showing how in my mind—and in that of most quality professionals and academics at the time—this whole thing about processes only applied to manufacturing. I had about 30 data points. I *selected* one and disregarded the others. I wanted to improve the course and was looking for ways to do it. One person had taken the trouble to give me pointers. It did not occur to me that the fact that she was motivated to do so while the others were not made her an outlier (that is, different in some way from the rest of the class) and that I should deal with it as such. I thought her comments made sense and accepted them as truth, without further validation. In fact, I disregarded the evidence I had in my hands at the time.

Drawing the wrong conclusion from the evidence at hand is obviously much worse than not drawing any and keeping an open mind. Once you believe you know, it takes much evidence—and cost, time, and pain—to convince you to revisit your original conclusion. I drew the wrong conclusion and all the energy and efforts I placed, with the best of intentions, in improving my course resulted in destroying a very good process (the *training process* through which I was putting the participants).

As the example shows, learning and processes are intimately linked at a personal level. This link is even stronger for multi-person processes. Individual learning is one thing, organizational learning is another. An organization has not learned anything until it has changed a shared way of doing things, that is, a process, and has improved its capabilities as a result. Individual members of the organization may learn something and use this knowledge to change some activity. However, unless other members adapt their own activities accordingly, not much will be gained. They will not do so unless they understand and share the reasons for the change and are willing to try something new. Thus, organizations need shared mechanisms (processes) to build and disseminate knowledge.

Obviously, an organization cannot improve a process that it does not know. Organizations that do not know their processes may get a great result one day, but they are at a loss to know why, since they do not know what was done differently on that specific day. Such organizations suffer from a learning disorder—an often-fatal impediment for competitiveness.

When faced with data, we classify it in mental pigeonholes: invalid data, known fact (that is, fits with and reinforces existing knowledge), irrelevant piece of information (discarded), and valid data that contradict existing knowledge. To the learning organization, the latter are considered like gold prospects. Members of such organizations share a common method of ascertaining what is true, what is not, what is uncertain, what reinforces our beliefs, what challenges them. They have a huge advantage over those that do not. The latter have to proceed by arbitrary decree, creating cynicism among employees and cutting itself off from a vast reservoir of learning capability.

Imagine, for instance, someone intent on outliving his peers, who has *optimized* his eating and training habits to maintain an optimal weight. How should he react to a recent study by the U.S. Centers for Disease Control and Prevention concluding that mildly excessive weight does not reduce life expectancy? Options include going back to being a couch potato (and feasting), discarding the disturbing data, and analyzing it. Learning individuals welcome disturbing new facts as a challenge. They see them as learning opportunities, not as threats. So do learning organizations. They value inquisitiveness, rigor, and logical validity more than blind faith.

The continuous improvement mindset is one that pushes you to always be on the lookout for a better way of doing things. That means that you should never use one hundred percent of your resources to complete a process successfully, but rather that you should dedicate some resources to analyzing and understanding the current process, and trying to improve on it. Alexander Fleming's discovery of penicillin in 1928 was triggered by the chance observation (that is, a defect, just like the one discussed in Box 1.2) of a culture plate that had been inadvertently contaminated by airborne molds. The Staphylococci bacteria he was studying had spread in the area immediately surrounding an invading mold growth. He realized that something in the mold was inhibiting growth of the surrounding bacteria. He analyzed the mold and this ultimately led him to isolate penicillin. Someone merely intent on completing the experiment would have cleaned up the plate, griped about laboratory assistants, maybe gone through a little bout of depression, and started over. Fortunately, Fleming had an inquisitive mind, a part of which was on the lookout for anything to learn, including from disappointing process variations.

Designing and running experiments is costly. However, process variations make every repetition of a process an opportunity for learning, and thus a potential source of seeds for improvement. The curious mind will always be alert and wonder "why is this happening?", or "why not?". This will lead to the formulation and later testing of hypotheses. Of course, basic conditions must be in place for this to happen. In an environment where ideas get turned down, experimentation is discouraged and only blind discipline is rewarded, continuous process improvement is not likely to flourish.

1.3 EVERYTHING THAT YOU DO CAN BE VIEWED AS A PROCESS—ANYTHING? ANYTHING!

In this section, the process design methodology (described at length in Chapter 11) is illustrated, using a convenient (and intriguing) example drawn again from the realms of family life (see Box 1.3).

Box 1.3: What movie should we watch tonight, dear?

Prologue: *Anatomy of a defect*

Issue: *Rigorous design of a service process involving subjectivity*
I entered the living room just as Carole was getting the DVD out of its case. The cheese platter had been strategically placed in the center of the coffee table. We were all set for a great

Continued

Continued

movie-viewing evening! I pressed play on the remote control with great expectations as I sat down and reached for my glass of wine.

I thought the first few minutes of the movie were a little strange, but I kept it to myself. "Sometimes the best movies throw you off in the early going, only to surprise and delight you later on," I reasoned. However, as the minutes went by, I was finding it increasingly difficult to silence the little voice that was telling me that something was decidedly wrong. Any remaining doubts were dispelled about thirty minutes into the movie, as I realized that a faint noise, which had been growing stronger, was actually coming from the neighboring couch: Carole was sound asleep!

"There goes our Saturday night," I thought, "a total flop!"

How did this happen? We had planned everything! I had read laudatory comments about the movie in a newspaper article. The excerpts of reviews appearing on the case were sprinkled with superlatives. We had not, however, seen the trailer. Perhaps that was our mistake! Since I am both a movie and a quality aficionado, I saw beyond the defect to the opportunity for improvement that it presented. I also thought that it would be a good test of the robustness of quality approaches, and that I stood to benefit if it worked. I discarded process improvement per se, however, as there was no process to speak of, and thus no starting point from which to improve. The only alternative then was to design one. However, would the process design methodology work in the home environment, especially on such a fuzzy process, taking place as it does in the informal environment of the living room?

It consists of four sequential phases (Define, Characterize, Design, and Verify), each taking in an input from the previous phase and producing an output for the next one.

1.3.1 Define the Problem

Required output: A statement of a problem of strategic importance, together with the perimeter of the process to be improved to solve the problem.

As part of our quality of life, what Carole and I want are enjoyable Saturday nights, watching movies. Since I had been working long hours and traveling a great deal, including weekends, our Saturday evenings together were a rare and precious commodity, to be cherished and enjoyed to their fullest. That made the issue strategic for us.

However, how can we measure an enjoyable Saturday night watching a movie? (If you can't measure it, you can't improve it.) The simplest thing to do is probably for us to rate the movie on a scale of one to 10, where 10 is memorable and one, a total disaster. Those are two ratings (Carole's and mine), though. What if we disagreed? We could take the average of our two ratings, but, if Carole was thrilled and I was bored, that might result in our rating an evening as okay, which clearly it was not. Our notion of an enjoyable movie-viewing evening includes at least minimal enjoyment for both of us. Therefore, we decided to set seven as a threshold—we had to work at calibrating the scale—above which we consider a movie to be good, and calculate the percentage of evenings when we both rated the movie as good. We would consider the evening a failure whenever we did not. Thus the problem statement:

Currently, about one Saturday evening in four (25 percent) is being wasted because of a bad choice of movie. This should not happen more than once a year (5 percent, assuming twenty movies a year).

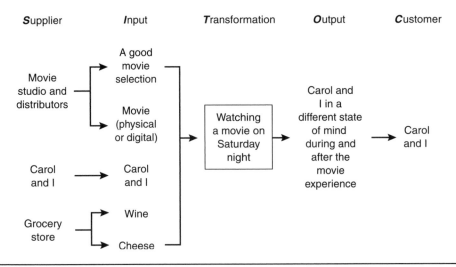

Figure 1.1 Movie selection: Defining the process.

We present the perimeter of the process to be improved in Figure 1.1, as a classic Supplier, Input, Transformation, Output, Customer (SITOC) diagram. The process starts when we both decide we want to see a movie. It ends when the movie has been selected and we are ready to watch it.

1.3.2 Characterize the Process

Required output: Clarification of customer requirements, appropriate metrics, and identification of critical variables

A process can be viewed as a number of variables, and designing a process as setting the values of those variables over which we have some sort of control. What is a variable? A measurable aspect of a process, that is, one for which we can use a scale of measurement. The scale may be strictly nominal (a list of all the values that the variable may take), ordinal (ranking), interval (such as the Fahrenheit scale where the zero value is arbitrary), or ratio (such as the Kelvin scale, where 20 degrees represents twice as much heat as 10 degrees).

If Y is the result of the process (or dependent variable) and X_i is the process variable i (or independent variable i), then the following generic equation occurs:

$$Y = f(X_1, X_2, X_3, \ldots, X_n)$$

which essentially says that what you get (Y) is a function of what you do (X's). In this case, Y is the joint rating of the movie (see Table 1.1). To identify process variables, it is useful to break down the process into its component functions (functional analysis system technique or FAST diagram, discussed in Chapter 3), as shown in Figure 1.2. We selected *Deciding which movie we are going to watch* as presenting the greatest leverage potential for reaching the goal. Thus, it was further

Table 1.1 Movie selection: Dependent variable.

Variable	Description	Value	Condition
Y	Joint rating of movie	0	The movie is rated below 7 by either Carole or I (or both)
		1	The movie rates at least a 7 for both Carole and I

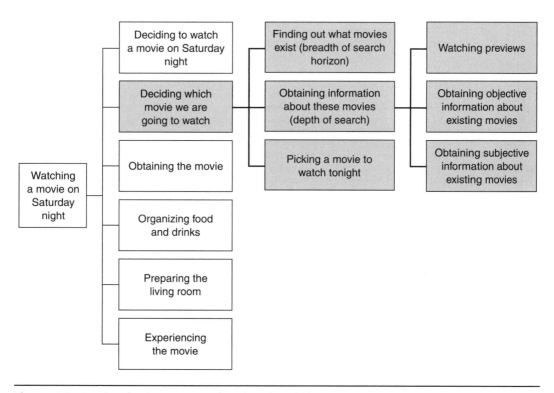

Figure 1.2   Movie selection: Functional analysis (FAST) diagram.

broken down. We thus identified three distinct aspects of the process, and, for each of them, we drew up a list of variables in a brainstorming session (see Table 1.2 for a sample). What might have looked straightforward at first glance is, now that it has been investigated with some rigor, seen to be complex.

In a business setting, this step would be even more complex, and design tools would be required. First, there would be several customer needs, not only one. Understanding them would be a challenge. We would translate them into appropriate metrics using the Quality Function Deployment technique (or QFD, Chapters 6 and 11). We would then identify the most important sub-processes (or process functionalities) by correlating the sub-processes identified in the FAST diagram, with the most important metrics identified using QFD again.

An essential element of the methodology is the recognition that some variables are more important than others. Indeed, Pareto's law suggests that a small number of independent variables account for most of the variation in the dependent variable.

We show a summary of these few vital variables (or critical to process [CTP]—as we will refer to them here), identified through exploration of the causes of past failures and successes, in the first two columns of Table 1.3. In a business setting, data would be available, or we would generate it, to positively identify these variables.

1.3.3 Design (High-level)

> *Required output: A general description of how the new process is going to work.*

Having zeroed in on the few vital variables that we have to improve, it is time to be creative! The next step in the methodology calls for the generation of *process ideas* using each of these variables as an initial prompt. For example: "Find specialized movie recommendation websites" is one

Table 1.2   Movie selection: Independent variables.

Aspect of process	Category of variable	Variable	Type of variable
1. Breadth of search horizon	Exposure	Number of new (not seen) movies we have heard about	Count
	Sources of awareness about movies	New releases Existing movies	List List
2. Depth of search	Samples	Pictures Trailers	Yes or no Yes or no
	Objective info	Director Actors Author (if book) Year Genre Color or B&W Country Language Subtitles Sound system	Nominal List Nominal Nominal Nominal Nominal Nominal Nominal Nominal Nominal
	Word of mouth	Number of opinions obtained Sources Richness of information Ability to relativize to ourselves all the opinions received Reliability of perception source (stability) Rating Awards	Count List Subjective Subjective Subjective Likert scale List
	Validation	Number of data points on any given movie	Count
3. Decision process	Information available at time of decision	Number of movies reviewed at time of decision Ability to retrieve info on movie at time of review	Count Yes or no
	Interchange Carole-Jean	Frequency Quality of communication	Count Subjective
	Joint decision process (once the info is in)	Influence Respect Empathy Honesty Trust	Subjective Subjective Subjective Subjective Subjective

possible answer to the question: "How could we ensure that we consider the broadest possible number of movies?" The last two columns in Table 1.3 illustrate two such process ideas (assigned sequential numbers for future reference) which we generated for each vital variable.

The next step in high-level design is to combine these ideas into alternative overall process concepts, and select the best possible one. These concepts are generated around a central theme which gives them cohesion and coherence. Giving them a name—especially a colorful one—helps make each theme vivid. We generated three initial process concepts (see Table 1.4) in such a fashion. We called the first one *Surf till we agree*, which involves basically sitting in front of the computer screen and surfing the web for information and recommendations whenever we are ready to pick a movie.

Table 1.3 Movie selection: Critical variables and process ideas.

	It is critical that:	Process ideas	
Aspect 1: Breadth of search	We consider the broadest possible number of movies	1. Build a personalized data-base of information on new releases and existing movies, using an Excel spreadsheet	2. Find specialized movie recommendation websites
	We consider both existing movies and new releases	3. Buy an encyclopedia that contains detailed information about all the movies ever made	4. Find a website that provides all this information
	We consider both movies we have never seen and movies that we have already seen	5. Buy rather than rent movies	6. When we see a movie we like, systematically capture that information on the spreadsheet
	We capture information about movies at the time of their initial release	7. Daily capture of movie information we come across on post-its (Keep a stack of post-its next to the TV). Weekly capture the post-its on the spreadsheet	8. Subscribe to specialized magazines
Aspect 2: Depth of search	We do not select a movie on the basis of a unique source of information	9. Identify and tune in to specialized TV and radio programs	10. Subscribe to web-based automated system that e-mails you weekly summaries of movie reviews
	We can relate any objective and subjective information received to our own preferences	11. Read the movie section of the Saturday edition of the newspaper. Capture on post-its. Enter weekly in the spreadsheet	12. Systematically make it a topic during social encounters: "What are some of the best movies you have seen lately?" Discuss the result with Carole afterwards and keep tabs
Aspect 3: Quality of decision process	We both have the option to eliminate from consideration a movie we do not feel like watching	13. Decision system: "List three movies you would like to see tonight, I'll pick one of the list"	14. Decision system: We both make a list of movies we would like to see tonight and discuss a final choice among the movies that appear on both. If there is no overlap, we make a second list
	The information gathered about movies should be easily retrievable	15. Print the spreadsheet weekly	16. Leave a computer open all the time so that the information can be readily accessed
	We both have a good understanding of what the other is likely to enjoy	17. Rate every movie on a 10-point scale after viewing and discuss. Capture the information on the spreadsheet	18. Build a list of "qualifying" factors for both of us—e.g. "Carole is very likely to enjoy any movie where heads get chopped off or with subtitles"

The second concept we called *The old economy solution*, which consists of using a paper-based rather than a web-based solution. The third concept we called *Let's talk till we drop* because it involves largely vocal communication. The ideas linked to each concept are shown in Table 1.4.

Figure 1.3 shows a comparative analysis of the three concepts using the Pugh matrix (discussed in Chapter 11). This involves a systematic comparison of the concepts against a set of criteria, including the metrics identified in the Characterize phase and other practical considerations, using

Table 1.4 Initial process concepts for movie selection and associated ideas from Table 1.3.

Concept name	Summary description	Aspect 1	Aspect 2	Aspect 3
Surfing till we're agreeing	Searching the web when you have to decide	2 and 4	10	16
Old economy solution	Paper based–read and write	3 and 8	9 and 11	14
Let's talk till we drop	Talk about it–no paper trace	5	12	17

one of the concepts (the S column stands for standard) as the baseline. A plus sign is used whenever the concept is superior and a minus sign whenever it is inferior. A weighted sum of the +s and -s is then calculated for each concept.

In Figure 1.3, *The old economy solution* concept turns out to be superior to *Let's talk till we drop*, but *Surf till we agree* comes out on top, being superior to the *The old economy solution* on 17 counts out of 20. This then becomes the new baseline, as further creative search for improvement takes place. A new concept called *Surf and turf* was generated by adding an idea to the baseline (ongoing updating and regular printing of new releases and movie critiques). The analysis eventually converged (other iterations are not shown here) with a process concept we called *Eclectic/ multimedia*. This indeed involves an eclectic mixture of TV and newspaper critiques, web-based searches, books, and discussion. The ideas it includes are presented in Figure 1.4.

1.3.4 Design (Detailed) and Verify

Required output: A detailed description of every aspect of process operation.

Quite a bit of work remains to be done to turn the process concept into an actual process. That is what the detailed design phase is all about: translate the concept into a process ready for pilot testing. In the home context, the detailed design and implementation phases were merged. Process elements to be specified include: the actual flow of the process, the specific commitments on deliverables

Criteria	Weight	Surfing until we're agreeing	Old economy solution (base concept 1)	Let's talk till we drop	Surfing until we're agreeing (base concept 2)	Surf and turf
		FIRST PASS			SECOND PASS	
Failure rate	9	+	S	–	S	+
Cost of initial setup	1	–	S	+	S	–
Time and effort required for initial setup	2	–	S	+	S	–
Time required weekly	4	+	S	–	S	+
Effort required weekly	4	+	S	–	S	S
Weighted "+"		17		3		13
Weighted "–"		3		17		3

Figure 1.3 Movie selection: Using the Pugh Matrix to evaluate and generate new process concepts.

Ideas included in the "eclectic/multimedia" concept
Build a personalized database of information on new releases and existing movies, using an Excel spreadsheet
Buy an encyclopedia that contains detailed information about all the movies ever made
Build a film library and make sure there are always several new ones to choose from
Buy movies on which we have information from many sources and we are convinced we are going to like
Buy movies that we have seen once and would both like to see again
Rent or see in theater movies about which we are unsure
When either one of us, in any situation, hears something about a potentially interesting movie, write it on a post-it note and mention it to the other so that he or she pays attention to any pertinent information that might come his or her way
When we see a movie we like, systematically capture that information on the spreadsheet
Daily capture of movie information we come across on post-its (keep a stack of post-its next to the TV)
Weekly capture the post-its on the spreadsheet
Identify and tune in to specialized TV and radio programs
Read the movie section of the Saturday edition of the newspaper. Capture on post-its. Enter weekly in the spreadsheet
Decision system: "List three movies you would like to see tonight, I'll pick one from the list"
Print the spreadsheet weekly
Rate every movie on a 10-point scale after viewing and discuss. Capture the information on the spreadsheet

Figure 1.4 Original and additional ideas included in final concept.

required from each player, the integration of the activities in the jobs (or activity cycles, in this case) of each player, the procedures to be used for performing the activities, the training involved, the technologies, equipment, and supplies, as well as the installations and layout required.

The last phase is the Verify Phase. *Required output: A fully implemented process, performing at the level initially targeted or better.* It involves verifying that the process's performance, once deployed, will be up to expectations. This is discussed in Chapter 11.

As the epilogue to the story shows, the process did produce outstanding results. However, nothing is perfect, and you have to be ready to switch to a continuous improvement mode, as soon as the process is fully deployed.

Box 1.4: What movie should we watch tonight, dear?

Epilogue: *A self-correcting method of discovery*

Issue: *Continuous improvement*

The movie ended shortly after the last action scenes, as the two protagonists go their separate ways. I did not have to ask a bored Carole how she rated it. Her opinion came right at me: "That one's a clear minus three," she said with a yawn. I personally felt it was more like a plus three, but I knew better than to say that. . .! The comment hit me right between the eyes, however, especially the unspoken part of her laconic statement: ". . .after all the effort we've put

Continued

Continued

> into this. . ." I almost gave in to the feeling of depression associated with failure. However, my lapse was short-lived, driven away by Pareto's famous words, as they came back to me: "Give me a defect, ripe with the seeds of its own improvement. . ."
>
> The good news is that this event took place some six months after the new process had been implemented, and was the first defect it had produced. Because we watch about two movies a month, it took a while to verify that the process had worked according to expectations. The last phase of the methodology does involve, in fact, verification that the process' performance is up to expectations. In the informal home environment, it blends in with the continuous improvement mode that sets in after implementation.

1.3.5 The Process View of the World

Besides the fact that I knew it would raise eyebrows, I chose this example to provide a quick illustration of the design methodology because of a number of its characteristics:

- The output is intangible and much subjectivity is involved in evaluating the quality of the outcome

- The transformation involves information selection, human judgment, and joint processing of soft data

- Even though the activity is not new, there is no process to speak of, as the players had been content to leave these issues to informal discussion and common sense

- This is the last thing you think of as a process

Such processes as evaluating new service ideas, managing the mix of service offerings, exploring new markets, supporting customers, introducing a new customer in the organization, and many more management and professional service delivery processes share these characteristics. Unlike the example discussed here, however, these business processes can be vitally important, and in many organizations still constitute a largely untapped reservoir of improvement opportunities.

Process improvement in organizations requires a concerted effort. An individual may get an improvement idea that can be implemented alone. Sometimes, an internal customer may be convinced to go along with an idea. However, many improvements require resources and concomitant changes in several parts of the process. Organizations learn through project cycles. These learning cycles are discussed in Chapter 9. There are many types of process problems and opportunities. They require different methodologies, different tools, and different approaches to change management. The methodology illustrated in the movie example is quite elaborate, and would thus only be used when the stakes are high and something needs to be designed from scratch.

There are processes that are well designed, but that we do not follow simply because we lack discipline. Reverting to personal examples, the process for driving a car is such a process. Before changing lanes, for example, a driver should not only glance at the side-mirror but also check the blind spot by turning the head. Yet, despite the potential dire consequences of not doing so, how many people do it all the time? Tired, careless, poorly trained, mind on something else, whatever the cause, the process simply needs a little discipline. Better information, education, and training would contribute greatly to better compliance through heightened awareness. Enforcement can go a long way as well. There is little value in designing new processes in organizations that lack the discipline to enforce any process, let alone implement new ones. Such organizations must first take stock of the state of their management. This, all too often comes with a wake-up call, through a culture-changing event such as a major setback.

When a process exists and displays poor capabilities, a question arises: does this process have potential or not? If we can confidently answer that it does, then we should try to fix it. The process improvement methodology is presented in Chapter 10. If the answer is negative, it is better to start from scratch. Sometimes the process does not even exist. In either case, the process design methodology, presented in Chapter 11, is needed.

When it comes to leading the change, the two major approaches available are the Kaizen event and the project. The former typically consists of one week, during which a dedicated team of process workers or managers is assembled and coached, with the express purpose of generating a quantum leap in the performance of an existing process. The latter takes place over a longer period, typically three to six months. A full-time expert, working with a part-time team of process workers and managers, leads it. The characteristics of these two different types of vehicles for change are discussed in Chapter 9.

A typical reaction we get when the idea of a kaizen event is first suggested in an organization: *You can't be serious? We're all up to our eyeballs as it is, how do you think we can spare a team of workers for a full week?* I typically reply with the toaster analogy. Imagine a restaurant whose toaster is not functioning properly, burning most of the toast. Things are so bad that a full-time employee is needed to scrape the toast before it can be served to customers. When it is proposed to the owner to take the scraper away from the task to devote time to adjust the toaster, the owner replies: "Free up someone to fix the toaster? Are you crazy? They're far too busy scraping burned toast!" Things will not get better until some resources are taken away from the daily chores of minding the store to focus on improving the process. In fact, when this happens, things are likely to get worse for a while. Those that remain on the front line will just have to scrape twice as fast for a while, and yes, some burned toast may slip through the cracks while the toaster is being fixed.

You are what you do, and you can choose to see anything that you do—anything really, including such counterintuitive examples such as selecting a movie—as a process, and make it better. This requires resources, which in most cases are obtained through redeployment. The pain will be immediate. The gains will take time (training, process selection, project ramp-up, growing pains, etc). Thus, organizations that embark on such a journey have to cross *Death Valley*. This is the difficult period when the reduction in operating resources and the pain involved in learning new ways hurts, but the promised benefits are still *in the pipeline*. The pressure to revert to the old ways is then such that the initiative is often dropped before the new process capabilities start to kick in.

The process view of things is like a pair of X-ray glasses that allow you to see that activities that might have previously appeared totally unrelated do respond to a common underlying logic. Admittedly, you might feel at this point that all you have been shown is the frame of the glasses, but hopefully that will only result in added motivation to read on.

If I may translate and paraphrase Christian Huygens, a noted 17th century scientist from the Netherlands: nothing is more glorious than to give rules to phenomena, which, lacking any fathomable structure, seem to recognize none and thereby lie beyond the grasp of the human mind. Huygens was talking about statistics. I am talking about processes. At the risk of stretching the point, I might make a last analogy: just as the long sought double-helix structure of DNA unlocks the door to gene engineering, understanding processes gives the key to improving in any activity that is important to an individual. Understanding the underlying constructs of processes will also give you the ability to transfer fundamental lessons learned in one field to others that had hitherto appeared totally unrelated. As your abilities in process analysis and improvement grow, this potential will be unlocked.

1.4 STRUCTURE OF THE BOOK

The quest for value drives customer behavior in the service marketplace. The quest for personal value drives employee behavior in the labor marketplace (both topics are covered in Chapter 2). The quest for economic value drives investor behavior in the financial services marketplace. Companies are competing simultaneously in these three marketplaces. They seek to profitably provide their customers of choice with more value than their competitors provide. The added financial resources made available to them by investors reward those organizations that succeed in generating more economic value added than their competitors generate. They can, in turn, use these resources to recruit and keep the best people. They do so by providing them with more personal value than their competitors can provide, and thus start a positive cycle of reinforcement as better, more motivated employees will provide more value to customers.

Strategy is the company's overall game plan for doing this. Operations strategy is that specific part of the plan that deals with how things will be done (Chapter 5). It is translated into specific goals, farmed out throughout the organization, triggering processes into action (Chapters 5 and 6). Companies must identify, design, manage, improve, and eventually redesign these processes in such a way that the game plan unfolds as intended. Organizations must decide on which processes to focus their limited improvement resources (Chapter 7) and how to mobilize the organization behind the change (Chapter 9). They must choose between trying to improve an existing process (Chapter 10) and designing a new one from scratch (Chapter 11). More difficult yet, they must ensure that the global coherence of their operations is not gradually lost through a series of such finely targeted changes (Chapter 6).

Understanding the inner workings of processes and the principles regulating sets of processes forming a business system is a central underpinning of the book (Chapters 3 and 8), and a prerequisite to understanding the distinctiveness of professional service processes—a species of processes with unique characteristics (Chapter 4). Finally, the book aims to present the reader with a broad framework for understanding how a set of shared fundamental beliefs drives the best professional service organizations in learning (process design and process improvement) faster than their competitors (Chapters 1, 9, and 12). This is the only sustainable source of competitive advantage. Indeed, all other sources (such as new products, patents, or a brand name, for example) are readily copied, while learning faster than your competition cannot be—witness the sustained and growing competitive advantage of Toyota over successive decades. This is why this book is worth the reader's time and effort.

Figure 1.5 presents a simplified model of the learning organization. Processes must simultaneously create value for customers (market), employees (labor market), and shareholders (financial market). The organization's game plan to beat competitors in these three marketplaces is outlined in its strategy. The *learning pump* pumps selected broken or inexistent processes from the organization, fixes or designs them, and puts them back, better. The chapters of the book are classified in Figure 1.5 according to which part of this value creation framework they address. The first six chapters explore the relationship between strategy and processes. Chapters 1 through 5 do so in a conceptual way, while Chapter 6 presents the techniques required to put the theory into action. In Chapter 5, Figure 1.5 (see Figure 5.10) is revisited, exploring its components in more depth, and specifying further the roles of the remaining chapters. Chapters 7 (project scoping), 10 (improving), and 11 (designing), along with Chapter 6, are the *technical* (how to) chapters. Chapter 8, dealing with process management, includes a mixture of theory and techniques, aiming at providing the reader with a more detailed analytical framework to analyze processes. Chapters 9 and 12 explain how and why the learning pump works.

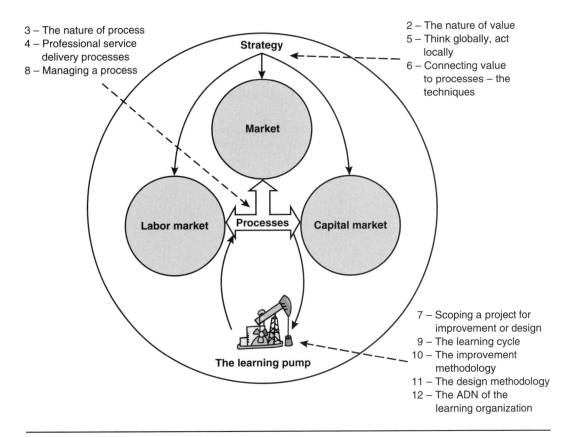

Figure 1.5 Structure of the book, as it relates to the learning organization.

The fact that you are reading this book indicates that you are dissatisfied with the way things are going in your organization, and you would like to find out if there is a better way to run your business. Intelligent people first try to understand. If they do, and if it makes sense, they try it out, cautiously. Try the end-of-chapter exercises, and let the concepts, methodology, and tools grow on you. Remember that the learning mind is like a parachute: more useful when open.

Many end-of-chapter exercises build on each other, that is, you need to do exercise 2.1 to be able to do 2.2. Further, some exercises build on each other from one chapter to the next, leading you, one brick at a time, toward a holistic understanding of connection of strategy to processes. These relationships are shown in Figure 1.6. While all of the exercises will help you gain hands-on experience and appropriate the concepts and tools of the chapters, those that produce an intermediate result that you will need in future chapters, as shown in Figure 1.6 are particularly important.

1.5 SUMMARY

Any organization's strategy is not worth the paper it is written on, unless the organization is able to carry it through. Strategies are executed through an organization's processes. It is in the doing (that is, through processes) that value is created. It is in the doing, as well, that opportunities for learning lie. It is finally also in the doing that what has been learned (that is, newly acquired knowledge)

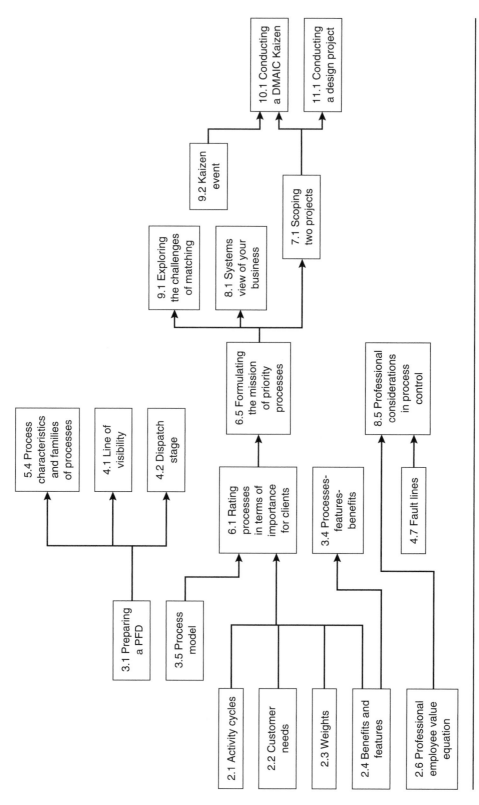

Figure 1.6   Logical flow and precedence relationship among some of the end-of-chapter exercises.

is put to use, creating competitive advantage. The process view of an organization constitutes a different way to understand value creation. The Define, Characterize, Design, and Verify (DCDV) process design methodology stands in sharp contrast with the normal way of doing things. It zooms in, with laser-like precision, on critical aspects of a process, judiciously mixing creativity with rigor.

EXERCISES

1.1 Personal and family processes changed

Identify three personal or family processes that have been changed during the last year or so. This may include such activities as keeping in shape, eating, smoking, planning vacation or a night out, or helping Tommy or Sally do homework. Surely, you have never thought about these activities as processes. For each one:

  a) Describe the inputs and outputs.

  b) What was the trigger that led you to change the process? How long did you wait before you decided to take action?

  c) Describe how you went about the change. How successful were you?

  d) What would you do differently, if you had the chance do it all over again?

  e) Would a more rigorous approach have helped?

1.2 Personal and family processes to change

Identify three personal or family processes that you want to change. For each one:

  a) Identify the reasons behind the change.

  b) Formulate a goal for the change. How important is it to you? How urgent is it?

  c) Describe the inputs and outputs.

  d) Who are the other process players (if any) who have to be involved in the project?

1.3 Rigor—personal

  a) Would you characterize yourself as a rigorous person? Why or why not?

  b) What is the greatest result you have achieved because you were rigorous?

  c) What greatest personal failure can you attribute to a lack of rigor?

1.4 Business processes changed

Identify three business processes that you have changed during the last year or so. For each one:

  a) Did you consider the activities you changed to be a process?

  b) Describe the inputs and outputs.

  c) What was the trigger that led you to change the process? How long did you wait before you decided to take action?

 d) Describe how you went about the change. How successful were you?

 e) What would you do differently, if you had the chance do it all over again?

 f) Would a more rigorous approach have helped?

1.5 Business processes to change

Identify three business processes that your organization has to change in the near future. For each one:

 a) Identify the reasons behind the change.

 b) Formulate a goal for the change. How important is it to the business? How urgent is it?

 c) Describe the inputs and outputs.

 d) Who are the other process players who have to be involved in the project?

1.6 Rigor—business

 a) Would you characterize your organization as rigorous? Why or why not?

 b) What is the greatest result the organization has achieved because it was rigorous?

 c) What greatest business failure can you attribute to a lack of rigor?

1.7 Benchmarking

Are there any rigorous organizations (excluding direct competitors) that you admire, and to which you could gain access (through friends and acquaintances)? If so, organize a visit with a few colleagues and ask them to explain how they manage processes. If not, the local ASQ chapter can probably point you in the right direction.

2

The Nature of Value

To win at the business game, a company must master the art of simultaneously creating value for its customers, its employees, and its shareholders.

In this chapter, three critical notions that will be needed throughout this book are introduced: quality of service, value, and positioning. Quality of service is about satisfying customer's needs, a key aspect of value. Value is *where the rubber hits the road*, that is, the end-point of business processes where the customer receives the benefits wanted in exchange for the time and money invested in the service encounter. A good understanding of how a company creates value in the marketplace is the only possible starting point to design, improve, and manage business processes. The journey toward this goal leads to a discussion of positioning—both in the market[1] and in the labor market. In other words, the only way for the organization to create long-term value for its shareholders is through simultaneous value creation for customers and employees. This is the topic of this chapter.

Figure 2.1 presents a map to help the reader navigate through the chapter. It explores the parts of Figure 1.4 that are relevant to this chapter. Customers' needs push them into action, triggering activities. These activities, in turn, drive customers to seek help. They want this help, or service, as it is called here, to meet their needs, that is, they want quality (Section 2.1). At the same time, they want the *biggest bang for the buck*, called value (Section 2.2). There are many customers out there, with many competitors vying for their business: the company must target the right ones (positioning, Section 2.3) and design a service concept (Section 2.3.3) capable of delivering a superior value proposition. Service employees are the key players in this delivery. Selecting the right ones, offering them a superior job concept (Section 2.4.3), and keeping them happy (that is, positioning in the labor market, Section 2.4) is equally important. All of this must happen as part of a concerted game plan (strategy) capable of keeping shareholders happy (Section 2.5). The key concepts are presented briefly in Table 2.1.

2.1 QUALITY OF SERVICE

A service episode consists of a sequence of events, activities, and encounters that take place between the moment a person becomes aware of a need and the time when the need is addressed, that is, when the person feels that no further action is required. For example, a hunger service episode would start when a person thinks, "I've got to eat something," and ends with the thought, "OK, that's enough." Therefore, our discussion of service quality and service value goes beyond the

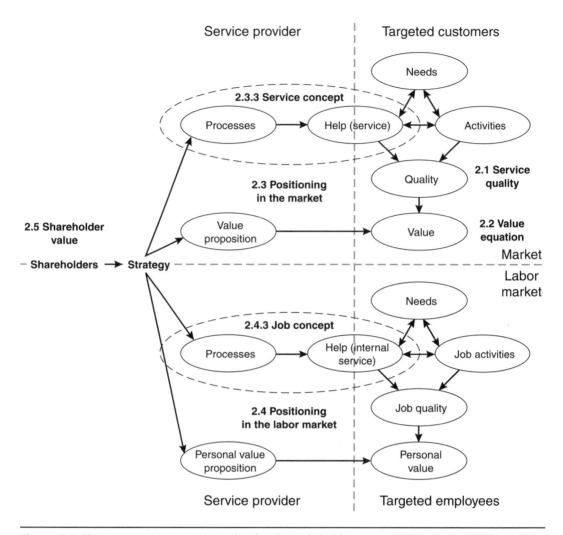

Figure 2.1 Chapter overview: Creating value for the stakeholders.

restaurant service encounter per se, to also include the decision to go to a restaurant, the reservation, the driving, the parking, etc. Using such a broad definition makes it possible to compare alternate ways to satisfy the need, such as cooking a meal at home or having pizza delivered.

The discussion of quality of service is divided into two parts: customer satisfaction and technical quality. Each concept is presented before turning to a discussion of how they are related. Customer satisfaction[2] consists of three components: results, service experience, and self-service experience. First, customers want results. *Results* are the degree of fulfillment of the customer's need. Satisfaction with the results does not tell the complete story, however. It is modulated by satisfaction with what the customer had to do to get the result, that is, with the service experience (what the customer had to do in interaction with the service provider), and with the self-service experience (what the customer had to do to achieve the results wanted). For example, one may enjoy the meal eaten at a restaurant (that may be the result wanted), as well as all aspects of the experience at the restaurant (service experience[3]), but if the driving time was found to be long and

Table 2.1   Key concepts discussed in Chapter 2.

Customer activity cycle	Description of the activities of the customer from the beginning to the end of a service episode.
Needs	A lack of something that a person or an organization wants.
Segmentation	Action of grouping customers in categories that are significant for the organization.
Service episode	Sequence of events, activities and encounters that take place between the moment a person becomes aware of a need and the time when the need is addressed.
Service	The act of helping a person or an organization.
Self-service	The act of helping oneself.
Result	The outcome of the service episode with regard to the main goal of the customer.
Service concept	Service features (or offerings) together with the benefits (effects) they produce for the customer.
Satisfaction	The state of being content with what happened during or after a service encounter.
Value	The ratio of what was received to what was given to obtain it.
Technical quality	The degree to which a professional service was provided in a state-of-the-art fashion.
Job concept	Job features together with the benefits (effects) they produce for the employee.
CTS	Critical to satisfaction: Key customer needs.
Value proposition	Short specific statement about the key benefits provided by a service to a market segment.
Positioning	The place that a company occupies in a market. Defined by the segment, service concept, and value proposition.

unpleasant (self-service experience), next time, an otherwise inferior restaurant that involves less driving may be selected. Of course, a very bad interaction experience can outweigh any positive feelings generated by an otherwise successful service episode. A lack of respect by a service provider, for example, may lead a customer to never come back.

Each of these elements will be discussed in turn, to highlight their meaning for professional services.

2.1.1 Results

A decision is made to purchase a service because of the want to address a need. Because of the need to protect the value of money over time, an individual decides to buy a guaranteed investment certificate. Home owners may hire a real estate agent because they feel that it is the best way to sell their house. Insecurity about an individual's financial future may lead to a consultation with a financial planner. Consequently, customer satisfaction with the result (or outcome) of the service is the customer's perception of the extent to which the initial need was met. How one values a result is strictly subjective and the extent of satisfaction depends, among other factors, on the expectations the person held at the outset. Past experience, the nature and importance of the need, word of mouth, and advertising are other factors that bear on customers' expectations.

2.1.2 Service Experience

Empirical studies (Berry, Parasuraman et al. 1988) of service quality in many industries have resulted in the isolation of four aspects of the service experience that bear on customer satisfaction:

- Responsiveness: The employees' willingness to help and provide prompt service

- Assurance: The knowledge and courtesy of employees and their ability to inspire trust and to reassure customers

- Empathy: Individualized attention that results in the customers' feeling that the employees understand them

- Tangibles: The appearance of the personnel and of the physical setting, installations, equipment, premises, and signage

Again, customer satisfaction derives from a comparison of perceptions after the encounter with initial expectations held before it. This may be misleading, however, as expectations are dynamic constructs that can be influenced by experience and by communication. Indeed, as one is induced—through some chance event—to reduce expectations concerning a forthcoming service experience, an experience that merely exceeds these reduced expectations may leave pleasant surprise, but not satisfaction.

2.1.3 Self-service Experience

A service episode, as defined above, also requires the customer to perform some actions alone, such as finding a phone directory to order a pizza, or taking a walk to the corner grocery store to buy a frozen dinner. Customer satisfaction with the self-service experience is therefore similar to the satisfaction one gets from performing any task, and may include any or all of the following aspects:

- Did it work the first time?

- Were instructions clear?

- Were the tools appropriate and available?

- Was my skill level appropriate?

- When I needed additional information, was I able to access it immediately, on my own?

- When I needed help from someone, was it immediately available?

- Was the work environment pleasant?

- Was the work itself interesting or enjoyable?

- Did I learn something that improved my personal capabilities, that is, something that I may use in the future?

The self-service experience can be broken down into four parts:

- Actions performed in the service provider's *physical service system* (that is, on the premises). Using a terminal to access a database on a real estate agent's premises or filling out a form (alone) in a bank fall in that category. Person-to-person phone calls are also included in this category–even though physical presence is not involved–because it consists of synchronous human-to-human interactions (this is discussed in Chapter 4).

- Actions performed in the service provider's *virtual service system*. This refers to web-based services such as tracking one's portfolio in a financial portal or searching for comparable properties to estimate market value.

- Actions performed in *other providers' service systems* (physical or virtual). Carrying on with the portfolio example, this includes checking out a competitor's site, simulating the long-term effect of various investment strategies in yet another site. For the customer of a discount real estate broker, designing a classified ad online to sell a house would also fall into that category.

- Actions performed in the customer's own environment, that is, in one's *personal service system*. Using financial planning software, capturing and editing photos electronically, reading about investment strategy, or re-painting the backyard fence fall in that category.

Table 2.2 presents complete examples of the components of service quality for hypothetical customers of insurance and accounting services.

This section is concluded with three caveats. First, while understanding these distinct concepts is important, you should not forget that they are correlated. The separate and joint efforts of the provider and the customer are required to produce results. A poorly designed or poorly managed service encounter or self-service experience will not only produce an unsatisfactory experience, it will also deny the desired results. Witness the faulty diagnostic that can result from a patient's failure to mention a symptom, because of embarrassment discussing that information with the doctor. The same is true for risk-averse investors leading their financial advisors to think they are risk prone.

Second, in services—such as professional services—where the customer may not be able to evaluate the true result (because of limited knowledge in the field, see Section 2.1.5), satisfaction with the experience has an important impact on the perceived results, even though the two may be totally unrelated. For example, an airline passenger may surmise from a well-run passenger cabin that the cockpit crew or the maintenance crew also run a tight ship, while there is little if any relationship between the two. Clean restrooms in a fast food restaurant might lead customers to infer that the kitchen is equally clean. Hence, in many services, and particularly in complex services where results are difficult to evaluate, the immediate negative impact of an unsatisfactory service encounter on service quality is compounded by its delayed impact on the perception of results.

Third and last caveat: there are services (tourism and entertainment, for example) where customers are essentially looking for an *experience* (Pine & Gilmore, 1999). One watches a movie for viewing pleasure or maybe to change the mood. One goes trekking in Tibet to experience new sensations, enlarge perspective or get in touch with the inner self. While the quality of such service still consists of the three elements presented above, results are very hard, if not impossible to distinguish from the experience itself.

2.1.4 Technical Quality and Leadership

One factor that complicates matters in understanding customer satisfaction and trying to improve it, is that people (apparently) purchasing the same service may well be looking for different results. One person buying real estate services to sell a house, because of dire need to pay a debt, may be mostly preoccupied with speed and much less with the actual sales price. Another seller's sole concern may be to generate enough money to buy a condominium he wants, with speed being merely a *nice to have* aspect of the service experience.

Further adding to this ambiguity is the fact that customers do not always know what they want. Indeed, professional services are characterized by a knowledge gap between the professional and

Table 2.2 Components of value: Two examples.

Components of Providers value →		Insurance claim	Income tax preparation
	→	Insurance company (primary) car dealer (secondary)	Accountant
Results		Car is fixed	Accurate return is filed on time (legal obligation is fulfilled; I'm not paying a cent more than I have to)
Service experience		Phone conversation with adjuster. Personal encounters with service manager (at the Dealer's)	Phone calls and meetings with head accountant and technicians
Self-service experience	In physical service system	Keeping busy reading a magazine in the waiting room	Filling out a couple of forms
	In virtual service system	Checking various addendas to the policy online	Consulting the checklist so I don't forget any paper I may need
	In other providers' service systems	Checking regulations on the overseeing agency's site. Getting other expert opinion and cost estimates on my own	Checking the latest government budget. Getting some receipts I needed (some face-to-face, some online, some by phone). Calling an online expert (on a per minute fee basis) to verify a deduction the accountant thought would not be allowed
	In personal service system	Writing and sending a letter to the insurance company	Building an Excel spreadsheet to check the totals and compare with previous years
Price		Insurance premium	Accountant's fee
Total cost		Premium + deductible + charges for other cost estimates + mileage + allocated cost for computer and internet access	Fee + online expert fee + some cell phone, computer and Internet charges + mileage

his client. We use the word *client* instead of customer to underline the fact that the relationship goes beyond the mere commercial relationship–implied by the word *customer*—between a buyer and a seller[4]. The knowledge gap means that the client is often unable to specify the true needs. The client does of course know the symptoms and is able to express a wish that they go away. However, the client also often goes further and attributes—often mistakenly—the symptoms to a specific source or sources. Indeed, this may lead to a choice of professional whose perceived specialty is fixing these specific sources of problems.

Hence, the customer's inability to formulate a diagnostic generally does not prevent an attempt to do so, instead of leaving that most complex part of the service to an expert ("I'm quite sure that my heartburns come from a gastric ulcer"). Consequently, the client may end up at the door of the wrong specialist or reach the right specialist but ask for the wrong procedure. This is a common occurrence in all professional services, from the management consultant responding to a flawed request for proposal, to a patient asking the doctor to prescribe a specific medication or procedure, to the engineer realizing that the slight machine performance problem is really a major design flaw.

Formulating a diagnostic is a distinctive feature of professional work (see Chapter 4). Since this diagnostic is often at odds with the client's own preconceived idea, the ability to convince the client to abandon the latter for the former is an important professional skill. That same skill is also needed to convince the client to accept the prescription as well. These are not selling skills, but leadership skills. Leadership is the ability to form in one's mind a crisp image of a reality that does not yet exist, to make that same image—equally crisp—appear in the mind of others, to make it believable and desirable, and to show the path to take to make it become real. This applies very well to professional work.

Be it the surgeon in the operating room, the notary public in an office, the financial planner at a computer, or the architect at the drawing board, when a professional makes a mistake, the client pays a price. The importance of the service to the client, coupled with the knowledge gap mentioned earlier, imply that the provider is in a position of power over the client during service delivery. Where there is power, there is potential for abuse. Therefore, society deems it essential to insulate the professional–client relationship from any undue influence that the commercial dimension of the transaction may exert on professional judgment. This is achieved by removing some decisions from the realm of business authority and entrusting them to professional regulatory or self-regulatory bodies. This adds to the complexity of managing professionals in general, and professional service organizations (PSO) in particular.

It would indeed often be easy for a professional to use the power or influence achieved over a customer through the service encounter to slant advice and prescription in such a way as to gain financial advantage. Professional ethic is about respect–that is, using the power of influence solely in the client's best interest. The potential for abuse is even greater in situations where the latter will not be able to detect it–that is, in situations where the result of the service episode is very difficult to assess with any objectivity in the short to medium term, let alone trace to professional abuse.

Client satisfaction (dissatisfaction) is defined in this book as the extent to which the customer's perception of benefits received after the service episode exceeds (falls short of) initial expectations. The foregoing discussion makes clear that, as important as it is, customer satisfaction cannot be a complete measure of the quality of professional services. That is why a professional service is characterized as having *technical quality* (to distinguish it from customer satisfaction) if it is performed in accordance with the state-of-the-art in the field. Most of the time, clients are not good judges of this. That does not hold them back, however. They interpret what they see and hear, however unrelated, and draw conclusions on important service aspects that they are in no position to assess. These conclusions guide them in current and future decisions.

2.1.5 Customer Satisfaction and Technical Quality

Figure 2.2 shows four possible situations resulting from various combinations of technical quality and customer satisfaction (Harvey, 1998). Quadrants 1 and 3 are particularly interesting (clinically speaking). In quadrant 1, professionals perform with a high degree of technical quality, but customers are not satisfied. This can occur in PSOs that value technical proficiency and ethics and pay no attention to customer expectations and perceptions. In other words, the firm produced the best possible results for the client, but the client does not know. This is often associated with professional arrogance and is not sustainable unless competition is somehow limited—otherwise the firm would soon be out of business.

Examples of this may include highly specialized medical services and notaries in underserved remote areas. This may also occur in internal professional services from the finance, engineering, or IT departments. Moving to quadrant 4 requires a change in the professional mindset. They must become more inclined to listen to the feelings of their customers and explain what they are doing and why it is needed. This is essential in order to adjust and meet clients' expectations and perceptions, and to assume fully their leadership role.

In quadrant 3, the situation is reversed: aspects of the service delivery that influence client satisfaction are well managed, but the clients are essentially being cheated, that is, they are not getting the service they should get, but they are (as yet) unaware of it. Such a manipulative environment may prevail as long as the organization can get away with it. Some forms of alternative medicine fall in that category. Despite scientific evidence that they do not produce any effect, some people will be duped, assuming that they are effective and never being able (or actually trying) to verify this assumption. Individual professionals in all fields can also *lead clients down the garden path* using their superior knowledge or intellect to conceal, interpret, or manipulate events, data, and facts to their advantage. Some use statistics as a drunkard uses a lamppost, for support, not for illumination (attributed to Mark Twain). Sometimes the behavior is clearly fraudulent. More often, it may simply involve complacency, lack of rigor, or convenient *little white lies* or omissions. These individuals and organizations are, of course, vulnerable as, when clients learn the truth—helped in this, at times, by competitors—they are liable to feel cheated and become inexhaustible sources of negative word of mouth.

2.1.6 Before and After

Before the service encounter (ex-ante), the professional is dealing with expectations; after, with perceptions. Thus, the customer bases a purchase decision on experience with similar services, modulated by any factor such as brand name, publicity, word of mouth, and interaction with sales-

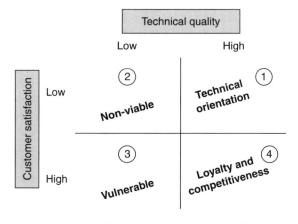

Figure 2.2 Customer satisfaction and technical quality.

persons, which may lead to an expectation that the experience will be different. The actual service experience, including all the subtle clues that customers read from verbal and non-verbal aspects of service encounters, affect perceived quality (an ex-post concept). As well, while service failure may deny results to the customer, impeccable service recuperation is an integral part of the service experience, and its impact on perceived quality may be determinant. It can lead customers to expect high quality results in the future, thereby enticing them to come back despite the failure.

Figure 2.3 illustrates the time relationship between customer satisfaction and technical quality. The grey funnel-shaped area shows the evolution of the breadth of expectations and perceptions about a service encounter. Initial expectations may vary widely. The service encounter modulates initial expectations, transforming them into (ex-post) perceptions, which are less variable then expectations–that is, closer to technical quality. Technical quality does not exist before the service encounter. The gap between perception and technical quality, which can be substantial at the time of the encounter, will tend to decrease over time, as customers learn (from experience and other sources) and as some delayed consequences start to appear. For example, design flaws in a house may show up in time or limitations, or a financial plan error may become more obvious as the economy goes through its multiple possible states.

2.2 THE CUSTOMER VALUE EQUATION

In this section, the notions defined above are used to introduce one of the most important—and debated—notions in business today: value (see Figure 2.1). It is first defined as a ratio, before turning to a discussion of how to use it as a framework to better understand customer behavior, both in the case of the static single transaction and in the dynamics of an evolving relationship.

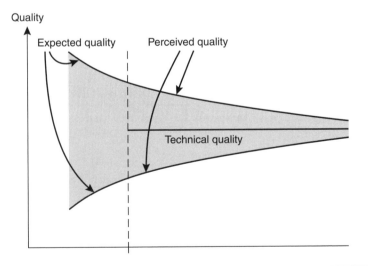

Figure 2.3 Time evolution of the relationship between expected quality, perceived quality, and technical quality in professional services.

2.2.1 Value as a Ratio

In any commercial transaction, value is the ratio of what the customer obtained over what it cost. Thus, in its simplest form, the basic value equation can be formulated as follows:

$$\text{Basic value} = \frac{\text{Results}}{\text{Price}}$$

No organization can survive without being competitive in basic value creation for its targeted customers. However, this equation does not tell the complete story: it does not take into account the customer's experience. Consequently, if the overall cost of a service is defined to include (in addition to the price) any additional expense incurred outside the service system, such as mileage cost to drive to a restaurant or Internet access cost for online banking, a more complete equation can be formulated:

$$\text{Value} = \frac{\text{Results} + \text{Service experience} + \text{Self-service experience}}{\text{Overall cost}}$$

where each term stands as defined earlier. The additional terms (price and total cost) are illustrated in Table 2.2 for the case of insurance and income tax preparation. Carrying on with the restaurant example (see Figure 2.4), on any given night you have a choice between preparing a meal at home and eating out. The decision hinges on such factors as:

- Your cooking skills (results)

- Your enjoyment of going to the grocery store, that is, walking or driving to the grocery store (self-service experience)

- The actual shopping (service experience)

- The pleasure you may derive from preparing the meal (self-service experience)

- The fact that the restaurant may cost $75.00 (including the cost of a 30 minute drive) compared with $10 (including the cost of the ingredients, energy, and appliance amortization) for the home meal.

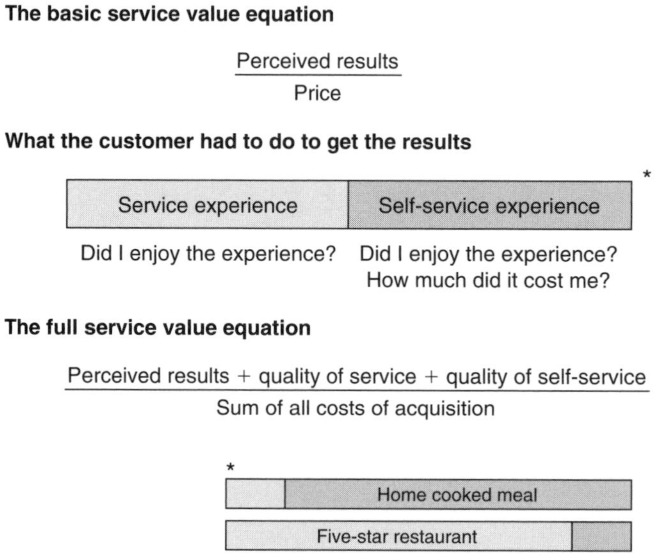

The basic service value equation

$$\frac{\text{Perceived results}}{\text{Price}}$$

What the customer had to do to get the results

Service experience	Self-service experience *
Did I enjoy the experience?	Did I enjoy the experience? How much did it cost me?

The full service value equation

$$\frac{\text{Perceived results} + \text{quality of service} + \text{quality of self-service}}{\text{Sum of all costs of acquisition}}$$

*

Home cooked meal

Five-star restaurant

Figure 2.4 The value equations.

If you are trying to lose weight, the very nature of the results you are seeking is different from those of a customer looking for a gastronomic experience. In that case, the value of the added control over calorie intake that you get from preparing a home meal (self-service experience) may outweigh your enjoyment of a five-star service (service experience).

In the age of Internet, understanding the value equation is imperative. Technological advances and the coming of age of a new generation—one that, having been raised in an environment where technology is omnipresent, enjoys the control and convenience that it provides—gradually and continually tips the balance of value, in many service industries, toward solutions that include an important dose of self-service.

Economic theory holds that a person spends money in such a way as to maximize the satisfaction achieved per dollar spent. In most situations, however, customers are content with *satisficing*[5] rather than *optimizing*, that is, stop the search and settle as soon as they find a service that meets their minimal requirements. A person could, however be expected to consider any new value proposition which appears likely to produce a *bigger bang for the buck*, that is, have greater expected value than the perceived value received from the current provider.

2.2.2 Transactional and Relational Approaches

The very notion of value is different, depending on whether you look at it from the point of view of a one-time transaction or that of an on-going relationship. In a transaction, both parties are solely interested in getting the most out of the exchange at hand. In a relationship, since both parties expect that they will be doing business again in the future, they look at every interaction as both an immediate source of value and an opportunity to influence future value streams. As a result, either party may be willing to settle for less value than they would normally expect out of a transaction, in exchange for expected future benefits. In other words, both parties may be willing to invest in the relationship.

The investment the customer may be willing to make often has to do with quality of self-service. As the customer is learning how to use the provider's physical and virtual service systems, there may be acceptance that it takes longer at first and that mistakes—even service failure—can occur. As customers become more familiar with the system and adapt to it, however, and as the provider gets to know the customer better, both stand to benefit: the customer will get more value and become more adept at evaluating the result and the provider will get a bigger *share of wallet*, reduce costs, and benefit from well-targeted referrals.

2.2.3 How the Search for Superior Value Drives Customer Behavior

Expected value (ex-ante) and perceived value (ex-post) preside over people's decision to come back for more, search for alternatives, respond to ads, respond to a friend's inquiry, or give advice to a friend. Perceived value lies at the root of business success or failure. Thus, it pays to understand the service value equation well.

Table 2.3 shows possible customers' responses to five situations. A low basic value equation (1) will lead customers to actively search for an alternative, irrespective of the quality of the associated experiences. A high basic value equation, coupled with positive service and self-service experiences, (2) leads to the development, maintenance, and growth in the relationship, with all the benefits that this entails.

In situation (3), results are good, service quality is high but the self-service experience is unsatisfactory. To illustrate, imagine an investor who is gradually achieving investment goals and enjoys the financial advice and the regular interaction with administrative personnel. However, an inordinate amount of time is spent following up on investments, that is, putting all transactional and account statement information together to find out financial standing. One solution may be for the investor

Table 2.3 Customers' reactions to various satisfaction conditions.

#	Basic value equation	Satisfaction with service experience	Satisfaction with self-service experience	Action required
1	Low	*	*	Explore all options right away
2	High	High	High	Maintain or increase relationship
3	High	High	Low	Look for full-service supplier or improve your self-help process
4	High	Low	High	Look for alternate–especially with more self-service
5	High	Low	Low	Look for full-service provider and keep an eye open for breakthroughs in self-service technologies

to improve the personal service system through building an electronic spreadsheet or buying specialized software. The investor could also ask the provider to improve the virtual service system—that is, develop a more user-friendly, real-time statement of account. The investor could look for another provider for that virtual service, or simply contract out the service to another provider, such as an accountant.

In case (4), the situation is inverted: The customer enjoys the self-service experience, but dislikes the service experience itself. Imagine that an investor does all investing online in the provider's virtual service systems and enjoys all the features of the system. However, visiting the provider's office to sign forms regularly and the fact that some transactions are only performed on the phone are both disliked. This investor would then be tempted to look for an alternate provider whose virtual service system is more complete, thereby doing away with the unwanted interactions.

In case (5) finally, the customer does not enjoy any aspect of what has to be done to get good results. This investor is therefore on the lookout for a full-service (turnkey) provider or for a breakthrough in self-service technology (such as the quantum improvement seen in recent years in financial management websites) that would turn an unpleasant experience into an enjoyable one.

A number of factors may cause a customer's value equation to shift from one state to another in Table 2.3:

- The performance of the provider may change.
- The customer may be enticed—through word of mouth or publicity—to sample another provider's fare with higher expected value, with the outcome dependent on the perceived value (ex-post).
- A competitor may come up with a breakthrough service concept.
- Needs may change.
- Self-service technology may improve, that is, a user-friendly, voice-activated 24-7 answering machine.
- The customer may improve capability for self-service through training or personal experience.
- The customer's values may change through a number of occurrences. For instance, the customer may suddenly have more time available or need more face-to-face contact.

It pays to understand, monitor, and manage this dynamic well. Technical quality of service has a direct bearing on it. Customers may come out of a service encounter with high perceived value, only to find out later that they have been duped. On the contrary, they may have received fantastic value and never realize it (see discussion in Section 2.1.4).

2.3 POSITIONING IN PROFESSIONAL SERVICES

Having defined quality and value, how companies can target specific customers and formulate a game plan (strategy) to create more value for them than competitors can now be discussed (see the upper part of Figure 2.1). To do so, a number of strategic concepts are addressed: customer activity cycle, segmentation, target market, value proposition, positioning in the customer market, and positioning in the labor market. A number of examples are given along the way to make these conceptual notions more concrete.

2.3.1 Understanding Where the Customer Is Coming from: An Illustration

Understanding where the customer comes from and where the customer is going is essential to understanding needs and preferences—that is, wearing the customer's shoes. An example is best to explain this (see Box 2.1). Jack and Linda's path is illustrated in Figure 2.5. You can zoom into any activity along this path to better understand the micro-activities involved. Figure 2.6, for example, shows the details of the activity sell the house. At this level, for anyone who knows what kind of people Jack and Linda are, it becomes fairly easy to understand their needs (see the illustrative bubbles in Figure 2.6). Specifically, they can be obtained by grouping the elements (using an affinity diagram [see Figures 2.18 and 2.19]) shown in the bubbles in Figure 2.6 (see detailed instructions in the end-of-chapter exercises).

Box 2.1: Jack and Linda have a vision

Issue: *Identifying customer needs. Formulating a service concept. Positioning a service.*

The week before Jack turned fifty, the younger of Jack and Linda's two daughters moved out of the house, turning it into the proverbial *empty nest*. After considering all their options, Jack and Linda decided to sell their suburban house and to have a new one built in the countryside. They picked a nice village that would still allow Jack an easy commute to his office in town, while affording the couple a better quality of life. Reaching that decision was not easy, involving hours of discussion to build a shared vision of the future they wanted. To turn the vision into a reality, however, they need help, that is, services. Their plan of action started with the selection of a location and the purchase of a piece of land. Then they would design the new house while they were waiting for a buyer for the old one. Construction would then start when they found a buyer, hopefully being completed by the time they moved out.

The results Linda and Jack want can be stated as follows: Getting the best possible net price, reaching a deal quickly, and being able to stay in their house till the new one is ready—that is, for about six months. They would also like the process to be as smooth as possible, that is, to have pleasant encounters and to minimize risks (including surprises). To Linda and Jack, an encounter is pleasant when they deal with someone honest, competent, and trustworthy, and when they do not feel any undue pressure—indeed deal with someone with whom they could become friends. They would like to avoid such risks as fraud, delays, or NSF checks. Jack and Linda's requirements are summarized in Table 2.4, together with the relative importance they attach to each. The weights are

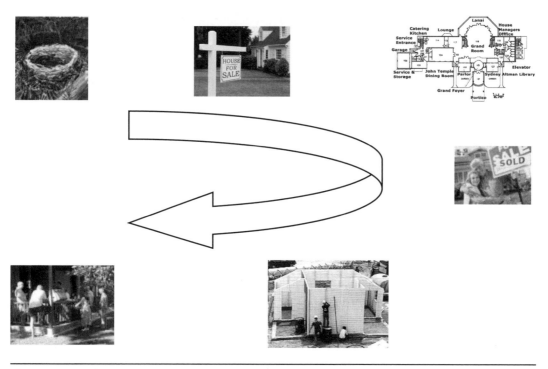

Figure 2.5 Jack and Linda's activity cycle.

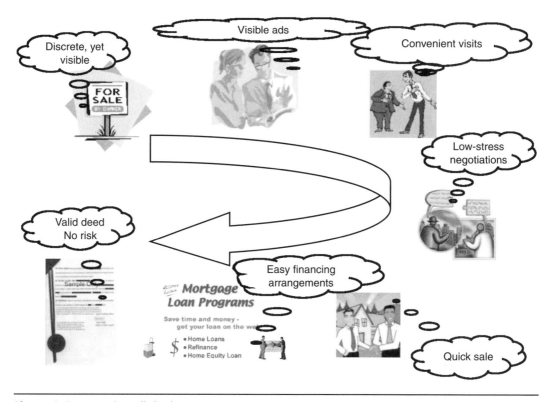

Figure 2.6 Zoom in: sell the house.

Table 2.4 Baby boomers are selling their house: comparing needs.

	Needs	Weights	
		Linda/Jack	Mike/Diane
Results	Quick deal	15	0
	Maximum net price	30	80
	Occupancy in 6 months	15	0
Service and self-service experience	Low risk (fraud, technical glitch)	10	0
	Pleasant encounters	10	10
	Know what's happening	5	0
	Remain in control throughout	10	0
	Ease	5	10

obtained by asking them to spread 100 points between their requirements. Often, the most important requirements, that is, the ones with the largest values in Table 2.4, are called *critical to satisfaction* elements (or CTS).

Interestingly, as Linda and Jack met Mike and Diane—long-time friends who had sold their house the previous year—they asked them what their weighting would have been at the time. They were amazed to see what they came up with (see Table 2.4). In the discussion that ensued, it came out that Mike and Diane were really just testing the market, having noticed a strong increase in property value in their neighborhood. They were ready to move out the next day if anyone met the asking price—and would even find the challenge of finding a place to live exciting. Mike and Diane were trusting people who thought that all real estate agents and notaries were nice and honest people, and that fraud is only seen on TV. Clearly, even though at first glance the two couples had the same needs, they were in fact looking for very different benefit packages.

2.3.2 Exploring How Customers May React to Various Service Offerings

The customer's capability and willingness to get involved in the satisfaction of need is a critical determinant of the nature of the services required, and therefore of the relative value that a customer places on alternate service options. This capability, in turn, is a function of the customer's knowledge of the subject area (medicine, finance, architecture, and so on) and of the ability to use information technology (IT) to access and use the information, advice, and capabilities that can help solve the problem. If Jack feels comfortable with the real estate business and with managing a website, he has many more options open to him than if he feels completely out of his depth in both fields. However, even in the former case, he may still opt for a full service agency based on his evaluation of its cost-effectiveness. This has to take into account his own opportunity cost (that is, things that he will not be able to do if he undertakes this task by himself), whether or not he finds the task interesting, and feels he may learn something by doing it himself.

To sell a house you need to: advertise it; provide information to interested parties; negotiate with potential buyers; close the deal; formalize it in a binding agreement; sign the deeds; and finalize financial arrangements. This is represented in a FAST (Functional Analysis System Technique[6]) diagram—see Figure 2.7. Three basic ways to sell the house are available to Jack and Linda: do it on their own; use a discount web-based real estate service, or use a traditional full-service real estate agent. Figure 2.8 shows, based on the FAST diagram, what each of these might involve for Linda and Jack.

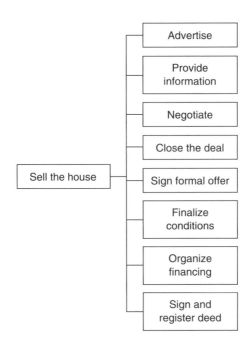

Figure 2.7   FAST diagram: Selling the house.

Assuming that Jack is quite proficient with technology, he can: place ads directly on many websites (some involving a fee); place ads directly in newspapers; design a sign to post in front of the house; or build his own web page to provide photos and information on the house, asking price and conditions. Initial contact can be made through e-mails, messaging service, or cell phone. Visits, negotiations, and closing have to be face to face, without intermediary (called *contact modes*, these are discussed in Chapter 4). They can use a notary, and banks can be used to finalize the transaction. Using a web-based real estate agent would make things easier on the technology side (at a price) and provide greater exposure through access to a widely advertised website. They could also contract additional help, as needed, in negotiation, formalization of an agreement, or any other legal and technical services.

Full-service brokerage, of course, provides the easiest route, but here again at a price. Because of the commission, Linda and Jack thought that this would probably not result in the best net price (criterion 2). However, they felt that the house would quickly get exposure to more potential buyers this way, thus beating the other two options on criteria 1 and 3. As for criteria 4 and 5, they depend on the choice of agent. The discount brokerage option is discussed later in this chapter.

Figure 2.9 shows a hypothetical expected value equation for Jack and Linda. For the sole purpose of illustrating the type of comparisons that go on in the mind of our fictitious characters, we have given quantitative values to each element of the equation. Let us say that Jack and Linda were able to rate perceived results on a scale of 1 to 100, where the latter represents a result perfectly in line with their expectations. That would allow for quantification of the basic value[7] of each of the options. Selling the house through a discount agent would thus come out as the option with the highest expected value.

However, the service and self-service experiences must be considered. Selling on their own involves dealing directly with several providers of specialized services, and Jack and Linda do not expect the service experience to be so good. They also have misgivings about some aspects of the self-service experience. Therefore, "+" and "−" signs are assigned to various aspects of the service experience as upward or downward modulations to that value, gave these an illustrative arbitrary

Function	Sell by myself	Discount agent	Full-service agent
Advertise	Hire help for the website software. Find printer for sign.	Send electronic photos for posting on his web-site. Takes care of sign.	Takes care of everything
Provide information	E-mail, fax, phone messages	Mostly through agent's website	Agent, by phone, or face to face with buyer
Negotiate	Face to face	On a fee-for-service basis, if required	Agent acts as intermediary. Offers advice.
Close the deal	Count on own inter-personal skills	As above	As above
Sign formal offer	Buy a standard form on the web	Agent supplies standard form and validates it	Takes care of everything
Finalize conditions	Face to face	Face to face	Agent acts as intermediary. Offers advice.
Organize financing	Shop around for a good deal	On a fee-for-service basis, if required	Agent acts as intermediary with banker. Offers advice.
Sign and register deed	Shop around for a notary	On a fee-for-service basis, if required	Takes care of everything

Figure 2.8   High-level customer process: Selling the house.

numerical value, and could thus compute the full value equation. In that instance, the negative aspects of the service experience in the sell-on-our-own option combined with the positive aspects of the full-service experience to turn the latter into the preferred option.

This is a reflection of their personal preferences, attitudes, and apprehensions based on (pertinent or not) experience. The actual service and self-service experiences with the full-service broker may turn out to be vastly different from their expectations, leading (should they choose that option) to a perceived value that is higher or lower than expected value. Understanding Jack and Linda's value equation is critically important for the agent trying to sell them brokerage services. A skilled agent who quickly zooms into the customer's priorities and fears will be in a good position to present a value proposition under its best light, and to later focus on critical aspects of service delivery.

Nobody quantifies value equations as seen in the previous illustration. Everybody, however, makes choices based on personal preferences. When a regular customer switches to another service

	Self	Discount agent	Full-service agent
Results	15 — It will take longer to find a buyer willing to pay the right price and wait six months for occupancy. In fact, we may never find it alone. Sale may fall through because of legal glitch or a customer that has not been correctly screened.	30 — Will go faster, but we still fear that a part of the market will not be reached.	75 — Best way to get the right buyer quickly.
Price	NA — Charges from all providers ($000)	5 — Agent's fixed fee	25 — Agent's commission (once sold)
Total cost	3	5	25
Basic value	5 — 15/3 (for sake of comparison)	6 — 30/5	3 — 60/25
Service experience	− − Organizing for a web-expert to help me when I need it will be complicated. − My web service provider has a local monopoly. They are not easy people to deal with.	− − We're not sure how they will respond (speed and quality) if we urgently need help.	+ Interactions will be enjoyable. + + He'll reassure us throughout the process.
Self-service experience	+ + Handling e-mail inquiries will be convenient − I will waste time with customers that are not serious. − − Negotiations will be tough. + + Making the web page will be fun.	− − Easier than doing it alone, but we still bear the brunt of making sure there is action. − −	− I'm a bit wary of final negotiations. + Not much to do really.
	−6	**−15**	**+25**
Value	3 $(15 − 6)/3$	3 $(30 − 15)/5$	4 $(75 + 25)/25$

Figure 2.9 Expected value equation: Illustration for Jack and Linda's sale of their home.

provider, it means that some element or other has changed in the equation, tipping the balance toward another provider. Understanding (through interviews, analysis, or deduction) what and why is very important to learning and improvement. The value equation provides a useful framework to do so discriminately.

2.3.3 Positioning in the Market

Positioning involves segmenting, targeting, and formulating a value proposition. After explaining what these terms mean they are illustrated by pursuing the real estate example.

2.3.3.1 Segmenting

Wanting to be all things to all people is a sure-fire recipe for failure. Positioning[8] is the art of selecting the right target market and gearing up to reach it. It can be broken down in three logical steps: Segment the market, select the segments you want to target, develop the value proposition and service concept.

Segmenting involves grouping customers into homogeneous clusters. There is no set way of doing this and it is more art than science. Demographics, geography, and social condition are obvious criteria to consider. Frequency of use is another. However, this results in categories that can be very heterogeneous—far too much to be able to compete in many industries. Targeting an excessively broad market segment places a company in the uncomfortable position of choosing between a standard service that does not really please anyone, or having to customize its offerings in a way that is prohibitively expensive to deliver.

Hence, including behavioral and psychological characteristics in segmentation criteria is essential. There are few guidelines available and you need to be creative. Such traits as enjoying technology, wanting to control the service encounter, and being passive or active by nature can be used. Financial planners, for example, target such segments as *fast-track to wealth* and *buy and hold* reflecting fundamentally different attitudes and beliefs toward life and retirement. Some drugstore chains are targeting people who need personal attention and reassurance, while others are trying to appeal to those who want to walk out with their medication as fast as possible without being bothered.

Understanding the path of people like Jack and Linda is a good starting point for segmentation, potentially leading to a segment that we might call *empty nest*. *Broken nest* might represent another segment, grouping couples whose union has faltered and who are in a hurry to settle their accounts and get on with their life. *Young nesters* may constitute yet another segment, grouping childless young working couples (which can be further segmented by such criteria as income and proficiency with technology). The way an organization dissects market reality in individual bits, and groups them in discrete chunks, can be an asset or a liability. It becomes a pair of glasses through which the organization sees the market and may prevent it from seeing opportunities right under its nose, but out of focus. Breaking the glasses occasionally and taking a fresh look can be a very profitable—if difficult—exercise.

2.3.3.2 Targeting and Value Proposition

Strategy is about beating your competitors. Targeting is about picking your fights. It requires a good analysis of your competitors' strengths and weaknesses as well as your own. You must evaluate each segment in terms of its size, growth, and satisfaction with current offerings. A package of benefits must then be developed to better meet the needs of targeted customers than competitors do, and the service itself must be designed in such a way that its features deliver these benefits. We will refer to the features-benefits pair as the service concept. It focuses on the numerator of the value equation and specifies it further, including the features of the service offerings designed to produce these benefits. Listing a number of benefits is easy. Specifying why these are the right benefits to win over and keep targeted customers and what service features are needed to produce these benefits is another matter.

A service provider's value proposition specifies the benefits offered to the customer in exchange for his money, that is, it is the expression of the service concept, formulated as a promise made to the target market. In the competition for the heart, mind, and wallet of the customer, the best value proposition wins—but woe befalls the service provider that does not make good on this promise. A benefit is something promoting or enhancing well-being. More precisely here, it is the effect felt by the customer when a provider satisfies an (implicit or explicit) need. Therefore, the value proposition is the specific promise made to the customer about the value received (as defined by the value equation) if our services are used.

A web-based service, for example, through which you can comparison-shop for cars, access the dealer's cost, and buy a car, offers benefits such as convenience, speed, best price, and assurance that you are not leaving any money on the table, as well as a low-pressure buying experience. The features of its web portal include links to the best sites for benchmarking technical data on cars, blue book prices, dealer discount programs, and so on. The customer sends a bid by e-mail to a participating local dealer and, if the latter accepts it, the car is delivered to the customer's door. For the targeted market, this concept (that is, the benefits and features of the service) is vastly superior to that offered by traditional dealership. The targeted market includes rational customers rather than impulsive buyers, people with strong analytical capabilities who are comfortable using web-related technology and abhor the sales tactics used by dealers.

2.3.3.3 Positioning: Pursuing the Real Estate Example

Back to real estate now, imagine a small community where the real estate market can be broken down into the aforementioned segments (empty nest, broken nest, and young nesters). Two full-service brokers dominate the market, each well established with a local office. Both are trying to serve all segments and investing heavily in advertising to promote their brand name. They are essentially undifferentiated, offering the following value propositions[9] :
For sellers—Using our services, you will:

- Expose your house to the highest number of serious buyers

- Receive many serious bids

- Receive the objective advice of seasoned experts who are well-acquainted with your specific neighborhood

- Obtain the services of a trained negotiator who will ensure that you get the best possible price

- Be guided safely through the maze of legal and financial technicalities

- Find it much easier to move or find temporary storage or temporary accommodations you may need

- Deal with a single expert who will manage it all in your best interest

For buyers—Using our services, you will:

- Have the widest possible choice of houses

- Receive advice from professionals who will help you find a house adapted to your needs

- Obtain the services of a trained negotiator who will ensure that you pay the best possible price

- Be guided safely through the maze of legal and financial technicalities

- Facilitate your move, temporary storage or temporary accommodations you may need

- Deal with a single expert who will manage it all in your best interest

Figure 2.10 illustrates the corresponding service concept offered to the seller. It shows the benefits offered to the customer (that is, the what?) with the feature or characteristics of the service package itself (that is, the how?). The full-service broker can consequently be seen as an integrator, analyzing the specific needs of the customer (diagnostic), and custom designing a service package to his needs. Through a single point of contact, the broker manages the integrated delivery of multiple services in the best interest of the client.

Imagine now a new entrant in the market, wishing to target people who are dissatisfied with the services offered by the full-service brokers. For *empty-nesters* and *broken nesters* (who have done this before) such dissatisfaction may stem from experience with brokers who, one way or another, did not deliver on their value proposition. They pass this on to *new nesters* through word-of-mouth (What do you think of real estate agents, Dad?). Understanding where the soft spots lie in your opponent's armor is as critical in business as in war. Full-service brokers, for instance, may be vulnerable to the following systemic delivery problems:

- Creating excessively high expectations on sales price and on a quick sale

- Under-spending on specific advertisement (as opposed to brand-name advertisement)

- Putting excessive pressure on the seller to close the sale

Further, breakthroughs in Internet and IT make for potentially better results, better self-service experience, and lower prices. The new entrant could focus on unsatisfied customers who have higher than average self-confidence and are technically literate (*techies* would be a sub-segment), who are willing and able to take control of the sales process, and who are looking for access to the right network and for specialized support and advice. The value proposition for sellers could thus read as follows. We will:

- Give your house as much visibility as you want

- Help you remain in control of the sales process from the day you decide to sell until you hand over the keys to the new owner

- Give you access, on a fee-for-service basis, to any specialized service or expert you may need (you will not pay for services you do not need)

- Assist you with any emergency that may occur throughout the sales process

Figure 2.11 shows what a service concept for this new entrant may look like.

Figures 2.12 and 2.13 summarize the various notions related to positioning introduced in this section. In Figure 2.12, the market is fragmented (figuratively) into segments—the circles represent the needs of a market segment (overlaps indicate common needs). Targeting (illustrated by arrows) is based on a market analysis, a competitive analysis as well as on a strategic internal assessment of mission, capabilities, strengths, and weaknesses. Figure 2.13 illustrates how the concept must represent superior value for the customers of choice, that is, for the targeted market segments stemming from Figure 2.12. The thermometers refer to customer value (see the equations

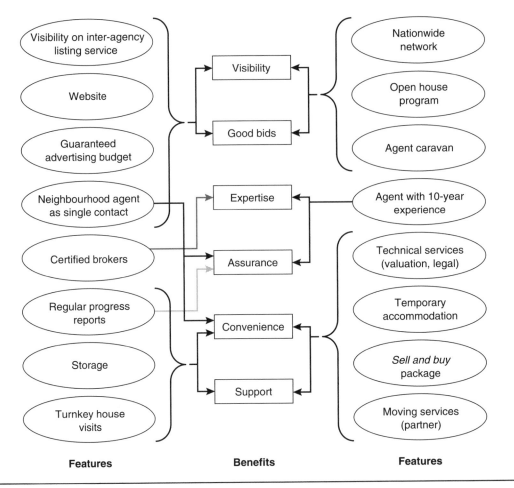

Figure 2.10 Full-service real estate agency: Service concept.

discussed earlier). The provider must translate that concept into a value proposition that advertisers will find a way to communicate so that it reaches the right people.

The discussion in this section focused on consumers, that is, a discussion mostly B2C (business to consumer). Business to business (B2B) is more complex in several ways. Several players are involved from various departments, often pursuing different goals, and even working at cross-purposes. They are acting on behalf of a third party (the company or the shareholders). They may have access to sophisticated resources and their buying power may be substantial. Finally, their activity cycle (processes, in this case), and thus the needs stemming from these activities, are generally much more complex.

2.4 POSITIONING IN THE LABOR MARKET

A company cannot create much value for its customers unless it is creating value for its employees. Indeed, unhappy service employees tend to produce unhappy customers. Of course, an organization does not relate to its employees as it does to its customers. Conceptually, however, there are many

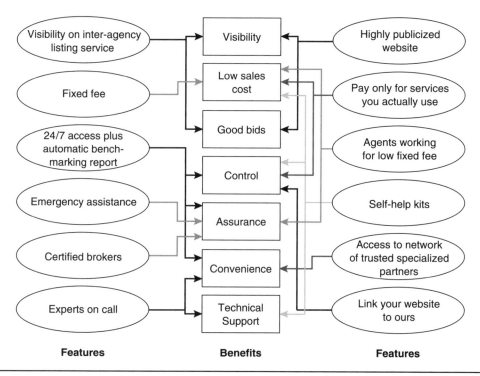

Figure 2.11 Discount real estate: Service concept.

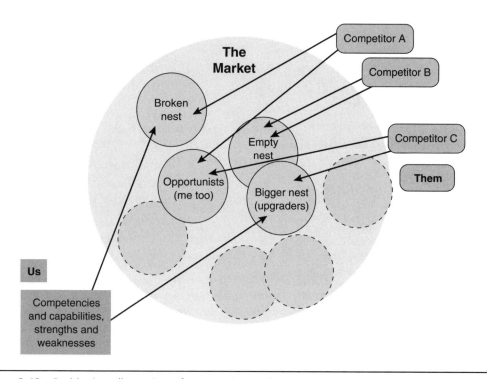

Figure 2.12 Positioning: Illustration of segmenting and targeting.

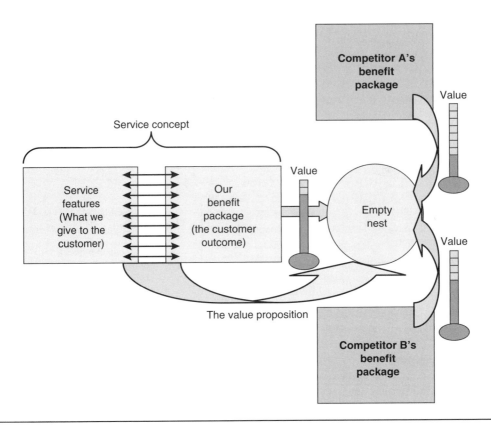

Figure 2.13 Positioning: Formulating a superior value proposition.

similarities. In this section, it is shown that the notions presented above regarding positioning in the market can advantageously be used (see the bottom part of Figure 2.1) to understand the challenges involved in recruiting and keeping the right people.

2.4.1 Personal Value Equation

Employees receive benefits from their employer, just as customers do. The latter buy these benefits with money, the former with their time and energy. Just as customers are searching the market for the best value, employees are searching the job market for the most benefits they can get for what they have to offer, that is, for the best personal value. The components of the personal value equation are the following:

- *Personal results.* People look for a job for various reasons: money, wanting to be useful, self-actualization, learning, and so on.

- *Internal service.* Organizations use various means to help employees do their jobs, that is, produce the results the company needs—and, through this, achieve their own personal goals. These means include such activities as training, coaching, providing tools, placing the employees in situations where they can grow, and helping with personal problems.

- *Employee self-service.* The burden of getting the employee to perform on the job does not rest solely with the employer. The organization expects the employees to take an active role in acquiring the required capabilities and maintaining knowledge and skills.

The employees must look for situations where they can learn and grow on and off the job and make the most out of them. They must improvise and be creative when faced with unexpected situations or when internal service fails.

The basic personal value equation (see Figure 2.14) is simply the ratio of results achieved to time spent on the job. A youth who has a job flipping hamburgers in a fast food outlet may summarize the personal value received from the job as follows: "I get $7 an hour, I've made new friends, and we generally have a lot of fun working together. The end-of-season party is always memorable."

To get the full value equation, the internal service and autonomous work (self-service) experiences are first included in the numerator. The youth, for instance, from the fast food example may appreciate or not the advice received from the supervisor (internal service) and may find it difficult to get up at 5 a.m. on Sunday morning and face the 6 o'clock rush on Friday nights, when two loaded busses pull into the parking lot at the same time (self-service). Consequently, the denominator is changed from time spent on the job to opportunity cost, which is defined as the sum of all benefits foregone to secure the benefits of the job.

The full value equation is a ratio of what the employee believes is being received from the job to what the employee feels could be received doing something else. When that ratio falls below 1, because of either a decrease in the numerator (salary reduction, more frustration on the job, and so on), an increase in the denominator or both, the employee is driven to reconsider the present employment. Anything that may lead the employee to believe better working conditions, more job satisfaction, or greater opportunities could be received elsewhere will have that effect. As well, if leisure time becomes more valuable for any reason, such as the arrival of a new baby or a close relative in dire need of assistance, the personal value equation of the job decreases.

The time aspect (ex-ante, ex-post) and the notion of technical quality discussed earlier also apply, *mutatis mutandis*, to the personal value equation.

2.4.2 Professional Service Workers

Advising a corporation on how to manage its financial affairs, for instance, bears little resemblance to flipping hamburgers. Indeed, professionals, as a class of workers, share a number of characteristics that separate them from other categories of workers:

- They value their knowledge and skills. They want to use them to the fullest by having the best tools available and not waste any time on tasks that would best be performed by less qualified workers. They want to improve on them.

The basic personal value equation

$$\frac{\text{Personal results}}{\text{Time spent on the job}}$$

What the employee had to do to get the result

Internal service experience	Employee autonomous work experience

Did I enjoy the experience?   Did I enjoy the experience?

The full personal value equation

$$\frac{\text{Personal results} + \text{quality of internal service} + \text{quality of autonomous work experience}}{\text{Opportunity cost}}$$

Figure 2.14   The personal value equations.

- They understand the central role they play in the creation of value for customers and want to be compensated accordingly.

- They are experts in their fields and do not tolerate intrusion—or anything they consider as such—in their professional realms.

- All of the above factors make them more independent. They can leave the company and take their expertise with them, and often some clients as well. They can often strike out on their own or set up a competing business with a group of colleagues.

For all their specificity however, the value equation presented above applies to them, *mutatis mutandis*. The results they seek include much better compensation and an important professional growth component. The self-service component (keeping current and honing the skills) tends to be more substantial. The opportunity cost is also higher because of the mobility their recognized (diploma and professional certification) skill set affords them in the labor market.

2.4.3 Positioning in the Professional Labor Market

Just as the organization must position itself in its service market, it must position itself in the labor market. To become the employer of choice for the type of professionals it needs, it must:

- Have a clear idea of who they are and where they can be found (segmenting and targeting)

- Understand where they are coming from and where they are going, both in the short and long term (activity cycle)

- Understand what they want from their job and how important each element is (affinity diagram and importance weighing)

- Develop an employee benefit package (job concept) that they will prefer to that of competitors (positioning)

- Find a way to translate the concept into a value proposition, and communicate it in such a way that it will reach and be understood by the targeted individuals

- Find a way to translate the job concept into work processes and internal service processes, which will truly generate the results and experience that they are looking for, and thus induce them to stay and prosper in the company, spreading the word to potential new recruits

Referring back to Figure 2.12, you can see that the notion of positioning it represents is conceptually analogous whether it refers to the market or the labor market. If you think of the labor market rather than the market in Figure 2.12, then the smaller circles represent groups of people with similar needs, skills, attitudes, or values, and the arrows illustrate how competitors (who may or may not be the same competitors met in the market) are targeting various labor market segments for employment. In this context, positioning in the labor market involves the elaboration of a superior benefit package for these employees of choice, and its translation into a personal value proposition, to be communicated in its recruitment drives, and to serve as guide in the elaboration and management of relevant processes (see Figure 2.15).

Imagine for instance that real estate agents are grouped in the following categories:

- *Young techies*, who enjoy dealing with computers as much as with people

- *Cruise control* (earn my keep) agents, who make a living but are happy with what they have and do not wish to change or reduce their leisure time

- *Moonlighters*, who do this to supplement their regular income

- *High rolling traditionalists*, who manage this as a business in an old fashioned way, (they sell and farm out some of the execution to *cruise control* and *moonlighter* agents)

Figure 2.16 illustrates how companies must position themselves simultaneously in the market and in the labor market. Reaching and maintaining this positioning dynamically, as markets, competition, and technology change, is an essential component of the strategic challenge that any organization must address. This is further discussed in Chapter 5. The reader who wants to explore the notion of personal value in services further should read Schneider and Bowen (1995).

2.5 MANAGING THE SHAREHOLDER VALUE EQUATION–EVA

Having discussed the dynamics of simultaneous value creation for customers and employees, the discussion now turns to shareholders, whose money rides on the success of the venture (see Figure 2.1). In capitalism, businesses exist for the sole purpose of generating profits for their owners. They achieve this by beating their competition at value creation in the market and in the job market. Societal benefits derive from this competition and the survival of the fittest. Economic value added (EVA) consists of what remains when all resources (human, material, and financial) that have been used to generate income have been paid for. The sole purpose of creating value for customers and employees, as discussed in this chapter, is the maximization of EVA. Just as the search for value

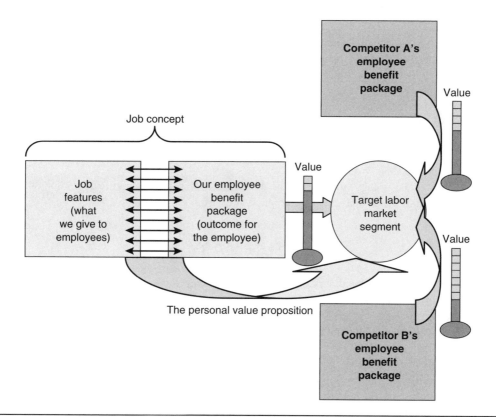

Figure 2.15 Positioning in the labor market: Giving more value than competition does to employees of choice.

drives consumer behavior and the search for personal value drives employee behavior, the search for EVA drives shareholder behavior. To avoid being sidetracked by the intricacies of EVA calculation (the interested reader should refer to Stewart, 1999), profit rate has been chosen as a proxy. It is defined by the following equation:

$$\text{Profit rate} = \frac{(\text{Number of clients X volume per client X profit margin})-\text{fixed costs}}{\text{Investment}}$$

The higher the percentage of clients who come out of the service encounter with disappointment or receive service of low technical quality, the lower the volume through:

- Loss of disappointed client

- Dissuasion of potential client through negative word of mouth

- Defection to competition of clients (and potential clients) through word of mouth from these disappointed clients, who have now been delighted by competitors

- Initially lower frequency of purchase from the new clients that have to be attracted to compensate for the loss

The lower the profit margin through:

- Increased advertising expense to attract new clients

- Initially lower margins for these new clients, as clients tend to become cheaper to service over time

Zero defection of targeted clients is therefore the only viable target for a firm that wishes to maximize its long-run profits. Technical quality and client satisfaction are crucial levers to move profit in the right direction. Good positioning in the market[10] and in the labor market makes this possible. The former will make it possible to (nicely) turn away, and refer to a competitor, clients who are likely to defect because the firm cannot provide them, for some reason or other, with services of high technical quality that will produce durable customer satisfaction. The latter will make it possible to select and keep only those professionals who will find it to be in their overall best interests to give the best service they can to these customers. Single-minded focus on short-term profits clearly precludes any of this.

Ways (operations strategy) to increase the numerator while decreasing the denominator of both value equations, and thus run away from the pack, are discussed in Chapter 5.

2.6 SUMMARY

Just as customers pick their providers, PSOs should pick their customers and tailor-design a benefit package for them. Customers are looking for the best results they can get for the money they have to spend, and they want the process of obtaining it to be painless. Like heat-seeking missiles, they change targets when they feel that a hot deal, promising a *bigger bang for the buck,* is available elsewhere. Service providers must seek to understand and manage the implicit underlying value equations that preside over such switches in various market segments. Understanding the mindset with which various market segments approach a service encounter is an essential first step to that end.

Value equations are particularly complex in professional services, where the joint effect of often hard to evaluate results, and the presence of a knowledge gap between service providers and

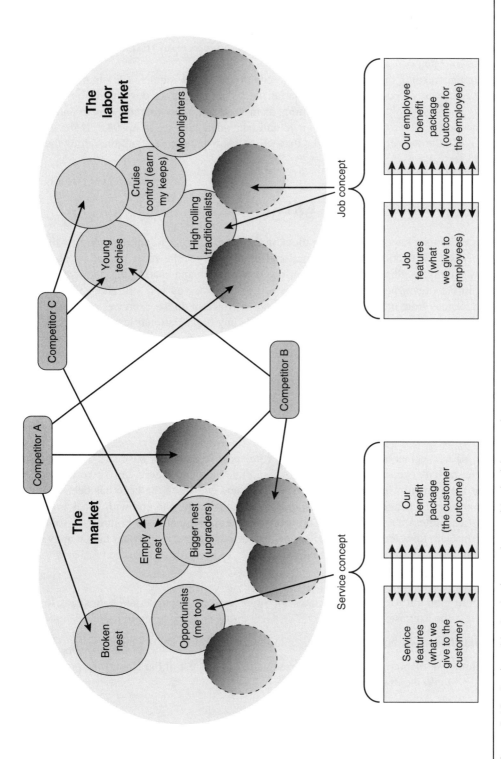

Figure 2.16 Dual positioning in the market and in the labor market.

their clients, allow for manipulation and abuse. Professionals must often lead their clients in directions different from where the clients' intuition would lead them. They must do so with sufficient tact that their customers will not defect to less scrupulous or complacent competitors. This introduces a layer of complexity to professional service delivery processes (PSDP), which is addressed in the next two chapters.

Finding and keeping the professionals who can do all of this requires the organization to pay as much attention to its positioning in the labor market as it does its positioning on the market. Maintaining and adapting this dual positioning, as markets and labor markets evolve and competitors strive to preempt the organization's move and take advantage of its mistake, is the challenge facing PSOs. To the winners go the profits that will reward shareholders and thus draw the capital necessary to stay ahead of the pack.

EXERCISES

These exercises are an important building block in the learning process, a bridge to cross the chasm between theory and practice. A multi-functional team will get the most out of it. This is best achieved by pulling together a team from various departments and sharing the book with them. If your level in the organization does not allow you to do that, you can still share the book with selected colleagues from other departments. Of course, you can do the exercises alone, which will produce the intended individual learning, but preclude any organizational learning. This may be a valid strategy if your intent is to vet the book and first find out for yourself if and with whom you want to share it. The formulation of the exercises assumes that a multifunctional team does them. Consensus must be the *modus operandi*.

Most of these exercises require only a flip chart, stacks of sticky notes of various colors (stick to pastel colors and large format), and black markers.

2.1 Activity cycles

Select two market segments from your current or prospective customer base and draw the respective customer activity cycles such as those shown in Figure 2.5 and Figure 2.6. Make sure you start the cycle at the moment when the original need arises and end when the need has been addressed. In the case of a sports health clinic, for instance, start with "ouch" and end with "back in competition." Use sticky notes on a flip chart and draw arrows to connect them (see Figure 2.17 for an illustration). If the team finds it difficult to agree on what the customer does, several factors may explain this situation:

- Nobody really knows what the customer does.

  Action: Find out! Conduct interviews and organize focus groups, then come back to the exercise.

- Marketing knows, but has never shared that with the rest of the organization.

  Action: Ask marketing to prepare a presentation to the rest of the team, then proceed to do the exercise.

- You are not thinking about the same people.

  Action: Review your segmentation or create one together if you have never done this explicitly.

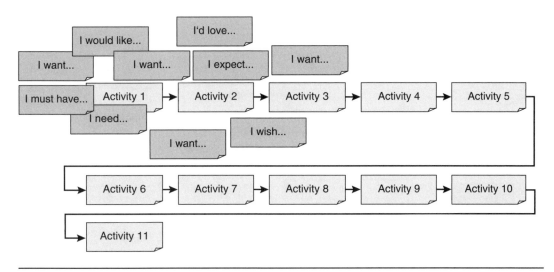

Figure 2.17 Customer activity cycle and needs (Exercise 2.1).

If you find that the activities of the two market segments only differ in a few activities, draw a unique activity cycle, highlighting differences between market segments using sticky notes of different colors.

2.2 Customer needs

Put on the customer's shoes, and slowly walk through the customer's activity cycle as depicted in the previous exercise, thinking about what you may need, want, or simply enjoy as you go about performing that activity. The best way to do this is for team members to sit silently, write down each individual element (write in the first person, that is, start with "I need ..." or "I want...") that comes to mind on a separate sticky note, and put it at the right place along the cycle. Team members may look at the elements their colleagues are adding, thereby stimulating their own creativity.

When they are finished, members jointly eliminate duplications and clarify the meaning of each element. They then take these elements off of the activity cycle and organize them in an affinity diagram to summarize them. This involves grouping them in homogeneous categories, that is, elements that reflect a common theme, and giving each category a name (see Figure 2.18). If you end up with more than 15 categories, see if you can group them under a broader heading. Politeness, respect, and courtesy, for instance, might be grouped under a broader heading such as *treatment*. If, on the other hand, you end up with four or five categories, see if you could split any of those into smaller sub-categories. We refer to the sub-categories as *level-two needs*, as shown in Figure 2.19. Depending on the business you are in, you should typically end up with seven to 15 needs (at the lowest level—ten categories are shown in Figure 2.19). In complex services, it is sometimes required to split some level-two needs into level-three needs (that is, yet smaller categories).

2.3 Weights

Wearing again the customer's glasses, rank the needs you just defined from the most to the least important, and spread one hundred points between them, reflecting the importance that customers attach to them. If the needs are divided in two levels, first rank the level one needs, then spread 100

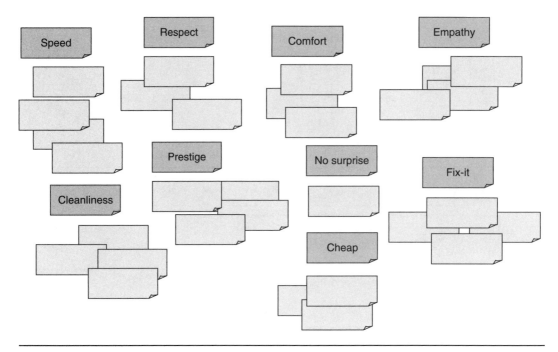

Figure 2.18 Affinity diagram of customer needs (Exercise 2.2).

points between them, and finally spread the points attributed to each level-one between the level-two needs, as shown in Figure 2.19.

Translate your understanding of the differences between the two segments into different weights, as shown in Table 2.4 above.

2.4 Benefits and features

Identify the current features of the services you are offering to each of the market segments you identified above and link them to the needs of each segment, as identified above, producing a diagram similar to those shown in Figure 2.10 and Figure 2.11.

2.5 Customer value equation

Build the value equation for these two market segments, as you perceive it, first explaining specifically what it includes (see Table 2.2 for an illustration) and second describing in one or two short sentences, such as those shown in Figure 2.9., what you think is your customers' current appreciation of each element of the equation. Compare this result with what you believe to be the customer's experience at your major competitor.

2.6 Professional employee value equation

Repeat the four preceding exercises (2.2 through 2.5), but this time thinking of your positioning in the professional labor market, rather than on customers. Select your major category of professionals—lawyers for a law firm, dentists for a dental clinic, and so on. If your major competitor is not your major source of competition in the job market, pick whoever is.

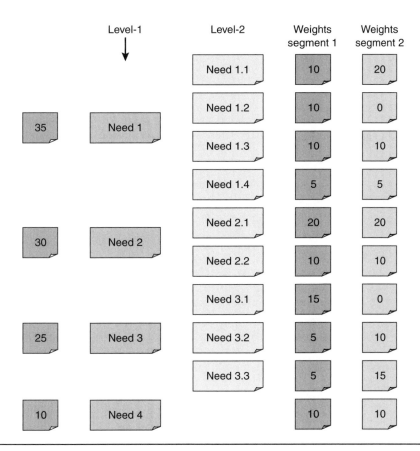

Figure 2.19 Weighted customer needs (Exercise 2.3).

Notes

[1] Refers to the market for services, unless otherwise specified.

[2] The expressions *service quality* and *customer satisfaction* are used interchangeably in this book. *Technical quality* of service, another aspect of service quality, is always referred to as such.

[3] Depending on the customer's need, this may be, in whole or in part, the result being sought.

[4] However, to reduce repetition, the words customer and client are used interchangeably throughout the book.

[5] Finding a solution that meets basic requirements.

[6] This is discussed in the next chapter. It is a decomposition of a process into its logical steps or function.

[7] In the case of *selling on their own*, there is no basic value to speak of, since Jack and Linda are not using the services of a real estate agent. A value is calculated here using total cost, so that the three options can be compared.

[8] What is being discussed here is *desired* positioning, not to be confused with *achieved* positioning. The first is a goal the company wants to reach, while the latter is *in the mind* of customers. In the car industry, for example, most customers will readily associate Toyota with reliability, Volvo with security, and Rolls Royce with prestige, reflecting their respective *positions* in the minds of consumers.

[9] Since brokers are intermediaries between buyers and sellers, depending on an agent's role in the transaction, the broker may have one or two clients: the buyer, the seller, or both. The discussion so far has focused only on the buyer.

[10] Unless otherwise stated, when used alone, the word *market* refers to the physical or virtual place where the services that a firm produces are traded.

3

The Nature of Processes

Companies create value through processes. Organizational know-how is to be found in processes. Focusing on them rather than on functions is the key to profit and learning.

Having explored the notions of value and positioning in the previous chapter, this chapter will take a more detailed look at how things are done in the organization, that is, at processes. Without a good understanding of the game plan for creating more value than the competitors for customers and employees of choice, processes are meaningless. A quick glance at Figures 1.4 and 2.1 will remind the reader of the role of processes in business.

After explaining what processes are in the next section, the various dimensions of the process space are explored, which means looking at various ways to classify and categorize processes. In the following section, a different look is taken at the nature of processes, viewing them as chains of commitment. The chapter is concluded with a discussion of the linkage between process and value and the importance of improving the right process. Table 3.1 gives a short definition of the major concepts discussed in this chapter.

3.1 WHAT IS A PROCESS?

A very broad definition of *process* serves as the beginning, using examples drawn from everyday life, and introducing some basic process definition tools. These tools are then applied to the business world and developed further. The section closes on a list of requirements for a process to exist (that is, to be defined).

3.1.1 Definition

Performing a process consists of taking an input and transforming it into a desired output. A simple example of a process would be *making toast* for breakfast (note that here is an action verb and a noun—this holds true for any process). You take a slice of bread (input) out of the refrigerator or breadbox and put it in the toaster (transformation) to get toast (output). The supplier (the baker) provides the input and the output goes to a customer (you). Consequently, a process is represented by the acronym *SITOC* (Supplier, Input, Transformation, Output and Customer, as illustrated in Chapter 1). The process starts when some input requirements are met (a slice of bread of the required type, size, and shape), and finishes when some output requirements are met (for instance, toast of the required color and temperature).

Table 3.1 Key concepts discussed in Chapter 3.

Service system	All the elements (human resources, machines, facilities, installations, software, roles, and relationships) standing ready to perform a service.
Process	A system put into operation to transform some inputs into desired outputs.
Know-how	The capability to transform some inputs into desired outputs. It lies in processes.
Organizational learning	The act of improving an organization's know-how.
Functions	Center of expertise in the organization such as finance or marketing, around which most organizations are structured.
Chain of commitments	Organizational view of a multiperson process, whereby responsibilities are distributed in a workable way throughout an organization, thus forming a chain linking inputs to outputs.
SITOC	A process tool used to delimit the perimeter of a process
Interfacing processes	Processes that are *adjacent* to each other, i.e. that receive or provide deliverables (intermediate or final) to or from each other.
Functionality	Some essential action that a process must be able to perform.
FAST	A technique to decompose a process into functionalities.
PFD	A graphic technique to bring out the (high-level) sequential flow if a process.
CTP	One of the vital few variables that has a determinant impact on a dependent variable.

Suppliers and customers of a process are often other processes. *Preparing financial statements*, for instance, may have *review company books* as a provider, and *prepare income tax return* as a customer. In B2B situations, there can be many customers, with different, often conflicting, needs.

A *process* is defined as a system put into operation to transform some inputs into desired outputs. In its broadest definition, a *system* is a group or combination of interrelated, interdependent, or interacting elements forming a collective entity (Collins Dictionary, 1981). This is broad enough to include, for example, the solar system, the atomic system, the human body, or an ecosystem. More specifically then, a *business system* is defined as a system standing ready to perform. The process puts it into operation. Even more specifically, a *service system* is a system standing ready to perform a service. At a fast-food restaurant, for instance, the service system would include the parking lot, the customer facilities, the cashier, the cash register and its software, the cooking facilities, the back-office personnel, the agreed-upon procedures, and so on. In this context, a process is the dynamic (intelligent) use of the system (and of all its needed elements or components) to transform an input into an output.

Many processes may take place in the same service system. Designing a service system requires thinking about all of the processes that will take place within that system, such as taking an order, fulfilling an order, eating breakfast, eating lunch, cleaning up the facilities, using the washroom, and so on. Designing a process to operate in an existing service system may involve modifying, improving, or redesigning the service system. As a rule, the word process is used in this book to mean the process and the relevant parts of the service delivery system. When referring to an organization's processes, the complete service delivery system is included.

Assembling a car and brushing your teeth are both processes (action verb and noun). In this sense, everything said about processes so far in this chapter applies equally well to both. The former, however, is a complex process that can be decomposed into hundreds or even thousands of interrelated sub-processes, many of which are repeated many times over. How can these processes be identified? They can be decomposed layer by layer, or level by level, using a technique (alluded to in the previous chapter) called the Functional Analysis System Technique, abbreviated as FAST (already illustrated in Chapters 1 and 2).

A FAST diagram proceeds—left to right or top to bottom—from the highest-level process (making a cup of coffee, say) to the lowest by asking the question *making a cup of coffee: how?* The answer is the list of level-two sub-processes shown in Figure 3.1. The analysis can be pushed further by asking the same question of each of the level-two processes: *buy beans: how?* Hence, choosing a supplier and placing the order are level-three sub-processes. Complex processes can easily consist of 10 such layers. A cursory coherence check can be performed by asking a series of directed questions (why?) from right to left, for example: *placing an order: why?* Answer: to buy beans. *Buy beans: why?* Answer: to make a cup of coffee, and so on. The purpose of a FAST diagram, however, is not to describe the way the process is currently performed (a technique called process mapping is used for that—see Chapter 8), but solely to identify the functionalities that are required of the process. Any process for making coffee must include the functionality *grind beans*, and there are many possible ways to do this.

How far is it possible to *drill down* (the often referred to way of decomposing the actions of a process)? Figure 3.1 illustrates this, admittedly to a ridiculous degree of detail in this case. At this point, we are not merely identifying functionalities, we are describing (partially) a specific process. Consider the process of brushing your teeth. This process may be repeated over 70,000 times in your lifetime. Consider the effect of doing any of the following:

- Using a toothbrush that does not have rounded bristles (gum problems at 35; variable: shape of bristle tip—0 for flat, 1 for rounded)

- Using toothpaste with an excessively high content of abrasive (receding gum and decay; variable: percent abrasive content by volume)

- Not brushing all the way to the last molar (extraction at 30; variable: gap in cm between reach of brush and extremity of last molar)

- Putting too much pressure on the gum (bleeding, sore and receding gums; variable: pressure in kilopascals or psi)

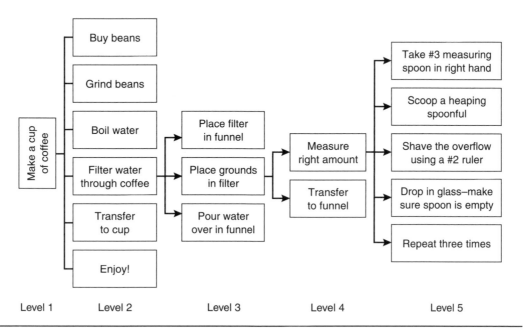

Figure 3.1 Functional analysis (FAST) diagram for the process of making a cup of coffee: selective drill-down to level five.

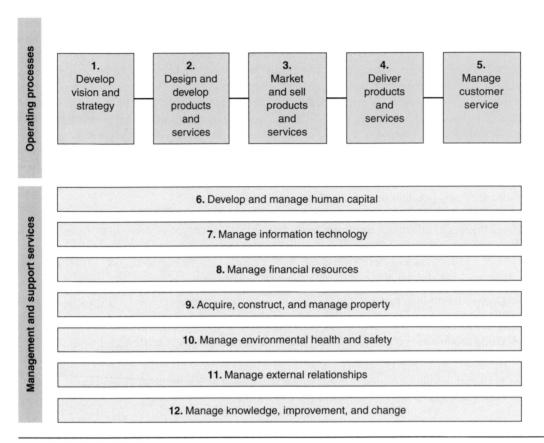

Figure 3.2 APQC's processes classification framework (level one processes).
Source: Developed by APQC's International Benchmarking Clearinghouse, in partnership with Arthur Andersen & Co., SC.

The devil is in the detail! The outcome of any process rests on a few critical variables or aspects of a process. Identifying and controlling these is a complex but essential task (see Chapter 8). Doing things right requires that processes (or selected sub-processes) be drilled down to the level of detailed process variables. What is a process variable? It is a measurable aspect of a process, that is, one for which a scale of measurement (see parenthetical illustrations in the above example) can be used. A crucial step in designing and improving processes is to differentiate the vital few (or critical-to-process [CTP] variables) from the many trivial variables (refer back to the examples in Section 1.3.2). This cannot be accomplished unless all of the variables are first identified, and that requires selectively drilling down the process in detail through process mapping.

3.1.2 Viewing an Organization as a System of Processes

An organization can be viewed as a complex system of (interconnected) processes. An organization's process model is a high-level representation of these processes. Figure 3.2 shows a generic process model produced by APQC[1]. Note that each process is still described by an action verb and a noun (the transformation part of the SITOC).

Figure 3.3 shows a breakdown of one of these processes into sub-processes using a FAST diagram. This is achieved using the transformation performed by the process (deliver products and services) and asking the question *how?* The five level-two sub-processes (4.1 to 4.5—called level-two processes because they are identified by two digits) are the logical answer to that question. Each level-two sub-process can be further exploded using the same technique: Deliver product service to the customer: *how?* The four level-three processes (4.4.1–4.4.4) are the logical answer to that question.

Figures 3.2 and 3.3 are neatly organized and Cartesian. This provides a false sense of orderliness that begins to crumble when we look at Figure 3.4. This figure shows a selected subset of processes arranged in a flow pattern, that is, following the SITOC logic. Inspection reveals, for example, that process *Define skill requirements*, produces an output (skill requirements) which becomes the input for process *Recruit, select, and hire employees*. The latter, in turn, transforms this input into an output (an employee) to process *Provide the service to specific customers*. This last process produces an output (information that the service has been provided as—or differently

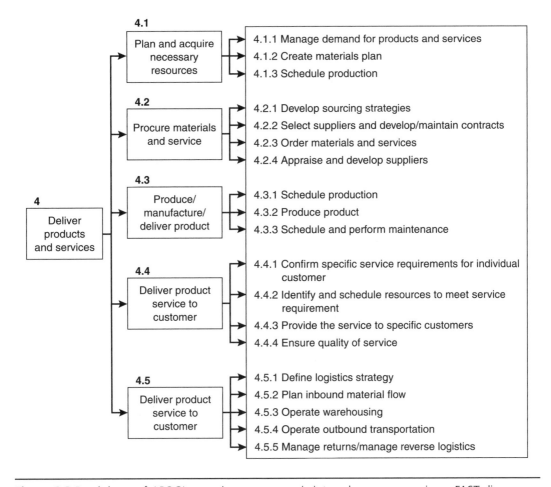

Figure 3.3 Breakdown of APQC's generic process no. six into sub-processes, using a FAST diagram (level-two and -three processes).
Source: AQPC.

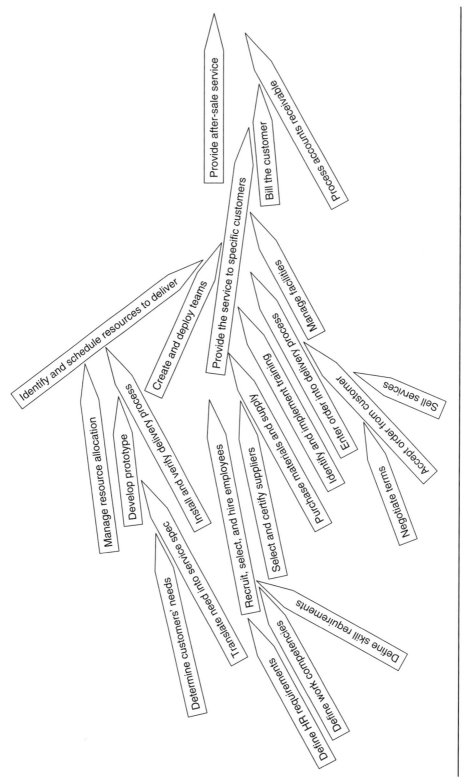

Figure 3.4 Viewing an organization as a system of processes: Selected generic processes organized in a flow (input-output) pattern.

from—what was originally requested and accepted by the customer) which is in turn input to the *Bill the customer* process. In a process system, processes can be suppliers to other processes or clients of other processes, and internal processes always play both roles. Processes, the output of which goes directly to the end-customer or client (these are said to be *in contact* and are the subject of Section 4.2.2 in Chapter 4), are the value-creating tip of the value chain (see the discussion on the value connection in Section 3.4.1 below).

So far, the discussion has been strictly generic, that is, it applies to most organizations. To better understand processes, it is useful to work on a specific example. The case of Medsol has been chosen for that purpose. Medsol is a health center which includes a general hospital, an outpatient clinic, an emergency service, and a specialized cancer treatment unit. The Medsol Clinic will be the focus for now, and more particularly one of its processes, of the type *Provide the service to specific customers*. The SITOC diagram shown in Figure 3.5 defines the perimeter of that process. It shows the patient to be simultaneously the key provider, the main input, the main output, and the customer, which is generally the case in health services. Indeed, the process transforms the patient, hopefully by making him healthier. The *begins when* and *finishes when* boxes delimit the time boundaries of the process—much like bookends—by specifying the process start-up and ending conditions (input and output requirements).

The last element in the diagram relates to key interfaces (or adjacent processes). Because an organization is a system of processes, changing any process is bound to have an impact on other processes. If Medsol were to somehow modify the way it provides services to specific customers, it might have to adjust (see Figure 3.3) how it purchases material and supplies, or how it ensures quality of service, for example. Identifying the most important of these processes—in the specific organizational circumstances at hand—at the outset of any change initiative is critical to change management.

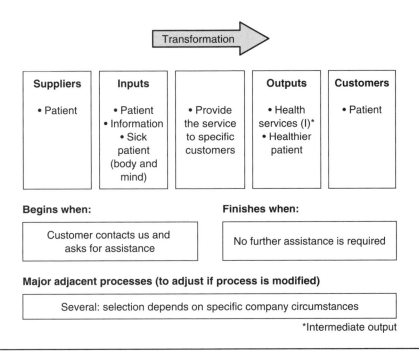

Figure 3.5 Circumscribing a level-three process: *Provide the service to specific customers.*

To dig further into the process of providing the service to specific customers at the Medsol Clinic, a different tool will now be used. Figure 3.6 shows the process flow diagram (PFD) used for that process, with each arrow-shaped box representing a level-four sub-process. The list of sub-processes is generated pretty much as done in a FAST diagram, that is, by asking the question *providing services: how?* However, since answering that question yields 12 sub-processes, organizing them in a way that illustrates the general flow of the process becomes important to understanding its nature.

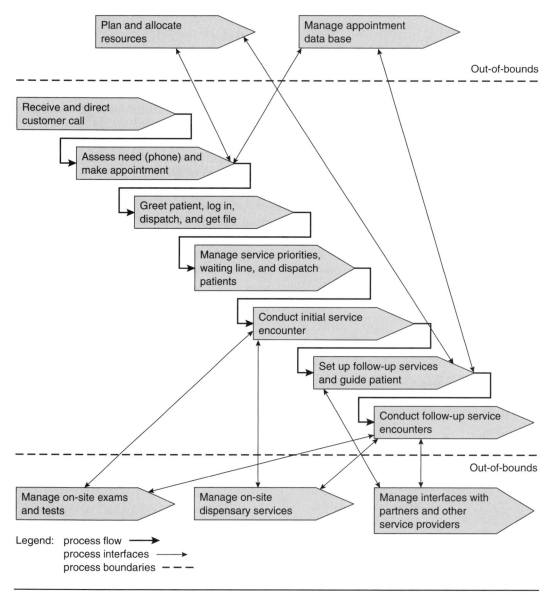

Figure 3.6 Exploding *provide the service to specific customers* in a process flow diagram at Medsol Clinic (identifying level-four processes).

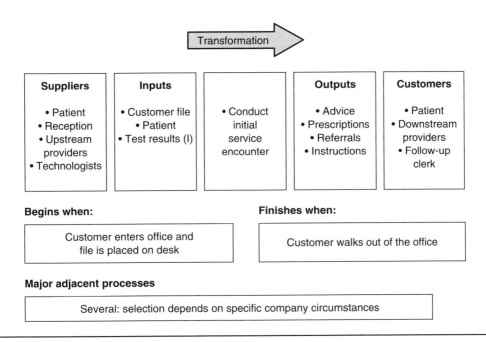

Figure 3.7 Circumscribing a level-four process: *Conduct initial service encounter.*

This is done in the PFD by representing the process (roughly) along a time line (horizontal axis) showing a logical sequence, and spreading it along the vertical axis to show (approximately) sub-processes that can take place in parallel. The thick arrows show the process flow and the thin ones show the most important interfaces with adjacent processes. Keep in mind that this representation, like all the others used so far in this chapter, is based on logic and not on a detailed description of what actually goes on at the Medsol Clinic.

The process drill down could be pursued further by selecting one of the level-five processes—*conduct initial service encounter*, say—and, using the same tools (see the SITOC, for example, in Figure 3.7) to establish its perimeter, exploding it into more detail.

Figure 3.8 further illustrates the use of the PFD in the case of the real estate agent discussed in Chapter 2. The generic process depicted there is the same as that shown in Figure 3.6 for Medsol.

3.1.3 When Is a Process Defined?

The word *process* is part of everyday language and is used in a variety of contexts to mean a host of different things. What does it take for a sequence of more or less repetitive activities to qualify as a defined process? While there are many opinions on this, the following criteria (or minimal requirements) will be used to make this determination:

- We (the organization) know how well the process is performing and thus can validly say whether its performance is improving, stable, or getting worse.

- Someone in the organization (a manager) is accountable for the performance of the process.

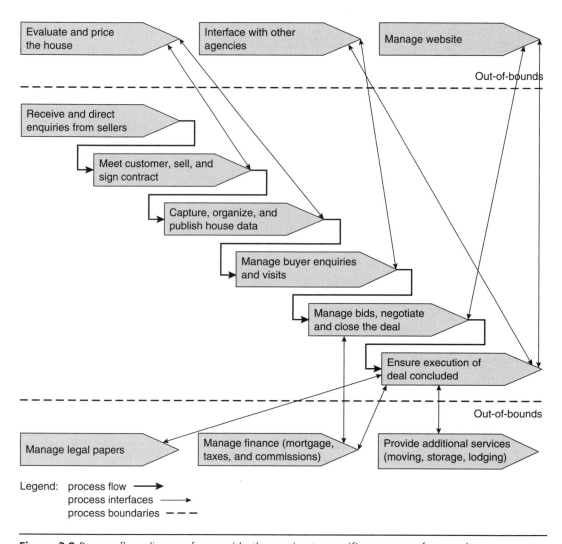

Figure 3.8 Process flow diagram for *provide the service to specific customers* for a real estate agency.

- All of the process workers[2] could, if it were explained to them, complete the SITOC of the process; specify the role they play in that process, that is, identify their internal providers, transformation, and customers; and spell out what their internal customers' requirements are, as well as their own requirements of their internal suppliers.

- The above knowledge would not be lost if one or two workers were to suddenly leave the organization (that is, organizational memory goes beyond one or two individuals).

- The workers' commitment to meeting their internal customers' requirements is real (this is discussed in Section 3.3 below).

Processes that meet these criteria may vary in their degree of formalism. However, tacit knowledge (Nonaka and Takeuchi, 1995) does not constitute a process, as it cannot be communicated or shared with other employees until it is made explicit.

Table 3.2 Evaluation of various situations with respect to the existence of a process.

Statement	Do we have a process?	Why
We have a process but it is not followed.	No	Maybe we have a process design, but we don't have a process because commitments are not real.
The process produces much variation and the customer is threatening to leave.	Maybe	The process may not be capable, but it may still exist.
We're the best in the business, but nothing is documented.	Maybe	The process may be undocumented, but it may still exist.
The procedures are all charted and duly documented in our quality manual.	Maybe	The key is whether or not they are followed.
Paul never delivers, I often have to do it myself.	No	If Paul can get away with it, it's because his commitment is not real
Only Joe can do this, if he leaves we're in big trouble.	Maybe	If Joe's departure would cause the company not to know what to do anymore, then we don't have a process. If the only problem is that Joe is the only one with the required skills, then we do have a process, but lack depth (or backup).

To clarify these criteria further, Table 3.2 shows a number of situations, illustrated by typical statements an organization may make about its process, as well as their interpretation, that is, whether or not a process is defined.

3.2 EXPLORING THE PROCESS SPACE

With such a broad definition, processes need to be classified into categories in order to understand them better. Being able to classify things, that is, to develop a typology, is the beginning of knowledge. In this section, some dimensions are presented (see Figure 3.9) along which this can be done. They are discussed in turn in this section, except for the *commitment* dimension, which is important enough to justify a section of its own (Section 3.3).

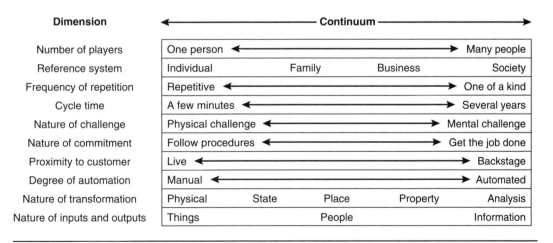

Figure 3.9 Various ways to classify processes.

3.2.1 Number of Players

Single-person processes are in a category of their own. Included in that category are all processes wherein a single person is involved in the transformation from input to output. The distinguishing feature of single-person processes is that no human interaction is involved. Single-person processes fall in two sub-categories: processes where the person is the customer, that is something the customer does for self, such as brushing teeth or planning the day, and those directed at external customers, such as producing a painting, writing a book, or cleaning the house (the whole family being the customer in this case). These are referred to as personal or one-worker processes, respectively. Although the latter involves an external *judge* of the results, in both cases all the decisions about the way things are done involve a single player, which makes things much easier. Complexity increases exponentially with the number of players.

3.2.2 Reference Systems

Individuals, families, businesses, and societies are all systems within which processes take place. The relationship they bear to one another is much like that between Russian dolls: the first fits within the framework of the second, the second within that of the third, and all three are included in a broad societal system. These systems will now be explored, to see how individuals fit in.

Processes in the family unit, whatever its composition, are unique because of the strong emotional bond that unites its members. The family plays a central role in any society and much of our well-being rests on it. Children raised in dysfunctional families face a long uphill battle in their quest for happiness. The roots of family problems are numerous, deep, and tightly interwoven, and addressing them goes far beyond the scope of this book or the competence of this writer. Numerous processes, however, are found in a family. Social workers and specialized educators direct much of their intervention effort toward fixing some family processes that have broken down, or designing and implementing new processes (*monitoring a child's social activities*, *administering punishment*, or *preparing meals for the kids*). Even healthy families which function well devote much effort—implicitly or explicitly—to improving processes, from getting one child to do chores to organizing the house for Halloween.

The existence of a customer, paid employees, and a decision-making hierarchy characterize organizational processes. In a business, a special type of organization, processes are further characterized by paying customers, the profit motive, and the existence of competition. The goal of business processes is to profitably deliver a superior value proposition to customers and employees, as discussed in Chapter 2. Maintaining this superiority is vital to the survival and growth of the company. This continuous search for superiority and dominance accounts for the vitality of business processes in capitalist systems.

Next are processes in society, involving the relationship between individuals, families, organizations, and communities. Capitalism is an economic system within a society. *Allocate capital*, for example, is a process—albeit at an extremely high level—within the capitalist system. At the other end of the spectrum, transferring money from a savings account to a mutual fund is a minute sub-process within that macro-process. Indeed, a FAST diagram linking the former to the latter would have many levels.

The democratic system is another critical societal system, and processes are at its core. The basic inputs are the individual opinions and preferences of a people about the way their society should be managed. The output is a set of elected representatives, empowered to legitimately wield the levers of government. The notion is simple enough. Making it stick is another story, as the history of civilization amply demonstrates. Witness the recent vagaries of the democratic process in two of the longest-standing democracies: the United States and France.

In the United States, two of the most mundane sub-processes went haywire (punching cards and counting punched cards—see discussion in Chapter 1), producing enough defects to raise doubts about the fairness of the process, and thus the legitimacy of the president. A process alternative—the touch screen—had distinct problems of traceability. In a democracy, playing by the rules and being seen to play by the rules are both critical to legitimacy. In France, the two-ballot majority vote process functioned without a hitch, even though it is assumed that the vast majority of French people would have thought it more appropriate if Jospin, rather than Le Pen, had faced Chirac in the second ballot. Thus, in process terms, the U.S. process showed poor *con*formance and the French process showed poor *per*formance (or design)[3].

Where do governmental processes fit into this classification? The answer is, somewhere between business processes and societal processes. The relationship between governments and individuals falls into one of four categories, according to the role played by the individual (Mintzberg, 1996): consumer, client, citizen, or subject. The consumer buys services from government on a commercial basis, such as electricity or garbage collection. The client receives professional services, such as educational services. The citizen utilizes services, such as public infrastructure, to which there is a right. The subject must perform the duties that follow directly from the rights as citizen, such as abiding by the law or serving in the army. Processes associated with the first two roles can be assimilated into business processes. Processes related to the role of citizen have characteristics of both business processes and societal processes, in that both the user and society are customers of the process. Processes where the individual is compelled—by moral suasion or by force—to act in a predetermined fashion, uniquely belong to societal processes.

Finally, processes that cross the boundaries of an organization are worth mentioning here. They face an added level of complexity. Crossing the boundaries of functions, as most processes do, has its challenges, but crossing different organizational cultures and structures is much more difficult. Buying a book on the web, for instance, may involve several organizations for a single transaction, such as web service provider, online bookstore, online payment service provider, and express package delivery service.

The reader can see how generalizing the preceding discussion to other systems such as ecosystems and international systems can be accomplished. Of course, this book focuses on business processes. However, many process notions apply to any reference system. The discussion of personal, family, and societal processes thus serves the following purposes:

- Illustrate the material with simple examples to which anyone can relate, and facilitate understanding by drawing examples from different reference systems

- Provide the reader with a convenient field of application to test the newly acquired knowledge

- Help business to better understand and therefore interact more effectively with individuals (employees and customers) and society (regulations, community integration, social responsibility)

- Provide the reader with a valuable by-product: improve personal processes and those of the family

3.2.3 Repetitiveness

Some processes take place only once. These are called *projects*. Examples may include learning to drive a car, building the family house, merging with another company, or revolting against a colonial power. This is in contrast to repetitive processes, such as preparing a cup of coffee, helping a student do homework, billing a customer, or collecting taxes. A major difference between projects and processes is the learning aspects. If you are going to do something only once, only the result matters. You are not concerned at all about being able to do it better next time. *Results, no matter how* may constitute a valid marching order at the outset of a project. However, if this order refers to a repetitive process, it is a counterproductive one. The importance of successfully concluding a repetitive process must always be balanced against the need to be able to do it better, cheaper, and faster the next time.

The distinction between projects and processes is not, however, as clear-cut as it may appear at first glance. Writing a book is a project: you are not going to write the same book twice. However, you may write several books, in which case the sub-process of preparing a table of contents or of harmonizing writing styles is repetitive. Further, even within a single project, some sub-processes, such as proofreading a chapter, may be repeated hundreds of times. Thus, there are very few pure projects where the *how* does not matter. Conversely, many repetitive projects involve changes from one cycle to the next. A company may repeat the strategic planning process, but it can make improvements every year and also the company's circumstances may vary widely over time.

Improving a process is a project, and this project can be described using a SITOC. The key input will be a broken process; the key output, a repaired process. The project will be conducted only once, but the process that will be fixed as a result will be repeated many times over—albeit differently from the way it had been run before it was fixed.

3.2.4 Cycle Time

Related to the difference between a project and a repetitive process are the notions of cycle time, complexity, and frequency of repetition. Most people brush their teeth two or three times a day. That may translate into roughly 70,000 repetitions over a lifetime. Cycle time is about five minutes (including two minutes of actual brushing) and the process is simple. Clearly, the process remains *frozen* for long periods of time during which you try only, with more or less success, to repeat the same activity without variation.

Preparing monthly financial statements requires hundreds, if not thousands of person-hours, depending on the size of the company. While it remains a repetitive process, the sheer complexity of the task makes it unlikely that it would ever be repeated in exactly the same manner—nor should it be. To carry the process through to a successful conclusion, some players have to continually find new ways to deal with unforeseen circumstances. Complex processes cannot be fully programmed and blindly repeated: they require judgment and skills. If repeated often, and if a continuous improvement philosophy prevails, they will evolve towards a better and more complete definition of vital aspects and the grey areas and ill-charted sections will be reduced.

Fixing short-cycle processes and long-cycle processes require a different approach.

3.2.5 Nature of Challenge

Some processes involve a mostly physical challenge on the part of process workers and others a mostly intellectual one. Even though no human action other than a reflex one can take place without the conscious brain being involved, moving a piano up a flight of stairs is a mostly physical challenge. Making a decision, on the other hand, is a mostly intellectual task. Most processes fall somewhere between these two extremes. Whenever physical challenges are involved, so are the laws of physics and chemistry. Improving such a process requires at least an intuitive understanding of these laws. Characterizing and optimizing it requires an explicit one. In addition, since parts of the process do not talk to you (that is, objects and machines), designed experiments will be required to make it *talk*, that is, to learn about it[4].

When an intellectual task is involved, the process takes place more between your ears or between two people than between two hands. Thus, a substantial amount of subjective information has to be processed, requiring a different approach and different tools. Table 3.3 illustrates this dimension of processes, as well as the previous one (cycle time), with a number of personal examples.

Improving processes where physical flows dominate falls largely into the realm of industrial engineering, and will not be discussed in any depth in this book.

3.2.6 Service and Customer Contact

Service processes are characterized mainly by the intangibility of the results they are producing and by the contact between provider and customer-face-to-face or otherwise (this is discussed in Section 4.2). Thus, an important difference between manufactured goods and services is that the former can be separated from the production process per se, but the latter cannot. Indeed, consumers are not present when the good is built, and will often never find out (nor care) how it was built (though things may be different for business customers). In services, the customer witnesses part of the process (the *contact* part, versus the *back office* part). In fact, the process itself is an important part of the service. The very fact that the name of a service often involves an action verb (repairing cars, cleaning houses) reflects this linkage. Put another way, the service *is* the process (or an important part of it, depending on the industry). When making a phone call for technical assistance for a computer problem, for instance, the process of helping the customer solve his problem *is* the service. Hence, designing a service is designing the service delivery process-and that goes for internal services as well.

Service takes place *live*. If you do something wrong when assembling a product, you can fix it before it is shipped. If you do or say something wrong in a face-to-face encounter, you cannot take it back: the damage is done (though you can, and should, try to apologize and make up for it). A service is a human experience. It is lived, not bought. The difference between a good and a bad service is well illustrated by the difference between seeing *The King and I* on Broadway and buying the DVD of the movie, starring actress Jodie Foster. It is the same story, but both the actors and the audience will have quite a different experience. The processes involved are radically different as well. After all those years on Broadway, one would expect the process to be *optimized* to the finest level of detail. Still, professional actors will tell you that reproducing the same emotions, performance after performance, is always a challenge, even if the required level of adrenaline is there. The movie captured on DVD has been *optimized* scene by scene, some of which may have required as many as 30 takes, and assembled in a *bottled* experience that can be delivered where and when desired, without any variation.

3.2.7 Inputs and Outputs

Processes can also be classified in terms of the nature of their inputs, transformations, and outputs. Inputs and outputs may be people, things, information, or any combination of these. The

Table 3.3   Illustration of personal processes, their major challenge, approximate cycle times, and lifetime frequencies.

Physical challenge	Intellectual/mental challenge	Cycle time	Lifetime frequency
Brush teeth	Plan your day	10 min	60000
Shop for groceries	Plan meals for next week	1 hour	1500
Prepare reception	Plan next year's vacation	4 hours	300
Winterize house	Annual home budgeting	1 week	40
Re-do landscaping	Teach daughter how to drive	3 months	2
Learn how to play golf	Learn how to write	1 year	1

transformation of things or people involves some sort of change: physical or chemical properties, personal state (sick, well, happy, and so on), ownership (retail, sales processes), or place (transportation processes). Data can be structured and organized to become information. Information can be analyzed to become knowledge and thus used to facilitate decisions. Designing, managing, or improving a process requires familiarity with the nature of the input. An industrial engineer, say, who excels at improving manufacturing processes, would probably be at a loss to deal with processes involving human emotions as information.

3.2.8 Automation

Finally, processes that can fully accomplish the transformation without human intervention differ from those that require it. Human intervention involves motivation, judgment, and skills. As much as these may be standardized through training, testing, and selection, the outcome will always remain unpredictable to some extent—witness the *human error* to which plane crashes are often attributed. Machines are generally much more predictable. As technology progresses, they surpass human processes in increasingly complex areas, such as some aspects of hip surgery and flying an aircraft. Thus, automated processes are in a class of their own.

As seen in this section, the breadth of the process space is vast-as varied, in fact, as human endeavor itself. For all this variety and complexity, however, processes share the simple definition of being ways to transform some inputs into outputs that better meet some human requirement or other. In this book, this commonality is exploited to show how processes can be better managed and superior ones can be developed. To show the wide range of applicability of the process framework, examples will be drawn from all corners of the process space.

3.3 CHAIN OF COMMITMENT

Processes involve people making commitments to one another and trusting that these commitments will be fulfilled, within a reference system—in our case, within an organization. In this section, the nature of commitment is explored first, and then a personal and a government example will be presented. Subsequently, a look at the difficulties large functional organizations encounter with processes will be taken.

3.3.1 Commitment to the Task or to the Result

When understanding of a process is poor or when it operates in turbulent environments[5], the ability to innovate and make adjustments on the fly is at a premium. Without a team fully committed to end results, failure is virtually guaranteed. Think of the early start-ups in the field of e-commerce, such as Yahoo and eBay, facing new technology, new markets, and new business models. Only unflinching commitment and talent—driven by leadership and vision—allowed some of them to pull it off. This type of commitment translates into *push-pull* behavior (helping internal providers [pulling] or customers [pushing] when they are experiencing difficulties), creativity, and team problem-solving.

In processes that are completely defined and programmed in the most minute detail, and where few chance events are involved (because of the stability of the environments), commitment to the task—its timing or the way it is performed—rather than to the end result may be the only thing that matters. This is typical of bureaucracies—not only of the governmental type, but also of the corporate type. Getting a construction permit at city hall or borrowing a book from the library are typical examples. In these processes, woe typically befalls anyone who tries to be creative or asks for special treatment.

Nowadays, the rules of e-business are becoming clearer (for the survivors) and the processes required to ensure flawless execution are slowly emerging. Commitment to end results is still required, but commitment to performing the activities correctly is becoming increasingly important. Performing open-heart surgery or controlling air traffic at a busy airport, for example, require both a strict adherence to procedure and great commitment to deal with unexpected situations.

In the process world, these three types of situations (commitment to end result, to the task, or both) have to be dealt with differently. However, they have something in common: without a real commitment by each player, the process fails miserably. A more detailed discussion of the link between commitments and processes will now take place.

3.3.2 Real Commitment: a Personal Example

When Louise and Paul are invited by Diane and Mark for dinner (see Box 3.1), they are the customers. Diane and Mark are the productive resources, delivering *a pleasant evening with good friends* (output) to their guests and themselves. The reference system is the family home. The global process of creating that result can be broken down into several sub—processes: preparing a meal, creating the right ambience, serving the meal, managing conversations, and so on. Each of these processes involves specific inputs, transformations, and outputs. Here, the customers play several roles: they are productive resources in the process (that is, they contribute to the conversation), they are suppliers of information (their preferences about meals, time constraints, and so on), and they are transformed by the process (from being hungry, for example, to being satisfied).

Box 3.1: Honey, Louise and Paul are coming over for dinner tonight!

Issue: *Process adaptability through a dynamic chain of commitments (in the home environment.)*

The following story is told by Mark Parker, a middle-aged lawyer working out of a home office and living in the countryside near a small town.

"Honey, Louise and Paul are coming over for dinner tonight!" Those are not necessarily welcome words, as I hear them through the closed door of my office where I'm busy trying to put the finishing touches on a complex contract. Louise and Paul are good friends, but it is Saturday and I have my heart set on going out to see a movie. I walk out of my second floor studio and meet Diane as she reaches the top of the stairs.

"I thought they were only coming back from Florida tomorrow," I say.

"They decided to come back early—weather was lousy and Louise was homesick!" she responds, "and you, sir, are needed!"

"How's that?" I ask.

"It's four o'clock dear," she says, "and I'll need about an hour to finish painting that chair before I can do anything about preparing dinner—and I would like to tidy up a little. I did tell Louise when I invited her that it would be a potluck affair, but she said that the last time she invited us, and I can still smell the roasted duck she prepared. My only option now is fondue!"

"Great idea!" I reply, "I would never have thought of that. What do you want me to do?"

"I can take care of the fondue," she says, "but I need you to take care of all the rest: appetizers, salad, wine, coffee, and dessert."

"Sir, yes sir, ma'am!" I respond, clicking my heels. "Permission to speak freely, sir, ma'am."

"Permission to speak cautiously and quickly," she quips. "They'll be here at seven o'clock."

Continued

Continued

"I'll be ready with appetizers at eight sharp," I say. "Salad will be ready as well by then, so we can sit down for dinner whenever we feel like it. I'll do the serving if you don't mind—I've been sitting all day at my computer and you've barely stopped for 20 minutes for lunch."

"Oh yeah! By that time, I'll need to sit down. Thanks! I've got a couple of hot dips I want to prepare. I'll set it up so that they're ready at 8:30. What about the rest?"

"I'll get to it right away," I say. "I've got a got a couple of good bottles downstairs, so I'll leave right now for the supermarket to get everything else we need. But I'll call Mr. England at the bakery right away to see if there's still time for a Saint-Honoré. That would add a nice touch to the evening."

I get Mr. England on the phone right away. After the usual greetings, we get down to business.

"Something just came up and I would like a Saint-Honoré on very short notice," I said. "In fact, I would like to be able to pick it up at 6:30. Do you think you can make it in time? I know it's late and Saturday is your busiest day of the week, but I would really appreciate it."

"Let me see what we can do," he responds.

While I wait, I hear muted voices involving three people talking about, *last bake*, and *oven temperature*. He comes back to the phone.

"Mr. Parker?"

"Yes?"

"It's your lucky day," he replies. "I just talked with the guys in the back and they say they'd be able to squeeze it in at the end of the shift. It'll be ready at 6:30."

"Thanks Mr. England! I really appreciate this." I say. "I could have picked something up at the supermarket, you know, but it would have been just dessert. Now I know that my guests will have a memorable experience."

"That's what we're here for, Mr. Parker," he says, obviously pleased with the compliment.

After a short drive, I enter the supermarket and head directly for the dairy counter. I'm halfway there when the cell phone starts vibrating in my shirt pocket. I answer as I pull away to a corner so that I'm not in the way of all these busy shoppers—mostly men, I notice (probably under strict marching orders like me):

"Mark? Boy, am I glad I got hold of you! Louise just called," says an anxious Diane over the phone. "She wants to call it off for tonight. They've got to pick up little Jenny from ballet at nine o'clock tonight, so they have to leave at 9:15. I told her I would have none of it; that if they could get here at 6 o'clock, we could still have a pleasant evening, with time enough to chat about their trip and plenty of time to pick up Jenny. Oh! I'm sorry dear! I should have talked to you before."

"Don't worry honey, you did the right thing," I answer with a conviction I do not really feel, as I glance at my watch. "Do you have Mr. England's phone number handy?"

Preparing this meal illustrates very well the notion of a process as a chain of commitments, with Diane as *process owner* (see below) and major player. A commitment is a promise to deliver. It is real when the person who makes it is responsible, which means accepting the personal consequences of not delivering on the promise. If there is no personal consequence, then there is no real commitment, and therefore there is no process. A commitment does not have to be written or formal. Eye contact may be enough, as illustrated by Mark's story. The consequences can be of any nature, as long as they are meaningful enough to the person making the commitment to motivate him to do what he has promised. Diane knows the consequences of not being able to have dinner before the guests have to leave to pick up their daughter; Mark, those of not bringing dessert on time; Mr. England, those of disappointing an important customer; and the baker, those of placing the boss in that position. Thus, everybody knows what he or she has to do to avoid these consequences. Note that, before making the commitment, each player in the process evaluated the feasibility of the request. This included verifying that each supplier was willing to commit as well.

What happened when the customer changed his mind illustrates well the strength of a chain of commitment. Before changing the commitment, each player assessed the feasibility of the change request. Because each player was accountable and felt empowered, neither one went to the boss, but rather went directly to the person who had made the initial commitment, who then disposed of the matter. Customer-provider negotiations may occur anywhere along the chain, but, since they are direct, they occur quickly. They start with the customer (downstream) and move all the way upstream (that is, customer-in). The revised chain of commitment then moves in the opposite direction, all the way to the end-customer. Thus, the process is agile, that is the response is quick and reliable.

3.3.3 Real Commitment: a Government Process Example

These process notions are just as relevant in business. Processes involving many players only work if everyone who has a role to play—providing some intermediate output to one of the players—is willing and able to play the part. Designing such a process thus involves decomposing the result desired into a set of intermediate results. The responsibility for each of these is then farmed out to the various players[6], who must accept this responsibility, that is, commit to it. They will not do so unless they are motivated (positively or negatively). They should not do so unless they feel that they are able to meet their commitments, that is, that they have the resources, tools, and skills required, as well as any required upstream commitments from other players.

In this context, a process is viewed as a logical chain of commitments. Since a chain is only as strong as its weakest link, processes are vulnerable to lack of commitment on the part of any player. To illustrate how these notions apply in complex processes, focus for a moment on the processes involved in airline security (see Chapter 1). The mission of these processes[7] is to prevent anyone or anything that might constitute a security risk from boarding or being brought aboard the aircraft. It starts when security officials are ready to start boarding and loading. It ends when the doors are closed and the captain asks the tower for clearance. How many distinct agencies are *responsible* for security throughout this process? If local airport police, federal agencies, private agencies, and airline personnel are included, the number would probably be close to 25, not counting the fact that different divisions of the same agencies are involved (in airlines, for example, there are ground crews, ticket agents, luggage handlers, gate crews, flight crews, and security).

Look at the interfaces and commitments along the chain as a passenger boards the plane. First, an official waves the passenger through as the luggage is X-rayed. This official trusts that the X-ray machine has done its job, and that the luggage does not represent a threat to security. If the luggage is randomly flagged for inspection, a security agent searches the passenger before allowing check-in or boarding at the airline's gate. The agent checks the papers and puts an "Inspected" seal on the luggage, thus communicating to downstream players that the commitment to search the bag thoroughly has been fulfilled. When the counter agent and baggage inspectors downstream see that seal, they trust that the job has been done. As the pilot gives a thumbs-up for pushback, there is trust again that the baggage control personnel, and those in charge of the computers and databases being used, have made sure that each piece of luggage loaded on the plane belongs to a passenger. The pilot also trusts that everyone involved has delivered on his or her respective commitment.

How effective is the process? The answer to that depends on a host of factors, including process design, people selection, training, and technology, as well as on the effectiveness of the processes intent on impairing it, that is, the processes used by terrorists. Failure can occur equally well within an individual task or at the interface between two or more players.

Any one player who is not committed to producing the intermediate result that was imparted to the task by process designers will simply go through the motions in order to protect his back, an approach typical of a bureaucracy. An agent inspecting a bag, for example, might seem to an observer to be totally immersed in the task, whereas in fact a fight he had with his wife the night before may be foremost in his mind. Such lack of commitment often occurs when failure to do the job right is perceived not to have any personal consequence. In a recent trip (yes, after 9/11), the only security person nearby as I walked through the metal detector was standing at the end of the X-ray machine conveyer, about 10 feet away. I emptied my pockets, stepped though the detector, picked-up my things, and went on to pick up my computer. I could easily have had several blades in there, and nobody would have noticed. Someone was not meeting the commitment, and nobody cared, probably thinking, *It's not my job.*

It is a critical part of the process designer's job to ensure that nothing falls between the cracks in terms of individual responsibilities, and that the connections or interfaces between various subprocesses allow for maximal verification of the quality of intermediate outputs. Placing a color-coded security seal on a bag is one way to avoid it being opened in the line that forms between the search point and the counter. It also informs the counter agent that the bag has not been totally overlooked.

3.3.4 Process Commitment and the Functional Organization

Clearly, the creation of team spirit and the sharing of a common understanding of the global process, as well as its individual components, are great contributors to the maintenance of the integrity of a process under various conditions; that is to say, they are critical to the adaptability (see Section 5.2.1) of the process. Without the right incentives and training, individuals will focus on their own tasks and lose sight of the purpose of the process. The 400-m women's relay in the Sydney Summer Olympic Games (2000) makes this abundantly clear: individually, American runners were the fastest—sports fans might vividly recall Marion Jones almost catching up in the last leg—but their baton did not cross the finish line first. Each runner focused on her 100-meter leg, obviously with little thought or preparation for the transition. The narrow-minded pursuit of excellence in the task does not make for excellence in the process as a whole.

Large functional organizations—famous for their lack of adaptability in an environment that increasingly requires it—are particularly challenged as they try to adopt a process orientation. A functional organization is one where people with similar expertise are grouped together under a functional leader, for example, vice-presidents for finance, human resources, strategic planning, marketing, and so on. Most processes, however, do not respect these functional boundaries (*silos* or *smokestacks*, as they are frequently called) and flow back and forth between functions. An invoicing process, for example, may require input from people from sales, pricing, inventory, production, shipping, customer service, and finance. Producing a mortgage loan in a bank involves people from account management, credit, collateral, legal, and the back office.

While the employees of such organizations may pay lip service to the concept of the next function in the sequence being their internal customer, their only true commitment is generally to their functional boss. That makes processes very rigid and slow to adapt. Often, even requests for minute changes have to go up the hierarchy and come back down, involving long and disruptive delays every step of the way. Hence, there are no processes to speak off in such organizations, only a disjointed, loosely related, and static set of activities, much like that of the U.S. women's relay team in Sydney, with each runner centered of running her part of the race, and not willing to adjust her own individual contribution to the process for the common good. The reader interested in digging deeper into this area should read Pall (1999). In later chapters, the notion of process owner as a countermeasure to this problem will be discussed (see Chapter 12).

3.4 PROCESSES: AT THE HEART OF VALUE CREATION AND LEARNING

This last section should help the reader who is wondering what any of the material presented in this chapter has to do with the notion of value discussed in the previous one. The need for continuous improvement is also highlighted here, and the challenges involved in selecting the right process for improvement. Finally, an additional typology to facilitate this improvement is presented.

3.4.1 The Value Connection

Processes create value, not functions. Functions contribute to value creation through the part they play (that is, the tasks they perform) in processes. Processes create the benefits customers want by delivering the service, or by making this delivery possible in one way or another. This point is illustrated by referring back to the discount real estate broker example discussed in Chapter 2. Figure 3.10 builds on Figure 2.11 to show the three-way connection between selected processes of a real estate broker, the features of the service, the delivery of the service they affect, and the benefits thus created for the customer. As discussed above, while in manufacturing, the output of a process is clearly distinct from the process itself (that is, a car is distinct from the assembly line that put it together), this is often not the case in services. For instance, the output of the training process, that is, training, cannot be separated from the training process itself. Thus, while you can design a car first and then the assembly line to build it, it is often impossible to distinguish service design from service process design. Hence, there is a wide grey area between marketing and operations in services. The price that the service organization will pay for a poor connection between marketing and operations is even higher than that paid by a manufacturing organization.

3.4.2 Why Should Processes Be Improved?

The space station orbits the earth at an altitude of about 390 kilometers. However, this altitude decays at a rate of about 40 cm per revolution. Consequently, unless some action is taken to lift it up, the station will eventually re-enter earth's atmosphere and burn. Processes decay over time as well, and tend to stray further and further away from their initial state (this is analogous to the principle of entropy in thermodynamics). Now, humans are a great source of variation. Humans become tired, forget, grow careless, and make mistakes. Priorities shift. Feelings may interfere, and co-workers under pressure may blame one another or become angry with one another. As anyone using a computer will know, however, machines are not exempt from variations either. Moreover, man-machine interaction and environmental factors are further sources of variation. Thus, processes have to be improved just to maintain current performance.

However, fixing processes because they show signs of problems is only half the answer. The world is a dynamic place. Technology changes and creates new opportunities. Markets change as well, also creating new opportunities. In business, every opportunity comes with a concomitant threat: if you do not seize it, your competitor will. At an individual level, your body and mind change. All social organizations, such as families and companies, are subject to dynamic influences. Process improvement skills are vital to survival and prosperity in such an environment.

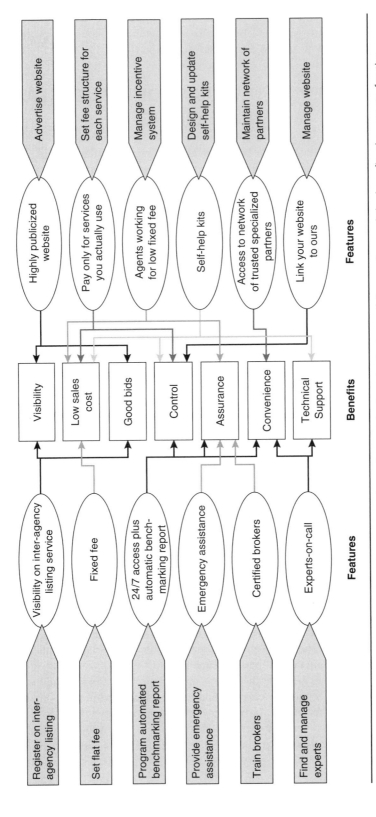

Figure 3.10 Connections between selected processes of a real estate broker, the features of the service, and the benefits they create for the customer.

Finally, and perhaps most importantly, as discussed in Section 1.2, processes lie at the core of organizational learning, the key to becoming a world-class organization.

Data is digits. When relationships are built into the data, it becomes information. When decision rules link the information, it becomes knowledge. Knowledge is static. While it can and should evolve dynamically, it does not produce anything by itself. Know-how refers to the organization's ability to produce a given result, repeatedly, and with minimal variation, that is, to processes. Processes, however, need to access information, data, and knowledge bases. When referring to the learning organization in this book (see Chapters 5, 9, and 12), we mean the organization that dynamically improves its know-how.

3.4.3 Which Process Should Be Improved?

Processes are many, and time and resources limited. Which ones should be picked for improvement? It is worthwhile for a person or organization trying to answer this question to classify their processes into three categories:

- *Value-adding processes*, which are those that are directly involved in the achievement of goals. For an individual, this may involve obtaining a degree or reaching some other personal goal such as completing a marathon or getting a book published. For a family, it may mean spending more time together or getting the kids to stop fighting all the time may be the priority. A company may want to reduce its time-to-market or increase the turnover of its inventory. At a societal level, reducing child abuse and ensuring airline safety are good examples. Table 3.4 shows illustrative value-creating processes associated with these and other goals. Corresponding enabling and support processes are shown as well. *Provide the service to specific customers*, for instance, including all the sub-processes shown between the boundaries in Figures 3.6 (Medsol) and 3.8 (real estate), are value-adding processes. In business, value-adding processes include transactional processes (from order-taking to order fulfillment) and developmental processes (involved in the development of new services and new markets).

- *Enabling processes*, which are those that enable value-adding processes to work well. Whereas the impact of value-adding processes on goals is direct, that of enabling processes is indirect. They are no less important than value-adding processes; they simply play a different role. They are often about the acquisition or development of basic competencies and capabilities. After training a team of design engineers for a week, for example (see Table 3.4), time-to-market has not been shortened by one second—in fact, it is probably longer because the engineers were away for a week—but training may be a prerequisite (enabler) for the product design process to ever reach the desired capability. Recruiting doctors at Medsol or recruiting agents in the real estate business would be enabling processes as well. Governance processes, such as capital budgeting, strategic planning, and succession management, belong in this category. Some management processes may fall in this category.

- *Support processes*, which are related to building or maintaining the required infrastructure for value-creating and enabling processes to work. Some management processes fall in this category. Failure of support processes may well impair the functioning of other processes, and thereby have a negative impact on value creation. These processes, however, are quite remote from the core of the business and thus require vastly different expertise. As such, they are often good candidates for outsourcing. Indeed, why not delegate some of these processes to organizations whose core business it is to perform them (potentially resulting in higher quality and lower cost)?

Table 3.4   Illustration of personal process classification for personal, family, business, and societal processes.

Goal	Value adding processes	Enabling process	Support processes
Personal Book published Marathon completed	Write a book Train for endurance	Improve writing style Eat the right food	Proofread Renew track club membership
Family No fights between kids Quality time together	Identify causes of fight Synchronize our schedules	Monitor the kids' activities Develop common tastes	Transport to mini-league Get good seats at the theater
Business Quick to reach market Fast inventory turnover	Develop new product Eliminate low turnover items	Train design engineer Train people in JIT	Build common parts database Manage in-plant traffic
Society No child abuse Safe airline	Protect endangered children Spot terrorists trying to board	Raise awareness in population Select the right technology	Type reports Manage telecommunications

Unlike the typologies presented in Section 3.2 above, this classification is based on the goals currently pursued. Clearly, as the goals change, so does this classification. Once someone has completed a marathon, the individual may well decide that the knees hurt too much, and so quits sports altogether and decides to write a book. The process of training for endurance then ceases to exist and a writing process has to be designed from scratch. On another level, since the events of 9/11, the salience of such processes in ensuring the safety of airlines and immigration processes has increased dramatically.

Setting the right goal and finding the most important sub-processes require one to take a global view of things, starting from a strategic (business) or philosophical (personal, familial, or societal) approach. It requires clarity of purpose, sound macroanalysis of environments, and rigor in priority-setting and process identification. Such an analysis (discussed in Chapters 6 and 7) could, for example, lead the discount real estate broker discussed in Chapter 2 to scope a process such as *write up property description for Website* in response to a problem statement such as while the *click-through*[8] rate is about 2 percent for our properties, it should be 5 percent. Improving this specific process is then *the right thing to do*, and focus can now move on to *doing things right*, which moves into a very different realm (discussed in Chapters 10 and 11).

Doing things right involves digging into the process to characterize it, that is, to understand in detail its dynamics and critical variables. The mindset, skills, and tools required at the two levels—which can figuratively be referred to as the 10,000 meters versus the ground-level view—are vastly different. Failure at either task is fatal. Failure to identify *the right thing to do* results in investing time and effort *doing the wrong thing right* (that is, things that are not important), which adds little value and distracts us from the important issue we should be addressing. Failure to *do things right* results in *doing the right thing wrong*—also a recipe for disaster.

One last thought on selecting which process to improve: Salience cannot be the only criterion. Current performance is also very important. Among value-adding processes, those that display the worst performance (relative to what it could or should be) are prime candidates. This is discussed in Chapter 7.

3.5 SUMMARY

Performing a process consists of taking an input and transforming it into a desired output. This notion applies equally well at a very high level (making a car) and at a very detailed one (snapping on the bumper). SITOC, FAST, and PFDs are essential tools to understand and delimit the perimeter of a discrete process functioning within a system (such as an organization). These tools help us on the path from the macro view to the vital few variables within.

For a process to be defined, a loosely related sequence of ill-defined activities is not sufficient. A number of conditions are presented.

Ten different ways to classify processes are presented, ranging from the number of players, repetitiveness, and cycle time to degree of automation. They are helpful in coming to grips with this very broad concept. Classification is the beginning of knowledge. One additional classification—of particular importance to organizations—relates to the nature and degree of commitment the players in the process make to each other. Without real commitment, there is no process.

Processes create value, as defined in Chapter 2. Understanding the nature of value for customers of choice is prerequisite to the design and management of processes. The ability to identify the most important processes to focus on at any point—doing the right thing—and the ability to improve, design, or redesign it-doing things right-are strategic business capabilities.

EXERCISES

3.1 Preparing a PFD

a) Prepare a SITOC (see Figures 3.5 and 3.7 for illustrations) for the two following processes, *"Sell products and services"* and *"Invoice the customer."* Use the form shown in Figure 3.11.

b) For these same two processes, prepare a PFD using the approach used in section 3.1.2 (see Figures 3.6 and 3.8).

c) In each of the PFD diagrams you have just prepared, check off the processes that are defined in your organization (as defined in Section 3.1.3).

d) From each of the same PFD diagrams, pick two processes: one that is checked off, one that is not. Prepare SITOCs for each of these four processes.

3.2 Commitment

Explore the nature and strength of the commitments associated with the two processes you identified with a check in c) above, and for which you prepared a SITOC in d). Talk to each of the players, and discuss with them who their providers and customers are and what happens when they do not deliver.

3.3 Experience with cross-functional processes

Identify a cross-functional process that has been modified recently or that is currently being implemented. Find out about inter-functional issues that arose and how they were resolved—if they were

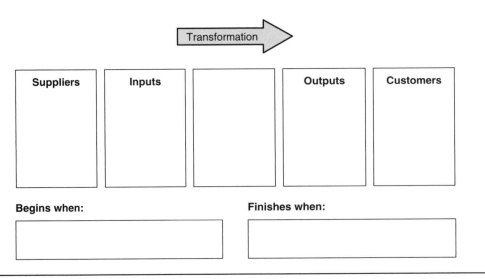

Figure 3.11 The SITOC form used to circumscribe a process (Exercise 3.1).

resolved. Draw a conclusion from this and from the previous exercises about your organization's *process-friendliness* and about the challenges that await it, as it embarks on a process-oriented style of management.

3.4 Processes—features—benefits

Prepare a diagram similar to that shown in Figure 3.9, connecting benefits, features, and processes. Start from your answer to Exercise 2.4 in Chapter 2.

3.5 Process model

Before doing this exercise, review Section 3.1.2 dealing with viewing the organization as a set of interconnected processes and Section 3.4.3 classifying process in three major roles.

a) Prepare a process model for your company. Refer to the APQC process classification framework presented in Figure 3.2 and 3.3 (you can download the full model free at www.apqc.org). This model is generic and is applicable to any industry. Make it specific. A medical clinic, for instance, might replace *produce and deliver for service organization* with *diagnose and treat patients*, and *manage external relationships* with *manage relationship with laboratories*, and *manage relationship with hospitals*. Only include processes that currently exist in your organization (do not for now add processes that you think should exist). You should get between eight and 15 processes.

b) Prepare a FAST diagram for all value-adding processes, such as the ones shown in Figures 3.1 and 3.3. Keep them at a high level, generating three to five sub-processes for each of the typically three to six value-adding processes. This should yield 15 to 25 processes. Bear in mind that designing the service and service delivery process, reaching the right customers, delivering the service, and managing customer data are all value-adding processes.

c) Prepare a FAST diagram for each remaining process. From the resulting list of level processes (you should have between 20 and 40, depending on the industry you are in), identify the ones you consider to be value enablers and the ones you consider to be support processes.

d) Identify the major processes performed by partners and suppliers. For a pharmacy, for example, this may include *manage inventory* (in the case of a supplier-managed inventory) or *provide online drug interaction information.*

Notes

[1] This model was developed as a facilitating tool for benchmarking, that is, a reference to help compare apples to apples.

[2] The term used in this book to describe people who work in processes.

[3] This latter point is admittedly moot. You could argue that the system was designed to do just what it did, and thus that it performed superbly.

[4] This is called the *voice of the process* in Chapter 8.

[5] Including the political, economic, social, technological, and ecological environments.

[6] The word player is used in this specific context to refer to a function (for example, marketing), department (for example, publicity), or section (for example, graphic design) with a role to play.

[7] A notion discussed in Chapter 6.

[8] The rate at which browsers exposed to the ad will click on it.

4

Professional Service Delivery Processes

The relationship between a professional and the client has many facets. So do the relationships among professionals, and between them and the rest of the organization. Selecting modes of contacts and managing interfaces is critical to all stakeholders.

After the general introduction to processes presented in the previous chapter, the focus turns now to the specificities of professional service delivery processes (PSDP). First is a discussion of what makes them different—and more complex than other processes. Then, the focus is on the intricate questions associated with how the players in the process interact with each other. After discussing the specific modalities through which customers and providers come in contact with each other, the discussion broadens to include contacts between professionals, and interaction with the rest of the organization. Short definitions of the major concepts discussed in this chapter are in Table 4.1.

4.1 FUNDAMENTAL NOTIONS ABOUT PSDPs

The way a PSDP is designed has a determinant influence on value creation for a PSOs three stakeholders: customers, employees, and shareholders. First, there is an explanation of how a PSDP consists of four generic stages, before a discussion of the first stage (dispatch or bidding). The chapter then revisits (from Chapter 2) the leadership role expected of professionals during co-production encounters. The varying challenges presented by different tasks in the process are then tackled, before concluding on the role of emotions throughout the service encounter.

4.1.1 Generic View of PSDPs

Any professional service delivery process can be broken down into four generic stages:

- *Matching.* As discussed in Section 2.1 (quality of services), because of the knowledge gap the professional and the client, the latter often does not know which professional is best qualified to solve the problem. The first generic stage in the process is therefore to somehow get the customer to meet with the right professional. A mistake at this stage results in a waste of time for the customer (that is, delayed solution) and in wasted resources for the organization. Matching takes place in one of two ways: dispatch or competitive bidding. In the former, the potential customer calls on the

Table 4.1 Key concepts discussed in Chapter 4.

Diagnosis	A conclusion reached by a professional regarding the nature and source of a problem. It is the defining characteristic of professional services.
Dispatch	The act of directing a customer in need to the right professional.
Customer contact	Any point in a service episode when the client and service provider must communicate or interact in some way.
Moment of truth	Any moment in a service episode that is determinant in shaping the client's opinion of the service provider.
Modes of contact	Communication channels selected for the various customer contacts that punctuate a service encounter. The notion also refers to internal contacts among service providers.
Line of visibility	The imaginary line that marks the limits of the client's field of vision during a service encounter. What lies beyond the line of visibility is called the back-office.
Co-production	The joint interactive activities of the service provider and his client to produce the desired result.
Leadership in professional services	The responsibility of a professional to guide the client toward the right course of action, even if it runs counter to the latter's preference. It is a fundamental difference that distinguishes the role of a professional from that of other service providers.
Task challenges	The nature of the most demanding aspect of a task or activity in a PSDP: discipline, judgment, or creativity.
Fault line	A particularly vulnerable aspect of a PSDP created by conflicting objectives between the client, the organization, professionals, and other employees.

organization and the organization dispatches the customer to a professional. In the latter—more commonly used by business customers—the customer invites a selected (or pre-qualified) number of firms to submit a proposal to supply the desired services. In both cases, the customer must first conclude that help is needed, identify potential providers, and evaluate them.

- *Diagnostic.* Together with the next stage (prescription), these are the defining functions of professional work. Professionals first interact with the client to obtain information. They then take the required actions to validate this information. They finally apply a number of decision rules, learned during their training and honed through experience, to reach a conclusion about the nature and origins of the client's problem. A diagnostic generally emerges gradually throughout this stage, through a series of iterations involving the formulation and testing of hypotheses. Validation is required before moving on to the next stage.

- *Prescription.* This is the professional's statement of the course of action required to solve the problem. Again, it results from the application of professional judgment and decision rules. Of course, any prescription founded on an inaccurate diagnostic will not solve the client's problem and may do more harm than good. Without a diagnostic and a prescription, the other productive resources of the organization (technicians and technologies of all types) are incapable of helping the customer.

- *Treatment.* This is the execution or fulfillment of the prescription. The actions spelled out in the prescription generally involve the professional and the clients themselves, separately and together (see Section 4.1.4 below), and may involve a number of other players, including other professionals, technicians, and other categories of workers.

The professional is normally responsible for ensuring the correct execution of prescribed actions, in the required sequence, and their continuous monitoring and adjustment as needed throughout the treatment.

Hypothesis testing and formulation in the diagnostic and prescription stages often require engaging adjacent processes that will return information to the professional. A real estate agent, for instance, may ask a clerk for a web search of comparable houses for sale, and an engineer may ask a technician to test the properties of some material. The reader may want to peek at Figure 5.8 to see what this may look like in a hospital. PSDPs are also surrounded by a host of other processes such as *develop pricing strategy* (upstream), *process accounts receivable, credit,* and *collection* (downstream), and *acquire and collect information* (throughout).

The next two sections explore the short but critical matching stage (dispatch or competitive bidding) in more detail. The chapter then turns to some implications of this particular process structure.

4.1.2 Dispatch

As the need for professional services gradually takes shape in the mind of the customer, the search begins for information. The customer needs to decide on three basic questions:

- Can I fix this myself or not?

- What kind of professional do I need?

- Who should I choose?

There are many sources of information to help in the search for answers: experience; discussions with friends, relatives, and associates; advertising (newspaper, television, web); literature (articles, books, electronic and web sources); as well as information brokers of all kinds. While there is no shortage of valid information on just about any topic, telling it from the rest and understanding it may be a challenge. People vary widely in terms of their ability to access, validate, and process this information. As a result, the self-diagnostic (that is, *I need to see a physical therapist*) may very well miss the mark.

The first contact with a professional service organization (PSO) is very important for both the customer and the organization. As the aphorism goes, "you never get a second chance to make a good first impression." Imagine a potential patient calling a sports medicine clinic. The patient talks to a receptionist whose job it is to manage the appointment books, greet customers as they arrive, process payments, and give receipts. This one-minute conversation with that busy receptionist will determine whether the customer comes or not, and which professional will see the patient.

The best outcome, of course is that the patient decides to come and sees the right professional. The second best outcome is that the wrong professional is seen, but the patient is redirected to the right one. This involves a loss of time (and maybe money, if there is a charge for the professional's time) for the customer. It also involves a loss of professional time for the organization, as well as a potential loss of goodwill and negative word of mouth. A PSO creates value for the right customers by first matching them with the right professional, at the right time. A good match from the organization's perspective is one that maximizes the organization's long term earning potential. This involves the judicious application of a number of dynamically evolving criteria, such as available skill-mix, workloads, complexity, urgency, and long-term potential income from a customer, as well as the personalities involved (see Chapters 10 and 11).

The patient could also hang up and call another clinic, but even that would not be the worst outcome. The worst outcome would be that a misdirected customer gets worse because of an inappropriate treatment and starts spreading negative word of mouth.

There are several ways to handle the dispatch phase. This discussion will be limited to two examples: a simple dispatch process (through a receptionist) and a more elaborate one (through a series of filters).

The simplest solution, as described above, is to have a receptionist greet the caller or visitor, enquire about needs, interact briefly—according to a programmed script—with the potential customer, and either direct to an available professional or make an appointment, using agreed upon decision rules. A receptionist in a law firm, for instance, may try to find out if the caller needs a tax expert, a criminal lawyer, or a specialist in immigration law. The receptionist may then assess the urgency of the need, see who is available, and use dispatch criteria established by the firm. What are the qualifications required to perform that function (receptionist)? Interpersonal skills are obviously very important. Given the stakes, however, and the challenges involved in reaching the right decisions quickly, substantial knowledge, judgment, and experience is required to do it well.

Organizations that leave that job to junior personnel might pay dearly for that mistake. Some do so because they do not realize the critical importance of the job. Internal considerations, however, such as the inability to draw the right people to the job (or keep them there) or failure to adjust career paths, incentive systems, or organizational culture to reflect that importance, also play a big role in the neglect of that function.

Hospitals need a more elaborate dispatch process. All emergency rooms, for instance, use some form of triage. Some patients roll in (on a stretcher) directly to the trauma room or intensive care unit where a doctor takes care of them. Most, however, are identified and checked, for ability to pay or admissibility under a health regime, before being directed to sit in a waiting room and wait for a triage nurse to call them. After a short examination, the nurse assigns a priority code (for example, a code two should not wait more than five minutes, a code five can wait all day) and the case is placed into a dynamic queuing system. The system factors in the urgency of the situation as well as arrival time (and maybe ability to pay). The system is dynamic in that later arrivals may jump the line if they are given a more urgent code, thereby increasing the remaining waiting time for patients given a less urgent code.

Figure 4.1 provides a generic illustration of such complex dispatch processes used to match customers and professionals. The process shown here involves three filters: a receptionist (unqualified, applying simple rules), a dispatcher (a senior technician such as an experienced dental assistant in a dental clinic), and a generalist professional (such as a general practitioner in a medical clinic). In the case of Medsol Emergency Clinic, the dispatcher would be a triage nurse, the generalist a general practitioner, and the specialist would a resident medical specialist—and there would be an additional level involving the resident's supervisor. The receptionist sends the customers with an easily identifiable need directly to the right professional, while informing the dispatcher, who keeps tabs on resource utilization. The dispatcher evaluates the needs and dispatches remaining cases, except those that require a professional judgment. The latter are sent to the generalist on duty who makes the dispatch decision (and informs the dispatcher, who keeps track of customers). The rationale behind the process is to try to use qualified resources only when their expertise is required, that is, after a less qualified resource has concluded that this is the case. For instance, the receptionist may dispatch 50 percent of the customers; the dispatcher may dispose of 80 percent of the remaining cases; leaving the generalist to assess the 10 percent of customers who require his expertise. The process would therefore result in a lower cost per customer dispatched and in fewer dispatch errors.

The weakness of the process is that it makes customers, especially those with the most complex cases, pay the price (delays, intermediaries, repetition) of the added efficiency. It is used extensively when resources are rationed, such as they are in public systems, or when the resources are extremely costly, and customers would rather put up with the process than pay more to gain direct access to the resources they want (but may not need).

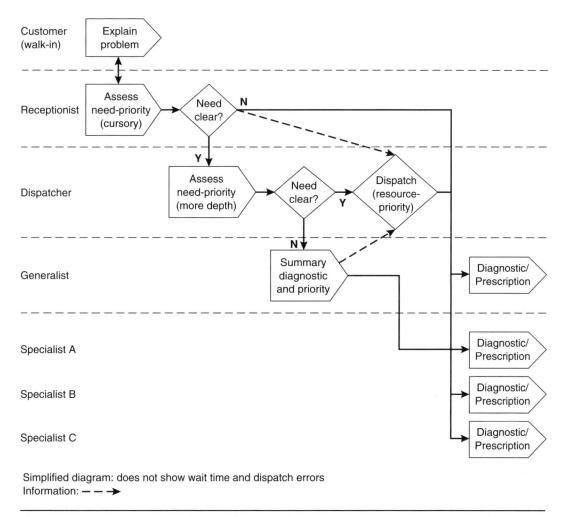

Figure 4.1 Generic illustration of a complex dispatch process to match customers and professionals.

PSOs must decide how much *filtering* of customers they want to do and how they want to do it. Questionnaires—of the physical or electronic kind—may be used, even tests. PSOs should measure the performance of the dispatch process and they should improve or redesign it (see Chapters 9 and 10) as need be.

4.1.3 Competitive Bidding

An example best illustrates the nature of competitive bidding (see Box 4.1).

Box 4.1: Quality knowledge management (QKM)

Issue: *A consulting firm develops proposals in response to open call for tenders*

QKM is a small consulting firm involved in helping a variety of organizations improve their quality systems, including, among others, such assignments as auditing existing systems, train-

---

Continued

Continued

ing, quality improvement consulting, and building integrated quality information systems. Long established, with a good reputation, the firm employs about 30 professionals, mostly drawn from the fields of engineering, quality, and management. QKM also employs a number of technicians, all graduates of technical colleges, in such fields as quality, metrology, and programming.

In its line of business, potential customers frequently ask QKM to submit proposals for contracts that are awarded competitively. Business customers approach this from the standpoint of designing and managing a competitive bidding process to acquire services. Service providers view it as designing and managing a selling process to beat competition in securing contracts. The two processes obviously overlap, with the bidders designing their processes to meet the parameters (or ground rules) set forth by the customer.

Figure 4.2 shows a macro-map of QKM's process for selling and providing services to specific customers. A macro-map provides more info than a PFD (see Figures 3.6 and 3.8 for illustrations of PFDs). It is more detailed, as it shows the major players involved in the process at the left of each row, or *swim lanes* as they are often called, and thus highlights organizational complexity. It also discriminates between activities and decisions (or branching points), and may show major delays. The macro-map, however, does not show everything that goes on in the real-life process, such as all delays, errors, volumes, reworks, and inefficiencies. Detailed mapping is the tool used to do this (see Chapter 8). Hence, the macro-map still has a *theoretical* flavor to it (that is, *how we think it goes*). Figure 4.3 zooms into the left-hand side of Figure 4.2 to show the "sell services" process in more detail.

4.1.4 Co-production and Leadership

As discussed in Chapter 2, the customer is a vital player in the process. The result depends, among other factors, on how the customer's part of the process is performed. An inaccurate statement of need or lack of follow-through on recommended courses of action will deny results.

Compare, for instance, the following two financial planners. The first one asks all the questions that must legally be asked of the client, reads a prepared text on the risks involved in investing, and provides a form to complete and sign about attitude toward risk—all said and done in 10 minutes, to get to the next customer. The second one takes an hour to interact with the client, asks about past investment experience, feelings about it, lessons learned, and plans. Imagine that this succeeds, through several such meetings (over a period of a year or two, say), in making the customer truly understand such fundamental notions as your own attitude toward risk and the costs involved when you compromise a long-term strategy through impulsive decisions, based on momentary greed or fear. Through such a process, the planner may lead the customer to a radically different investment strategy than the customer had asked for when originally walking into the planner's office.

The first planner is protected, legally. The client is none the wiser, not really knowing what to expect, and may be very upset with the outcome of the investment. The client may end up doing much damage to the business of the provider through negative word of mouth. While the planner may feel very productive (four clients an hour, 30 clients a day), no value is being created for the customer, the shareholder, or the planner. The second planner has exerted professional leadership, showing caring, competence, and trustworthiness. This led the client to accept putting initial beliefs on hold, listen, and gradually open up. A win-win-win (customer-professional-shareholder) relationship may ensue.

A professional must lead customers of choice, train them, and coach them to do their parts correctly. Professionals should give their clients the services they need, not necessarily the services

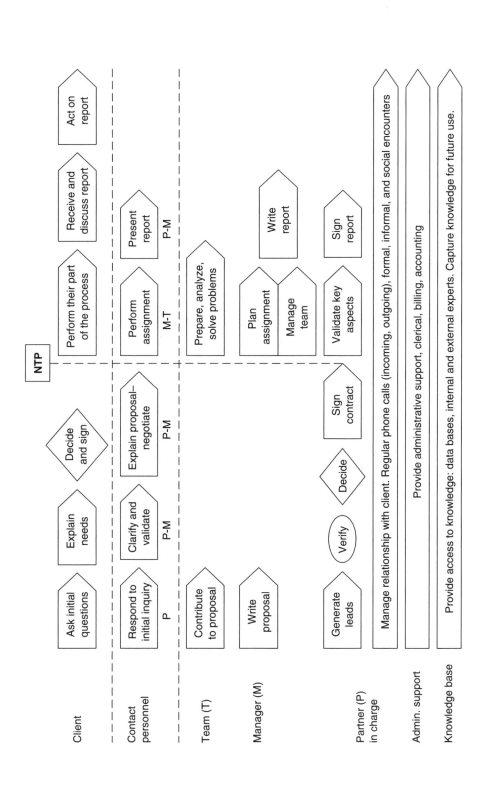

Figure 4.2 Macro-map of the *sell and provide services to specific customer* process at QKM.

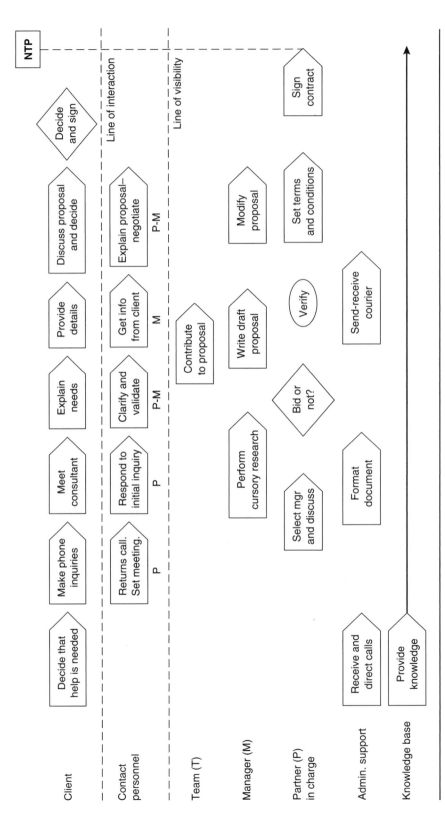

Figure 4.3 Macro-mapping of the *sell services* process at QKM.

they ask for. They should give them the advice they need to hear, not necessarily what they want to hear. Thus, professionals serve through leadership rather than subservience. Doing what is right for the client (see the notion of technical quality in Section 2.1.4) may result in short-term dissatisfaction on the part of the customer. The skilled professional should, however, be able to make the case convincingly enough to get the customer to do the right thing, and to trust enough to wait for results. In some fields of professional endeavor—such as health, insurance brokerage, and financial planning—this may take years. Once results are achieved, however, the bond between the professional and the customer will be very strong and hard to break.

When two persons work together, as the professional and client do, they must decide who does what. Therefore, an important service design decision involves how to divide work between the customer and the service provider. The professional leadership role includes getting the client to understand failure to play the role correctly will deny the result being sought. As discussed in Chapter 2 (Section 2.3.2), customers are very different in terms of their capability and willingness to get involved in the satisfaction of their needs. Doing more for the customer does not necessarily create more value. Indeed, you are never better served than by yourself. Some customers prize the added control over execution and the speed that self-service provides—witness the fact that many customers will prefer a cafeteria to a restaurant, or a self-service gas station over a full-service one.

Depending on the tasks the professional would like the customer to perform, the customer may need tools, training, and coaching. Physical therapists, for instance, train their patients to perform some exercises through demonstration, asking the patients to reproduce the exercise and correcting them until they get it right. Together with a complex prescription, pharmacists give patients a medication organizer as well as an instruction sheet. Lawyers often prepare their clients for testimony in court through role-playing. Therefore, PSOs should design very carefully the tasks they want their customers to perform; assess their current knowledge level (which may differ from segment to segment); develop the required instructions and tools; and develop and manage a training process. At times, the provider-client relationship seems to invert itself. For instance, an airplane cabin crew giving instructions to passengers: "I need you to place your seatback in a vertical position . . ." and verifying compliance, leaves little doubt about who has to comply with whose requirements. Prefacing this sentence with "If you want to arrive safely . . ." makes the reason for this inversion of role clear.

This section may leave the reader with the impression that in some respect the customer is treated as an employee. Indeed, leading, empowering, giving tools, training, and coaching are all key management roles vis-á-vis employees. However, the fact that, contrary to employees, the customer is paying us and not the converse, changes fundamentally the nature of the relationship. The professional has no formal authority over the customer. The sole source of authority is that which the customer grants. It stems at first from the professional's status (degrees and professional certificates) and reputation. However, it quickly moves on to leadership. Failing that, the relationship deteriorates and eventually peters out.

4.1.5 Discipline, Judgment, and Creativity

As the foregoing discussion makes clear, PSDPs involve more players than just the professionals themselves. Technicians, technologists, administrators, and clerical personnel for instance, are involved in close interaction with the professionals, with the clients, and with each other. It is useful to classify the tasks that each of these players must perform on the basis of its major requirement:

- Tasks that require discipline. These are tasks for which it has been decided (by regulatory agency, the PSO, or by agreement among the colleagues who perform the process) that some specific aspect of these tasks would be performed in a given way.

For instance, there is one way to administer an intravenous painkiller. Signing a contract always require a witness. An engineer approving a drawing should always put a seal on it. You must always staple the contract to the rear cover of the folder. These accepted procedures generally specify acceptable deviations (or tolerance), such as: "you must wait between 10 and 15 minutes after the injection to . . ." All process players must be committed—to one stakeholder or another—to perform these tasks in the agreed upon manner. For such tasks, straying from this procedure is not a demonstration of flexibility, but of a lack of discipline.

- Tasks that require judgment. Professional knowledge is largely codified in decision rules. Professionals are trained to understand, use, and combine these rules in various ways, depending on the client and situation they are dealing with. Applying these rules correctly requires judgment, which professionals hone through experience. Therefore, different professionals will differ somewhat on the judgment calls they make in similar circumstances. In this type of task, trying to enforce rigid rules can be counterproductive. The path to improvement—and improving their judgment is a crucial responsibility for any professional—lies in learning from mistakes and successes, as well as identifying and sharing best practices. The organization's role here is to create the right conditions for peer groups to function and achieve maximum effectiveness.

- Tasks that require creativity. Because a situation encountered lies at the boundary of the profession's domain, because it is uniquely complex, or because it falls in an uncharted (controversial or disputed) area, generally accepted professional practices sometimes fall short. In these situations, professionals are left to their own devices and must be creative. If these situations are recognized, and the organizational climate is such that professionals feel supported, innovation may take place. Otherwise, failure or paralysis occurs. The former not only benefits the customer, it energizes the professional and creates a virtuous cycle of learning. It can be a dynamic source of rejuvenation for the organization. The latter triggers a cycle of failure and leads to defensive practices and sclerosis.

Telling these tasks apart is of vital importance for process design and management in a PSO. Developing processes that impose discipline where creativity is required, or failing to introduce guidelines for professional judgment where they are needed, result in poor performance, confusion, and frustration. *Creative accounting practices*, for instance, have destroyed auditors and their firms. The best ad agencies do not lack discipline, but they have clearly staked the zone where it should not infringe. Orthopedists, in good hospitals, hold *fracture* meetings to exchange their views on complex cases and explore original solutions together, thereby sharing best practices and improving their judgment.

4.1.6 Emotions

Emotions are always present in human relations, no matter what the functionality or purpose of the encounter. While a customer's interaction with a service provider in a fast-food restaurant may last less than a minute, a greeting and a smile might leave both parties with a pleasant, if short-lived, feeling. An encounter that ends on a negative note, however, may leave an unpleasant feeling that will linger on much longer. A physical therapist, on the other hand, may spend 50 hours or more with a patient over a one-year period. A trainer may spend twice as long with trainees. The stakes in such encounters are much higher for both parties than they are in short encounters. The knowledge gap (see Section 2.1.4) between the customer and the provider places the customer in a situation of relative dependence and the provider in a situation of responsibility. Thus, the stage is set for the whole gamut of human emotions to take place: hope, anxiety, fear, trust, anger, friendship, and so on. These emotions may facilitate or impede the positive interaction needed to bring the service encounter to fruition.

The attendant in a fast-food restaurant is not expected to lead, but to serve. The professional must lead. It is the nature of the job. As already mentioned, this leadership includes service, not subservience. The line between the two is sometimes very fine, and a professional whose vision is blurred by the prospect of short-term profits may easily cross it unwittingly. Since clients are often vulnerable, professionals must use their authority with respect. This means complying with the needs of the customer, in a non-judgmental, accepting fashion (see discussion on the potential for abuse in Chapter 2.1.4). The emotional skills required to manage the emotions involved on both sides of this complex interaction, often called emotional intelligence, are thus an essential part of the professional skill set.

4.2 EXPLORING THE MAJOR LINKS IN THE CHAIN OF COMMITMENTS

As discussed in Chapter 2, a chain of supplier-customer commitments is required throughout the transformation from the original input to the final output. For you to make a commitment, you must understand what is expected of you, be motivated to do it, and feel capable of doing it. As noted in Chapter 3, a commitment is real if it involves significant personal consequences for not delivering. A process is only as strong as the weakest commitment along the chain. Therefore, designing, managing, and improving processes involves ensuring that these commitments exist.

While commitment to yourself, to a superior being, an idea, or society can be very real, this discussion is limited to commitments made to other persons (who may or may not represent a larger entity or group of people). The section starts with a discussion of the commitment made to the customer, and then explores the various modalities through which such contact can take place. The section is concluded with a discussion of the other commitments required, that is commitment between professionals and other employees—in order to meet the commitment made to the customer.

4.2.1 Customer Contact, Visibility, and Moments of Truth

Whatever the customer hears and sees during service encounters, that is, what takes place within the *line of visibility*, may have an impact on the perception of the provider and the organization. In the case of QKM for instance, before the agreement (NTP in Figure 4.2) it influences the decision to do business with the organization; after, the decision to keep doing business with it. Process maps (such as the macro-map shown in Figure 4.2) represent these activities above the line of visibility, spread on both sides of an imaginary line of interaction. Whoever in the organization is interacting with the customer will be referred to as a server. The same person may at times work as a server (that is, on stage) and at other times in the back office (that is, beyond the line of visibility, or backstage). The theater analogy is a vivid way to highlight the direct impact of every aspect of a provider's *performance* (while *on stage*) on the client. In Figure 4.2, the *player* involved in each task that appears in the *server* swim lane is identified by a letter.

Service delivery starts when the customer agrees to the (explicit or implicit) terms and conditions set forth by the provider. The form that such consent may take ranges from a simple nod to a formal signature, and may include verbal acknowledgement ("OK") and handshake. Whatever means is used to communicate it, the agreement must be clear to both parties. When it is, the parties are thus mutually committed to perform their part of the agreement. From that point on, any contact between the customer and the organization (SAS's Ian Carlzon called these encounters *moments of truth*) is an opportunity for the former to verify that the latter's behavior is compatible with the commitment and form an opinion about whether this is a good place to do business. This monitoring may be active or passive, overt or covert, explicit or implicit, depending on the stakes riding on the outcome and on the customer's trust in the provider. Bear in mind that because of the client's possible inability to assess technical quality (see Chapter 2), the *moment of truth* may be a *moment of lie*, that is, the potential for manipulation exists.

To perform the service task, the server needs to interact with colleagues (that is, internal servers). This is represented in a macro-map as activities taking place on both sides of a line of internal interaction, often beyond the line of visibility. As these *internal servers* in turn need help, further such lines can be added, and thus dig deeper into the inner strata of the organization. In Section 4.2.2, customer contact is discussed, and internal contact will be discussed in Section 4.2.3.

4.2.2 Modes of Contact at the Customer Interface

4.2.2.1 A Typology of Modes of Contact

The possible ways through which this two-way communication between provider and customer takes place will be referred to as *contact modes*. Figure 4.4 shows various modes of contact organized in a tree structure, based on three criteria. It provides specific sub-categories and examples.

Contact modes are first classified broadly as synchronous or asynchronous, depending on whether or not the players are interacting in real time. This is a very important distinction in services. This is an age of little patience. A sense of urgency permeates most actions. People want

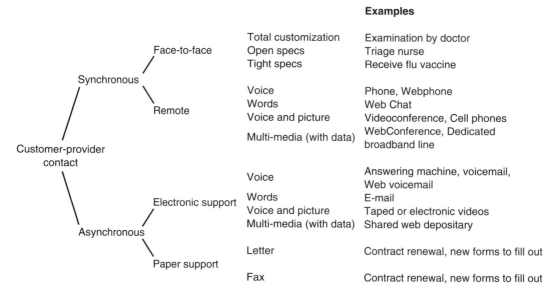

Included here are contacts involving a possibility of response and that can be initiated by either party. Contacts may be one-to-one, one-to-many, many-to-one, or many-to-many.

Figure 4.4 Classification of the various two-way or multi-way contact modes.

immediate satisfaction and immediate answers to their questions. As long as competitors are willing and able to provide it, business has little choice but to meet this requirement of immediacy. Synchronous contact allows for quick interactions, and thus has to be the preferred mode of contact whenever it is technically possible and economically justified. *Carpe diem!* Now is the time to seize the moment, when the need is urgent enough to push the customer into action, that is, to make it an immediate priority. Failure to do so may result in losing the business to a more responsive competitor or the customer finding another way to meet the need.

Different modes of contact deal differently with emotions. Emotions are very much involved at the time of making a serious commitment. Asynchronous contact affords the interlocutors time to think about their responses. While this may be a blessing in some circumstances, salespersons know that the probability of closing a sale is much less if the customer has free time to think about it and to explore alternatives. Also, a sequence of e-mails may at times be more likely to escalate a small problem, if the correspondents have time to meditate their revenge. Asynchronous response, however, allows for optimal dispatch and batch processing, and may thus be considerably cheaper than organizing to meet demand in real-time. A poor performance at this, however, will result in long queues and waiting time, and thus, finally, in an asynchronous response, that is, a response for which the customer has to wait.

A second important distinction is that between those contacts that take place face-to-face and those that take place remotely. The former are necessarily synchronous, while the latter may be either synchronous or asynchronous. The face-to-face contact environment is the best in terms of richness of human interaction. It also meshes simultaneous verbal, visual, tactile, and olfactory clues in a way that no website will ever reproduce. It is the preferred mode of contact of a multitude of customers. It is however also very expensive for the provider.

Face-to-face modes of contacts (see Figure 4.4) can be further subdivided into total customization (TC), open specifications (open specs), and tight specifications (tight specs) (Chase and Tansyk, 1983). To formulate a diagnostic and prescription (as presented in Section 4.1.1 above), professionals prefer a contact environment where they can freely interact with their clients, solely guided by their professional judgment, that is, a total customization environment. In an *open-spec* contact, the server's (who may or may not be a professional) leeway is somewhat limited by available service offerings. An insurance agent, for example, is limited by the types of insurance policy available and by the limited possibility to customize them. In a *tight-spec* contact, the employee's performance is totally scripted. There is little leeway for using judgment. As you drop your dirty laundry at the neighborhood cleaners, the employee's routine is perfectly predictable, sometimes down to the smallest details.

Contact modes listed near the top of the chart (Figure 4.4) are referred to as *high touch* to reflect their intensity in human contact and those listed near the bottom as *high tech* or *industrialized*, highlighting the remoteness (in both time and space) of the interacting parties and the important intermediation role played by technology.

The last distinction made here is that between paper-based and electronically supported interaction. The long awaited paperless society is still not here. This is not to diminish the impact of IT, but there may be a wait for that particular outcome to materialize. Digits are much cheaper to transmit, store, retrieve, and process than words, images, or numbers printed on paper. However, the written word has a legal value that digits still do not. In many circumstances, the customer finds it handier to have a printed document or to write one than to have to use an electronic medium to access or produce information. In addition, written documents (letters, leaflets) are sometimes the best way to circumvent the line of defense of customers against unwanted information. The preference for the written versus the electronic variety of information varies widely across customers, depending on such factors as technological literacy, education, wealth, and availability of equipment and support networks (such as wireless networks and high-speed web-access).

The foregoing discussion is about two-way contacts—that is, human interaction. *One-way contacts*, that is, when the service provider or the customer takes unilateral action to obtain or give information, are a different matter. Figure 4.5 presents a classification of the various modes available to send or access information (that is, *contact* with or access to information). The first dimension shown refers to the originator of the contact—the customer or the provider. The customer may access passive information—either electronically (PDF format, for example) or through a paper document. Electronic access can also be gained to structured information, which may be browsed through menus or search engines. Finally, access may be made through *smart* information—that is, interfacing with expert systems that can request data, analyze it, and select the best information to provide back to the customer.

An expert system can best be understood by seeing it as an *automated expert* or *automated professional* (depending on its capabilities). What takes place between the expert system and the customer is similar in many ways to what takes place between a professional and the client. Based on the information received, the system accesses a database and a set of logical rules to formulate a diagnostic and a prescription. The rules may be very basic ("if debit card is selected, request PIN") or very sophisticated ("if risk aversion factor is between x and y, total asset is less than z, and target retirement date later than v, then . . ."). While this is referred to as a one-way contact, because no employee of the provider is involved, for the customer, it shares many of the characteristics of a two-way contact (or multi-way contact, as we may open several *windows* in parallel or in short order).

While provider-initiated transmission of information is not further broken down in Figure 4.5, if the customer is a business, the provider may also have the option of accessing (on an extranet) structured or smart information made available by the customer. A customer may, for instance, give selective access to structured product or process information, and even to smart information on how to set up electronic billing.

Refer back to the real estate agency example discussed in Chapter 2, and more specifically to the process flow diagram shown in Figure 3.8. Figure 4.6 shows a simplified macro-map of that same process together with possible modes of contact. The modes indicated at each point of contact may be selected individually or in combination. For instance, the agent's assistant may set up the first meeting with the potential seller over the phone, through e-mail, or in a face-to-face tight-spec

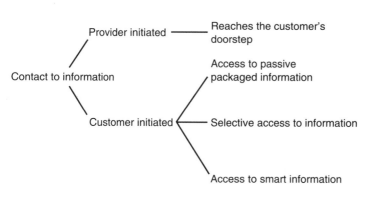

Example

Provider initiated ——— Reaches the customer's doorstep — Spam, junk mail, statement of account, change of fees, leaflets

Access to passive packaged information — Download a PDF file, get a brochure from a stand

Contact to information

Customer initiated — Selective access to information — Web search, site search engine, accessing a database or a well-organized website (by topics, tree)

Access to smart information — Movie recommendation, analyze your risk of heart attack or colon cancer, drawing your risk profile, etc.

These are one-way contacts, involving the customer receiving or accessing information

Figure 4.5 Classification of the various modes available to send or access information.

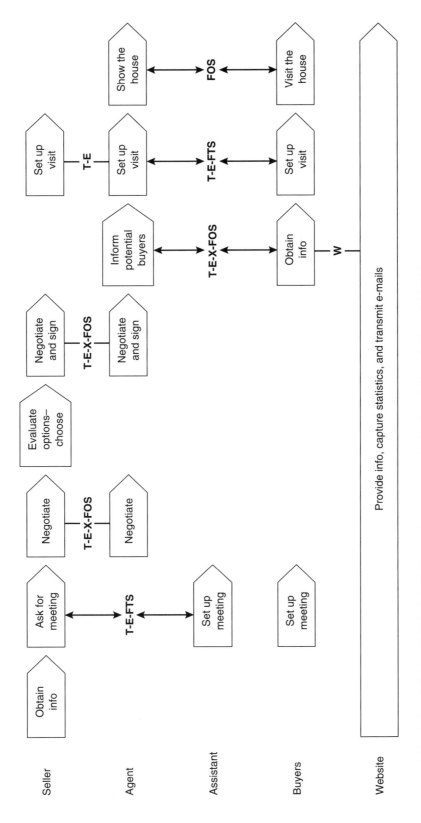

Legend: **T** (telephone), **E** (e-mail), **X** (fax), **FOS** (face-to-face, *open spec*), **FTS** (face-to-face, *tight spec*), **W** (Web)

Figure 4.6 *Provide the service to specific customers* for a real estate agency—simplified macro-map with modes of contact.

mode. Negotiations may be conducted again though phone and e-mail, as well as through the fax or face-to-face open-spec modes. In this later case, a combination of modes is likely to be used: a sequence of phone messages followed by an exchange of faxes and a face-to-face meeting, for instance. Potential buyers can use these same means to interact with the agent to obtain information on the property or, alternatively, they may choose to get it directly by accessing the agency's website.

In designing the process, the agency has to decide which modes of contact it wants to make available to which clients. The client can pick the mode or sequence of modes preferred from amongst the alternatives offered. For instance, a discount agency may try to substitute web interactions for two-way contacts to handle progress reports on the sale of a property. It may limit phone calls and face-to-face open-spec contacts to initial contact and final negotiations. Its advertising (refer to the discussion on positioning in Chapter 2) would then stress the convenience of 24/7 access from your home, to induce customers to switch. Its full-service competitor may retort by stressing that it, too, offers that convenience for customers who want it, when they want it, but that whoever wants personal attention can also get it. An ad such as "don't fight with your computer: we will visit you at home, in your own sweet time," would provide an incisive reply.

4.2.2.2 Customers' and Employees' Perspectives

While a customer may enjoy the possibility of walking into a law firm and asking one or two quick questions to a lawyer while standing at a counter, such an encounter may not be much to the liking of many lawyers. Since there are two players in a two-way contact, the server and the customer, selection of a contact mode has to take into account the needs and preferences of both parties.

Understanding who the customer is, what the need is, and how the customer ticks, is therefore critical in selecting contact modes. Understanding the customer value equation (Figure 2.3) can be very useful in that pursuit. Knowing, for instance, that the customers of the target market segment spend most of their free time on the web because they enjoy it is an important clue for any service provider.

The contact person is also participating in that encounter to get value—personal value, that is. Understanding the personal value equation (see Figure 2.14) of the employee thus becomes very useful. Banks, for example, have been trying to turn their branch contact employees from *transaction workers* (generally called customer service representatives or CSRs) into salespersons. Indeed, as banking transactions were increasingly being automated, profit margins on transactional services were decreasing. This created the need to reduce costs and generate more revenue by introducing *higher value added* services, such as financial counseling and investment banking. Since the resources they had available were the CSRs, they pressed them to turn the transaction encounter into a sales encounter whenever possible. The results were generally dismal as customers who, at that time, were expecting a quick transaction, reacted negatively. The CSRs were not prepared and did not have the right personal attitudes to face such rejection. A poor understanding of customers' and employees' needs at that particular contact point resulted in a three-way loss for the employees, the customers, and ultimately for the shareholders, having to deal with increased turnover and customer defection.

4.2.2.3 Shareholders' View

There is a third stakeholder, of course, in the selection of an appropriate mode of contact: the shareholder. Different contact modes involve different costs and have different revenue generation potential. Table 4.2 presents a rough-cut comparison of the cost and revenue effects of various modes of contact. Since it is generic, Table 4.2 is only indicative of trends in costs. Fixed costs include initial investment and regular maintenance cost. Variable cost is the cost of processing an additional customer. Also shown in Table 4.2 is the opportunity each mode of contact affords the provider to

Table 4.2 Rough-cut comparison of the cost and revenue effects of various modes of conduct.

Type of interaction		Mode of contact	Costs		Relationship***	Strength and nature of relationship
			Fixed**	Variable		
Human interaction	Synchronous	F-t-F TC****	+	−	+++	HI-TOUCH
		F-t-F open-spec	+	−	++	
		F-t-F tight-spec	+	-	=	
		Human, remote — Videoconference	-	−	++	
		Phone-open-spec	++	−	+	
		phone-tight-spec	++	-	-	
	Asynchronous	Phone (messages)	+++	=	−	
		E-mail*	+++	-	−	
Human-machine interaction	With dumb machines	Voice recognition or tone	-	+++	−	
	With smart machines	Access structured information	−	++	+	
		Access expert systems	−−	+	++	HI-TECH

*Excludes the investment in PCs and training, assumes tight specs
**Includes initial investment and regular maintenance cost. Variable cost is the cost of processing an additional customer.
***Opportunity to create/reinforce relationship with customer.
****F-t-F TC: Face-to-face, total customization

Legend: "−" means bad, "+" means good, that is, referring to cost, "-" means a high cost.

create or reinforce its relationship with the customer. A "+" sign in the body of the table means that selecting this mode of contact is relatively advantageous on that criteria (column)—that is, a "+" in the first two columns means lower cost, a "+" in the third column means higher relationship potential. Multiple signs (such as "+++") are used to allow better discrimination between the modes.

Phone and e-mail stand out as having the lowest fixed cost, with structured information and expert systems on the web, the highest. Simple, tree-structured phone systems (for example, "for departure time on flights leaving from New York La Guardia, press 1 . . .") have the best variable cost, and face-to-face TC, the worst. The first two columns show the classical trade-off between fixed and variable costs. It has to be resolved based on current and forecasted volumes, the cost structure of the technologies involved (based on installed technology infrastructure), as well as expected future costs.

While face-to-face TC contact is the most expensive, it also affords the provider the greatest opportunity to build and maintain a profitable, enduring relationship. Indeed, no other mode of contact can provide the customer facing a complex problem with a diagnostic and a solution better suited to the need. This fosters trust and loyalty. It also gives the contact expert an opportunity to understand the client's needs, attitudes, and aptitudes well enough to assess the potential represented for the organization. This allows for tailoring the company's offerings and modes of future contacts to the client's requirements, thus optimizing the relationship.

A face-to-face *open-spec* contact or a videoconference cannot reach the same degree of *fit* possible through TC, the former because a finite number of options are available, the latter because of the limitations of the medium. Accessing expert systems on the web still has its limitations, though these are receding with every wave of technological advance. While expert systems may vie in richness of information obtained and accuracy of diagnostic and prescription—at least for some types of customer—with face-to-face TC contact, it will never compete in the ability to convey such critical emotions as empathy and trust. For mass markets, however, its variable cost increasingly makes it a compelling choice in many sectors.

The cheapest modes of contact—e-mail and automated phone—also offer the lowest relationship potential, thus highlighting the trade-off between cost and relationship potential. Since modes of contact with the highest relationship potential are more costly, they should only be used whenever the additional cost thus incurred can be considered an investment in a future relationship. The service provider should allow access to these modes of contact to selected customer and market segments only, provided of course, that they *want* to use them—or that they can be induced to do so.

The latter assertion means that dispatching each customer to the modes of contact the professional would like them to use in various circumstances will require some doing. A combination of push and pull approaches—inducements, penalties, and actual control—may be needed. Indeed, you must offer something valuable to a high potential customer with the right skill set and attitudes for web-based interaction (for the design of a house or portfolio management, say) to accept face-to-face TC contact. On the other hand, pricing mechanisms or outright denial of access may be required to keep a low-potential customer from using TC contact.

4.2.2.4 Designing Customer Contact Modes

Designing a sequence of modes of customer contact is a critical part of service process design. Four families of considerations bear on this task:

- *The nature of the task to perform.* If both parties (customer and server) must simultaneously interact with something material—such as a surgeon with the patient's body or an engineer and client with a prototype of a product—then some form of face-to-face contact is required. The same holds true—at least at first—when trust must be established between the provider and the client.

- *Customer's needs, attitudes, and aptitudes.* Relevant questions include the following: How important and urgent does the customer perceive the need to be? How competent does the customer feel in the field of knowledge involved? How competent in using IT? How self-assured and pro-active is the person? How strong is the desire for control?

- *Employee's needs, attitudes, and aptitudes.* The questions here are a bit different, but no less important: With what dosage of personal contact is the employee comfortable? How well is rejection dealt with? How tolerant of repetitive tasks? Can the client's behavior be recognized, and the employee's behavior be adapted to meet the client's behavior (empathy and personal flexibility)? Can leadership be exercised with the clients?

- *Cost and revenue implications.* As discussed in the above section, there are many trade-offs to consider. The provider wants the cheapest effective contact mode, but is willing to invest on high-potential customers, that is use a costlier mode than cost considerations alone would justify. The customer however, does not care much about maximizing the provider's profit. The customer's preferred mode of contact may be considered by the provider to be ineffective or too costly.

Figure 4.7 presents a general model, adapted from Huete and Roth (1988), that can be useful in selecting contact modes. The oval shows that simple services lend themselves well to high-tech contact, while complex services require high-touch contact. Of course, the notion of simplicity is relative to the customer's level of knowledge. For example, to many people, managing a portfolio is complex; to someone who holds a master's degree in finance, it is simple. To someone who is inexperienced with IT, filling out a simple form online may be a huge challenge. Thus, when venturing to the left of the diagonal in Figure 4.7, increasing risks of service failure are faced. When venturing to the right, growing potential for waste (using an excessively expensive contact mode) and frustration (imposing a high-touch contact on someone who would prefer high-tech) are faced. Hence, the client's levels of knowledge about the professional service and about IT are important segmentation criteria. Segments can be plotted across the top of the model and used as a guide in selecting modes of contacts.

The model is also useful in understanding the dynamic evolution of contact modes. Customers can move along the horizontal axis. As contact technologies mature, they become more user-friendly (for example, going from DOS to Windows), and some services become simpler and high-tech more prevalent. Clients can also be trained (both in IT and in the professional domain itself—see the case study discussed in Chapter 1), thus displacing them toward the right on the horizontal axis. Further, since the older population strata are the most technology-averse, as time passes the proportion of technology-prone clients keeps increasing.

The large line in Figure 4.7 illustrates the pressure that the above forces are constantly applying to change high-touch for high-tech contact modes. Price competition from developing countries is also adding to the pressure in some sectors. As clients can increasingly gain instant access to a competent engineer on the phone in India, at a very small fraction of what a face-to-face encounter with a local engineer would cost, the pressure on the latter to reduce the cost, and thus move some contacts to high-tech, is building. One of the challenges that this entails is to maintain differentiation, as high-tech contact is a commodity: you have it today; your competitor has it tomorrow. Without differentiation—and face-to-face contact is a prime source of it in professional services—profit margins are razor-thin.

Customers are offered a portfolio of contact modes, together with instructions on how to use them. The instructions range from quick verbal instruction to training manuals or in-class training. Each mode has distinct features, which makes them more or less attractive for different customers.

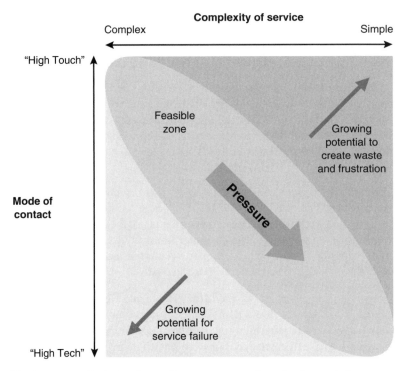

Figure 4.7 Choosing modes of contact: A model.
Source: Adapted from Huete and Roth, 1988.

Depending on customer preferences, which may change over time, some modes will be overused, and thus congested, while others may be underused.

Managing the traffic here to avoid congestion can be a daunting task. It involves offering different contact portfolios to different customers ("Gold card gives you access to a specific 800 number . . .") as well as communication, inducement, and deterrence. The evolving capabilities of IT further complicate the task. As voice-recognition technology becomes increasingly reliable and sophisticated, for example, a task that was previously offered through phone contact with an employee could at some point be offered through an automated phone service.

4.2.3 Chain of Commitments: the Rest of the Chain

4.2.3.1 Internal Contact

In Chapter 3 (see Section 3.3), a process was described as a chain of commitments running upstream from the end customer up to the initial supplier. In Section 4.2.1, there was discussion about how the commitment the organization makes to the end customer translates into a series of moments of truth, throughout a sequence of contacts during a service episode. Here, the rest of that chain of commitments is briefly explored, that is, from the server inwards.

The major players involved are professionals, technicians, non-technical support personnel (clerical or administrative), managers, suppliers, partners, and government (regulatory agencies, taxes, and so on). As discussed in Chapter 3, a commitment is real if the person making it accepts the personal consequences of failing to deliver. A process is nimble if every player has sufficient leeway to renegotiate their commitment directly upstream with suppliers and downstream with customers[1] as need arises, without always having to consult a superior.

The notion that once a commitment is made, every contact with the provider becomes a moment of truth, is not limited to commitments made to the end customer, but applies to this context as well. There are however, some differences. Most importantly, the internal customers are not involved in the satisfaction of their own needs, but that of a third party. If both the internal customers and the internal providers belong to the same organization, the purpose of the contact is not solely the satisfaction of the former's need, but also the efficient use of resources. The pursuit of efficiency makes the relationship between them more like a partnership, where the internal customer does not necessarily have the upper hand. Rather, the expertise and circumstances of both partners are considered when time comes to select modes of contact.

However, the above assertion must be qualified. Professionals wield much power in the organization. Some professions are more powerful than others, and some professionals have more power than others within the same profession. Therefore, the respective power of the players involved is likely to affect choices of modes of contact and the outcome of the contacts.

4.2.3.2 Example

An example is the best way to highlight issues regarding internal contact modes. Imagine a financial planner in FPA (see Box 4.2) interacting with a tax expert (a colleague from the tax department) and an accountant (working for a consulting firm with whom the planner has a long-term agreement) in an endeavor to prepare a long-term retirement plan that was promised for delivery to a client in 10 days time. After getting a commitment from the customer to send the company's financial data immediately, the accountant is asked to extract from it and format the required information. The accountant agrees to provide it in a given format within two days, if the data is received the next day. The planner then calls the tax colleague to ask for an analysis of the tax implications of several retirement scenarios—based on the accountant's report being delivered in two days—and meet within a week.

The modes of contact selected by the professionals involved depend on their relationship with each other. Let us explore various situations:

- The planner is working with that specific colleague for the first time. Each contact— the initial call, a request for further information, an initial meeting, and so on—then becomes a potential moment of truth. The planner is likely to intentionally select high-touch contact in this situation, to better assess the provider, both to find out about reliability and to determine how best to work together.

Box 4.2: Financial planning associates (FPA)

Issue: *Following a merger, a PSO wants to identify the key processes on which it should focus its improvement efforts*

FPA is a small firm dispensing professional services in the area of financial planning to a customer base of wealthy individuals. Created by the recent merger of three independent companies, it now has a staff of 200, including 70 certified financial planners (FPs) as well as a

---

Continued

Continued

number of specialists in tax, insurance, and investment. One of the companies involved in the merger had a strong IT group, which had been involved in the development of investment decision support systems and portals for large players in the industry. Though the company serves various market segments, its core market consists of busy professionals and managers with assets under management of at least $500,000. Their services revolve around the development, maintenance, and implementation of a personal financial plan, reflecting an individual's specific financial goals, assets, earning potential, family situation, and attitude toward risk.

Personal relationships and trust lie at the heart of financial planning. An FP must know and understand the client very well. They also must be able to explain to the client all relevant options and their implications, custom design a financial plan tailored to expressed needs, and explain all its implications, to the point where the client clearly understands what is involved. Technology also plays a crucial role in facilitating interaction with customers and suppliers—the latter consisting mostly of brokers, mutual fund companies, traders, insurance companies, trusts, banks, and notaries. An increasingly sophisticated and very busy customer base now demands online access to their FPs and their accounts, as well as to user-friendly analytical and simulation capabilities.

Following the merger, the partners (all FPs own at least some company stock) had expected profits to grow because of economies of scale and synergism, but this had not happened. On the contrary, back office costs had soared and response time had increased.

- The colleague is well-known, trusted, and liked. Contacts may be all *high-tech* (e-mails, spreadsheet attachment) until the joint face-to-face meeting with the client.

- The colleague is disliked, but trusted to deliver on the commitment. Results will be received, but getting those results may be painful. The contact modes will be chosen to minimize the pain. For instance, a written report may be requested, and the colleague may be excused from the meeting with the client.

- The colleague is not trusted. The sequence of contact modes will be designed to minimize the risks of failure. An initial face-to-face meeting may be chosen to avoid any confusion that could take place in a phone call. Regular calls or e-mails may be made to check on the progress. An early meeting may be called to check the analysis before meeting the customer. The colleague's secretary may be asked to inform when the boss will return from a trip.

In the above discussion, the planner is assumed to have a choice of mode of contact. That may not be the case. The tax department may have an *official* policy as to what mode to use in various circumstances. In addition, the tax expert may also have preferences and selection may ultimately depend on who has the most power. Finally, of course, business or personal circumstances (workload, previous engagements, travel plans) also play an important role.

While the preceding discussion generally applies to contacts with the accountant as well, there are a number of differences:

- Since they do not work on the same premises, face-to-face contact is more costly.

- The planner is less likely to be *stuck* with a disliked accountant, since the planner is a paying client.

- Interfacing technologically may be a little more difficult as two companies with different systems are involved.

Professionals also have to interface with external professionals that they have not selected. This would be the case, for instance, if the planner had to get the data from the client's consultant. Here again, the outcome depends on the power relationship between the two professionals. This, is turn, depends on a number of factors such as the respective prestige of the professions, the prestige of the professional, and the strength of either one's relationship with the client.

4.2.3.3 The Professional's Contacts

The above example illustrates some aspects of contacts between professionals. Much of the behavior of professionals is guided by their desire to protect their autonomy. They use various defense mechanisms to respond to any demand that they consider as potential interference in their professional practice. They tend to be very circumspect in working with other professionals, especially more powerful ones, that they do not know well, for fear that their comfort zone may be invaded. When such contact is unavoidable, they seek the less *invasive* mode in order to minimize the risk to their egos.

This desire for autonomy also creates risks of conflict with management. What professionals expect from management are clear marching orders about business targets to achieve, appropriate tools, resources, and support. Professionals may at times perceive—rightly or wrongly—that management's desire for control infringes on their professional duties and privileges. Selecting management among professional ranks—particularly highly respected professionals—is one way to reduce such tensions. An appropriate management style involving collegiality and peer groups also helps considerably.

Relating with technicians is a different issue. Here, the line of authority is clear. The relationship, however, is not exempt from systemic friction factors. Indeed, technical disciplines, whether or not their sector of practice is specified by laws or regulations are, much like professions, always seeking to enlarge their fields and reduce the restrictions placed on their freedom of practice. Hence, there are always zones of contention at that interface that can create turbulence.

Finally, the interface between professionals and administrative personnel is normally much smoother, with the former having much latitude about their choice of contact modes. Conflicts may arise when management, having failed to achieve the control it desires, goes though the back door and uses administrative personnel as gatekeepers. The latter then find themselves the unwilling (and sometimes unwitting) players in a power struggle. Employees controlling access to scarce resources (such as computing resources, specialized equipment, budgets, and conference rooms) are particularly vulnerable.

Just as professionals are expected to lead their customers, not serve them complacently, they are expected to lead the team of technical and non-technical employees who meet customers or work in the back office. In an ideal world, management understands that and concentrates on creating the right organizational environment and providing the team with the tools and resources it needs to operate at peak effectiveness, with as little management interference as possible.

4.3 FAULT LINES

Many factors can contribute to a moment of truth with the customer not turning out the way all stakeholders would like. Awareness of a process's particular vulnerabilities or fault lines is an important ally in any effort to avoid such failures. The interfaces discussed above are a potential source of such systemic weaknesses, which can result in the hijacking of an encounter from its real purpose of addressing the client's problem to that of contributing to some other goal or internal power struggle.

Identifying and managing these is a critical management function in PSOs. Building safeguards, identifying countermeasures, and installing monitoring systems are part of management's arsenal in dealing with these interfaces.

In the case of the real estate brokerage example discussed in Chapter 2, there is a fault line at the initial determination of the asking price for the house to be sold (see Section 2.3.3.3). Depending on the customer and context, the agent's interest may be to list the house lower than its market value (to increase the odds of selling, if no other real estate agency is competing for the contract) or higher (in an effort to outbid a competitor and get the contract—later reducing the price, when the customer is solidly *locked in*). Another fault line occurs at the time of interacting with potential buyers and presenting a purchase proposal. Here the agency's long-term reputation, the client's interests, and the agent's remuneration may come into conflict.

4.4 SUMMARY

PSDPs consist of four generic stages: dispatch (including bidding), diagnostic, prescription, and treatment. In each stage, the customer is closely involved as co-producer, working with technical and support personnel, under the leadership of the professional. Emotions are ubiquitous when people are working so closely on important and complex matters. Dealing with them is an important professional skill. Professional tasks can be grouped in three categories, based on their major requirement: discipline, judgment, and creativity. Professionals must always distinguish clearly between the three.

Customer contacts are decisive moments when the customer makes or validates an opinion of the provider. Choosing the contact mode is an important enabler for the co-production task. Many modes of contacts are available to choose from, each with its specific requirements, cost, and revenue implications. The provider offers the customer—globally or by market segment—a portfolio of contact modes. While the former may try to influence the latter's choice, the customer is free to choose.

Selecting a mode of contact has an effect on both parties: the customer and the server. Hence an employee's needs, skills, and preferences must be considered in making that decision. Internal contacts and contacts with external partners and providers must also be carefully considered. Here again, the question of who chooses the contact mode depends on many factors, not the least of which is the respective power of the players involved.

EXERCISES

4.1 Line of visibility

a) Review the PFD of your invoicing process (prepared in Exercise 3.1b). Prepare a macro-map of that process.

b) Explore possibilities of changing the location of line of visibility, either increasing or reducing what the customer sees. Would any of these changes make sense?

4.2 Dispatch stage

a) Prepare a macro-map (such as that shown in Figure 4.1) describing the dispatch process currently used in your organization. If your organization is also involved in bidding competitively for contracts, prepare a macro-map (such as that shown in Figure 4.3) of that process as well (you should start from the PFD prepared in your answer to Exercise 3.1b).

b) If possible, prepare a macro-map of your two major competitor's dispatch process. See if you can identify and explain the major differences that you find.

c) Compare the location of the line of visibility in your process with that of your competitor. How do you explain the differences?

4.3 Major task challenges

a) Analyze the macro-map you prepared of your dispatch process (Exercise 4.1a) to identify one task whose major challenge involves the discipline to apply a rule or a procedure without deviation. Repeat this exercise for judgment and creativity.

b) Based on your answer to the previous question, ask the opinion of a number of players involved directly or indirectly with these tasks. Compare their answers and draw your conclusions.

4.4 Modes of client contact

a) Starting from your macro-map of the bidding process prepared in Exercise 4.2a, identify available contact modes (both for customer contact and for internal contact) by the corresponding letters, following the model shown in Figure 4.6.

b) Identify two distinct market segments and describe how you would like each segment to use each mode, and why.

c) Refer to Figures 4.4 and 4.5, as well as to Table 4.2 and the discussion about the characteristics of each mode of contact to assess, in general terms, if your current policy makes sense.

d) Evaluate the mechanisms (inducement, dissuasion, control) currently in place to push or pull the two segments to the contact mode you would like them to use in various circumstances.

e) Discuss with contact personnel to find out how each segment actually uses the various modes of contact available to them. How could you improve on the current push/pull mechanisms used?

4.5 Customer training

a) Prepare an inventory of all the approaches your organization uses to train its customers.

b) For each major market segment and product category, evaluate the appropriateness of the training method selected, based on the importance of the segments, the level of knowledge and skills of the customer, their motivation to learn, and the available time that they have.

4.6 Modes of internal contact

a) Starting from your answer to Exercise 4.3a, select a point of contact between two professionals. Describe how you would like each segment to use each mode, and why.

b) Evaluate the mechanisms (inducement, dissuasion, control) currently in place to push or pull the two professionals to the contact mode you would like them to use in various circumstances.

c) Discuss with the appropriate professionals to find out how they use the various modes of contact available to them and why. How could you improve on the current push/pull mechanisms used?

4.7 Fault lines

a) For this exercise, refer to your reading of the chapter and your answer to the previous exercises. Identify three tasks or contact points in your processes where a potential systemic conflict of interest exists between the client, the professionals, or the organization.

b) Describe what the interest of each party is and how they are conflicting. Review your current policy about how to manage these fault lines. Is it relevant and appropriate?

c) Interview the managers and some of the professionals involved to evaluate how these problems are resolved in practice. Assess the application of your policy.

Notes

[1] In this section, the word customer is used to describe the person to whom a commitment is made. This may include any player in the process. The end customer will be referred to as such or as the client. The person making the commitment is referred to as the supplier or provider.

5

Think Globally, Act Locally

Processes come in many varieties. Operations strategy states how processes will turn the organization's game plan into a reality. The design, improvement, and management of processes must ensure that they all work in harmony towards that end.

The last three chapters have evolved around value creation—the very purpose of business—and the processes that create this value, and particularly professional service delivery processes. This has laid the groundwork necessary to present the big picture. This chapter turns to the connection between processes and value. To do that, two unifying notions in business will first be discussed: business strategy and operations strategy (a subset and extension of the former). Then the logic connecting positioning, operations strategy, and processes is presented. Following that, that connection is explored in the specific case of professional services before turning to an exploration of the major family of processes and their fit with various strategies. Table 5.1 presents a short definition of the major concepts discussed in this chapter.

5.1 STRATEGY IN PROFESSIONAL SERVICES

Capitalism is about competition. Business has borrowed the notion of strategy from another competitive field: war. This notion is explored first, before investigating in more detail a related notion, which is closer to processes: operations strategy.

5.1.1 What Is Strategy?

No amount of rigor in the design of services and processes can make up for a poor strategy. In this section, an introduction is presented to the essential building blocks of a winning service strategy. It is however beyond the scope of this book to enter into a detailed discussion of how an organization should go about performing a strategic analysis and preparing a strategic plan.

As discussed in Chapter 2, a company's strategy is its overall game plan to beat competition. It requires a company to know:

- Why it exists and what it wants to achieve (mission)

- What are the opportunities and threats in the environment (industry and market analysis)

- What it does well and what it does poorly (strengths and weaknesses)

Table 5.1 Key concepts discussed in Chapter 5.

Strategy	The company's game plan to beat competitors in creating value for its customers, its employees, and its shareholders. Positioning decisions are made in the context of strategy formulation.
Operations strategy	Statement of how the company's operations will contribute to beating competition.
Operations policy	Important modality of execution of the operations strategy. They provide guidelines in the design, improvement, and management of processes.
Service standards	Performance levels, derived from the service concept, to which value-adding processes must perform. Performance standards for value enabling and support processes are derived from the requirements of value-adding processes.
Coherence	The quality of SDPs that implement operations strategy and policies cohesively (in a complementary and mutually reinforcing manner).
Families of processes	Major kinds of processes (fully automated, line-flow, job-shop, and craftsman are discussed here), sharing a flow pattern and different characteristics.
Process characteristics	Desirable features of a process (effectiveness, efficiency, productivity, capacity, flexibility, and reliability are discussed here). Designing a process involves trade-offs between these features: you cannot have it all. We use operations strategy and policies as guiding principles in making these trade-offs.
Customization	The extent to which the service, and therefore the SDP, lends itself to adjustments to meet the specific needs of various customers, or various market segments.
Learning organization	An organization that is capable of improving its know-how faster than competitors.
Learning cycle (pump)	The unit of learning: selecting a process, designing it or fixing it, and putting it in action with a new level of capability.

This overall game plan spells out how the company plans to beat its competition in creating value for its customers, its employees, and its shareholders. An example will best illustrate this. Box 5.1 presents the BMI case. The mission statement specifies why the entrepreneurs are investing their time, money, and energy in this venture. The short statements about competitive weaknesses and BMI's strengths and weaknesses are the result of competitive analysis. The strategy statement is the overall game plan, and the service concept (see Figure 5.1) outlines the major benefits and service features.

Box 5.1: Body and mind (BMI)

Issue: A startup reflects on its positioning

BMI is launching an innovative concept in the field of training. Mike Gross, a former sports club manager and globetrotter, has noticed that moderately vigorous training stimulates the mind. Once, when he was pressed for time to learn the rudiments of Spanish before a planned trip to Spain, he had bought a training DVD and studied while doing his daily workout, with the stationary bike placed in front of the TV. It had struck him that the unusual combination of activity had saved him much time and resulted in both activities being easier, less tedious, and

Continued

Continued

more productive. (He felt his retention rate had been higher and his training more intense than usual.) Discussion with a friend who teaches foreign languages had led to their original service concept.

Mission: Profitably create stimulating experiences involving mental and physical fitness for and by active and ambitious young people.

Competitors' weaknesses (opportunity): They serve a broad, indiscriminate spectrum of customers. They sell as many yearly memberships as they can, to anyone who can pay. Once customers have signed, they leave them to their own devices, knowing that there will be an 80 percent abandon rate. They often leave equipment in a state of disrepair. There is an important pool of unsatisfied customers and ex-customers who would be receptive to a low-risk proposition that addresses their frustrations.

BMI's strengths and weaknesses: The founders live what they preach. They have the required expertise and network to find the right people. They have first-hand knowledge of the systemic weaknesses of competition. Their access to capital is limited, forcing a small-scale startup, to reduce the initial risk to investors, but risking quick copycatting by already established and better financially backed competitors.

Strategy: Beat competitors who keep mental and physical activities separate, on cost, quality (performance and ease in both physical and mental activities), and time by exploiting innovative combinations of *body and mind* learning activities. These activities are adapted to the life-style of busy, stressed, ambitious, active, and well-off professionals (target segment). Exploit the social synergism created by these activities to become a magnet (and broker) for all industries offering related services to this prized market segment.

Service concept: A professional who wants to take both language and fitness training sessions has to find two suppliers with schedules compatible with his own—an often-impossible feat. BMI makes that possible for him and achieves superior results in half the time. Thus the key benefit: "stay fit and learn a new language with the least possible time investment, combining two activities that, alone, can be boring, into a stimulating physical, mental and social experience, as you interact with a group of like-minded professionals."

Operations strategy: Language instruction will be given by an instructor to a group of 12 executives, working out on training bikes laid out in a half-circle around the instructor. The course will be very interactive and personalized. BMI will provide clients with headsets to facilitate communication with the instructor and with other class members. BMI will also provide them with interactive DVDs to train and learn at home, in between gym sessions, and thus speed up their learning. For such value, customers can be charged somewhat more than they would pay both suppliers (gym and language school) together. However, since the two sessions are combined into one, BMI's cost will be lower (the gym and the classroom are combined). That is how BMI makes money. BMI will perform themselves only the tasks that are vital to the concept and outsource the rest.

Operations policies: The strategy will generate enough cash to build and maintain facilities that exceed the standards customers are used to, in their work and home environment (including the training rooms, lobby, bar, restaurant, and locker rooms) and to recruit and retain as instructors the type of professional they feel comfortable with. The clients themselves will be involved in supervising the composition of the classes and in organizing special activities, such as action trips (*use your language skills while biking along the Loire*) or viewing the *Tour de France* on a giant screen. BMI will favor word-of-mouth advertising and require referrals from existing

Continued

Continued

member. Partners' (such as specialized travel agencies, providers of interactive training material, and vendors of home training equipment) sales activities will be seamlessly integrated with our own in a relaxed, low-pressure environment, and they will pay a commission.

Financial strategy and marketing strategy are missing.

Job concept: Fitness trainers and language instructors will work in partnership. They will initially have day jobs in the public sector, leaving them much time and energy to invest in something meaningful. They will have the highest qualifications. As individuals, they will share the values of their clients (*mens sana in corpore sano*) and naturally enjoy the interaction with their groups. They will both be encouraged to get as involved as much as they can in the other dimension of the class and in other class activities. Whenever places are available, we will allow them to learn other languages and accompany their clients on organized trips at reduced rates. Hence, they will get much of the benefits that their clients are getting.

The overall strategy branches out into the financial, operations (more details below), marketing, and human resource strategies. These respectively specify in more details how BMI will get and use money, operate profitably, build and manage relationships with customers, and get and keep the people needed to do all this. The job concept is a summary portrait of who the major players are and how BMI plans to create personal value for them (refer to the personal value equation—Figure 2.14). The book focuses here on operations strategy. While the other strategies are not discussed, the reader should bear in mind how important it is that all these strategies fit together well.

The second and third columns of Figure 5.1 present a schematic view of the service concept, that is, the benefits and features of the service. The service features are what are actually given to the client to produce the benefits. In other words, the features are the *how* of the benefits. The connection between features and benefits, however, is not one-to-one. For example, the answer to the question: "how do we produce the social experience benefit?" is "through interaction with selected professional, organized trip, and social activities." Hence, a diagram like those shown in Figures 2.10 and 2.11 could be used to represent the service concept.

Of course, the benefits package only makes sense if the clients are known (see the segment column in Figure 5.1), as was the case with Jack and Linda in Chapter 2, after having described their personal activity cycle (Figures 2.5 and 2.6). Having identified the major competitors, the segment they target, and the benefits they offer them, BMI's positioning could be represented in diagrams such as those shown in Figures 2.12 and 2.13. The first column of Figure 5.1 lists some of the processes that BMI must develop. The process-concept connection shown here parallels that of Figure 3.10. The global model of service profitability involving positioning, operations strategy, and coherence has been initially proposed by Heskett et al. (1997) in their seminal book: *The Service Profit Chain*. Even though the many examples and illustrations they use are now somewhat dated, it is still an excellent complementary read to this book.

5.1.2 Operations Strategy and Profit Leverage

Positioning is about designing a service concept that is superior to those offered by competitors to targeted market segments. Good positioning, however, is not sufficient for business success. Operations strategies and policies are needed to deliver this concept to clients profitably. To generate profits, a business must be able to produce superior value with minimal costs. To dominate the

Service concept

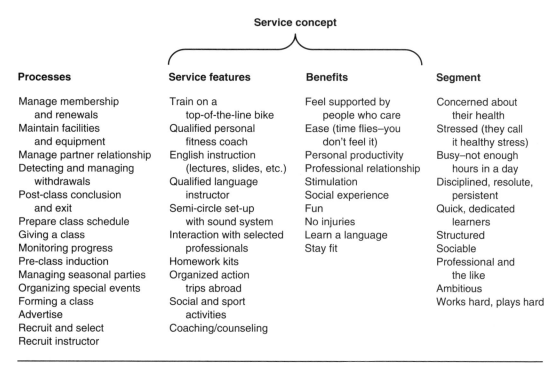

Processes	Service features	Benefits	Segment
Manage membership and renewals	Train on a top-of-the-line bike	Feel supported by people who care	Concerned about their health
Maintain facilities and equipment	Qualified personal fitness coach	Ease (time flies–you don't feel it)	Stressed (they call it healthy stress)
Manage partner relationship	English instruction (lectures, slides, etc.)	Personal productivity	Busy–not enough hours in a day
Detecting and managing withdrawals	Qualified language instructor	Professional relationship	Disciplined, resolute, persistent
Post-class conclusion and exit	Semi-circle set-up with sound system	Stimulation	Quick, dedicated learners
Prepare class schedule	Interaction with selected professionals	Social experience	Structured
Giving a class		Fun	Sociable
Monitoring progress	Homework kits	No injuries	Professional and the like
Pre-class induction	Organized action trips abroad	Learn a language	Ambitious
Managing seasonal parties	Social and sport activities	Stay fit	Works hard, plays hard
Organizing special events	Coaching/counseling		
Forming a class			
Advertise			
Recruit and select			
Recruit instructor			

Figure 5.1 Body and mind: Service concept, segment, and selected processes.

market, it needs to produce more benefits than its competitors at the lowest cost. The spread between benefits provided to the customer and the cost to the provider affords the service provider leverage to charge a price that will leave customers, employees, and shareholders with enough value to secure their on-going association with the company (that is, a win-win-win proposition). Thus, the service provider needs operating strategies that will maximize profit leverage.

An operating strategy (or operations strategy) is a defining aspect of how the company plans to deliver the benefit package. Put another way, it is a statement of how the company's operations contribute to beating competition. BMI's operations strategy clearly states how the proposed concept creates more value for the client while generating a relative cost advantage at the same time.

Referring back to the real estate example discussed in Chapter 2, appropriate use of the Internet, for example, may deliver great value to buyers and sellers alike, by providing virtual guided tours on a 24/7 basis. In addition, because it requires little human intervention on the part of the provider, it can give the latter a huge cost advantage over a competitor making extensive (and indiscriminate) use of costly face-to-face contact (see discussion in Chapter 4). Giving the customer control over service delivery through user-friendly technology is a great feeling (that is, value) for some people, and relieves the provider of the burden and cost of doing so. Creating seamless (both on the website and in actual delivery) links to trusted specialized partners is very valuable to customers and does not cost a penny to the provider. It may on the contrary generate additional revenues. Those are all operating strategies that create leverage.

Full-service providers on the other hand can elect to maximize their visibility in selected neighborhoods, initially *buying* market share through heavy advertising, discount pricing, and extensive house-to-house solicitation. This visibility then becomes a self-fulfilling prophecy: Sellers and buyers alike are more likely to take their business to the broker with more signs in their neighborhood, thus producing more sales and word of mouth. Intensive local penetration is a marketing operation-human resource strategy (it very much involves delivering personal value to agents actively involved in their community) that delivers superior benefits to customers, while reducing the cost to the provider through economies of scale (reaching a critical mass that becomes self-sustaining).

The real estate market is also characterized by wide cyclical fluctuations. In such an environment, an operating system that can expand its capacity rapidly to meet peak demand and then contract to minimize costs—without losing the key productive resources it will require to face the next expansion—is at a great advantage. Full-service brokers pay their agents on a commission basis to match their cost and revenue curves. However, if agents are not kept at least on survival income during market troughs, a vital linchpin in the delivery of their value proposition is lost. Our new entrant could potentially be very resilient to market cycles. However, considerable initial investment is required for creating brand awareness and systems development, resulting in substantial financial charges, a situation which may be hard to withstand during extended periods of low revenues.

An operations policy is similar to an operations strategy, except that it is more a modality of execution than a crucial aspect of the game plan. BMI's operating policies (see Box 5.1) are really spelling out the operations strategy in more detail, making it clearer and pinpointing how it materializes in specific aspects of the operations. In the real estate business, developing self-help kits may be an operations policy that goes together with the strategy of empowering the customer: It can be of great help to the customer and does not cost much to produce and distribute. Another operation policy that would create leverage involves the production and automatic e-mailing of a weekly benchmarking report. A software agent could easily be programmed to compare the number of hits on the house, average stay, number of requests for additional information, number of new houses sold in that price range, and so on.

5.1.3 Service Strategy and Processes

Having defined strategy, and operations strategy in particular, it is now possible to see how processes relate to it. In this section, the link between positioning and processes is discussed. The link between processes and positioning in the labor market is then presented. The section concludes on the critical notion of coherence.

5.1.3.1 Positioning and Processes

The notion of operations strategy just introduced sheds new light on positioning. Indeed, it does not appear anymore as stemming only from customer needs and market opportunities (*outside-in*), but from internal considerations about the possibility to exploit these opportunities profitably as well. The service concept can now be seen as the linchpin between strategy and operations. Figure 5.2 builds on Figure 2.13 to show a more complete picture. Strategy is formed as discussed in Section 5.1.3 (and illustrated in Figure 2.12), and deployed into finance, marketing, and operations. The search for the right formula (benefits and features) for the right market segment involves simultaneous prospection and introspection.

As shown in Figure 5.2, the value proposition (see the examples in Section 2.3.3.3), or promise to clients, stems from the service concept and defines marketing's job. The same service concept is also the source, together with the operations strategy, of service standards. Since service features (or service offerings) are the output of the provider's value-adding processes (see process classification in Section 3.4.3 and Figure 3.2), the service standards set the performance levels to which these processes must perform. Performance standards for value enabling and support processes are derived from the requirements of value-adding processes.

Notice that even though the promise to the market and service standards both stem from the service concept, they are formulated in very different languages. The promise to the market is the

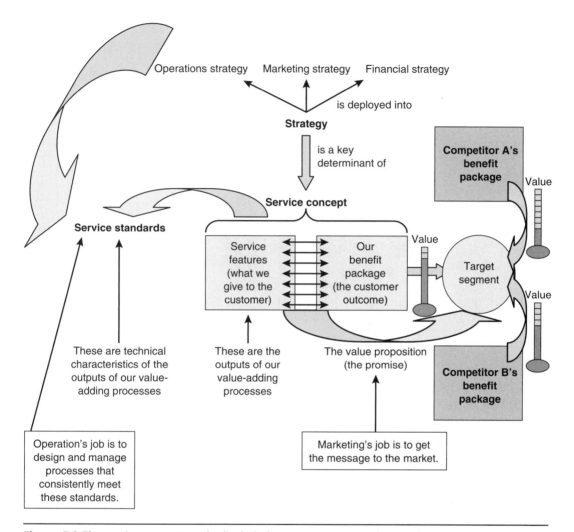

Figure 5.2 The service concept as the linchpin between strategy and operations.

translation that marketing and advertising creative staff make of the service concept, so that it reaches the target market segment. It may take such forms as 30-second TV spots, magazine ads, or e-mail spam. Service standards, on the other hand, have to lend themselves to measurement in a repeatable and reproducible manner (see Chapter 6) so that they can be used as the basis for process design, management, and improvement. The promise creates or adjusts clients' expectations. Processes managed in the light of appropriate service standards allow the provider to meet these expectations at the moment of truth (see Section 4.2.1). One condition for this to happen is that marketing and operations—both fluent in their respective languages, but generally largely illiterate in the other—see eye to eye on the service concept. Such communality of views allows *desired* or *intended* positioning to become *achieved* position, that is, in the minds of customers (see note 6 in Chapter 2).

Figure 5.3 builds on Figure 5.2 to highlight the role of operations strategy and processes in the value chain. In Chapter 3, processes were introduced as the sequences of activities transforming inputs provided by suppliers to produce outputs needed by customer (or SITOC—see Figure 3.5). Retracing the value chain backwards, it can be seen in Figure 5.3 that the service features are the

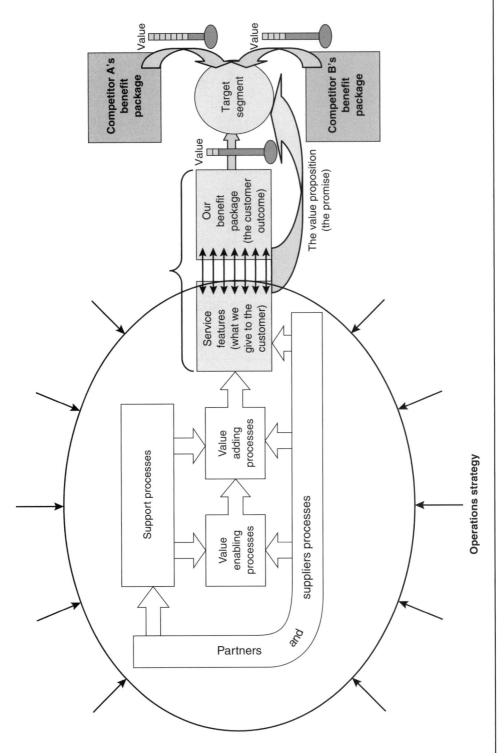

Figure 5.3 Operations strategy as the driving force behind process design, management, and improvement.

output of value-adding processes. They are the transformation of inputs received from upstream processes, including enabling, support, and suppliers' processes (and customers' processes as well—not shown in the figure). These inputs to value-adding processes are, of course, the outputs of the aforementioned processes. Value-enabling processes in turn produce these outputs from inputs received from support and suppliers' processes (as well as value-adding and customers' processes—not shown in the figure).

Just as service standards define the targets, operations strategy is the source of the vision and guiding principles required to insure coherence in all aspects of service delivery.

5.1.3.2 Positioning in the Labor Market and Processes

Referring to Section 2.4 (and Figure 2.16 in particular), the reader will recall that there is a dual aspect to the positioning challenge. Indeed, the organization is continuously competing to recruit the right employees, keep them appropriately challenged, support them in their jobs, and compensate them adequately. This is particularly difficult when dealing with professionals, since they are a workforce with unique characteristics: They value their skills and want to improve on them, they are mobile, they value their autonomy, and they are demanding of themselves and others. Hence, they have unique needs and requirements, requiring an appropriate benefits package. Their jobs must be designed in such a way (job features) that they reliably deliver these benefits (benefits and requirements together constitute the job concept, as shown in Figure 2.16).

Imagine that BMI has targeted a niche of energetic young educators working in public schools, who value fitness and are disillusioned with their jobs. BMI's benefit package for this labor market segment could include such benefits as a social experience, stimulation, additional income, fitness, and travel. The job features that would deliver these benefits could include working only at night and on weekends, doing part of the teaching while working out on a stationary bike, learning other languages free while training, accompanying groups in action trips abroad, participating in social events, and so on.

Of course, the job concept is delivered jointly by the organization's processes, which must simultaneously deliver the service concept. Figure 5.4 illustrates this dual value creation role of processes. It also shows the pivotal role of operations strategy as a set of guiding principles that ensure coherence (discussed in the next section) in the company's action (that is, in the company's processes) in such a way that positioning in the market and in the job market can be achieved and maintained. To better understand this duality, it is useful to take a closer look at processes than the one allowed by Figure 5.4. Figure 3.4 gives a somewhat more realistic perspective on the complexity of processes in the organization, using a subset of level-three processes drawn from the APQC model. Inserting it in Figure 5.4, in lieu of the earlier representation, results in Figure 5.5.

Of course, processes relating directly to human resource development and management play a central role in delivering internal services to employees. Referring to the APQC process model (Figure 3.2), these would all be included under process number six. The explosion of this process into level-two and -three sub-processes is shown in Figure 5.6. A well-designed and managed process *6.5.6 Manage deployment of personnel* (see Figure 3.4), for instance, ensures that members of work teams get mutual stimulation and support from each other, and that conflicts are minimized and manageable when they do occur. Indeed, interaction with colleagues is an intrinsic part of the benefits that you derive from your job. This same process, however, is also very important for delivering the service concept, as a team's dysfunctions inevitably disrupt service delivery, reducing quality and even denying the client results. Disgruntled customers, in turn, are liable to provide negative feedback to service providers, thus fueling a downward value creation spiral, triggered by the path shown by the dotted arrows in Figure 5.5.

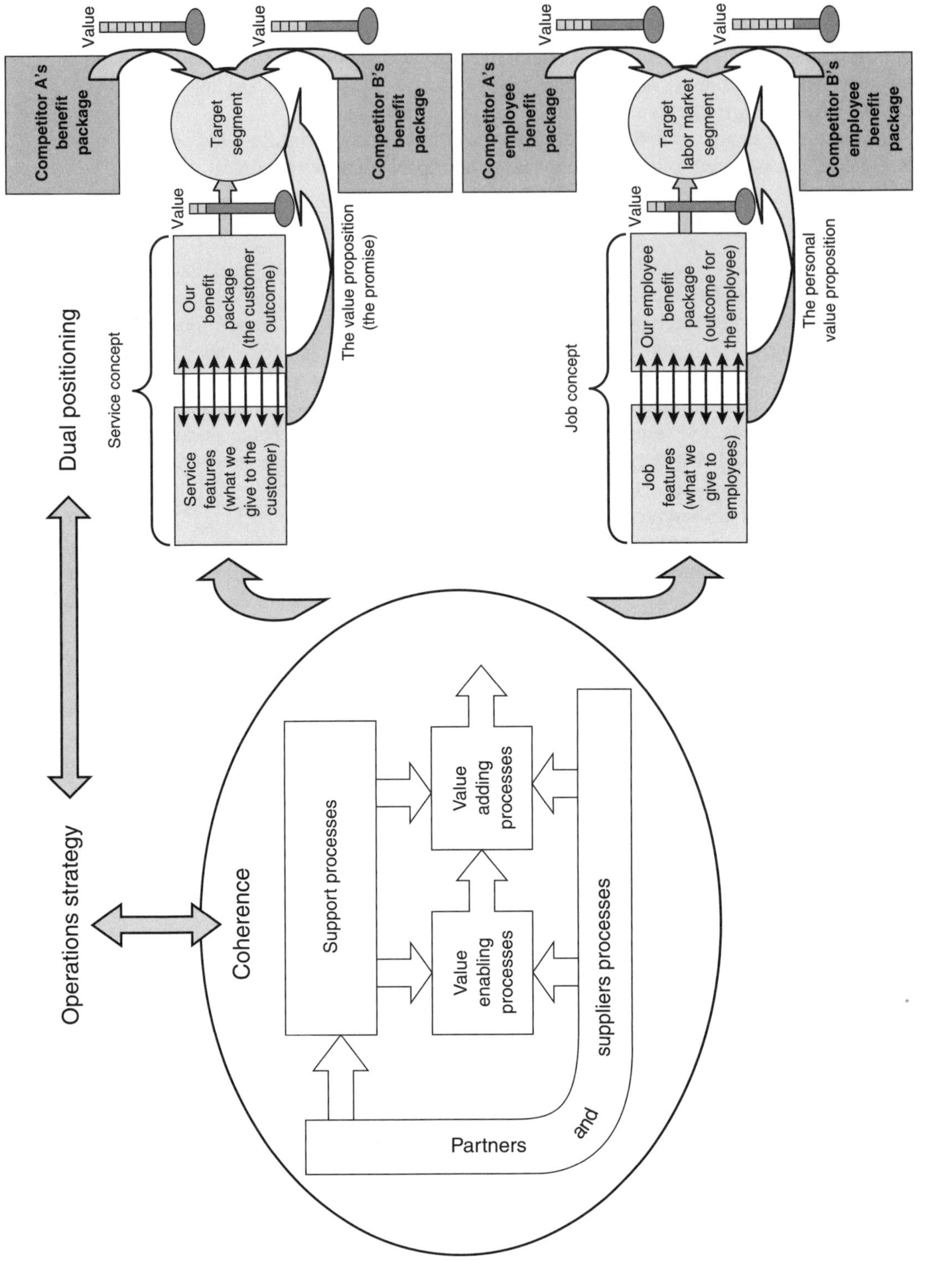

Figure 5.4 The three-way fit between operations strategy, positioning, and coherence.

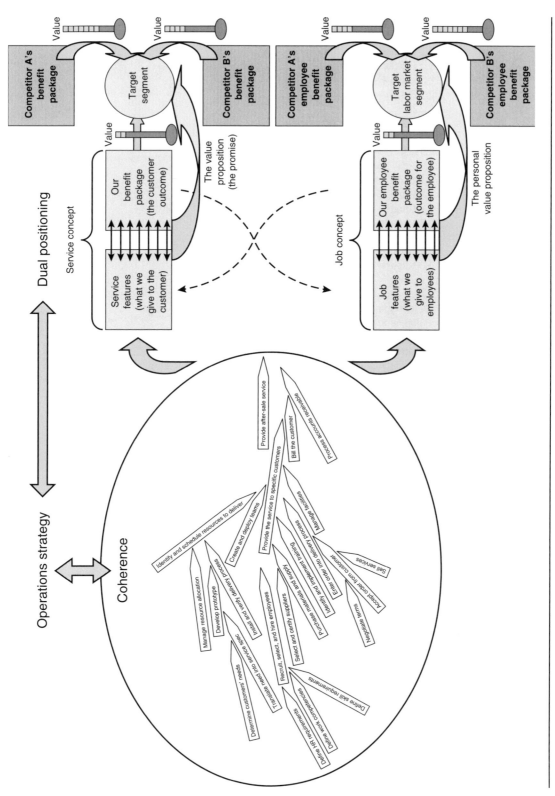

Figure 5.5 The three-way fit: with processes presented in a flow pattern, drawn from Figure 3.4.

6.1 Create and manage human resources (HR) planning,policies, and strategies
    6.1.1 Manage/align/deliver human resources strategy accountability
    6.1.2 Develop and implement HR plans
    6.1.3 Monitor and update plans
6.2 Recruit, source, and select employees
    6.2.1 Create and develop employee requisitions
    6.2.2 Recruit candidates
    6.2.3 Screen and select candidates
    6.2.4 Manage preplacement verification
    6.2.5 Manage new hire/re-hire
    6.2.6 Track candidates
6.3 Develop and counsel employees
    6.3.1 Manage employee orientation and deployment
    6.3.2 Manage employee performance
    6.3.3 Manage employee relations
    6.3.4 Manage employee development
    6.3.5 Develop and train employees
    6.3.6 Manage employee talent
6.4 Reward and retain employees
    6.4.1 Develop and manage reward,recognition,and motivation programs
    6.4.2 Manage and administer benefits
    6.4.3 Manage employee assistance and retention
    6.4.4 Payroll administration
6.5 Re-deploy and retire employees
    6.5.1 Manage promotion and demotion process
    6.5.2 Manage separation
    6.5.3 Manage retirement
    6.5.4 Manage leave of absence
    6.5.5 Develop and implement employee outplacement
    6.5.6 Manage deployment of personnel
    6.5.7 Relocate employees and manage assignments
    6.5.8 Manage employment reduction and retirement
    6.5.9 Manage expatriates
    6.5.10 Manage employee relocation process
6.6 Manage employee information
    6.6.1 Manage reporting processes
    6.6.2 Manage employee inquiry process
    6.6.3 Manage and maintain employee data
    6.6.4 Manage human resource information systems (HRIS)
    6.6.5 Develop and manage employee metrics
    6.6.6 Develop and manage time and attendance
    6.6.7 Manage employee communication

Figure 5.6 Developing and managing human resources: process list (down to level three, based on APQC).

Other processes, such as *6.3.5 Develop and train employees* and *6.2.5 Manage new hire/re-hire*, which are directly supportive of service delivery also have important bearing on the job concept. Even such operational processes as *Sell services* and *Provide services to specific customers* (illustrated in more detail in the case of Medsol [Figure 3.6] and real estate [Figure 3.8]) are just as important to the professionals as they are to the clients, even more so, in fact, because professionals repeat them much more often than clients. Recall that these two processes involve face-to-face contact (discussed in Section 4.2.1 and 4.2.2) and are therefore important, albeit in different ways, to both interlocutors. All of the other processes involve many interactions with other professionals, managers, partners, suppliers, and so on. As Section 4.3.3 illustrates, such interactions are important sources of satisfaction and learning when they work well, and of stress and frustration when they do not.

Quick inspection of Figure 5.1, which displays a selection of specific processes for BMI, makes it clear that many of these processes, such as forming a class, giving a course, and organizing seasonal parties, must be designed with both the client and the instructor in mind.

5.1.3.3 Coherence

A service delivery process (SDP) is coherent if:

- Its design reflects a clear understanding of the needs and preferences of the market segment and of the employees, of the benefit package to be delivered to each respectively, and of what it is that must be done right to beat competition while maintaining and growing the skills and motivation of our workforce

- All its components are complementary and mutually reinforcing

- It exploits operations strategies and policies to their fullest potential

The notion of coherence is best understood by looking at examples of incoherence. Indeed, a coherent service delivery goes so smoothly that it is seamless and effortless for the customer. Delivery is incoherent when the way things are done systematically works against the fulfillment of the promise made to any of the company's stakeholders.

Here are some examples of incoherence in different types of SDPs:

- A fast-food restaurant with a menu from which the customer will require more than 30 seconds to make his pick

- A five-star airport hotel where the only food available after 11 p.m. is whatever is available in the mini-bar

- An airline with slower check-in for first-class than for economy

- A gourmet coffee shop that serves coffee in a cardboard cup

- A phone banking service that asks the customer to key-in a host of information about account number, transaction, and PIN, and then asks for it to be repeated verbally

Anyone who is minimally attentive as a service customer can unfortunately recall many more observations of the same flavor.

Back to the real estate example, a full-service agent (see Figure 2.10) subtly putting pressure to accept on a customer who is inclined to reject an offer is being incoherent if the benefit package includes *assurance*, that is, *you are in the competent hands of a professional whose only interest is that you get the best possible price for your house.*

Other possible examples of incoherence for the full-service agency include:

- Agents are switched around regularly between sectors (local expertise is lost)

- It takes two weeks for the photographer to come around to take pictures of the house (speed of sale)

- The agent can never be reached on the phone after hours (easy access)

The new entrant's (see Figure 2.11) SDP would also be incoherent if its website is only listed on the second page of a Google search for *house for sale*. Other examples of potential incoherencies include:

- The automated report is impossible to understand (assurance, convenience, and control)

- Agents act like bureaucrats, not really motivated to help the customer sell the property (assurance)

- Partners are not really integrated with the brokerage firm and the customer has to reach an agreement with them from scratch, as though just an anonymous walk-in customer (convenience)

Notice that all of the examples of incoherence given so far are related to the delivery of the service concept to the customer. The notion of coherence, however, is broader than that: it also includes employees and shareholders. Therefore, incoherencies include delivery system dysfunctions that result in denial of benefits to any of the three stakeholders or that pit one stakeholder against another. Table 5.2 shows various potential process dysfunctions at BMI, indicating why it is incoherent and which stakeholder or combination of stakeholders it would affect.

Of course, the foregoing discussion does not go very far in helping the reader design coherent service delivery processes. This is a much more complex issue that will require much of the rest of this book.

5.1.4 Positioning Professional Services—Revisited

The challenge that positioning poses should now be clearer: Simultaneously offering and delivering superior benefit packages to selected customers and professionals in such a way that much

Table 5.2 Potential process dysfunctions at BMI, explanation, and stakeholders affected.

Incoherent element of service delivery process	Why it is incoherent	Stakeholders affected
Noisy or worn-out equipment with frequent breakage and adjustments	The noise and frequent interruptions will make learning impossible	Client and trainer
Recruiting a language instructor who does not care much about fitness	Will not fit in and will not be able to accompany the group in action trips abroad. Will stick out like a sore thumb at parties.	Client
Setting fees too low—less than the cost of the alternative	The alternative is taking two separate courses, with the time and inconvenience that this entails. Charging less than that will result in cheating the shareholders or in self-defeating decrease in service standards.	Shareholders
Not detecting early-on and taking immediate steps to correct excessive drop out rate		Client and shareholder
Assigning trainers daily, according to who is available	Convenient for trainers, but denies the clients continuity in learning and social interaction	Client versus trainer

money is left for profits and growth. Each of the components of this challenge, illustrated in Figure 5.5, have been discussed, and the chapter now turns to a discussion and illustration of the global challenge that it entails. To address this, first we will provide a brief review of the implications of the knowledge gap between client and service provider in professional services. Then, the chapter revisits the notion of positioning, this time with the benefit of the above discussion of strategy.

5.1.4.1 The Knowledge Gap and the Fog of Professional Services

Consider the plight of a patient who suffers from *whiplash*[1]. A medical book or search of the web can be used to find treatment advice. Any of the following service providers can also be consulted: physical therapist, orthopedist, general practitioner, osteopath, physiatrist, acupuncturist, or massage therapist. To make things more complex still, some physical therapists are free practitioners, while others work for orthopedists or physiatrists. The treatments offered by each vary widely, involving various mixes of service and self-service. Others also double-up as massage therapists, while some osteopaths are also trained as acupuncturists, and so on. Each of them will claim incontrovertible evidence that this angle is best, and after a 20-week treatment, the poor patient may well be left wondering what percentage improvement is really felt, and if that's attributable to the $2000 treatment received or to the mere passage of time.

As discussed in Chapter 2, the gap in knowledge between the service provider and the client and the latter's difficulties in ascertaining the effect of the service makes selection of a professional very difficult. The decision as to which provider to select will generally be based on beliefs, which in turn are induced by experiences, reality, and word of mouth. Hence, reputation and branding are even more important here than they are in other sectors.

Because all professionals are well aware of that, much competition takes place in the media. Clearly, the professional that provides the best value is at an advantage, but is not sheltered from competition from less scrupulous competitors, who manage advertising, perception, and public image better. Newspapers are full of stories about highly reputable professionals who have been caught red-handed, and whose professional practice turned out to be very different from best practice. Witness the Enron debacle and the subsequent demise of the audit practice of Arthur Andersen. Thus, the best professional service will not prosper in the marketplace on its own. The perception and branding war must also be won.

5.1.4.2 A Broader View of Positioning—a Legal Service Example

Consider the case of someone who wants to prepare a will. This customer is faced with two decisions concerning how to go about it. "To what extent am I able or willing to get involved in the process? To what extent do I want it customized to my own specific needs?" The first question relates to the issue of service versus self-service discussed in Chapter 2 (see Figure 2.4, for instance) and relates to the importance of the knowledge gap discussed above. The second one raises a fundamental issue, not discussed so far, about service and service delivery processes, that is, that of standard versus customized services. It has an important effect on all three stakeholders. Figure 5.7 illustrates the four basic possibilities resulting from the two decisions. The two axes really involve a continuum along which many possibilities exist, even though only two are presented in the body of the diagram. The bars on the degree of service axis refer to those used in Figure 2.4.

While the four possibilities are presented from the customer's perspective, they clearly imply positioning opportunities for service providers as well. A different operations strategy and different processes underlie each opportunity. Each also implies a different job concept. Assume that four providers (labeled 1 to 4 in Figure 5.7) are competing with each other in a given market. Provider

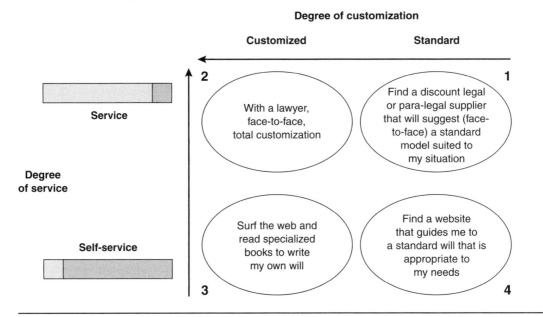

Figure 5.7 Four generic ways to prepare a will.

1 delivers a result that is quite close (for clients with simple needs) to that offered by provider 2, with the difference that it is faster and cheaper. This operations strategy might involve using personable legal technicians to leverage lawyers. Technicians are the primary service providers. They are selected for their people and professional skills. The contact mode is face-to-face (*tight specs* to *open specs*, depending on service offerings[2]), but because of the technicians' people skills and availability, customers do not feel this limitation. A few lawyers work in second line, mostly developing service offerings and acting as backup and support to technicians. Clients in the target market are delighted by the availability and human qualities of the technicians, who in turn enjoy the positive feedback they are getting (refer to the dotted line in Figure 5.5). Lawyers are selected for their preference for work that is more intense in professional content than in client contact. As it is much easier to manage technicians than lawyers, customer requirements weigh much more in the design of delivery processes, including selection of modes of contact, than on those of lawyers. This is an important advantage over provider 2.

Provider 4 offers clients who have some technical knowledge and who are willing to get involved in the process, the same result that provider 1 offers, except that the service is faster, more convenient, and cheaper. This operations strategy involves a substantial investment in automated service delivery, essential to provide the aforementioned benefits, that becomes profitable as extremely low variable cost allows setting a price that is attractive to a mass market. There are very few lawyers on staff and many IT professionals. Specialized technical expertise on a contractual or consulting basis is used, with in-house lawyers acting as interface with IT experts. The interfacing between these different professionals is vital to the success of the business, and much management attention is directed at ensuring smooth contact between them and early detection of conflicts. Provider 3 is in a different business altogether, acting as a content assembler, integrator, and distributor. However, emerging expert systems are gradually blurring the line between providers 3 and 4. As technology evolves, customer knowledge increases, and market matures, many synergistic merger and strategic alliance opportunities will emerge.

This example shows that the existence of a viable operations strategy is indissociable from the positioning exercise. The customer value equation serves as a reminder that value is not only a function of the benefits produced, but also of the price paid by the client. Price, however, is a function of cost, and the latter is, in turn, a function of the resources used. Since experienced professionals are generally the scarcest and most expensive resource in a PSO, it is advantageous to use their time with parsimony, allocating it to tasks which technicians, trained personnel, or machines cannot perform. The number of ways to combine professionals, technicians, customer service representatives, and IT into service delivery processes is virtually infinite. The number of viable ways to do so for a PSO, at any point in time, is much more limited. It is the purpose of operations strategy to find, formulate, and act as implementation guide and bulwark for the *right way of doing things* in the organization.

It is also impossible to dissociate the formulation of the service concept from that of the job concept. The different mixes of resources that are possible not only offer different value propositions to the customers but also imply different job concepts as well. To understand this better, it is worthwhile to explore further some important aspects of professional work, professional workers, and PSOs.

5.2 FROM STRATEGY TO PROCESSES

In this section, further exploration of processes and their characteristics takes place, with a view to illustrate the required fit with positioning and operations strategy. After presenting the major process characteristics, it is shown how these are unevenly distributed among the various families of processes, and thus shown that tradeoffs have to be made. Discussion then turns to the specificities of professional services in that regard, and the legal services example is pursued further.

5.2.1 Process Characteristics

There are many ways to achieve a desired result. In preparing a cup of coffee for example, you may boil water on an electric kettle, on a range, or in the microwave oven. Beans may be ground with an electric blade grinder, ground with a stone grinder, bought pre-ground, or ground in an industrial quality machine at the supermarket. Water may be filtered through the grounds through a funnel, under pressure (espresso), or using a piston (Turkish style). Are these all equivalent? Of course not. The taste, smell, effect, temperature, and texture of the coffee will vary. So will the cost, the cost structure (fixed versus variable), the tasks of the employee and skill requirement, input requirements, suppliers, and so on. How can these processes be compared and the best one selected? In order to do that, a little more about processes and their characteristics must be understood. In this section, a number of such characteristics are described and illustrated: *effectiveness, efficiency, productivity, capacity, flexibility, and reliability.*

A process is *effective* if it produces the desired effect (or result). If you are preparing a cup of coffee because you feel sleepy, effectiveness is directly proportional to the amount of stimulation received from the coffee. Consider the case of Midtown Child Protection Services (see Box 5.2, Midtown CPS), where process effectiveness is related to the security it provides to the children. In both these cases (the cup of coffee, and CPS), it is a question of degree. Sometimes, however, effectiveness is either zero or one—it worked or it did not—such as fixing a broken computer or transporting a letter from point A to point B by 10 a.m. the next morning.

Box 5.2: Midtown child protective services (Midtown CPS)

Issue: A complex public professional service dealing with a sensitive societal issue

Sam Alonzo looked worried as he cut the line by flipping off the switch with his thumb. A glance at the clock told him it was almost midnight. A flashing red light on the console indicated that Mark, his colleague at Midtown Child Protective Services (CPS), was busy taking another report. The caller was obviously concerned:

a) "The poor little things are 3 and 5"—the man had said—"they've been playing outside all evening wearing T-shirts and it's freezing out there. They had been banging at the door of their parent's house for half an hour when my wife decided to invite them in. They're downstairs having hot chocolate now. The parents must be having a really good time in there. I knocked at the door and rang. No answer. The music is so loud in there! Besides, we could distinctly smell that they're not smoking the normal kind of tobacco, if you know what I mean . . ."

The caller was worried and so was Sam now. CPS's mission was to enforce the State's child protection legislation. Sam, a trained social worker, was working in the emergency service department. On a 24/7 basis, the department received reports from professionals (doctors, nurses, teachers, social workers) and concerned citizens about children in need of protection. They had to assess these reports and decide, sometimes on the spot, on an appropriate course of action.

Sam was mentally reviewing his options. He could have the police department send a patrol car right away to pick up the children, and drop them at the city's reception center or at the home of a specially trained family willing to handle this situation. A team of specialists would then take over the case first thing the next morning as they came to work. That of course could trigger a chain of events, including legal procedures, that would be very consequential for the family, and thus for the children. He also had to consider that the team's resources were already spread very thin. Instead, he could ask a special intervention team composed of a family therapist and a specialized educator to make it their next stop. However, it would probably be a couple of hours before the team could get there, and then they would not be available if something more urgent came up elsewhere in the city. He could finally ask the caller if they were willing to keep the children over for the night and slip a note under the door for the parents. However, could they be trusted? What would be the parent's reaction as they read the note? At this point in his thought process, the red light on the console turned off.

"Oh good,"—he thought as he got up, grabbing his empty mug—"I need a sounding board on that one . . . and a good cup of coffee!"

A process is *efficient* if it uses the most economical means possible to achieve the desired results. If I buy Jamaica Green Mountain coffee beans at $60 a pound for the sole purpose of ingesting 120 mg of caffeine, that's inefficient, even though the inefficiency comes from the choice of inputs and not from the brewing process per se. If I brew a full 6-cup percolator and throw away the rest, that is inefficient as well. At Midtown CPS, if Sam sends the police and a special intervention team to place the children in a reception center for a week, when a good night's sleep at the neighbors and a simple visit by a social worker the next day would have been sufficient, that's inefficient (not to speak of the potential side effects of that approach). While the definition of efficiency is quite clear, how to measure it raises many issues. For instance, should you focus on the transformation per se, excluding the cost of the inputs? In many instances, it is convenient to use unit cost of output as a good proxy for efficiency (that is, including the cost of the inputs). This is impossible however if you want to analyze the efficiency of several interconnected sub-processes or in situations where you are trying to track efficiency over time, excluding the influence of market price variations.

Productivity is traditionally defined as the ratio of outputs to inputs—that is, the quantity of output per unit of input. Since that leaves out quality entirely, a better definition would be the quantity of good output per unit of input. However, you can see the difficulties that would arise in trying to define, let alone count, *good output* at Midtown CPS. The best measure—though measuring it remains a challenge—is the ratio of effectiveness to efficiency, commonly referred to as cost effectiveness. CPS being a public service, its mandate is to provide maximum protection to the children at risk in their community, given the budget they have. Thus, cost effectiveness plays an important role in every resource allocation decision they make.

The *capacity* of a process is a measure of the volume of work it can perform. The security process at a given airport gate may be able to handle 500 people an hour. A Boeing 767-200 accommodates 224 passengers, 206 in coach and 18 first-class passengers. Sam and Mark at Midtown CPS may be able to investigate an average of four calls an hour during their shift. A fast food drive-up service may be able to process 50 cars an hour. Often, however, capacity is not a fixed number. A full plane means less personal attention and a longer wait at the restroom. Sam and Mark could handle six calls an hour for a while, but if that rate was to be sustained for a whole night, they might become tired and the risk of a bad decision would increase. Short-term response to unforeseen increase in demand, as the process approaches maximum rated capacity, often means loss of effectiveness and/or efficiency. If the increase in demand is sustained, the process can generally be modified to adapt to the new level. Eight-abreast, with an all-coach configuration, a Boeing 767-200 can sit 290 people. However, you should make sure that the increase is not just a short-term blip before incurring the changeover cost. Thus, a good volume forecast is a precious tool for both process designers and process managers.

A process is *flexible* if it can deal with much variety with minimal penalty. The penalty refered to is the higher cost, lower quality, or longer cycle time that processes that do many different things suffer, compared to processes that do only one thing. The latter benefits from a high level of standardization, special purpose tools, less qualified employees, and an optimized layout and flow. Anyone who gets a hepatitis shot at a traveler's clinic and compares the procedure with that used in a general practitioner's office knows the difference. The time penalty is even more obvious if you compare your personal process for removing a flat tire with that used by the pit crew for a Formula 1 car. Hence, while variety always entails a penalty, a process that minimizes that penalty is said to be the most flexible. A five-star restaurant, for instance, offers a vast selection of coffee. However, if you ask for a Turkish coffee—which they only brew once a month when they have a special request—you may have to wait a while (time penalty) for a coffee that is not to your taste (quality penalty) and pay a hefty price for it (cost penalty). Midtown's emergency service process is very flexible. It can deal with any type of emergency on a 24/7 basis. To achieve this, they must often pay an expensive professional (university-trained, 10 years experience, working a night shift) for hours to wait for that truly urgent call and pay a premium to other specialists to remain on 30-minute call all night.

A *reliable* process is one on which you can depend. An unreliable process is one that generates an excessive number of failures. No process is infallible, but some are pretty close to being so, with a defect rate (see Chapter 6) under one per million. What is acceptable and what is not depends on customer's needs. A cleaning process that would be considered unreliable in an operating room, for instance, may be perfectly acceptable in a hotel. This notion is discussed further in Chapter 6. Other process characteristics, such as capability, stability, predictability, reproducibility, and repeatability are discussed in later chapters.

Designing a process involves making trade-offs between the characteristics presented above. Go back to the coffee example presented in the opening paragraph of this section. Buying the beans pre-ground saves time in preparing coffee, but the coffee does not smell or taste the same (ineffective). Preparing a filtered coffee one cup at a time allows you to personalize bean selection and grinding (flexible), but it takes much time (inefficient) and would be impractical for a large party. It may also introduce much variation in taste, caffeine content, or temperature from one cup to the next, and may thus be unreliable. Espresso tastes great (effective, if you like that) but may require a long lead-time and a substantial investment. It also utilizes much space on the counter and has the highest cost per cup (inefficient). Further, it is very rigid, producing a unique taste that will not please all guests. Its capacity is much lower than that of a percolator, and the labor content per cup, much higher.

Such trade-offs must be made with a clear understanding of the mission of the process (that is, what contribution does it need to make to the execution of the strategy—this is discussed in Chapter 6) and also based on a realistic look at the constraints of all nature that limit the choices: financial, technical, and circumstantial. Understanding the major families of processes and their characteristics somewhat simplifies that choice.

5.2.2 Major Process Families and Their Characteristics

Consider four major families of processes: artisan, job shop, line-flow, and continuous (or fully automated). In any service, three different elements are processed: people, things, and information. Things may include food, medication, the client's property (pool, house, or dog), and hard documents (deeds, drawings, certificates). Job shop and line-flow processes are illustrated first with a simple example.

Compare two types of cafeterias. One is a line-flow process where everybody follows the same sequence, directed by the guiding rails supporting the trays: trays, dishes, utensils, cold drinks, salads, cold sandwiches, soup, hot plates, desserts, hot drinks (placed last to improve the odds that it will not be too cold by the time you drink it), and cashier. The other one is a job shop, organized as a set of islands (hot drinks, cold drinks, salad bar, soup bar, hot plates, sandwiches, desserts, and so on). Each customer decides where to go and in what sequence to do it.

For a homogeneous set of customers, wanting a complete meal with salad, soup, dessert, and drinks, the line flow will tend to be the fastest, most reliable, and most efficient process, provided it is well balanced. Line balancing is about making sure that each station along the line requires about the same amount of time. Since the longest station determines the pace of the line, total process time is equal to the processing time at the longest station multiplied by the number of stations. If the group is heterogeneous, many people who do not want soup will end up waiting this station out, or trying to jump the line, with all the disruptions and frictions that this may entail. The same will happen when someone is coming back for seconds. Thus, the line is quite rigid and becomes inefficient (from the customer's point of view) as the group becomes more heterogeneous. In this context, reliability might involve delivering each plate with little variation in the quantity of food, temperature, and cycle time. Reliability and capacity (measured in number of customers served per hour) will tend to be superior to the job shop.

Assuming again a homogeneous group of people, a job shop would result in unpredictable and unmanageable bottlenecks surfacing here and there because of random customer decisions. More staff would be required, running around to replenish the food supply as shortages randomly occur in various spots, and to try to alleviate bottlenecks as they occur. To do so, employees should be cross-trained to be able to perform at any workstation where they may be required (there is a cost associated with that) and more variation would be introduced by frequent switchovers. For a heterogeneous group, however, the job shop would be the fastest and most efficient process. Customers wanting only a sandwich and coffee and customers wanting a soup and hot plate would not be in each other's way because they would use different parts of the service delivery facilities. The job shop is also more flexible for such a group, involving a lesser time-penalty to customers than a line-flow would.

Employees working in both environments receive different benefit packages. The task is very repetitive in the assembly line, which may be boring for some people, and employees have to work in close synchronization with each other. Job shop workers receive much more training and are called upon to use their initiative much more often, which some people may like and others not.

Of course, there are many intermediate options between the two processes presented above. Depending on customer needs, operational problems encountered, and layout constraints, you may create a sandwich counter to relieve some pressure from a regularly congested line. The job shop may add an express one-stop meal (including payment) for customers willing to sacrifice choice for speed (provided there are not too many). Having such a mix of job requirements may allow employees with different preferences to find something more suited to their tastes.

An artisan type of process involves a single worker producing alone most of the deliverables. To pursue the meal preparation example, a person preparing a meal at home uses such a process: planning the meal, buying what is needed, preparing, cooking, and, in this case, consuming the output as well. Compare to the line and the job shop, it is generally less efficient and less reliable. It is, however, more flexible and may, depending on the customer and the provider, be considered very high quality. Japanese steak houses, where the grill is on your table and the chef cooks your meal in front of you, come close to being an artisan process (the host serves the salad, soup, rice, and drinks, but the cook does the rest). To make this economically viable, however, the menu had to be reduced considerably (grilled chicken, shrimp, or steak, typically), thereby limiting the flexibility of the process.

Strictly speaking, a continuous process involves the continuous flow of a product (generally in liquid or semi-liquid state such as molten steel, crude oil, or paper paste). Electric utilities provide a continuous flow of electrical services along wires. Radio and TV stations provide a continuous flow of information carried by electro-magnetic waves. Food, obviously, cannot be served this way. Information, however, can be digitized and flow along wires, electronic components, and electro-magnetic waves. Such processes involve a continuous flow of data. They can be fast, efficient, and reliable. They can, however, be very costly to build, requiring an important investment in infrastructure, and are rigid, though this last limitation is receding as IT continues to push the frontier.

Table 5.3 summarizes the foregoing discussion of the four major types of processes and their characteristics. The four types of processes really represent discrete points along a continuum. Artisan processes are not very structured, leaving much leeway to the (typically highly qualified, and thus highly paid) worker. They are neither very efficient, nor reliable, and have a low capacity. They compensate for these weaknesses with a high level of flexibility. From artisan to continuous flow process (when this is possible), more structure is introduced and the process is standardized. The variety of services it can render are also limited, and cost-effectiveness, reliability, and capacity are increased, at the expense of flexibility. Hence, the general trade-off implied by the table is clear. An organization's positioning and operations strategy guides it in the selection of the appropriate family of processes. Organizations whose expertise lies in managing a particular type of process must also take this capability (and the corresponding limitations it implies) into consideration in its positioning decisions.

From artisan to line flow, work is increasingly divided, workers perform increasingly limited tasks, and less qualification and training are required. Workers, however, become more closely interdependent, and more coordination is required. A continuous, or more to the point in this case, a fully automated information process, is a different animal altogether. Much of the cost of such a process comes from its design, maintenance, and updating, as transactions themselves are extremely

Table 5.3   Major families of processes and their characteristics.

Family/characteristics	Cost-*effectiveness	Flexibility	Reliability	Capacity
Craftsman	–	++	–	—
Job shop	-	+	-	-
Line-flow	+	-	+	+
Fully automated	++	–	++	++

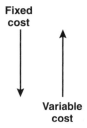

Fixed cost

Variable cost

Legend: ++ Very good
+ Good
- Bad
– Very bad
* at a high volume

cheap. A few very specialized, highly trained, and costly resources (mostly analysts and programmers) do this work. Obviously, management's job varies considerably from one process to the next.

The discussion of cafeterias essentially focused on the flow of people through the process. Thinking about customers first is certainly the right approach. However, the movement of food must be considered simultaneously as well. The design of process that ensures that no workstation ever runs out of food is based on both the needs of the customer and those of employees in contact, and thus on the process selected to serve customers. The shape, weight, and accessibility of food containers from which the customers' plates are prepared (as well as the ordering and refilling procedure), for instance, are unimportant for the customer, but are very important to the contact employee. The flow of people and food jointly determine information requirements. This forms the basis for the design of information systems. The three flows (people, things, and information) must stem from a unique vision that ensures coherence in the implementation of the operations strategy.

Process choices regarding the flow of things and people have implication on layout, as the cafeteria example should make clear. The line-flow requires sequential stations to be aligned and in close proximity. The job shop requires enough space to allow free circulation lanes between each functional island, and to accommodate waiting lines wherever they build up. An artisan process requires organizing all the tools and equipment around the artisan and ensuring the flow of all required material to each artisan, that is, since the artisan does not move, the material must.

One last consideration is required before coming back to professional services: the location of the line of visibility (see Chapter 4) is an important process design decision. Rather than have the customers go to the food, the food could come to the customer. In hospitals, for instance, where patient mobility is limited, food trays are assembled on a full-fledged assembly line connected by a moving conveyor. In a five-star restaurant, customers select from a vast array and the meal is prepared and assembled in a back-office job shop. The respective modes of contact are face-to-face *tight spec* and total customization, respectively.

As this chapter makes clear, the choice between one process and the other depends on positioning and strategy, including operations strategy.

5.2.3 Types of Professional Processes

The process typology presented in the previous section has general applicability in professional services. Care must be taken, however, when using it in that context, as they present a number of unique characteristics.

As discussed in Chapter 4, PSDPs consist of four stages: dispatch (or bid), diagnostic, prescription, and treatment. The flows within a PSO generally consist of a flow of information and decisions around the professional core of the service. Decisions flow out of that core to peripheral processes (technical, administrative, and support) and information flows back into it (this is shown in Figure 5.8, illustrating a cancer service episode) as these processes report back, after acting on the instructions they received. This information, in turn, triggers further interactions among professionals and with the client and, eventually, new decisions. In the professional core, generalists and specialists are found. Generalists normally act as case managers, dispatching customers to specialists or interfacing directly with them as required. They integrate all the technical information flowing back to them, interpret it, and translate it to a form that is understandable by the customer. They communicate this, together with recommended courses of action, to the client, for consideration and decision-making. Technicians work in the immediate periphery of the core, as owners or operators of various technical sub-processes. Support and administrative processes take care of logistical, informational, relational, financial, and other functions.

Professional SDPs are meant to manage the flow of people, things, and information throughout the service encounter. In health services, the body itself is processed, that is, it is a key input and output of the process. Thus, the flow of people takes on a very central place in process and facilities design. Most other professional services are very information-intensive and the flow of people is limited to the area defined by the line of visibility (see Chapter 4). This is not to say that human contact and emotions are not important, since information flows between the emotional persons that all human beings are. As discussed in the previous section, information can be captured in images, word of mouth, paper, or digits, and it can be transformed from one form to another.

Digits are particularly convenient, as they allow for massive and cheap storage and retrieval of information, as well as instantaneous and cheap flows of rich (multimedia) information between the various players in a process, including the client, irrespective of layout or distance. Workflow, for instance, is a family of software applications whose purpose is to ensure the semi-automatic flow of information along pre-defined process steps, irrespective of location, as long as each player is connected to the system, or to the Internet. Such a process shares many of the characteristics of a continuous flow process (speed, low cost, reliability), even though it can be viewed as a connected line, because it requires human input along the way, without the rigidity associated with this type of process in the physical world (where people or things have to be processed).

Some information (such as land titles and contracts) still has to be kept on paper, because of legal requirements. In addition, many customers do not have easy or convenient access to the technology required to digitize their instructions, requests, and responses. These are either transmitted on paper or by human voice (phone or face-to-face). The extent to which information can be digitized, and the point in the process where it is (customer, reception, dispatch, generalist) have a direct effect on the choice of contact modes (see Chapter 4). The nature of professionals and their work also introduce many constraints to these choices. You simply do not tell a professional to digitize information (such as entering instructions in a system). They must be involved in the decision process as part of a carefully planned change strategy. The same goes for deciding to provide a professional with a digital input rather than a paper one. It is not enough to install the *plumbing* of the process to change the flow of information and work. Somehow, you must secure the commitment of the various players. Securing the commitment of professionals is particularly important, as they generally have the power to kill any process change initiative they do not like.

5.2.4 Pursuing the Legal Service Example

There are many ways to combine professionals (generalists and specialists of all kinds), technicians, support workers, and technology in the design of a professional SDP. An example will make this

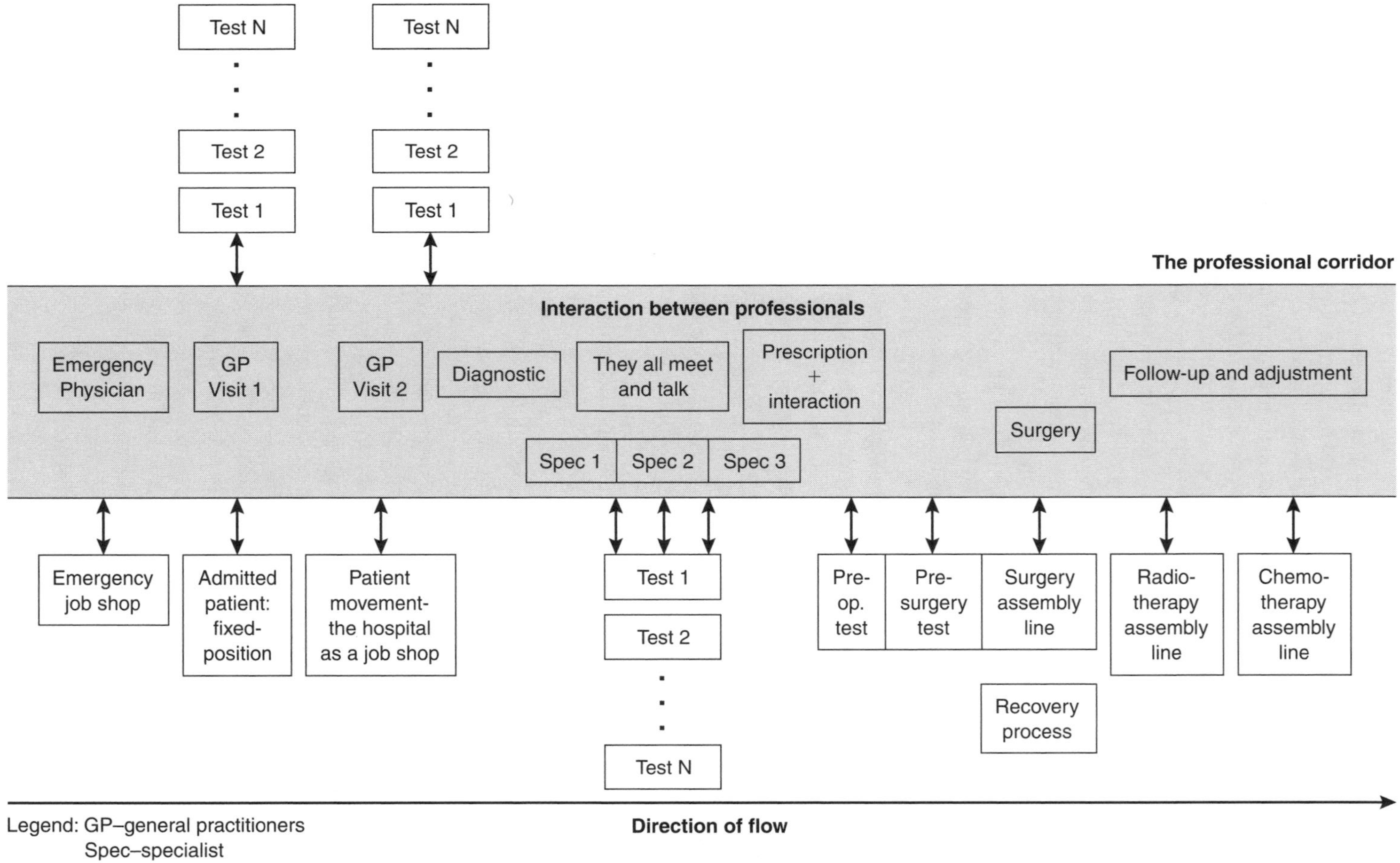

Figure 5.8 The professional core and peripheral processes: Cancer service episode in a hospital.

clear. Refer to the will preparation example discussed earlier (see Figure 5.7). Provider 4's process is fully automated (from the provider's point of view). The marginal cost is virtually zero, but the process can be very rigid: Adding new services or adapting existing services to changes in legislation can be very costly. Provider 2 could use an artisan process, where each lawyer, with the help of a clerk performing whatever task the lawyer delegates (such as word-processing, filing, appointment book, and billing), is in charge of the complete service, from input to output. That process is the most flexible, but it is very costly. Several alternate designs are possible, involving the use of technology to replace the clerk or use a mix of generalists and specialist lawyers. Management has to consider whatever takes place in the lawyer's office (the artisan) as a black box, essentially beyond its control. An assembly line or even a loosely connected sequence of tasks involving different lawyers is not an option—because of professional resistance, triggered by their fear of loss of autonomy. In this environment, professional leadership, teams, and peer groups are central ingredients in building and maintaining cohesion in service delivery.

To understand Provider 1's processes, first recognize that the market for will preparation is not large enough to sustain such a business. The firm would have to offer as well a number of similar legal services—such as simple contracts, proposals to buy a property, and leases—that technicians can perform under the supervision of a professional. Technicians can be specialized in specific services, or even specific steps of service (workflow works wonders in this environment), and the tasks and procedures can be optimized, standardized, and controlled. Customers call for an appointment and, depending on their needs (advertising only brings targeted customers), customers are routed through a programmed sequence. Tight design of the task allows for minimal variation in execution time (see Chapter 8), and thus optimal use of resources, limited waiting time for the client, and mostly on-time delivery.

Those are typical benefits of line-flow processes, and this may sound like paradise. In any context, however, such processes have their limitations, and even more so in professional services. First, they are inflexible. Technicians can only perform the tasks that they have learned. If demand shifts towards more leases and fewer wills, the firm may have to support the cost of idle resources and may not be able to meet the added demand. Cross-training its technicians to provide several different services, such as changing from face-to-face *tight spec* to *open spec*, would alleviate this problem. However, it would also increase cost (training), increase variation in duration, and reduce reliability. A second and related limitation, obviously, is that the provider is trying to address a complex need using an employee who is not a professional, and thus has not been fully trained to perform clinical work (diagnostic and prescription) in that field. Since the technician does not fully understand the ramifications and implications of the work, mistakes are likely and, in professional services, such mistakes can be very costly.

Because of their respective strategies and operations strategies, Providers 1, 2, and 4 have very different processes and cost structures (see Figure 5.9). Provider 1 has a lower cost than provider 2 as soon as the required volume is achieved. A larger part of the cost consists of allocated fixed costs, stemming from process design, implementation (including technology), and training (technicians). Provider 1's high variable cost stems from the intensity of its processes in costly professional time. Provider 4 has an even lower cost (volume allowing), consisting of an essentially fixed cost resulting from the full automation (from the provider's point of view) of the process.

This cost structure results from process choices by providers that are consistent with their respective positioning. It has obvious strategic implications for each provider, implying different opportunities and vulnerabilities. The implications for management cannot be missed either. The challenges of managing a loosely connected collection of artisans is vastly different from that involved in controlling the line-flow or making sure that the automated process stays online, that customers flock to it, and that they come back for more.

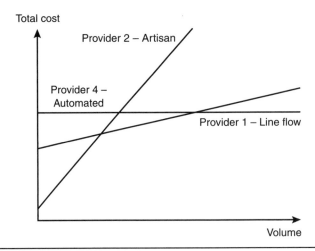

Figure 5.9 Different cost structures associated with different operations strategy.

Turning to the labor market now, provider 1 could target people-oriented legal secretaries or legal assistants with 10 years experience who, even though they like legal work, have reached a ceiling in their current position, in terms of both job richness and pay, and who would welcome a change and new challenges. Such persons are most likely to be found in firms like that of provider 2. The job concept would include benefits such as prestige, independence (not being at the disposal of an exclusive boss), job satisfaction (providing a service to a grateful customer), and personal growth (gradually learning new skills as the firm offers new services). Hence, training and incentive processes would be particularly important for provider 1. Lawyers, on the other hand, would be selected for their relative dislike of traditional law practice (typified by the artisan process), because they do not enjoy direct customer contact or court appearances or for some other reason. They could be offered a salary equivalent or higher than that of the artisans, because of the extent to which technicians would leverage them, allowing for a larger customer base per lawyer on staff. Because, by training, lawyers are naturally more at ease with artisan work, processes related to recruiting and keeping these lawyers happy are particularly important for provider 1. A similar positioning analysis (on the labor market) could be carried out for providers 2 and 4.

In this section, it has been shown that operations strategy, including process selection, does not flow linearly or sequentially from market positioning decisions. Indeed, it is in and of itself a key consideration in the simultaneous exploration of alternate positioning opportunities in the market and in the labor market, as shown in Figure 5.5.

5.3 THE LEARNING ORGANIZATION

In earlier chapters (Sections 1.3 and 3.4), it was explained that processes lie at the heart of value creation and learning. More specifically, processes must create more value than competition for its three stakeholders: customers, employees, and shareholders. The foregoing discussion shows that the strategy-process connection is central to this global purpose. Figure 5.10 illustrates this graphically. The organization's strategy addresses the simultaneous positioning in the market and in the labor market (as illustrated previously in Figures 5.4 and 5.5). The organization must deliver a service concept that creates more value than its competitors to its customers of choice (the *value-gap* shown in the *market* square). At the same time, it must deliver a job concept of superior value to its

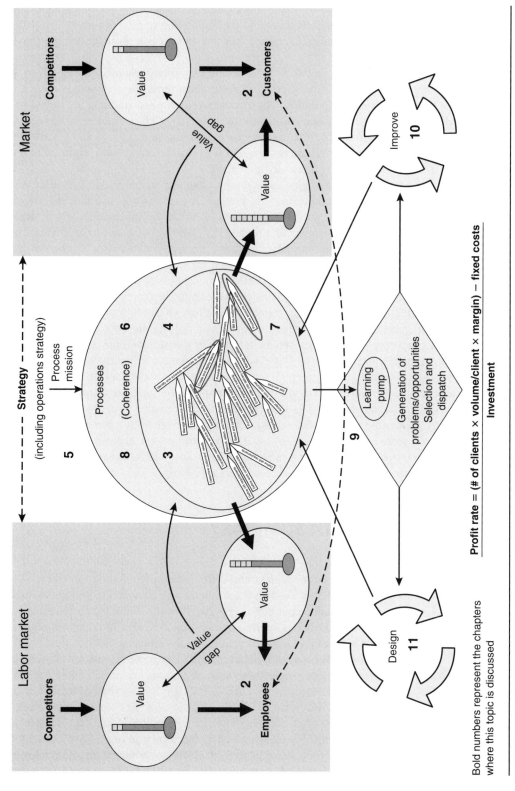

Bold numbers represent the chapters
where this topic is discussed

Profit rate = (# of clients × volume/client × margin) − fixed costs
──
Investment

Figure 5.10 The learning organization: Doing the right thing (picking the right process) right (designing or improving that process) as a key organizational routine.

employees of choice (competitors vying to obtain the services of these employees may be totally unrelated to those faced in the market). The curved broken line in Figure 5.10 illustrates that if the organization fails to deliver to either stakeholder, the other one suffers as a result, thus triggering a spiral of negative feedbacks.

As discussed in Chapter 3, the organization must decide how many resources it can afford to devote to improvement at any point in time, given that in the short term, these resources are withdrawn from those available for daily operation. Thus, processes that need attention are many and resources limited. Selecting the process that will contribute most to the enhancement of the organization's competitiveness at that point in time (that is, *the right thing to do*) is crucial. Fixing that process (using improvement resources efficiently) so that it performs at the level required by the organization (that is, *doing things right*) is equally important.

There are four basic inputs to process selection: strategy, value gap in the market, and value gap in the labor market. When an organization reviews its strategy, it explores opportunities and threats facing it in the markets and diagnoses its strengths and weaknesses. Out of this exercise, key strategic issues emerge. Addressing these issues requires first finding the processes that have to be modified or designed. This exercise often results in the formulation of new missions for processes to achieve (discussed in Chapter 6). It also highlights the competitive value gaps, which in turn point to different processes. Daily operations and entropy (the natural deterioration of processes—see Chapter 3) also create many more problems and opportunities, so that processes must be managed (Chapter 8).

Figure 5.10 revisits Figure 1.4, with a higher resolution. The bottom part illustrates the process that the organization uses to generate, select, and exploit improvement opportunities (*the learning pump*— Chapter 7) to generate more profits. One of its important functions is to decide if the process should be improved (Chapter 10) or designed (Chapter 11) and what change *vehicle* (Chapter 9) should be used to do it. This is the organizational learning loop (or learning pump, as we shall call it). It is the object of Chapter 9. The better and the faster it works, the faster the organization learns and adapts to its changing environment and the more competitive it gets. This is the most sustainable form of strategic advantage, as it is virtually impossible to copy. Maintaining coherence through such a continuous series of local changes, however, poses a particular challenge, which is addressed in Chapter 6. Bold figures in Figure 5.10 indicate the chapter where this topic is covered. The reader interested in reading further on the relation between processes and learning should read Garvin (2000).

5.4 SUMMARY

Strategy is the organization's game plan to beat competition. In that sense, positioning is about picking your fight, that is, selecting the market segment and differentiating your services. Operations strategy is that part of the game plan that deals with the way you will provide the service, in such a way that you will make money, and keep your employees happy while doing so. Formulating an operations strategy requires simultaneously considering market opportunities, internal capabilities, and competencies, as well as the need to find a viable position in the labor market.

It is in the light of such an *umbrella* orientation that processes must be considered. Processes are where *the rubber hits the road*, that is, where these abstract notions are made concrete. From artisan to continuous flow, processes have different characteristics (effectiveness, efficiency, productivity, capacity, flexibility, and reliability) that can facilitate or impede the creation of the strategic advantage sketched out in the game plan. An assembly line reliably produces high volume at low cost, but it is rigid. A job shop is flexible and responsive, but results in high costs. Designing processes is about making tradeoffs—you cannot have it all. Strategy provides the guidelines to make these tradeoffs.

An organization is a complex web of interrelated processes. These processes must work together, complementing and reinforcing each other in the delivery of the benefit package to the customers, to the employees, and to the shareholders. In other words, they must be coherent. They each have a specific contribution, or mission, to make to the execution of the game plan. Whoever designs, improves, manages, or partakes in that process must be well aware of that mission. Maintaining such coherence is the subject of Chapter 6.

EXERCISES

5.1 Strategic overview

Write up a short case study of a new service that you would consider launching, including (refer to the BMI box for an illustration):

   a) Target market segment

   b) Competitors' weaknesses (opportunity)

   c) Your strengths and weaknesses

   d) Strategy

   e) Service concept

   f) Operations strategy

   g) Operations policies

   h) Job concept (if there are several categories of employees, write a concept for the major categories: professional and technician)

5.2 Positioning and processes

   a) Identify your major competitors and position them in a diagram such as that shown in Figure 5.7, based on the degree of customization and the degree of service. Then, position your new service in it.

   b) List the major processes that you will need to deliver this service concept, in a fashion similar to that shown in Figure 5.1.

5.3 Human resources—processes

   a) If the job concept you described in Exercise 5.1h is different from the one you currently deliver to your employees, specify the differences and identify the processes you would have to change to be able to deliver the new benefit package.

   b) Is the new concept compatible with the existing one, from a cultural point of view? How will the new employees (assuming you would have to hire them) fit with existing employees?

   c) Does this involve minor changes or, on the contrary, would you have to design new processes from scratch?

5.4 Process characteristics and families of processes

a) Review your answers to Exercise 3.1. Characterize your sales process and your invoicing process, writing a short statement for each of the following characteristics: effectiveness, efficiency, productivity, capacity, and reliability.

b) For each process: what are the most important and least important characteristics, in view of what you believe to be the mission of the process? Does the current process reflect the competitive priorities of each process?

c) Select two of the processes that you listed in your answer to Exercise 5.2 b. What are the two most important characteristics required of each process, in view of the positioning and strategy you spelled out in your answer to Exercise 5.1?

d) For each of these two processes, prepare a rough-cut design using a PFD diagram of what an artisan process and an assembly-line process would look like. Which one seems to be the best (refer to your answer to Exercise 5.4c) to answer this question)?

5.5 Coherence

Carrying on with the same example, give two examples of incoherence (as defined in this chapter) that could happen if the designers and managers of these processes are unaware of the organization's strategy.

5.6 Positioning to processes: Visual representation of the value stream

a) Use your answers to all of the preceding exercises to complete the form provided in Figure 5.11, inspired by Figure 5.4. Refer to the latter to better remember what goes in each box. The form is called *positioning to processes*, or P2P for short. Its purpose is to allow you to produce a visual representation of the (simplified) value stream of your company. The profit rate equation has been added as a reminder of the purpose of the venture. Since the *Competitor X* boxes are very small, specify only the major benefit that differentiate each competitor's offerings from your own. Competitors in the labor market may or may not be the same as the ones you picked for the market itself. For the job concept, select a category of professionals. Service standards must be quantitative and specify target values (for example, customers should never wait more than 10 minutes). You cannot possibly write down all processes in that form: select the most important.

b) When you have completed the form, pick one key value-adding process that you would like to design or improve. Use arrows (pointing toward that process) to connect upstream processes to it. Use arrows (pointing away from it) to connect it to offerings, elements of the value propositions, and service standards. Use one-direction or bi-directional arrows to connect the process to elements of the operations strategy, as appropriate.

c) Use the resulting diagram as a basis for discussion at a management committee meeting. Try to reach a consensus on it, that is, build a common vision of the value stream. This is an important document to communicate management's vision to the team involved in the development of the new service.

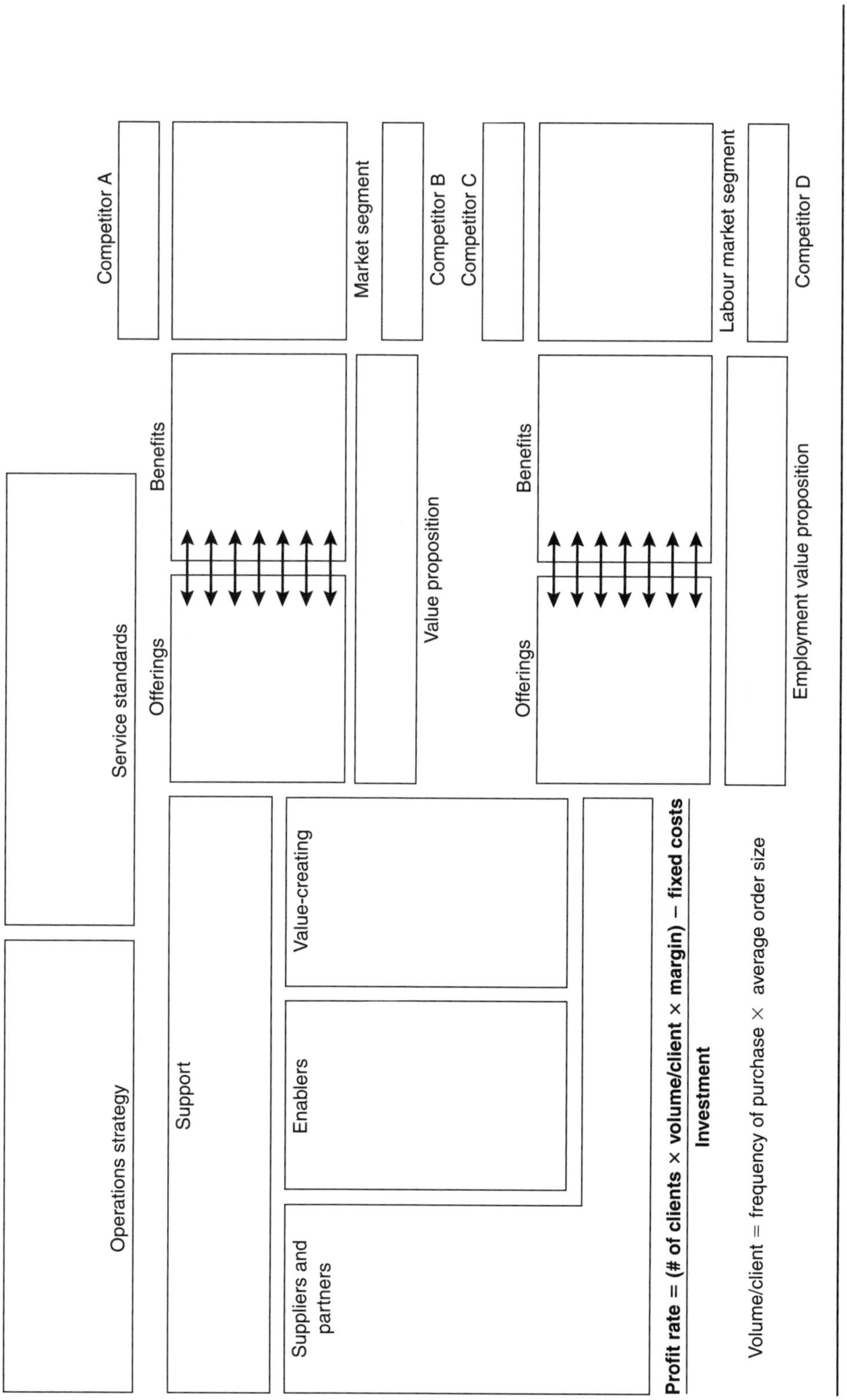
Operations strategy
Service standards
Support
Offerings
Benefits
Competitor A
Market segment
Competitor B
Suppliers and partners
Enablers
Value-creating
Value proposition
Competitor C
Offerings
Benefits
Labour market segment
Profit rate = (# of clients × volume/client × margin) – fixed costs
Investment
Employment value proposition
Competitor D
Volume/client = frequency of purchase × average order size

Figure 5.11 Positioning to processes (P2P) form.

Notes

[1]Neck pain that typically occurs after being hit from behind by a car, after coming to a sudden stop.
[2]See discussion in Section 5.2.3-Types of professional SDPs.

6

Connecting Value to Processes: the Techniques

Deciding on the right thing to do: a methodology to identify the processes that should be focused on to provide superior value, and create competitive advantage.

In the previous chapters, the notions of value, operations strategy, coherence, and processes have been discussed. Discussion now turns to methodologies and techniques that can help connect these elements together. The major technique used here is adapted from quality function deployment (QFD). It provides a structured approach to translating customer needs into service offerings (or features), service features into technical characteristics (metrics), and deploying the latter onto processes. It will take the reader from 30,000 feet to 5000 feet (so to speak), that is, it allows for the identification (at a high level) of the processes on which the organization should focus. In Chapter 11, the reader will be taken from 5000 feet to ground level, carrying on with the same example. The chapter is concluded with a short discussion of the central notion of coherence between operations strategy and operations, and more specifically, of the pivotal role that process mission plays in that regard.

This material is placed in its logical sequence in the book. However, the methodology presented herein is quite demanding in terms of executives' time. They will only be willing to make such an investment if they believe in the approach and are solidly behind it. That is generally not the case unless they have seen it at work and felt its benefits (this is discussed in Chapter 12, in connection with learning maturity level). If your organization is not at this stage, I recommend that you read the last item in Section 6.9 and skim through Box 6.1 before reading on. While you still need to read the chapter after that, you will be able do so more selectively, deferring a more detailed study of it until your company is ready for it.

6.1 SELECTING THE RIGHT PROCESS

Many trends in management thought and business practice stem from the idea of doing the right thing right (see Sections 3.4.3 and 5.3). The *doing* part refers to processes. *Doing the right thing* has to do with focusing on the processes most likely to create strategic advantage. *Doing things right* refers to optimizing the selected process. Studies aimed at demonstrating the long-term benefits of total quality management, business process improvement, reengineering, and other related process-based strategic business initiatives have yielded disappointing results (Brown, Hitchcock et al., 1994). This may be the fate that awaits more recent initiatives in this field, such as Six Sigma, ISO-9000 (version 2000), and the Capability Maturity Model, unless the missing link is found (Hammer, 2001). When faced with having to explain this poor showing, few if any authors fault the approaches and tools used for process improvement. Most attribute it to the fact that companies are simply picking the wrong process for improvement (Keen, 1997; Gardner, 2001). That is to say, the process improvement drive in many organizations only succeeded in doing the wrong thing right. Whereas the benefits of this may still outweigh its cost, it certainly does not amount to the strategic breakthrough that led them to embrace the initiative. Without a methodology to guide them in the search—particularly in the initial search—for the vital few processes on which they must focus, no process-based strategic initiative will ever be truly strategic, and will thus be short-lived. Organizations pick the wrong process because they do not know:

- What processes are and why they should bother to find out

- How processes are connected to creating value and beating the competition

- What their processes are and how well they are performing

Turn now to a methodology designed to address these problems. It proceeds in six steps:

- Review and clarify positioning and operations strategy

- Establish customer needs and wants

- Define a service package (or verify the coverage of current service package)

- Identify key metrics

- Identify processes and evaluate their impact on key metrics

- Select processes based on salience and performance

Figure 6.1 presents a bird's eye view of the methodology. It is based on Figure 5.3, which shows the logical connection between processes (suppliers, support, value enabling, and value adding), the service package (offerings), the benefit package, positioning, and competitive advantage in the market place. In Figure 5.3 (reproduced in Figure 6.1), value is created and delivered from the left-hand-side to the right-hand-side. Hence, the methodology used to identify processes for improvement proceeds in the opposite direction, that is, from the customer inwards. Bold black text, numbering, arrows, and numbered icons overlaid on Figure 5.3 show the methodological path followed in this chapter. It will be refered to in order to help the reader in this journey.

The reader is invited to review Section 4.2.3.2 (and Box 4.2 in particular) where the FPA short case in relation to modes of contact is presented and discussed. The same context is used to illustrate the methodology. The case has not been *engineered* so that everything would fall in place neatly. It is as messy as real life can be. No specialized knowledge in finance and investment is required to understand the analysis that is made of the case.

6.2 REVIEW AND CLARIFY POSITIONING AND OPERATIONS STRATEGY

A merger is a great opportunity for process redesign. Step one in the methodology sketched in Figure 6.1 is to define the target market and clarify what has to be done to beat the competition for the target market. Moving from the outside in means starting with a blank sheet of paper, that is, trying to answer the question: "How would you design this business if you were a new player in this

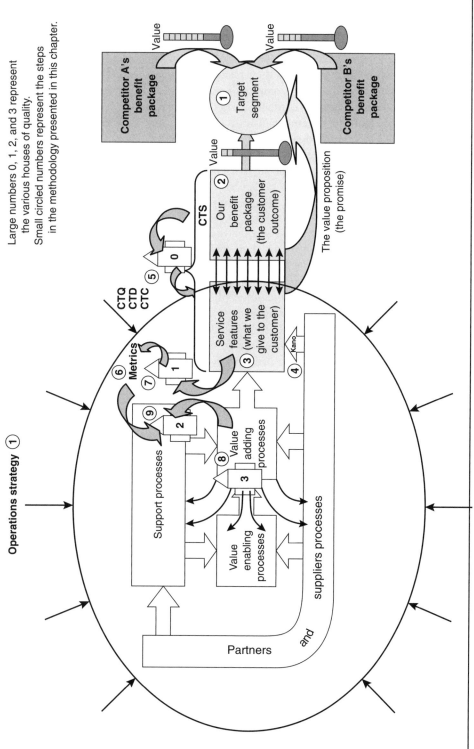

Large numbers 0, 1, 2, and 3 represent
the various houses of quality.
Small circled numbers represent the steps
in the methodology presented in this chapter.

Figure 6.1   Identifying the most important processes *from the customer in*: bird's eye view of the methodology.

industry?" Following a market study and a strategic planning session, FPA decides to target an affluent market segment, which the market research firm's report characterizes as follows:

> They are professionals and executives between 40 and 55 with portfolios of half a million dollars or more. They are busy individuals with a clear focus on ensuring that they are financially independent by the time they reach their planned retirement date. They are generally knowledgeable about financial matters—without being experts. They are users (with varying levels of sophistication) of laptop computers and the Internet, to which they have access. They tend to be analytical and systematic. They have cell phones and most of them travel widely. They are well educated and cultivated, and are generally good judges of character. They need time and solid evidence before they trust someone. They tend to be active and controlling, and will typically interrupt salespeople with directed questions. They are demanding of themselves and of others, particularly of their service providers. Since they are very busy, they expect to get service at their convenient time and location.

The market research firm points out as well that there is another larger and growing market segment, quite similar to this one, except for a lack of sophistication in financial matters. FPA's partners decide to keep this attractive segment in the back of their minds as they proceed with this exercise. FPA's operations strategy is predicated on using technology to leverage the client's knowledge and desire for convenience and control. Competitors split into two groups: those offering high-tech contact (see Chapter 4) with little if any high-touch expertise, and those offering (pricey) *tender loving care*. This leaves the target segment stuck in the middle. While these investors enjoy the control and access offered by the former, they also need the guidance and reassurance provided by the latter. FPA plans to deliver a value proposition just right for these clients, through high-touch initiation of the relationship, including a strong dose of training and education meant to build trust and make the client autonomous for day-to-day operation. Afterwards, high-touch contacts with financial planners (FPs) would gradually spread out, to eventually be limited to periodic (once or twice a year) face-to-face encounters or special events. FPA wants to use the hedge it holds in IT to develop an investment portal second to none. It feels that its resulting costs would be lower than that of *strictly high-touch* competitors, while offering a superior value proposition to this market segment.

FPA also wants to take advantage of major fault lines in its competitors' strategies. Indeed, many banks, trusts, and other financial institutions claim to provide independent financial planning services to their wealthy customers, while the planners are in fact pushing the institutions' own financial products. A truly independent FP can help the client achieve better performance through selection of the best products and through bargaining power with various providers. Further, many full-service providers of financial services have a stake in their clients remaining dependent on their services. By developing a fee structure based on a percentage of assets, adjusted by a performance factor, it will be in FPA's own interests to make the client as autonomous as the client wants to be, as quickly as possible. The risk for FPA in doing so is that autonomous investors might migrate to discount brokers. Thus, it is critical that FPA uses the close relationship it will enjoy with the client during training to build trust and sufficient value-added services for the client to perceive the value being received, and to decide not to *mess with a winning formula*.

6.3 ESTABLISH CUSTOMER NEEDS AND WANTS

The market research firm then holds focus groups with selected investors to establish their needs and their expectations of their FP. To put it succinctly, they find that clients are looking for a professional service provider to help them in achieving peace of mind about their financial futures.

However, much more detail than that is needed to design the services and delivery processes. Achieving peace of mind is the clients' overarching goal. It can be broken down into specific needs, grouped under two general headings: results and customer experience (the reader may wish to review the earlier discussion of the service and self-service experience in Section 2.1). The latter includes quality of service (that is, what the customer does in interaction with a service provider) and quality of self-service (that is, what the customer does alone or with technology).

Based on the focus groups, FPA draws a customer activity cycle, such as those shown in Figures 2.5 and 2.6, to place the needs in context, better understand how they arise, and to make them visual. With the help of the market research firm, FPA finally develops, based on available data, a weighting scheme (such as that shown in Table 2.4) that accurately reflects the importance that these clients attach to their various needs. Table 6.1 presents a summary of customer needs and wants in these two categories. Note that all the statements in this table are written in the first person, that is, as if the client was addressing the organization directly.

Results include performance, price, trustworthiness, and knowledge. The clients' experience includes treatment, access, relationship, ease, and information. Service and self-service experiences are not distinguished, because as yet, neither FPA nor the client know what the client should do with the assistance of a service provider and what should be done alone. In determining the

Table 6.1 Weighted clients' needs for target market segment.

Results		Weight	Service and self-service experience		Weight
Performance	Help me develop and maintain the best possible financial strategy and plan. Help me keep it constantly aligned to my evolving personal needs, income and tax patterns, risk profile, and evolving market conditions.	30	Treatment	Treat me like a VIP	10
			Access	Be reachable at all times through my medium of choice	2
Price	Charge me a fair price with no hidden or invisible costs	4	Relationship	Assign me a top-notch personable professional that will remain my single contact over the long term	10
Trustworthiness	Ensure that your financial interest is in line with mine at all times (no conflict)	8	Ease	Make the process simple and painless	4
	Always take my best interest in our dealings with financial institutions	4	Information	Give me all the information I need to make enlightened choices, while ensuring that I do not suffer from information overflow	4
Knowledge	Help me understand my true needs and attitude toward risk taking	9		Keep me informed of the evolution of my financial situation	4
	Facilitate my understanding of the major choices I am facing and their implications	8	Communication	Communicate in plain English	3
Sub-total: 63			Sub-total: 37		

respective weight of each need, FPA initially feels they should assign results two-thirds of the weight and customer experience, one-third. A finer analysis of the data leads to the final 63/37 split shown in Table 6.1.

The most important needs in Table 6.1 are referred to as critical to satisfaction (CTS) elements. *Develop and maintain a financial strategy and plan constantly aligned to my evolving personal needs, income and tax patterns, risk profile, and evolving market conditions*, for instance, is a CTS, or one of the vital needs. The four most important needs account for almost 60 percent of the weight, while the bottom four represent only 13 percent. Thus, process selection (and later process design or improvement) decisions must be strongly slanted towards the former.

In this case, it is felt that the customer experience constitutes mostly *hygiene* factors or qualifiers, while the most important needs under *results* are order-winners and differentiators. As discussed in Chapter 2, however, the two are closely interrelated, so that a poor relationship, for instance, may have a negative impact on trust and eventually on performance, as the client may not heed the advice of the financial planner. Therefore, FPA should not disregard any client need.

As discussed in Chapter 2, before moving on, FPA must assess competitive offerings, position FPA's customer benefits package vis-à-vis that of competitors, specifying how it will differentiate itself, and explicitly formulate value propositions such as:

"We will never hold back any knowledge, training, or information that could bring you closer to the level of autonomy you wish to achieve."

"We will always make sure that our interests are fully aligned with yours, and thus will only succeed as a business if we are better than competitors at helping you reach your financial objectives."

Such propositions go beyond customers' stated and implicit needs to specify the basis selected by FPA to compete, thus emphasizing the satisfaction of some needs over others. Formulating value propositions, however, would require a strategic analysis of external opportunities and threats, and of internal strengths and weaknesses, which is done in the context of a strategic planning exercise and lies beyond the scope of this book. The reader interested in learning more about understanding customer requirements and measuring customer satisfaction should read Fisher and Schutta (2003) and Hayes (1992).

6.4 DEFINE A SERVICE PACKAGE

The next step is to define the service package, that is, the offerings (including contact personnel behavior) that FPA will supply to its customers to meet their needs (see numbers 2, 3, and 4 in Figure 6.1). Every offering should contribute to the satisfaction of one or more needs, and the service package must address all the needs. With this goal in mind, FPA comes up, through brainstorming, with an initial list of services required:

- Great courses/conferences
- Efficient transaction service
- Performance-based prices
- Clear/accurate status reports
- Well-aligned financial plans

- Effective face-to-face Q&A sessions

- User-friendly web portal

- Fast and friendly 800 line

- Assignment of a top-gun FP

- Very few forms to fill out

- Courtesy and professionalism at all times

FPA then turns to two important questions: How will the customer react to each of these offerings? Is anything missing in the service package? They decide to use the Kano model to address the first one and QFD for the second.

6.4.1 Specifying the Effect of Each Offering on the Client: The Kano Model

Based on the effect they have on the client, the Kano model (developed by Japanese consultant Noriaki Kano) classifies the elements of a service package in one of the following categories:

- *Basic element:* An offering that does not produce any reaction when present but may trigger much dissatisfaction when absent (for example, *the restaurant could not even provide such basics as a clean plate*).

- *Performance:* An element directly related to the results sought by the customer in purchasing the service package. A hungry customer might be disappointed by a small portion and pleased by a large one. Performance elements may result in customer satisfaction or dissatisfaction.

- *Delighter:* An unexpected element of the service package that creates a pleasant surprise. The unexpected arrival of a violinist at a dinner table or being upgraded to business class on a flight, for instance, may delight some customers.

- *Inverse:* An unwanted offering. The customer will be pleased if it is not provided or if there is not much of it. Some customers at movie theaters, for instance, dislike watching previews of other movies or advertisements before the movie starts.

- *Bull's-eye*[1]: An element that the customer enjoys in limited quantity-too little or too much of it produces discontent. The service provider's challenge here is to do it just right, that is, provide the right amount of that element. Bringing the check immediately after serving dessert, for instance, may be considered impolite. Having to remind the waiter three times that one requires the check is no better.

- *Indifferent:* An offering that does not correspond to any customer need, but that does not cause irritation. For example, a bank posting a sign saying that it can provide service in Cantonese will not have any effect on non-Chinese speaking customers.

Consider an example closer to the case of FPA: a one-day seminar on derivatives. Also, consider two different audiences: a group of undergraduate business students and a group of busy senior executives and senior professionals. Consider the reactions of the two groups to various elements of the service package (see Table 6.2). While the executives would consider a personalized greeting as the participants arrive to be basic, it would delight the students. An offering is basic in the eye of a customer if *it goes without saying*. Having attended other such seminars in the past and well aware of their standing as potentially interesting clients, the executives fully expect to be treated as such. Thus, the handshake and greeting: "Good evening, Dr. Smith" does not create a *satisfaction*

Table 6.2 Reaction of two market segments to various elements of the service package in a seminar on derivatives.

Offerings	Students	Professionals
Personalized greeting	Delight	Basic
Cushioned seats	Delight	Basic
Cocktail with experts after seminar	Delight	Performance
CD to each participant	Wow!	Perfomance
Animated color slides	Delight	Basic
Free coffee at the break	Delight	Basic
China cups	"I'm in the wrong room"	Delight
Filling up the cups at the table during the seminar	"I'm in the wrong room"	Delight
Directed questions to the audience by the speaker	Inverse	"I'm in the wrong room"
Theoretical content	Performance	Bull's-eye
Practical advice	Indifferent	Performance
Speaker's phone number for personal questions	Wow!	Delight
Open bar during seminar	"I'm in the wrong room"	Delight

response—merely an unconscious: "OK, this is as it should be." A basic service offering goes unnoticed. Clients would, however, definitely notice its absence—in a negative way: "What? Nobody to greet me? What sort of shop is this?" The students, on the other hand, are quite accustomed to entering a seminar room and taking a seat without anyone noticing their arrival. Hence, being greeted at the door by name would create a positive surprise, and maybe even leave some a bit worried ("What does this guy want from me?"). Finding an open bar in the room, on the other hand, would probably delight many of the executives, whereas it may result in some students squarely turning back and marching out of the room ("I must be in the wrong room").

The students come to the seminar to learn the theory of derivatives: If they get very little, they will be disappointed, if they get much they will be pleased. Such an offering is alternately labeled performance, linear, or *more is better*. Contrary to delighters (which can only produce satisfaction when present) and basic elements (which can only produce dissatisfaction when absent), performance elements have the potential to either please or displease the customer, depending on whether they are present, or on the degree to which they are present. Since executives come to the seminar to get practical advice, they might consider a one-to-one chat with an expert, practical advice, or a CD with frequently asked questions to be the *performance* elements of the service package.

Theoretical content may be a *bull's-eye* element for the executive, as they require a minimum of theory to understand the topic, but that is not why they came to the seminar: They want practical advice. Directed questions by the speaker to participants are probably a negative for students (inverse). Further, if all they care about is passing an exam and have no money to invest, any practical investment advice may leave them indifferent.

As the foregoing example illustrates, whether a service offering is a delighter, performance, or basic element (or any other category) depends on customers' expectations and needs (as well as the price they pay), and these in turn depend on the market segment (needs, past experience, values, and so on) to which the customer belongs. The effect of an offering on a given customer also evolves over time. While the use of an electronic projector, for instance, may once have been a delighter in executive seminars, it is now basic. You can only delight (that is, surprise) the customers so many times with the same offering until they begin asking for it (performance) and eventually consider it basic. This phenomenon is often referred to as the *ratchet effect*, that is, once expectations have been adjusted upwards, they do not come back down. Meeting them then merely produces satisfaction, not delight anymore, and may even eventually leave them cold. Notice that competitive offerings also influence the expectations of your own customer. The minute one bank advertises a no-fee platinum card (thus delighting its own customer base), for instance, all providers of such services are flooded with requests for the same service feature, now considered a performance element rather than a delighter.

The Kano model brings out a limitation of customer surveys: When asked what their expectations are of a given service, customers are liable to respond mostly with performance elements, that is, the explicit result elements they want from the service. One has to probe to find out implicit elements, such as delighters and basics, because the former are *surprises*, and the latter *go without saying*. Hence, observing the customer in action in a service environment is a useful complement to surveys to fully understand customer needs.

As FPA is designing its service package, it must consider the effect each element will have on the clients. Will they consider it basic? Will they be pleasantly surprised? Will they consider it part of the performance they are looking for? The very process of searching for answers to these questions pushes the organization to try to get inside their clients' minds, thus countering the natural tendency to look at offerings from the service provider's perspective. It also helps to bring the targeted market segments into sharper focus.

Figure 6.2 shows a visual representation of the modified Kano model just presented, along with a classification of the element in the initial service package FPA has generated. The horizontal axis shows the extent to which a given element is present and the vertical axis, the client's reaction to the element, with the central line representing the *neutral* point, or absence of reaction. The diagram

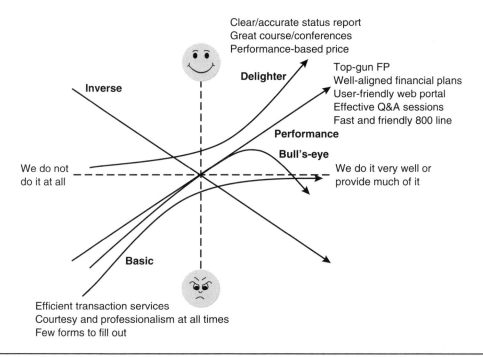

Figure 6.2   Classification of some elements of FPA's servce package, based on their effect on the customer (modified Kano model).

shows that a delighter (*great courses/conferences*) cannot create dissatisfaction and that a basic element (*courtesy and professionalism*) cannot generate satisfaction. Performance (*top-gun FP*, for instance) and inverse elements, on the other hand can lead to either reaction. To produce satisfaction through a bull's-eye element, you must find just the right dosage of that offering and deliver it with precision.

Note that if *few forms to fill out* had been formulated as *forms to fill out*, it would have classified (more appropriately) as an inverse element. Fees per se would also be an inverse element, even though the fact that they are based on performance per se is a delighter. Other potential inverse elements might include *sales pressure* or *waiting time to reach an FP*. The amount of effort required to become better investors might also fall in this category or be labeled a bull's-eye element, as the client may be disappointed and not perceive that they are learning unless they put in some effort.

The Kano model is indispensable for a team charged with the design of a new service package. Without all the basics, the client may not even consider the service provider: They are qualifying elements to enter or stay in the running. Inverse elements often play the same role in clients' decisions. Much competition takes place on performance elements. One or more of these are generally *order-winning* criteria for clients to select a service provider amongst those they consider qualified. Since delighters are unexpected offerings, they are not a part of the client's decision process at the outset. Advertising these elements, however, may induce trial and adoption. They also contribute to transform merely satisfied (that is, vulnerable to competition) clients into loyal ones.

6.4.2 Building QFD—House 0

Now, turn to the second question: Does the service package cover all clients' needs? To answer that, each offering could be examined, inquiring about which customer needs it affects. It could be said, for instance, that *performance-based price* is a direct way to reassure the client that FPA's interest is in line with the client's. It also reassures the client, to a somewhat lesser extent, however, that FPA will always defend the client's interests. "Having few forms to fill out" directly affects the client's need for simplicity and, to a lesser extent, the client's desire to be treated like a VIP. As can be readily seen, the needs-offerings correspondence is not one to one: most offerings correlate with more than one need, and most needs are affected by more than one offering. This suggests the use of a matrix for verifying the adequacy of FPA's service package.

The technique used here is adapted from Quality Function Deployment (QFD), or House of Quality, which is just such a matrix. The top row of the matrix in Figure 6.3 contains the initial list of service offerings, and the first column, customer needs (from Table 6.1). The body of the table is used to correlate each offering with each customer need: that is, specifying to what extent each offering contributes to the satisfaction of each need. Four possible correlation values are used: blank squares, triangles, circles, and bull's-eyes, standing respectively for zero, weak, average, and strong correlation between the offering and the corresponding customer need. Having a top-notch FP assigned, for example, is strongly correlated with helping the customer understand the true attitude toward risk (for instance), but not at all with ensuring that FPA's financial interests are in line with those of the customer (that is, that there are no conflicts of interest).

The best way to build this matrix is for a team to use sticky notes for columns and row headings, and sticky colored dots for correlation (*traffic light* color coding works well: red is a bull's-eye, yellow dots are circles, and green dots are triangles). Sticky notes can be moved around, discarded, and replaced—a flexibility that is essential as reaching consensus is an iterative process.

The last column contains the importance weight assigned to each client need, based on the focus groups (see Table 6.1). Had value propositions been formulated, these weights would have been modified to reflect the strategic choices made by FPA—that is, FPA positioning and differentiation decisions. The matrix can be used to assess the relative importance of each offering for the

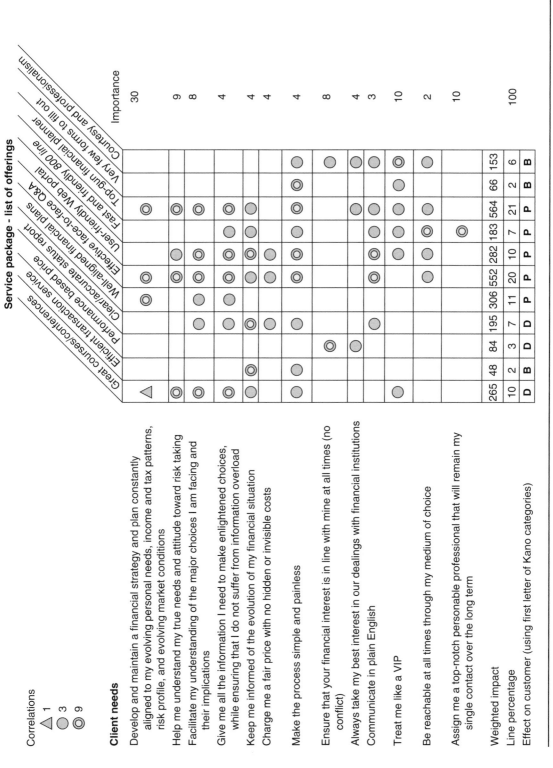

Figure 6.3 QFD—House 0: Adequacy of service package to meet customer needs.

customer. An important offering is one that correlates strongly with important needs, that is, having bull's-eye symbols in rows corresponding to important needs. Thus, importance factors (weights) can be calculated for each offering, as the vertical cross product of the correlation with every customer need multiplied by the importance weight of that need, using the customary QFD approach of assigning weights of one for a weak, three for an average and nine for a strong correlation. For example, the weight of *efficient transaction service* is calculated as (9X4) + (3X4), or 48. This weight is shown on the third row from the bottom of the matrix. The weight is shown as a percentage of the row total in the penultimate row (2 percent in this case). This relative weight is easier to interpret than an absolute number. According to Figure 6.3, *effective face-to-face Q&A*, for example is more important than a *user-friendly web-portal* by a factor of two (20 percent /10 percent).

This matrix (which will be referred to as "House of quality 0", or simply "House 0", for sake of consistency with the labeling used in Chapter 11) is a tool to verify whether the service package is necessary and sufficient to meet customer needs and to point out offerings that are particularly important to the customer. It is desirable that, for each need, at least one offering is available that correlates strongly with it (that is, at least one bull's-eye per line). For each customer need (or rows in Figure 6.3), FPA must also ask itself if all of the elements with a non-zero value are collectively sufficient to beat competition. Thus, you can compare different service packages, at a very high level, to verify their respective coverage of clients' need, adding and deleting service elements until the package is satisfactory. Figure 6.4 shows the offerings in order of importance. The top five services account for 75 percent of customer needs in terms of importance.

House 0 is represented in Figure 6.1 as a house icon bearing the number 0. It is numbered as step (5) in the methodology, correlating the benefit package to service features, thereby pointing out the critical features.

6.5 IDENTIFY KEY METRICS

What you measure is what you get. What are the key metrics that FPA should use to design and manage its services and processes? Measuring customer satisfaction is essential, but you cannot wait for the result of surveys to manage the business. The firm needs metrics, which will be referred

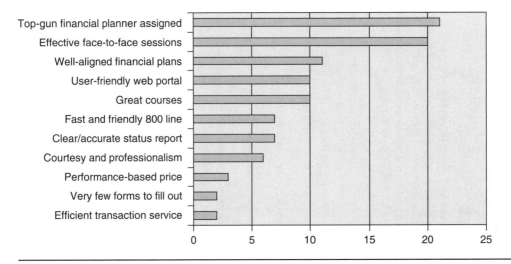

Figure 6.4 Most important service features for the client (from House 0, penultimate row).

to as technical characteristics that can provide useful and timely feedback about the performance of processes. Each service offering that is part of the service package is the output of one or more processes. Processes are needed to deliver these outputs with the right quality, at the right time, and at the right cost. Hence, metrics are needed for each of these aspects to ensure early detection of process shift or drift (discussed in Chapter 8). These metrics, together with the target values set for them, will serve as a guide in the identification and design of key processes.

Metrics appear in Figure 6.1 as a new element that was missing in Figure 5.3. Figure 6.1 allows relating the methodology to the strategic value creation framework presented in the previous chapters, but there is a need to *zoom in* to see the detail and better understand the connections and flow of the methodology. Figure 6.5 presents such a closeup. As shown there, the contribution of House 0 is to specify the connections between the benefit package (left-hand-side of House 0) and the service features or offerings (top row). House 1, which is presented in this section, connects the service features (with their importance weights, as established in House 0) to a set of metrics. Proceeding from an initial list of metrics generated through brainstorming, it uses a correlation matrix to complete the list, rationalize it, and determine the relative importance of each metric. The most important metrics relating to quality, cost, and time (or delivery) are often referred to as CTQs, CTCs, and CTDs (CT stand for *critical to*, and the last letter for quality, cost, and delivery, respectively). The ongoing example now continues.

Looking at each service feature, FPA partners now ask themselves how they could measure it. How do they know, for instance, if the courses are great, besides asking the participants if they enjoyed it, which FPA will certainly do? They come up with the idea of developing their own course *fog index*, that is, a metric based on various indicators such as the number of complex words, quality of slides, use of examples, and so on. They would conduct an internal *dry run* of each course and calculate the index beforehand, thus allowing for changing the course before it does any *damage*. They think that the index is related to other important offerings, such as having financial plans that are well aligned to the client's goals (hard to achieve if the client does not understand some important financial notion) and a user-friendly web portal (for the same reason).

Searching for a metric for the efficiency of transaction services, they come up with the number of transaction errors. They then define the various kinds of errors and the way they will count them. This metric also affects the accuracy of status reports. They also identify transaction cost as an important indicator of transaction efficiency. Since several metrics may be needed to measure all relevant aspects of any service offering, and since any one metric may capture aspects of several offerings, a matrix is again appropriate to develop a set of indicators that covers the complete service package.

FPA's partners put together, through brainstorming and using an affinity diagram (see Exercise 2.2), an initial list of indicators. They take the list of service offerings from House 0, together with their weights expressed as percentages, and stick them (literally, using sticky notes) as the left-hand-side column of the matrix (see Figure 6.6). They stick the metrics randomly across the top and move down each column, debating correlations as they do so, using colored dots again. Once the matrix is complete, the team can use it to verify if the list of indicators is complete, and if some metrics are redundant or trivial. This *rightsizing* exercise for House 1 (as it will be called) parallels that conducted for House 0. They obtain an importance weight for each metric by calculating, for each column, the cross product of the correlations by the respective weight of each offering. An important metric is one that correlates strongly with an important service offering. They then analyze the resulting matrix, eliminating metrics that scored poorly and brainstorming for new ones whenever a service offering failed to correlate strongly with any of the metrics appearing in the top row.

The results of their work are shown in Figure 6.6. The top 10 metrics appear in Figure 6.7, where it can be seen that the five most important metrics again account for about 75 percent of the total weight. The top four are essentially of equal importance. It will require some doing to turn the

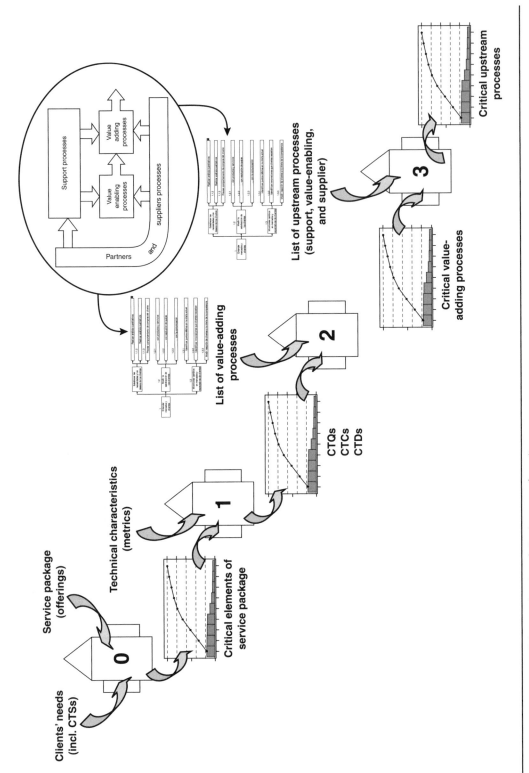

Figure 6.5   Overview of the mechanics of the houses of quality.

Figure 6.6 QFD—House 1: Adequacy of set of metrics to cover all elements of the service package.

Legend:
- → Less is better
- ← More is better
- ⊕ Bull's-eye

Customer requirement	Importance
Great courses	10
Efficient transaction service	2
Performance-based price	3
Clear/accurate status report	7
Well-aligned financial plans	11
Effective face-to-face sessions	20
User-friendly web portal	10
Fast and friendly 800 line	7
Top-gun financial planner	21
Very few forms to fill out	2
Courtesy and professionalism	6
Total	**100**

Metrics (with Weighted impact / Line percentage):

Metric	Weighted impact	Line percentage
Correlation (FPA profits with cust. portfolio performance)	27	1
# of queries re: status report	129	6
Transaction cost	18	1
Periodicity of revision of plans	99	5
Time spent filling out forms	36	2
Course log index	249	12
# of reporting errors	74	4
# of transaction errors	39	2
Alignment of plan to goals	298	14
# of years with same planner	281	14
Quality time face-to-face	281	14
Time required to learn system	103	5
# of golf games score of FPS	71	3
Average exam score of FPS	298	14
Phone response time	63	3

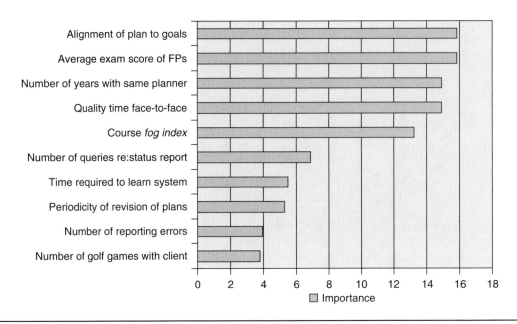

Figure 6.7 Most important metrics for the client (from House 1, last row).

top metric, *alignment of plans to goals*, into a numerical scale, and professional judgment will be involved. The average results FPs obtain in their certification exams constitute a good, easily available index of their technical proficiency. The average number of years an FP stays with a client increases the quality of the relationship, as well as the ability of the planner to match a customer's portfolio to the true needs. Quality time face-to-face is a direct measure of the satisfaction of an important customer need. The question of what truly constitutes *quality time face-to-face* is a big one for FPA.

Analyzing the last row of House 1 shows that the only correlate of *courtesy and professionalism at all times* is a mid-range correlation with *time spent filling out forms*: relevant, but far from complete. Thus, this is work in process for FPA. More brainstorming (*average time to return a phone call, average time to respond to a request*), benchmarking, and validation are needed. FPA will have to revisit House 1, as well as the other matrices, regularly.

While the metrics identified here will provide more timely feedback than customer surveys, make sure that their correlation with customer satisfaction is true and holds true as time passes. Correlating the values of these metrics with the corresponding elements of customer satisfaction surveys, is therefore extremely important to ensure that they remain valid proxies for customer satisfaction, and thus valid guides to manage processes.

QFD has several other interesting features that we do not discuss here:

- Perception benchmarking with all major competitors on each client need—that is, show how people in that market segment perceive FPA's performance on each need, compared to competitors—can be added as additional columns on the right-hand-side of the matrix. A market survey would readily provide the data. The importance weights of each need could thus be modified, giving more weight to those where FPA ranks poorly, thus increasing the weights of metrics and processes related to these needs.

- Technical benchmarking is also a competitive comparison, but this time based on technical characteristics (metrics). It might be found, for example, that clients of competitor

A spend on average one hour per year in face-to-face contact with an FP, compared to three hours for competitor B and two hours for FPA. This requires FPA to do some baselining (that is, determine its current performance). This is useful in setting a target for this characteristic.

- The *roof* of the house consists of technical relationships between the metrics appearing in the top row of the house. If phone response time is very long, fewer queries will probably be made, as impatient clients give up or find another way to obtain the information they want. Thus, these two metrics are inversely correlated. The number of transaction errors, on the other hand, is positively correlated to the number of reporting errors, as the former find their way into reports, causing the latter. These relationships can be captured in a triangular correlation matrix that sits nicely on top of the matrix being used here, thereby forming the *roof* that inspired the appellation *house of quality*. They are a useful complement to the technique, allowing setting more coherent targets for the critical metrics.

For a good discussion of these features, see Fisher and Schutta (2003).

6.6 IDENTIFY PROCESSES AND EVALUATE THEIR IMPACT ON KEY METRICS

Not much has been said so far about what it is that FPA actually does. That is the next step: identifying the processes and rating them in terms of importance for the customer. Figures 6.1 (see Step 8) and 6.5 show how weighted metrics go into House 2, which is built in this section, to be correlated with processes, which first have to be identified. Most organizations have an organizational chart but very few know what their processes are, let alone how they relate to one another. That is the role of a process model, such as that of APQC discussed in Section 3.1.2. In Section 3.4.3, three categories of processes were identified according to the role they play in value creation: value adding, enabling, and support. In Section 5.1.3.1, the upstream processes of partners and suppliers were added. All of these are represented in Figure 5.3. This representation is reproduced in Figures 6.1 and 6.5.

The methodology consists in first prioritizing value adding processes. This is done in House 2, as shown in Figures 6.1 and 6.5. Once the weights have been assigned to value-adding processes, House 3 is built, correlating the latter with other upstream processes, that is, enabling (such as *implement new technology*), support (such as *prepare budget* or *purchase supplies*) and partners/suppliers (such as *securities safekeeping* and *assessing end-of-day market position*). This allows assigning importance ratings to upstream processes as a function of their effect on value adding processes, and thus, ultimately, on clients.

Value adding processes includes everything FPA does that contributes directly to meeting the goal of being better than its competitors at helping people in the targeted market segment achieve peace of mind about their financial future. How does FPA do that? By getting the right FPs, attracting the right customers, preparing good financial plans, implementing them well, and managing the relationships with its customers. Each of these functions can be broken down in turn, thus producing a FAST diagram (see Section 3.1.1), which is shown in Figure 6.8. The diagram shows only value-adding processes.

Which of those 22 value-adding processes (level two processes in Figure 6.8) are the most important for clients? The rationale that FPA uses to answer this question parallels that used so far in this chapter: An important process is one that has a strong impact on important metrics. From

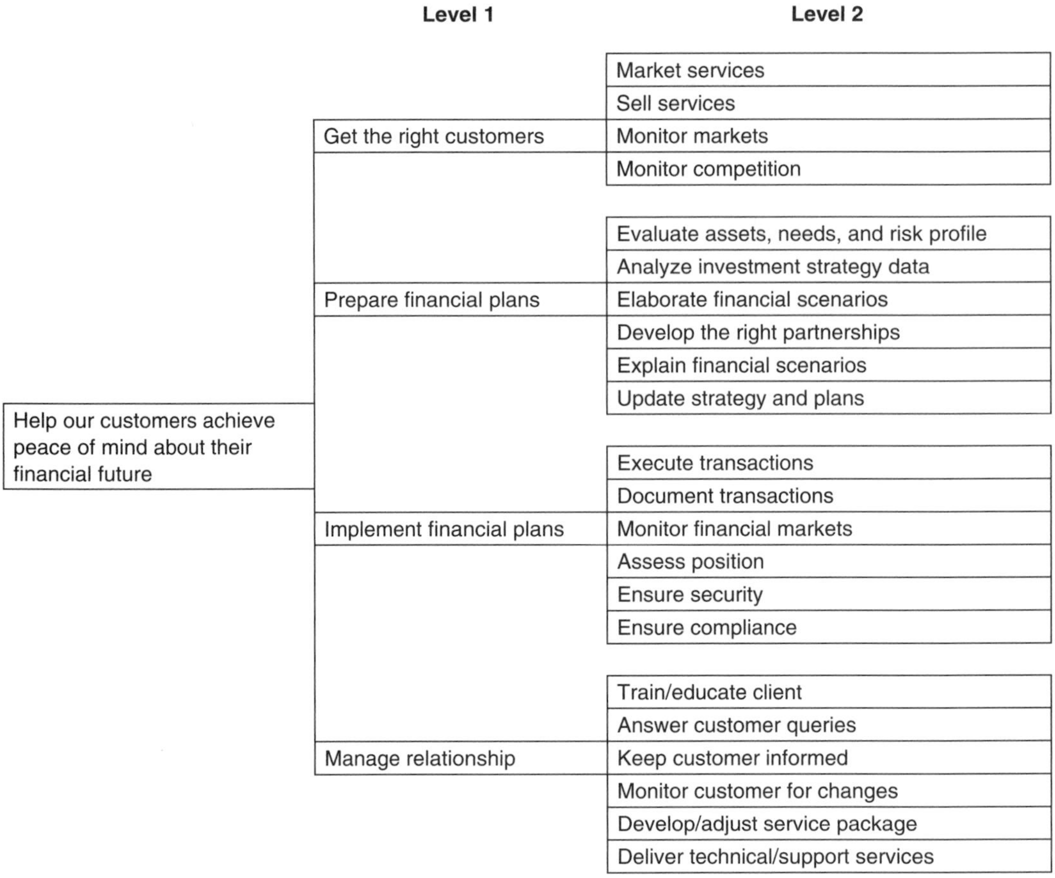

	Level 1	Level 2
		Market services
		Sell services
	Get the right customers	Monitor markets
		Monitor competition
		Evaluate assets, needs, and risk profile
		Analyze investment strategy data
	Prepare financial plans	Elaborate financial scenarios
		Develop the right partnerships
		Explain financial scenarios
Help our customers achieve peace of mind about their financial future		Update strategy and plans
		Execute transactions
		Document transactions
	Implement financial plans	Monitor financial markets
		Assess position
		Ensure security
		Ensure compliance
		Train/educate client
		Answer customer queries
	Manage relationship	Keep customer informed
		Monitor customer for changes
		Develop/adjust service package
		Deliver technical/support services

Figure 6.8 Partial FAST diagram for FPA.

House 1, these metrics are known, as well as their importance (weights) for clients. That leaves FPA with the task of establishing the impact of each process on each metric, using a matrix similar to those used earlier, which will be referred to as House 2. A matrix of 22 X 10, together with the further deployment of the value-adding processes onto upstream processes is too cumbersome for the purposes of the ongoing demonstration. Hence, an illustrative House 2 is built, based on 11 processes selected from among value-adding and enabling processes, and on the 10 most important metrics from House 1 (Figure 6.7). This modified House 2 is shown in Figure 6.9, and House 3 is not shown, as the reader, by now, must have caught on to the logic and mechanics of QFD and can extrapolate it.

Figure 6.10 shows the processes assessed in Figure 6.9 in order of priority. Recruiting and training FPs are shown to be the two most important processes (in the selected sample) for the customer, followed by *introducing new technology* and *training and educating customers*. Note that the results of House 2 are somewhat biased because of the shortcut that was taken. Indeed, the processes selected are a mixture of value-adding and enabling processes. They are related to one another: *develop courses* and *develop training aids*, for instance, are enablers of the *train customer* process. Hence, they are more important than what their weight in House 2 indicates. In practice however, if FPA was to select *train customer* for improvement (or design), those two enablers would most

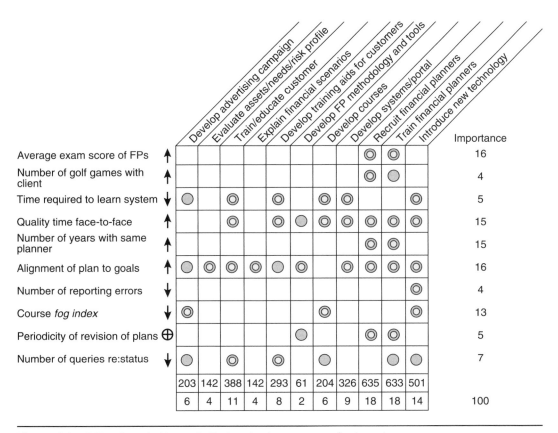

Figure 6.9   QFD—Sample House 2: Rating the importance of selected processes.

certainly be considered to be in scope. In the next chapter, a detailed methodology and tools to facilitate process scoping are presented. In Chapter 11, we pursue this example, using *train the customer* to present the process design methodology.

6.7 SELECT PROCESSES ON THE BASIS OF SALIENCE AND PERFORMANCE

Should it be concluded from the preceding analysis that the design and improvement dollar should be focused on these processes? Not necessarily. As important as a process may be in meeting customer needs, it is but one criterion in deciding which processes to improve. Two other factors must be considered: the strategic impact of the processes and their current performance.

6.7.1 Assessing the Strategic Impact of Processes

Any company has three generic stakeholders: customers, employees, and shareholders. This book has been focused on customer satisfaction, because it is central to the satisfaction of the other stakeholders. However, unless it provides personal value to employees and economic value to shareholders the company may not be viable over the long haul. The way to address the specific concerns

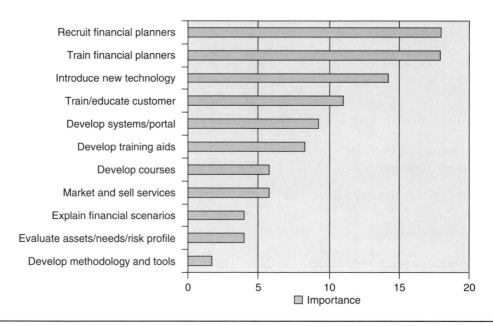

Figure 6.10 Most important processes in sample (from House 2, last row).

of these stakeholders is through the company's strategic plan. This is the company's game plan for beating competition. It typically identifies a small number of (defensive or offensive) key strategic issues. These issues may be related to any or all stakeholders. In the case of FPA, the list of issues identified[2] includes the following:

- Respond to our major competitor's recent introduction of an advanced next-generation web portal.

- Exploit an opportunity—recently created by the bankruptcy of a competitor—in a market niche of wealthy retirees less familiar with financial matters.

- Reassure a nervous customer base following recent unsettling events (9/11 and the Enron debacle).

- Correct the flaws in our professional practices that were harshly criticized following an inspection by regulatory authorities.

- Develop our activities in derivatives[3] to exploit upcoming opportunities in financial markets and respond to increasing customer interest.

The strategic plan specified as well that the second and fourth of these issues were by far the most important and that the other three issues were on a par with one another. Thus, the partners agree to assign the former an importance weighting of 35 each, and the latter 10 each, out of 100. They use a correlation matrix (see Figure 6.11) similar to the preceding ones (but which will not be called a house of quality, because it does not constitute an extension of the rationale behind QFD) to evaluate the impact of the eleven selected processes on each issue. For example, the process of explaining financial scenarios to customers has to be reviewed to better address a market segment less comfortable with basic financial notions[4]. This process also plays an important role in reassuring customers about the risks associated with their investments. One issue raised by the regulatory authority was that

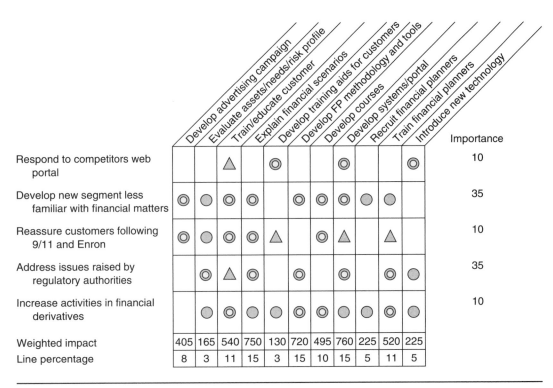

Figure 6.11   Correlation matrix showing the effect of selected processes on key strategic issues (strategic impact matrix).

they had found cases where this had not been done properly. Finally, as derivative products are introduced for the first time in the portfolio of some customers, considerable thinking has to go into how to make sure that they understand the intricacies and implications of these investments.

Thus, explaining financial scenarios, developing a financial planning methodology and tools, and developing systems and portals are three processes that are critical to the implementation of the strategic plan. The latter two, being very broad, would benefit from further division into subprocesses, to determine which parts of these processes are vital.

The fact that only one of these processes made it to the top five most important in House 2 clearly shows that this step addresses a different aspect of process salience. Whereas House 2 ranks the processes based on their effect on meeting customer needs, this step looks at their contribution to the company's game plan to beat the competition.

A *salient process* is defined as one that has a strong impact on both customers and strategy. The effect of each process on strategy has been quantified in Figure 6.11, and their effect on clients has been quantified in Figure 6.9. We present this data in Table 6.3 and plot it in Figure 6.12. An overall salience score can be obtained for each process by summing up the two scores. Results are presented in Table 6.3. Training financial planners and developing systems/portals are the two most salient processes coming out of this exercise.

6.7.2 Assessing the Current Performance of Processes

Having identified salient processes, an important question has yet to be answered to be in a position to decide which process should be focused on: How good are the processes currently in place?

Table 6.3 Prioritization of processes based on salience and performance.

	Salience			Performance			
	Importance for customers	Importance for strategy	Salience	Efficiency	Effectiveness	Performance	Priority
Develop advertising campaign	6	8	14	3	1	4	
Evaluate assets/needs/risk profile	4	3	7	1	2	3	
Train/educate customers	11	11	22	3	3	6	2
Explain financial scenarios	4	15	19	2	2	4	2
Develop training aids for customers	8	3	11	5	4	9	
Develop FP methodology and tools	2	15	16	2	3	5	5
Develop courses	6	10	16	5	5	10	
Develop systems/portal	9	15	25	2	4	6	1
Recruit financial planners	18	5	23	3	4	7	4
Train financial planners	18	11	28	5	5	10	
Introduce new technology	14	5	19	4	3	7	

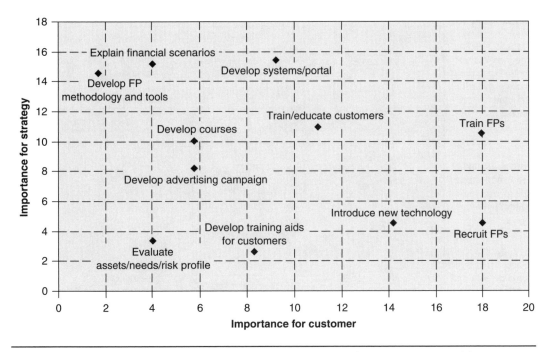

Figure 6.12 Salience diagram: Importance of selected processes for the customer and for strategy.

Clearly, a salient process that is performing at world-class level should be lower on the priority list than a slightly less prominent process that is in terrible shape. Thus, both salience and performance must be considered.

A high-performance process is one that is both effective and efficient. Effectiveness consists of producing the desired effect, that is, satisfying or exceeding customer requirements (this is equally true for processes serving internal customers). This can be measured on a five-point scale, ranging from *outputs do not meet any customer requirement* to *outputs exceed most customer requirements* (see Table 6.3). Efficiency is about the best possible use of resources in the pursuit of effectiveness. It, too, can be measured on a five-point scale, this one ranging from the process being plagued with defects, waste, and long cycle time, to being defect-free, and having a short cycle time and no waste (see Table 6.3).

A diagram (see Figure 6.13) adapted from De Toro and McCabe (1997) can now be constructed using these two dimensions of performance as axes. This diagram can be used to compare and classify processes according to current performance level, from *sick*, for any process which scores no higher than a one on either dimension, to *world class*, for a process that scores a five on both dimensions. Categories in between those extremes are labeled fair, satisfactory, and superior, respectively. To obtain an overall efficiency and effectiveness (or *performance*) score, simply sum up the effectiveness and efficiency scores. For example, Table 6.3 and Figure 6.13 shows that FPA's partners have assigned a score of ten to the processes for developing courses and training FPs, thereby indicating that improving these processes cannot be a priority. On the other hand, evaluating clients' assets/needs/risk profile and developing advertising campaigns are the worst performers and thus badly in need of improvement (or redesign).

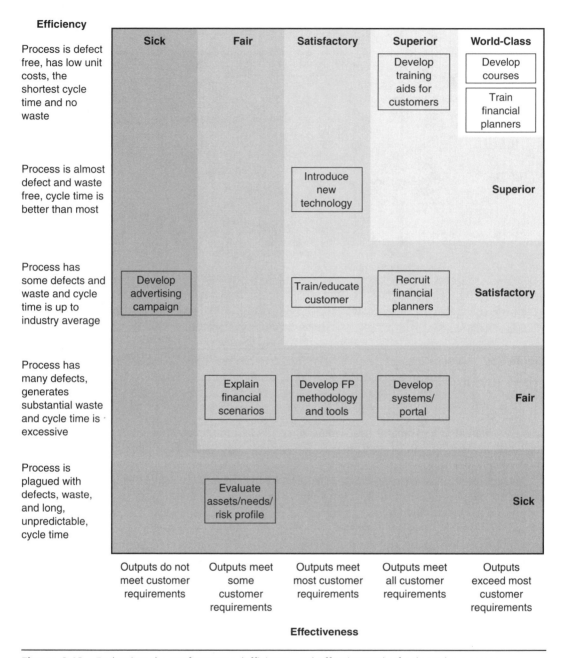

Figure 6.13 Evaluating the performance (efficiency and effectiveness) of selected processes.
Source: Adapted from Tenner and DeToro, 1997.

You must base process evaluation on data. However, recognizing that few organizations have such data available, they should not wait for them as they set out on their process improvement journey. They should instead direct process owners to plan and launch data-gathering initiatives themselves, and perform an initial subjective evaluation. There will be differences of opinion, just as there was in the preceding exercises. In many ways, bringing these differences to the fore is good for the organization, as it creates a need for data and measurement discipline.

6.7.3 Putting it All Together

Table 6.3 shows the salience score (importance for customer and importance for strategy) and performance score (efficiency and effectiveness) for the 11 selected processes. This data is plotted in Figure 6.14. The higher the salience and the lower the performance score, that is, the closer the process to the lower right-hand side in Figure 6.14, the higher is the process priority. However, FPA can develop its own prioritization rules, such as:

- Eliminate from consideration processes that score below average on both salience criteria

- Eliminate world-class processes (that is, a perfect 10 in the third column)

- Rank remaining processes from the worst performers to the best

- Use common sense and consensus to finalize the ranking

The last column in Table 6.3 shows the top five processes, in order of priority, using proximity to lower right-hand side (see Figure 6.14) as criterion. The process for developing systems/portal combines strategic importance with a dismal performance. *Explaining financial scenarios to customers* and *train/educate customer* display the same pattern, though the latter is more salient, and the former displays lower performance. *Recruiting FPs* and *Developing FP methodology and tools* thus rank fourth and fifth respectively.

Figure 6.15 traces back the methodological path followed in this chapter. Starting from FPA's positioning in the market, FPA's benefit package was deployed onto service features, metrics, value adding processes, and upstream processes using three houses of quality. A rating reflecting the importance of each process for the client was obtained. Key strategic issues were then deployed onto processes, thus obtaining a specific rating for each process. Next, these two ratings were combined into a salience score. After that, the current performance of these processes was compared,

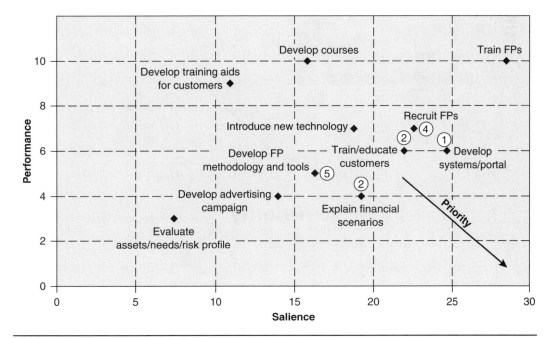

Figure 6.14 Salience and importance diagram: Prioritizing processes for improvement or redesign.

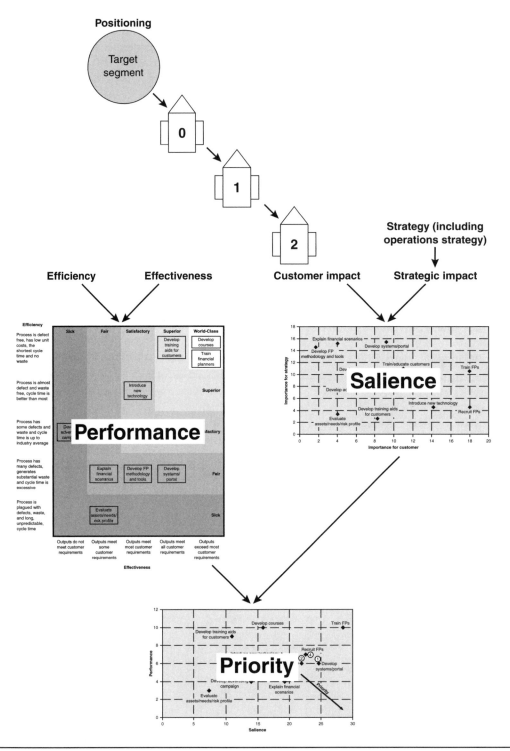

Figure 6.15   Prioritizing processes for improvement: Bird's eye view of the back-end of the methodology.

based on an assessment of their respective effectiveness and efficiency. The last step involved visualizing each process in a performance/salience diagram and setting priorities.

6.8 PROCESS MISSION: THE HINGE BETWEEN STRATEGY AND OPERATION

In this journey from a high-level and strategic view to the isolation of specific processes to improve, a mean is needed to ensure that the reasons for selecting a process are not lost when the time comes to make improvement and design decisions. Further, even though processes have been dealt with so far in this chapter as independent entities, clearly, they are not. They receive inputs and provide outputs from and to each other. They must be synchronized and work in harmony. A mechanism to make sure that these processes are complementary, do not overlap, and mesh well with one another is needed. In other words, a way to promote coherence is needed (see Section 5.1.1.3).

The mission statement is the hinge that ensures the integrity of the *strategy-process design* link and that promotes harmony among processes. It is a short statement about why the process exists and what its priorities are. Those who design, modify, and operate the process use it. It helps the process designer make unavoidable trade-offs in process flow, equipment selection, design of facilities, and so on. It ensures that anyone with a mandate to cut costs or otherwise improve the process will not *throw away the baby with the bath water*. It finally helps operators in making their own trade-offs as operating problems arise. It is obtained by analyzing its position in the FAST diagram (and process model or PFD diagrams, if available), the metrics it influences (from House 2 and House 3), and the key strategic issues that it relates to (from Figure 6.11).

The FAST diagram indicates that *train/educate clients* is part of FPA's way to build a relationship with the client. House 2 shows that a good training process should result in quick learning, quality time between an FP and the client, better alignment of financial plans to personal goals, and eventually reduce the number of queries made by the client. Figure 6.11 shows this process to be an important pillar for strategy as well. It affects the strategic issues of penetrating growing market segments of less knowledgeable investors, reassuring insecure investors following a series of traumas suffered by financial markets, and broadening the market for derivative financial products—an important advantage in an era of reduced yield expectations.

The mission of the *train/educate client* process could thus be formulated, for example, as follows: *to create for each client a learning environment conducive to personal growth in financial management, and to the parallel evolution (upgrading) of the client's portfolio management system, with FPA as trusted adviser and service provider*. Personal growth in financial management means that the client's level of knowledge and comfort with financial matters increases in such a way that the client gradually becomes more apt (astute, confident, and mature) to play the role to the fullest in the management of the client's own financial affairs. The mandate of the team entrusted with the task of designing this process (see Chapter 11) is to find the best way to achieve this mission, while respecting any constraint imposed by management (such as deadline, budget, human resources, or technical considerations).

The mission of the *evaluate assets/needs/risk profile*, to take another one, could be formulated as: *to obtain a complete and accurate picture of all the client's assets, current and future financial needs, and true attitude toward risk, so that FPA can help the client formulate an appropriate financial strategy*. Thus formulated, the mission does not specify the extent of customer involvement in the process, a decision that would be left with an eventual design team.

As mentioned above, the *train/educate client* example is used to illustrate the process design methodology in Chapter 11. The reader who wishes to seize the moment and move on directly to

Chapter 11 can do so without loss of continuity, and come back later to Chapter 7 and read on toward the improvement methodology presented in Chapter 10.

6.9 QUESTIONS AND ANSWERS ON THE METHODOLOGY

A number of questions arise from the methodology presented above. They are addressed here:

- Is it worth all this effort (why can't we just *wing it* as usual)? Executives cannot expect subordinates to be rigorous about *doing things right* if they are not rigorous themselves in deciding what is *the right thing to do*. Besides, even if subordinates were to overlook the body language and indeed be rigorous, it would only result in *doing the wrong thing right*, and this does not achieve much.

- What happens to selected processes? First, they deserve to have an owner (see discussion in Chapters 9 and 12), probably for the first time. Most processes are orphans, belonging to everyone, and thus to no one. The owner's first mandate is to identify the right metrics (House 1 should point in the right direction) and then obtain data. Doing a high-level mapping will come soon thereafter. This will allow the identification of key players and the building of a process team. FPA can then proceed to project selection, project scoping (Chapter 7), and to selecting a methodology and change vehicle (Chapter 9).

- How many processes should be selected? Very few (generally two or three). The better is the enemy of the good here. Trying to move on all fronts at once will only result in spreading scant resources too thin, with discouragement typically ensuing from a lack of focus and results. It is better to focus all the effort on the vital few processes, select the vital few sub-processes within them and zoom in on the vital few variables (Chapters 10 and 11).

- Is this is a one-time exercise? It would be a shame if it were. The methodology involves a substantial start-up cost and a learning curve. Management is learning to view the business in a different way, from the customer in, and investing time to develop a shared understanding of the way processes are connected to reaching corporate goals. Updating the matrices is much less demanding an exercise than building them, and can easily be integrated with the annual review of the strategic plan, with which it generates much synergism. Further, the benefits of the approach keep growing as the organization becomes more rigorous and management by facts gradually replaces seat-of-the-pants management.

- Could the organization be limited to the strategic impact matrix (Figure 6.11) and skip the intricacies of the three houses of quality? This is indeed a quick and dirty way to get a jump-start on process management for an organization in a hurry. If the organization follows up with a more complete approach as soon at it can, then it might be a valid approach. However, organizations that are happy shooting from the hip should never undertake this journey at all, unless they intend to do it right. While the strategic plan spells out organizational priorities in a rolling three to five year window, it does not provide the complete picture of the connections between customer needs, service offerings, metrics, and processes. The lack of such a framework will impede clear process focus, thereby denying the organization the full benefits accruing to customer-focused organizations.

- Since management has to invest considerable time in this exercise, is there not a risk of management losing faith in the approach, or being sidetracked by some emerging situation that requires their urgent and undivided attention? Definitely! Only strong leadership will guarantee that management sees this process through to its conclusion. However, an organization embarking into process-based management need not wait until the exercise is completed before embarking into improvement projects. Indeed, it is important to be able to show results as soon as possible. Starting training projects immediately after one or two *convenient* projects have been selected through brainstorming allows two types of learning to go on in parallel: how to pick the right thing to do and how to do things right. Since this learning takes place at different levels in the organization, doing them in parallel not only cuts cycle time in half, but also contributes to building support for the initiative and to achieving a critical mass of involvement and support for the initiative. There is one caveat though: it is important to adjust expectations up front. These are training projects and they most probably are not *on the money*. They have to be presented as training opportunities first.

- If, for some reason or other, your company is unwilling or unable to follow the methodology proposed in this chapter, the *quick and dirty* approach suggested in Box 6.1 provides an alternative. It is quicker, but less rigorous. It bypasses metrics and service offerings and provides a shortcut to reaching a consensus on important processes. It does not leave a *trace* that can be used to update the analysis and will leave many important issues unresolved. Using this approach, however, allows the organization that is still feeling its way in this field to take the shortest path to demonstrable results (Chapter 10). It can come back to this methodology later, when the initiative is better shored up and the organization is willing to invest further.

Box 6.1 Keeping it simple: the quick and dirty way

If you do not have time or will not do this, for any reason . . .

The management committee can do the following exercise. It is best to do it as an immediate sequel to the strategic planning exercise. You will need flip charts and small sticky notes, or colored dots. This will require one to two days of work:

1. Prepare a list of all customer needs (list 1).

2. Prepare a list of key strategic issues (list 2).

3. Prepare a list of your major business processes and draw four columns next to it (list 3).

4. Prepare a second working copy of that list.

5. Spread a hundred points between customer needs in list 1 and key strategic issues in list 2, through multi-voting (see procedure below). Keep these ratings in plain view of all participants while performing the next step.

Continued

Continued

6. Members should think about the impact of each process on the most important customer needs. Copy the ranking obtained in the first column of list 3. Then, remove the sticky notes from the working copy, so that it can be used again for the next steps.

7. Through multi-voting, using the working copy of list 3, rank the processes based on their impact on key strategic issues, and copy the ranking in the second column of list 3.

8. Through multi-voting, using the working copy of list 3, rank the processes based on their efficiency and effectiveness. Assign the highest value (10) to the most ineffective and inefficient process (thus making it more likely to be selected for improvement). Copy the ranking obtained in the third column of list 3.

9. List 3 is now the rough equivalent of Table 6.3. The committee should now have an open discussion and come to a consensus on priority processes.

Multi-voting: First, agree on a weighting scheme. For example, give each committee member 10 sticky notes, representing 10 votes, ranging from one to 10 points, where 10 reflects the highest importance and one the lowest. Each member can use a different color, or write down initials so that votes can be identified. To rate a list of items, each member assesses (silently—no discussion is allowed) the elements to be ranked or scored, and sticks the notes next to the appropriate elements in the list. When everyone is done, the votes on each element are discussed, with the members holding the extreme values explaining why they voted that way. Members are allowed to review and change their ratings when the discussion is over. The total points assigned to each element by all participants is then calculated, and they are ranked. Ties or near-ties are debated again until consensus is reached.

6.10 SUMMARY

Process-oriented improvement philosophies are about doing the right thing right. They are predicated on rigor—rigor in deciding what the right things to do are, and rigor in deciding how to go about ensuring that these things are done the right way. This chapter presents a methodology to do the former. Chapters 10 and 11 present methodologies to do the latter.

The methodology presented here is realistic, rigorous, and in harmony with the *doing things right* methodologies. It deploys strategy and market positioning through a series of matrices, called quality functions deployment or QFD, onto metrics and processes, ultimately allowing the organization to zoom in on important processes to manage and improve. It bridges the gap between strategy and processes, and is thus the missing link that has denied many organizations the breakthrough gains possible through doing things right. The mission statement is an important element connecting processes to strategy and promoting coherence of action across processes, throughout the organization.

The methodology requires top management to *walk the rigor talk*, not to simply ask the rest of the organization to be rigorous in the way they do things. Body language has more impact on employees than spoken language. When management shoots from the hip, so does the rest of the organization.

EXERCISES

6.1 Rating processes in terms of importance for clients

As in previous chapters, it is best to assemble a team to do this.

a) Review your answers to Exercises 2.1 (customer activity cycle), 2.2 (needs), 2.3 (weighted needs), and 2.4 (benefits-features connection). Use the Kano model to prepare a diagram similar to that shown in Figure 6.2. Do you think your service package is complete? If not, adjust it.

b) Your answers to Exercises 2.1 to 2.4 constitute your data to prepare House 0. It is your first task. Follow the directions given and the example shown in Section 6.4.2 and Figure 6.3. Once you have a first version of the House, adjust it to make sure that your service package is complete and sufficient.

c) Prepare an importance diagram of the elements of the service package similar to the one shown in Figure 6.4.

d) Analyze your service offerings and generate an initial set of metrics to be used as input into House 1. Follow the directions given and the example shown in Section 6.5 and Figure 6.6. Once you have a first version of the House, adjust it to make sure that your set of metrics is complete and sufficient.

e) Prepare an importance diagram of metrics similar to the one shown in Figure 6.7.

f) Review your answers to Exercise 3.5. Use the list of value-adding processes (about 20) generated through the FAST diagram in Exercise 3.5b as input into House 2. This will be correlated to the metrics in the Pareto diagram above, following the instructions provided in Section 6.6, and the example shown in Figure 6.9. To keep the matrix to a manageable size, you may limit yourself to the most important metrics. If you find that some metrics are not affected by any process, revise the FAST diagram accordingly. If some processes do not affect any metric, verify if they would affect some of the metrics left out of the matrix. If some processes do not affect any metric at all, you have an incoherence to resolve: either this is not a process or some service feature or metric is missing.

g) Prepare an importance diagram of value adding processes.

h) Review your answers to exercise 3.5c. Select from this FAST diagram all value enabling processes. You should get seven to 15 processes. Correlate these processes to the most important value-adding processes resulting from House 2, following the instructions provided in Section 6.6.

i) Prepare an importance diagram of enabling processes.

6.2 Identifying salient processes

a) Review the company's strategic plan and the key strategic issues identified therein. If you do not have such a plan, a brainstorming session should produce a coarse assessment of the major challenges of all natures facing the organization. You should have no more than 10 or 12 such issues. Spread 100 points between these issues based on their relative importance for the future of the company. Use these issues in a matrix similar to that shown in Figure 6.11 to correlate with all enabling and value-adding processes identified above. The matrix should have about 30 columns, but many cells will turn out to be blank. Calculate a weighted index (see Figure 6.11) reflecting the importance of each process for strategy. If the matrix is too large, limit your assessment to the direct correlates, marking them with a bull's-eye.

b) Prepare a salience diagram such as the one shown in Figure 6.12, plotting each process on the basis of strategic impact and performance.

c) Tabulate the strategic impact and performance scores of each process in a table similar to Table 6.3. Calculate a salience score by summing up both scores.

6.3 Assessing the performance of the processes

a) Prepare an efficiency/effectiveness diagram such as that shown in Figure 6.13, following the instructions presented in Section 6.7.2.

b) Tabulate the scores in the table you started in Exercise 6.2c, including a performance score, obtained by summing up the two ratings.

6.4 Prioritizing the processes

a) Prepare a salience/performance diagram such as the one shown in Figure 6.14. Identify the five priority processes, numbering them one to five, on the diagram itself and on Figure 6.14 as well, following the instructions given in Section 6.7.3. You may use the proximity criteria, the decision rules presented in Section 6.7.3, or any other set of sequential decision rules that your organization deems appropriate.

b) Select two processes you would like to use as pilot projects to test the improvement and design methodologies presented in Chapters 10 and 11 respectively. It is suggested that you pick for improvement a process that scores particularly poorly on efficiency. Pick as your design project a process that does not exist or one that is so informal, or whose global performance score is so low, that it is best to start from scratch.

6.5 Formulating the mission of priority processes

Follow the instructions presented in Section 6.8 to formulate the mission of the five priority processes selected above.

Notes

[1] Not a part of the Kano model.
[2] Discussing strategic planning methodologies lies beyond the scope of this book.
[3] Derivatives are products, financial instruments, or securities that are derived from another security, cash market, index, or another derivative, such as futures, forwards, and options.
[4] The firm will have to decide whether it is worthwhile building distinct houses 1, 2, and 3 starting from a different set of customer needs, or if it will be sufficient to adjust the results obtained with the original segment based on the differences between the two market segments.

7

Scoping a Process for Improvement or Design[1]

Effective change happens in bite-sized chunks, but you have to ensure coherence among the pieces. To achieve the proper scope, an organization must determine where the project fits into the global picture and pick the right part of the right process to improve. A methodology is presented to do that.

Chapter 6 presented a rigorous approach to deploy strategy onto processes, that is, to define the right thing to do. The approach presented requires much rigor. Few organizations are likely to embark on such a journey until they have had first-hand experience with rigor and its benefits. This chapter presents a methodology to scope a project for an organization that has not explicitly explored the relationships between clients' needs, strategy, and processes. Those organizations that did will find that they still need the methodology to break down selected processes into *bite-size* projects, fine tune the scope of the projects, and clarify the boundaries of the processes.

The methodology unfolds in 10 steps. To facilitate generalization, it is presented using three examples drawn from very different professional and semi-professional services: social work, accounting, and software development. After presenting the 10 steps, the delicate trade-offs involved in delimiting the perimeter of the process are discussed.

7.1 INTRODUCTION

Think globally, act locally. Strategic options and their implications are not visible unless you take a global view. However, since trying to change everything at once results in chaos, change must be executed through small, bite-sized projects. The same goes for process improvement and process design of a more tactical nature. Unfortunately, a series of beneficial local actions may result in a loss of global coherence (see discussion in Section 5.1.3.3), unless care is taken to ensure coherence by regularly looking at the big picture.

To get the correct project scope, you need a good cookie cutter. Too big a scope generates much frustration, and energy is wasted beating around the bush. The greatest risk is that you never reach the level of detail required to identify and fix the vital variables. By contrast, the greatest risk of too small a scope is to leave these variables out entirely, and waste time beating the wrong bush.

While these issues are well known in manufacturing (see, for instance, Lynch et al., 2003), mitigating the risks in professional services, where complexity arises from other factors, requires a different approach. The proper methodology in services includes tools designed to force an organization to see where the project fits into the global picture and to help it pick the right part of the right process to improve.

To illustrate this methodology, focus on the case of a child protection service (CPS) agency. It is useful to review Box 5.2 (Midtown CPS) to see the general context in which a CPS operates. While the methodology has general applicability, an example drawn from the complex field of human services shows how the approach lends itself to some of the most sensitive social problems. For those readers not familiar with CPS agencies, it will also be shown how the methodology applies to a software developer and an accounting firm. Here is an overview of the problems each organization faces:

- The CPS agency is concerned about recurring capacity problems, so the general manager hired a process improvement consultant.

- The software developer is not meeting its promised delivery date. Late project start-up was initially thought to be the culprit.

- The accounting firm is experiencing problems in collecting its receivables and thought inefficiencies in the billing department were to blame.

The methodology (see Table 7.1) proceeds from a high-level exploration of related metrics and processes (steps one through four) through the selection of the specific goal and process to be improved (steps five through eight) to a final delimitation of scope (steps nine and 10).

7.2 STEP ONE—IDENTIFY THE BIG Y: WHAT IS THE GENERAL GOAL BEING PURSUED?

The initial problem statement should be formulated to be SMART (specific, measurable, ambitious, realistic, and timely). The CPS agency wants to solve its capacity problems, so its problem statement says, "We want to shorten the time it takes for children in need of protection to be admitted to the reception center from 10 days to one day". A diagram such as that shown in Figure 7.1 makes this more vivid. While on the waiting list, these children are at risk and their situations generally deteriorate. Having recently completed a strategic planning exercise, management had no problem identifying this as its top priority.

This initial problem statement is known as the *Big Y*, referring to the high-level dependent variable. It provides a starting point in an organization's search for the right scope.

The corresponding statement for the software developer says, "We currently meet our deadline on 25 percent of our contracts, but we should on 90 percent". The accountant's SMART statement says, "We get paid 85 days after we've performed the work, but we should be paid in 30 days."

This first step of the methodology gives focus to a discussion that is often loose and unstructured. It forces stakeholders to be more rigorous and get data. Benchmarking can be very useful here to help set the target value.

Table 7.1 Overview of the methodology.

Step	Purpose	Instructions
1. Pick general problem, select metric (Big Y)	Avoid endless discussions around ill-defined issues.	1. Select a metric that best summarizes the problem you have in mind. 2. Get data to establish the baseline. 3. Find a rationale (benchmarking, market need or other) to set a target.
2. Investigate adjacent metrics and correlations	Refine choice of metrics, zoom out to a broader view, explore associations and start thinking about causality.	1. Identify related metrics (think of other metrics closely associated to the one selected in step 1). 2. Identify the relationship among these metrics using arrows and $+/-$ signs.
3. Identify potential processes and explore linkages	Take a first look at what the organization does (processes) that might have to be changed in order to reach the target. Group processes in discrete entities.	1. Starting from the above metrics and their internal dynamics, identify things that you do that have an impact on those metrics. 2. Specify how these things (processes) relate to one another.
4. Explore the impacts of processes on metrics	Raise awareness of process-metric linkages. Promote systemic thinking about the genesis of the problem and potential change levers.	Draw a diagram connecting each of the processes (step 3) to the metrics which they impact. Specify the direction of the impact ($+/-$). Verify for completeness: If some metrics are not touched by any arrow, search for the process that impacts it. If some processes do not impact any metrics: why were they included in the first place?
5. Assess performance of high-level processes	After highlighting salience, it is important to think about performance as a criterion for selecting the process on which to focus.	Perform a summary evaluation of the efficiency and effectiveness of all processes identified in step 3. A five-point scale is used for each axis on an x-y diagram.
6. Perform cursory cause-and-effect	Approaching the problem from a different angle is useful to validate results obtained using the process approach. Cause and effect is more intuitive and less restrictive than step 4—i.e. not limited to processes.	Starting from the *Big Y* (step 1), generate a fishbone diagram, classifying causes in categories.
7. Formulate specific problem and goal (small y)	Having gone through steps 2 through 6 since first stating the problem (step 1), management is in a much better position to be specific about the nature of the problem.	1. Revisit the previous step and pick a metric from the influence diagram (step 2) that you now feel should be the object of the improvement project. Pick one that is at the heart of the problem and that offers a good payoff/risk ration. 2. Formulate it as was done in step 1.
8. Delimit process perimeter and formulate process mission	Determining what should be considered in-scope and out-of-scope is as difficult as it is critical. All the intermediate output of the methodology are now brought to bear on this task. The process mission is the anchor that will insure continued coherence.	Revisit step 4, focusing now on the metric selected in step 7. Pick the smallest subset of processes that can be the focus of the project, taking into consideration linkages between projects (step 3) and current process performance (step 5). State why this process has to exist (refer to Section 6.8).
9. Identify sub-processes	To validate the scope by zooming in to the selected process to see what's in there exactly.	Perform a cursory functional analysis of the process delimited in step 8. Start from the one sentence (action verb-noun) process definition and list functions by answering the question: "How?"
10. Assess performance of sub-processes	This is a final validation and represents the finest level of analysis reached in the scoping exercise. The micro-level performance analysis allows management to use a fine-tooth comb to establish final scope	Repeat step 5, this time using the functions identified in step 9.

175

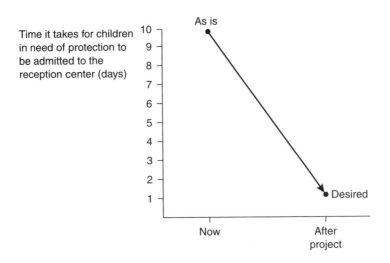

Figure 7.1 SMART problem statement: the big Y, CPS.

7.3 STEP TWO—DETERMINE RELATED METRICS: WHAT OTHER QUANTITIES (OR METRICS) ARE SO CLOSELY RELATED TO THE BIG Y THAT THEY COULD POTENTIALLY CONSTITUTE ALTERNATIVES TO IT?

Managers can generally land in the right strategic area, but if left to their own devices, they are quite unreliable when asked to pinpoint the problem. Thus, it is useful to explore the vicinity of the original problem to see whether a more meaningful problem statement can be found. The resulting metrics for the CPS agency are shown in Figure 7.2 in the form of a correlation diagram.

Adapted from the field of systems dynamics (see, for instance, Forrester (1969) and Senge (1990)), correlation diagrams illustrate patterns of influence. An arrow indicates a correlation, and its direction signifies the assumed underlying causality. Correlation diagrams allow visualization of patterns. Balancing loops, such as the one shown by the correlations numbered 1, 2, and 3 in Figure 7.2, show how a one-time increase in the number of reports when the reception center is near capacity will eventually (that is, with a time lag) lead to an automatic adjustment, as management responds to a lengthening of the waiting line by adding resources.

Reinforcement loops, such as the one shown by correlations 1-2-3-4 in Figure 7.2, are vicious circles. Because of a longer waiting list, children at risk are left in their home environments for a longer period, thus triggering new reports that have to be investigated. This puts added pressure on the social workers who receive and investigate these reports, leading them to cut down the number of validation calls they make. They tend to deal with this increased professional risk by erring on the side of caution and deciding more frequently to withdraw children from the threatening situation (correlations 5-6 in Figure 7.2).

Under the pressure of the longer waiting list, the reception center reinserts children earlier than clinically indicated, thus triggering new family crises and even more reports (correlations 7-8 in Figure 7.2). Delays in these reactions (that is, adding more personnel, earlier reinsertion, and so on) typically exacerbate the swings brought about by such situations, as new corrective measures are brought on to try to resolve a situation whose solution is already in the pipeline.

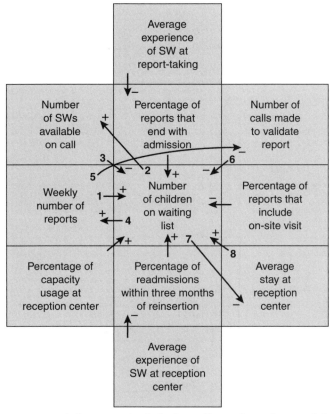

Arrows are correlations, + and − indicate positive and negative correlations,
the direction of the arrow reflects the assumed direction of causality

Figure 7.2 Step 2: Identify related metrics and their interrelationships, CPS.

This diagram helps managers understand the dynamics of the situation—a critical asset when the time comes to identify the best leverage point for breaking negative patterns. Though some of the critical correlations can and should be substantiated with data, it is generally impossible and even counterproductive to try to do so systematically. Keeping things simple produces the most benefit for the effort exerted. Assuming some quantities are exogenous to the model, such as the variable *average experience of social worker* in Figure 7.2, will contribute to the simplicity.

As for the software developer, its influence diagram (see Figure 7.3) identifies metrics such as the number of technical risks initially recognized, the number of staff changes that take place during the project, the number of supplier changes that take place between the bid and start-up stage, and the time required to fully free up designated core team members once the project is started. This brings out a complex dynamic involving a lack of serious risk analysis and planning at the bid stage. Because technical challenges are not discovered until the project is well on its way, the developer tends to pull the best resources from other projects to fix the problem, thereby spreading the crisis to these projects and triggering a domino effect.

The accounting firm's diagram (see Figure 7.4) identified metrics such as delays in producing invoices, errors on invoices, lateness of and errors on time and expense reports, clarity of invoices, and clarity of contract and customer queries. The firm uncovers the fact it often started projects on the wrong foot as the terms and conditions related to billing are often vague or not discussed in

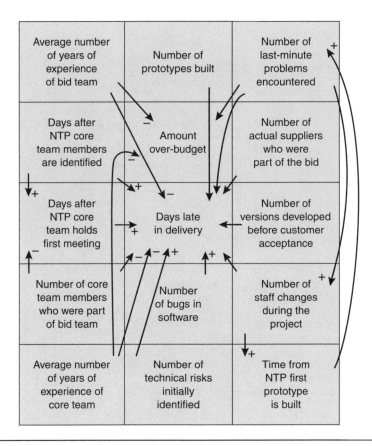

Figure 7.3 Step 2: Identify related metrics and their interrelationships, software developer.

detail with the customer. Thus, the staff working on the project do not receive clear instructions. This causes delays, ambiguity, or errors on time and expense reports and the invoices. These problems, in turn, trigger customer queries and further delays. The delays eventually build up and generate a backlog that takes months to resolve.

In step one, an organization is forced to be specific and gather data. In doing so, it realizes it has to exclude related metrics it believes are equally important. Step two allows the organization to revisit these metrics to identify and specify the dynamic nature of the relationships among the metrics. This helps focus the project on processes with maximum leverage to resolve the problem.

7.4 STEP THREE—LIST POTENTIAL PROCESSES: WHAT IS BEING DONE THAT HAS AN IMPACT ON THESE METRICS?

Underlying processes are implicit in steps one and two. This step makes them explicit. A potential set of processes relevant to the influence diagram of CPS (Figure 7.2) is shown in Figure 7.5. Managers readily identify these processes, but because no process exists alone, the major links still need to be acknowledged.

Correlations are not being looked for here. Functional linkages that can be found in the answer to this question are being looked for: If you were to modify this process, which other processes

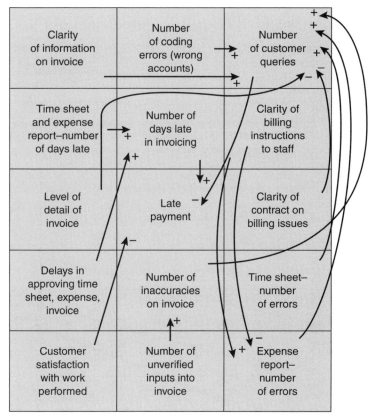

Arrows are correlations, + and − indicate positive and negative correlations,
the direction of the arrow reflects the assumed direction of causality

Figure 7.4   Step 2: Identify related metrics and their interrelationships, accounting firm.

would have to be included in the project and which would have to be tagged up front as related processes to be adjusted to maintain global coherence? The bold arrows in Figure 7.5 represent the former type of link; the regular arrows represent the latter.

As the CPS agency managers ponder which process to focus on, they realize that the way short-term reinsertion decisions are made is irrevocably linked to the way long-term decisions are made. If criteria are changed for one, they have to be changed for the other. They also realize that they cannot meaningfully separate these decisions from the other decisions that are made when the case is reviewed.

Thus, the three processes linked by bold arrows on the left-hand side of Figure 7.5 form an inseparable whole called the *review initial decisions* process. In a similar fashion, the three processes linked in the upper right-hand corner of Figure 7.5 must be considered together. The trio are thus referred to as the *make initial decisions* process.

The managers realize that if they want to change the process through which children are removed from their homes, they must be ready to make corresponding changes in the way families are helped and reinsertion is prepared. While these processes would be out of scope if the *remove child and admit to reception center* process is selected for improvement, they would have to be considered to be adjacent processes, and appropriate experts would have to be included in the project team.

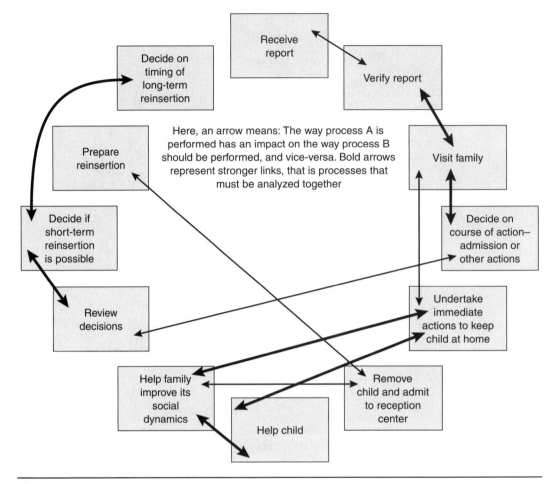

Here, an arrow means: The way process A is performed has an impact on the way process B should be performed, and vice-versa. Bold arrows represent stronger links, that is processes that must be analyzed together

Figure 7.5 Step 3: Identify relevant processes and their functional linkages, CPS.

The software developer (see Figure 7.6) ends up linking several processes related to risk management (assess initial project risk, prepare risk management plan, and manage risks), and staffing (select bid team members and core project team members). Several clusters of processes also emerge in the accounting firm (see Figure 7.7), such as those related to the preparation and verification of time and expense reports and those that related to the initial billing agreement.

7.5 STEP FOUR—CREATE A PROCESS METRICS DIAGRAM: HOW ARE THE TARGET METRICS AND PROCESSES RELATED?

Figure 7.8 shows the impact of each process on the relevant metrics at CPS. Processes that are inseparable are the same color. These relationships are especially useful if you look back at Figure 7.2, which highlights patterns of influence among the metrics. The *make initial decisions* process, for example, is at the center of the reinforcement loop mentioned in step two due to its impact on the intake valve. The *review initial decisions* process is also a strong factor due to its impact on the outlet valve.

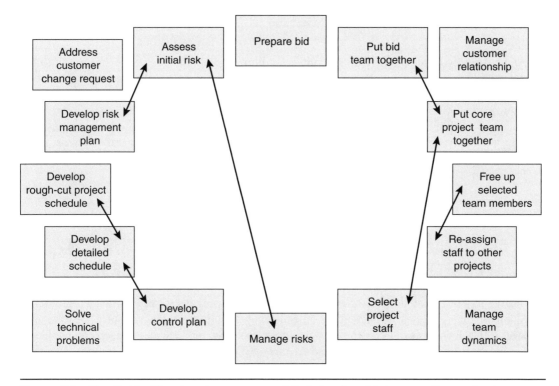

Figure 7.6 Step 3: Identify relevant processes and their functional linkages, software developer.

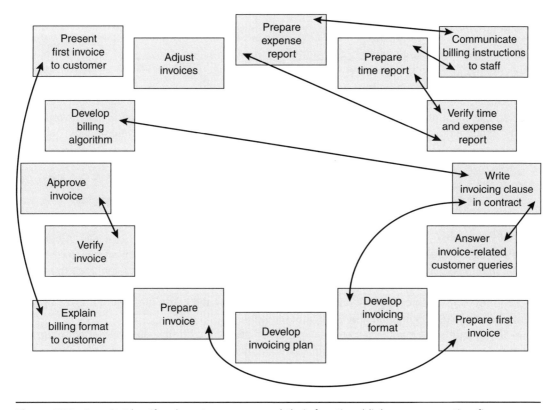

Figure 7.7 Step 3: Identify relevant processes and their functional linkages, accounting firm.

At the software developer (Figure 7.9), the late completion of software projects turns out to be a complex problem with several clusters of processes at its root. Several projects are needed to solve this problem, and each needs to focus on a different aspect of the business, such as team selection, staff movements, prototype development, and risk management.

This step confirms the accounting firm's suspicion (Figure 7.10) that the initial setup of the invoicing process is an important part of its problem because instructions to staff and customer expectations stem from that process. The firm also find the preparation and communication of the first invoice are pivotal in detecting and resolving any remaining internal or external issues.

7.6 STEP FIVE—CONDUCT A HIGH-LEVEL PROCESS PERFORMANCE EVALUATION: WHAT IS THE CURRENT PERFORMANCE LEVEL OF THESE PROCESSES?

The answer to that question provides critical input to the scoping decision. Figure 7.11 shows an evaluation of the processes at CPS using an efficiency/effectiveness diagram (see DeToro and McCabe, 1997). It consists of assessing, on a five-point scale, the performance of each process identified in Figure 7.5, in terms of efficiency and effectiveness (see Section 6.7.2 and Figure 6.13), and plotting the result in a diagram. Three processes are in dire need of improvement:

- Deciding which course of action to take initially

- Visiting the family

- Removing the children from their home environment

Dedicating an improvement project to any of these processes will likely yield a high return. On the other hand, dedicating a project to the decision surrounding the timing of long-term reinsertion will probably not yield important payback.

A similar diagram (not shown) for the software developer shows the risk management and prototype development processes to be sick. Low performers in the accounting firm included verifying time and expense reports, communicating billing procedures, and answering invoice-related queries.

7.7 STEP SIX—CREATE A CAUSE AND EFFECT DIAGRAM: WHAT ARE THE CAUSES OF THE PROBLEM?

Tentative answers arising from earlier steps can be further validated using a cause and effect diagram (also called Ishikawa diagram—see Figure 7.12). Detailed instructions about how to prepare such a diagram are given in Section 10.5.2. This tool forces an organization to approach the same problem from an angle not restricted by process and metrics. The organization's earlier conclusions will be reinforced if the most important factors identified by the cause and effect diagram point toward the same culprits identified in the preceding steps.

In the case of the CPS agency, correlating earlier analysis with the cause and effect diagram singles out *defensive practices*, *lack of uniformity in application*, and a *poorly scripted home visit* as the processes that should be fixed. If that were not the case, the agency would have to revisit earlier results.

Various issues related to risk management come out in the analysis that the software firm conducts, while the accountant's analysis reveals that billing procedures are poorly understood.

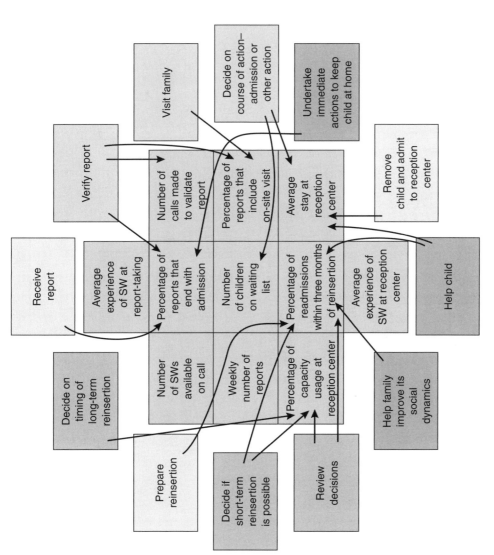

Here an arrow means: "The way process A is performed has an impact on metric B"

Figure 7.8   Step 4: Identify the impact of each process on each metric, CPS.

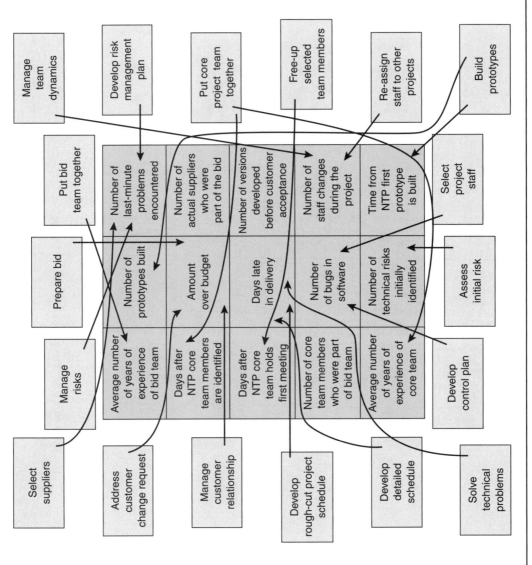

Figure 7.9 Step 4: Identify the impact of each process on each metric, software developer.

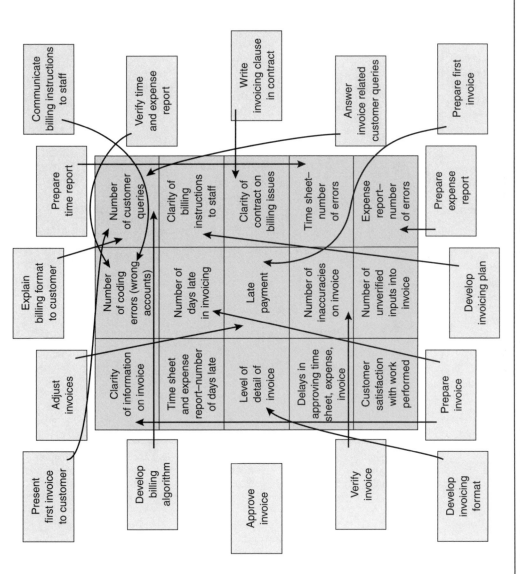

Figure 7.10   Step 4: Identify the impact of each process on each metric, accounting firm.

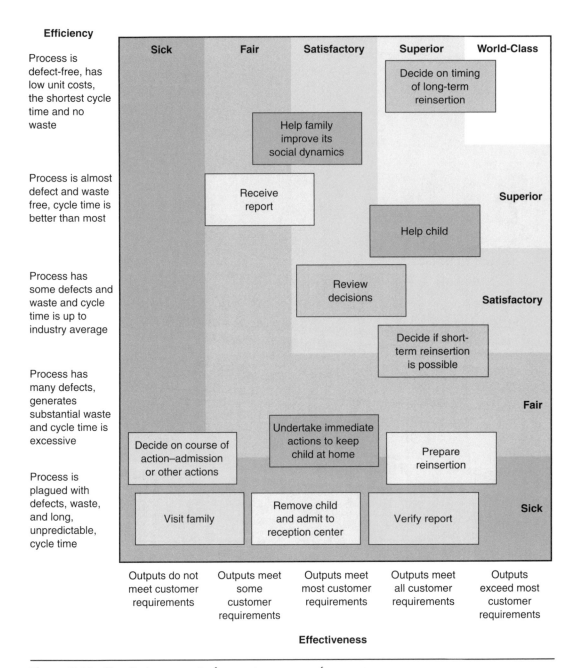

Efficiency

Process is defect-free, has low unit costs, the shortest cycle time and no waste

Process is almost defect and waste free, cycle time is better than most

Process has some defects and waste and cycle time is up to industry average

Process has many defects, generates substantial waste and cycle time is excessive

Process is plagued with defects, waste, and long, unpredictable, cycle time

| Sick | Fair | Satisfactory | Superior | World-Class |

Decide on timing of long-term reinsertion

Help family improve its social dynamics

Receive report

Superior

Help child

Review decisions

Satisfactory

Decide if short-term reinsertion is possible

Fair

Decide on course of action–admission or other actions

Undertake immediate actions to keep child at home

Prepare reinsertion

Visit family

Remove child and admit to reception center

Verify report

Sick

Outputs do not meet customer requirements

Outputs meet some customer requirements

Outputs meet most customer requirements

Outputs meet all customer requirements

Outputs exceed most customer requirements

Effectiveness

Figure 7.11 Step 5: Assessment of current process performance.
Source: Adapted from De Toro and McCabe, 1997.

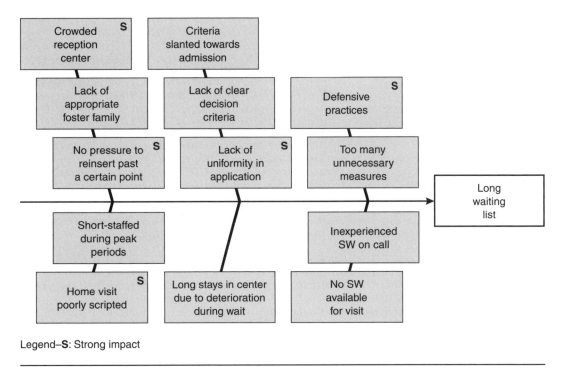

Figure 7.12   Step 6: Cause and effect (or Ishikawa) diagram, CPS.

7.8 STEP SEVEN—IDENTIFY THE SMALL Y: WHAT IS THE SPECIFIC GOAL BEING PURSUED IN THIS PROJECT? WHAT IS THE YARDSTICK THAT WILL BE USED TO MEASURE THE PROJECT'S SUCCESS?

Based on the information obtained in the preceding steps, the percentage of reports that end with the decision to admit a child appears to be at the center of the problem at CPS. It is a bull's-eye type of metric, and there should be a target range within which the processes would be considered within specifications. The specific SMART statement for the CPS agency (see Figure 7.13) says: "Currently the admission rate varies between 10 percent and 50 percent. It should remain within the 15 percent to 25 percent range, 99 percent of the time."

The software developer's specific SMART statement says, "Our risk management plan currently rates a three on our 10-point quality scale. It should rate eight or higher". The quality scale has to be developed based on a weighted sum of criteria, such as validation of the list of technical issues, the depth of the initial exploration of a technical solution, the number of risks signed off by experts, and the number of risks with associated contingency plans. It is a common misinterpretation of the measurement imperative (that is, if you cannot measure it, you cannot improve it) that unless a metric is readily available for an objective you would like to reach, it should be dropped in favor of another. On the contrary, it should be kept, and an appropriate metric should be sought or developed.

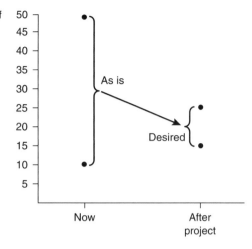

Figure 7.13   SMART problem statement: The Big Y at CPS.

The accounting firm decides to focus on the errors on the expense reports and time sheets used to prepare the first invoice for a new contract. The error count was eight, and it should have been zero.

7.9 STEP EIGHT—DELIMIT THE TURF: WHAT IS THE PERIMETER OF THE PROCESS TO BE IMPROVED OR DESIGNED TO REACH THE GOAL FORMULATED IN STEP SEVEN?

The process of making initial decisions links directly to the goal (see Figure 7.14). It starts when a report is received and ends with a decision on what action to take, if any. While the process of verifying the report is effective, its low efficiency is likely to have an effect on the waiting list in the resource-bound context of the agency. The process owner is the director of child and youth protection. A concise mission statement is formulated, to ensure that the process remains anchored on its reason for existence and that no loss of coherence takes place because of the change.

The process to be improved or designed by the software developer was defined as *prepare risk management plan*. It starts with receipt of the request for proposal and ends with approval of the plan by the owner of the proposal.

The accounting firm chose *specify and communicate billing procedures to all concerned* as the target process. The process starts with the point from terms of reference (pre-contract) and ends with all concerned parties (internal and external) receiving explicit reporting and billing instructions.

7.10 STEP NINE—CHECK THE SCOPE: IS THE SCOPE TOO BROAD?

Is management abdicating its responsibility to scope the process down to a manageable size? If that were the case, the team would feel abandoned because it was forced to use a rigorous analytical methodology to perform a task that required managerial judgment.

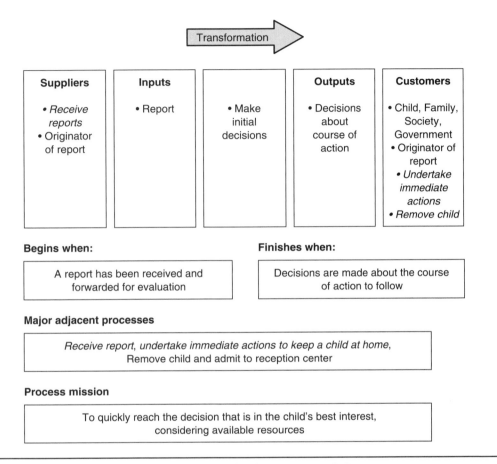

Figure 7.14   The SITOC form used to circumscribe the process at CPS.

A cursory functional analysis, such as the FAST diagram (Figure 7.15) can help assess the size of the process. Instructions about preparing such a diagram are presented in Section 3.1.2. The diagram can be pushed further to the right one level if management still doubts the breadth of the process, or a macro-map that adds the players involved to another axis can be prepared. Of course, management will need the counsel of a process improvement expert to make an enlightened decision as to the process's adequate size.

7.11 STEP TEN—REVIEW THE SCOPE: HOW COULD THE SCOPE BE FURTHER REDUCED?

A low-level efficiency/effectiveness analysis (see Figure 7.16) can be performed on the functions in Figure 7.15 to determine whether a viable high leverage (low performance) subset can be isolated. This may create a loop back to earlier stages of the methodology because management may be tempted to leave out sub-processes that display high performance but were previously judged inseparable from the others. Thus, the methodology is iterative, not linear, because early judgment calls may be questioned later, and may turn out to be critical to the scoping decisions as things unfold.

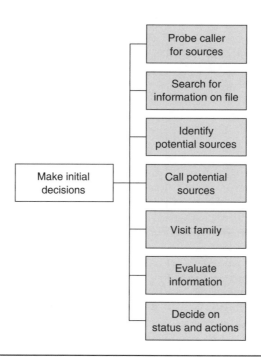

Figure 7.15 Step 9: Functional analysis (FAST diagram) to identify sub-processes, CPS.

7.12 A BALANCING ACT

Determining the scope of a project involves managing a complex trade-off. Scoping must be performed from the top down and should be as scientific as possible, but the top view (management and strategy) deals more with art than science. Establishing the scope of a project means deciding where the boundary between the two realms should lie, at least for the period during which a rigorous analytical framework is to be deployed within the domain of the project. This places managers who must make that decision in the uncomfortable position of spanning the proverbial boundary between art and science. It assumes they will know when to be guided by intuition and good judgment and when to be guided by facts.

Drawing the boundary between art and science is not easy, and doing so requires highly qualified people. They have to be comfortable distilling the experience of the organization one moment and, say, evaluating the normality of a dataset the next, accepting a manager's judgment call one moment and rejecting an undocumented assertion the next, taking the broad view one moment and the near view the next.

7.13 SUMMARY

Effective change happens in bite-sized chunks, but you have to ensure that coherence is not lost because of a series of such changes. To achieve the proper scope, an organization must determine where the project fits into the global picture, pick the right part of the right process to improve, and anchor it well using a clear mission statement. The systems' dynamic has been adapted to play a central role in initial exploration of scoping decisions. The methodology and toolkit presented here helps bring structure to a complex task and diminish the unavoidable turbulence that occurs at this crucial interface between intuition and rigor.

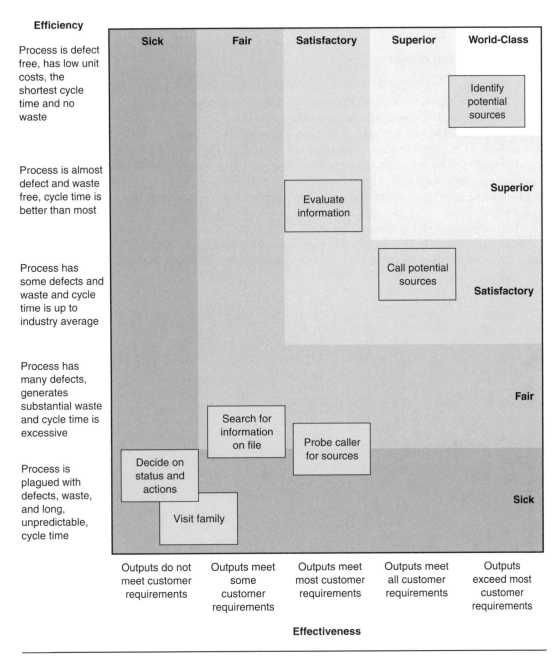

Figure 7.16 Step 5: Assessment of current performance of sub-processes, CPS.
Source: Adapted from De Toro and McCabe, 1997.

EXERCISES

7.1 Scoping two projects

Refer to the work you did in the end-of-chapter exercises in Chapter 6, and particularly to the five projects for which you formulated a mission statement, in exercise 6.5. Select two projects among these: one that needs improvement and one that needs to be designed (or redesigned) from scratch. The former should be one that you deem to have potential. Base this assessment on such indicators as past versus current performance (are there moments when the process showed that it can perform much better?) and on benchmarking data (how big is the gap with competition?). The latter should be a process that does not exist (something you have never done), that virtually does not exist (you perform some activities, but an actual process was never designed), or that you deem to have no potential.

Follow the 10-step procedure outlined in this chapter to scope two process change projects based on these processes. A well-scoped improvement project is the central input you will need to perform the end-of-chapter exercise in Chapter 10. The same goes for the design project in Chapter 11.

Notes

[1] This chapter is largely drawn from: Harvey, J. "Scoping Improvement Projects in Professional Services—A 10 Step Approach," *Quality Progress*, 37 (8), August, 2004, pp 64–72.

8

Managing a Process

Variation is the voice of a process. It is the enemy of value, but the friend of anyone who wants to characterize a process and learn how it works. Statistics is the language of variation. Adopting a system's view of the organization potentiates the process approach.

In the previous chapters, the importance of identifying and focusing on the right processes was explained and a methodology and tools to help the organization do this were proposed. These important processes must be managed. In this chapter, some basic notions about managing a process are presented. The critical role that variation plays in process control is first explained, and a systems view of the latter is presented. The distinctive features of process control in professional services are then discussed, using the examples of a drugstore, social services, and consulting. Much of the rigor discussed in Chapter 1 is rooted in the approaches and tools presented here. Table 8.1 gives a short definition of the major concepts discussed in this chapter.

8.1 VARIATION AND PROCESS CONTROL

To introduce basic notions about variation and process control, a simple example is used (see Box 8.1). It is critical to Judy's satisfaction (CTS) to live in a comfortable home environment. Comfort can be defined by two technical characteristics or critical to quality (CTQ) criteria: room temperature and relative humidity. Say that Judy is comfortable when room temperature is within the 68 to 72 degrees Fahrenheit range and relative humidity within the 35 percent to 45 percent range. While the average daily temperature and humidity provide useful information, this is not enough to evaluate Judy's comfort level. Indeed, half a day at 60 degrees and the other half at 80 degrees, while very uncomfortable, yield an average temperature of 70 degrees, that is, right on target. Hence, a measure of variation in temperature and humidity is also needed.

Box 8.1: Judy's environment control

Issue: *Basic notions on variation and process control*

Judy has just moved from Jacksonville, FL to Edmonton (Alberta, Canada) where she had a new house built. In early December, she is discovering the wonders and challenges associated

---

Continued

Continued

with her first winter at northern latitude. One of these unexpected *pleasures* is the difficulties she faces in maintaining a comfortable home environment, that is, the temperature, and humidity in various areas of her three-bedroom cottage. Upon handing her the keys to the house, the contractor had indicated that there were three simple controls at her disposal to make adjustments as outside conditions changed:

- A thermostat (controlling a central electrical furnace)

- A knob (with settings labeled one to seven) to set the lower humidity level at which a humidifier would start (circulating the air through a humid filter) to reduce dryness

- Another knob, to set the upper humidity limit beyond which an air exchanger would start, expelling hot (pollutant charged) humid air and taking in dry cold air, thus avoiding excessive humidity

For all this *simplicity*, after three weeks of a Canadian winter, hardly a day had gone by when Judy had felt comfortable in the house. Unless set correctly, the humidifier might well work against the air exchanger (injecting humidity while the exchanger expels it): a costly situation, since the furnace would be functioning most of the time to compete against the cold air coming in all the time. When she felt cold, she would raise the temperature setting on the thermostat. Soon after, however, her throat would feel dry and she would raise the humidifier setting. As outside temperature mellowed, however, the furnace would stop and humidity would rise, eventually triggering the heat exchanger and reducing both temperature and humidity. She was well aware that the more the exchanger functioned, the higher her heating bill would be, and was thus tempted to set the humidity level at which it would start rather high. Thus, she would lower the humidifier setting, only to find the dryness problem coming back when outside temperature dropped again, and then humidity would never rise high enough to trigger the air exchanger . . .

The most commonly used measure for this purpose is the standard deviation, often represented by the Greek letter σ (sigma). It measures how far away from the mean each observation lies, on average. The further the observations lie from the average—that is, the higher the standard deviation—the more variation there is and thus the lower Judy's comfort level. Suppose that Judy decides to use some rigor to solve her problem. She goes to the hardware store and buys a thermometer and a hygroscope. Every day, at a convenient time, she jots down on a piece of paper the readings on both instruments. The results are shown in Table 8.2. Also shown are the mean and standard deviation of each sample. The standard deviation is the square root of the average squared deviation from the mean. That is not as complex at it sounds. The standard deviation of the humidity data, for example, is calculated as follows:

$$\sqrt{\frac{(37.9 - 38.7)^2 + (40.4 - 38.7)^2 + (49.2 - 38.7)^2 + \ldots}{29}} = 7.6$$

The division by 29, that is, the sample size minus one, rather than by 30 is a correction factor required because this is really an estimate of the unknown value of the standard deviation of a much broader reference set (referred to as *the population* in statistics) of temperature value. The real standard deviation could only be obtained by continuously monitoring the house. A sample size of 30 is generally considered sufficient to produce a valid estimate.

Table 8.1 Short definitions of major concepts discussed in this chapter.

Concept	Definition
Systems view	A way of thinking–often supported by a visual representation—about a group of elements as a dynamically interacting set of variables, taking inputs and providing outputs to one another within an environment.
Variations	Changes in the value of a dependent or independent variable.
Interaction	Reciprocal action between two or more variables, which make it essential to consider the value of the other variables when setting the value of one of them.
Statistics	The science of variations and risks. As complexity increases, statistics quickly become essential to make up for our limited unaided capacity to analyze variations, and thus understand processes.
Standard deviation	The most common statistical measure of dispersion of values around the mean. The smaller the standard deviation, the tighter the values cluster around the mean.
Normal distribution	A statistical distribution that describes well many naturally occurring phenomena.
Voice of the process	The range of values (including typically three standard deviations on either side of the mean) within which the results of a stable process fall most (99.7%) of the time.
Voice of the customer	A translation of customer requirements into a quantitative specification that the process must meet.
Process capability	A quantitative assessment of a stable process's ability to consistently produce results that meet client's specifications. It involves a (statistical) comparison of the variations produced by the process to the client's specifications. The ratio of the voice of the customer to the voice of the process is a commonly used metric for this.
Special causes	A factor or variable interfering with the normal operation of a process, thereby modifying the patterns of variations and making predictions of future behavior unreliable.
Shift	A special cause that causes a sudden change in a process's performance, leaving it stable at different operating parameters (i.e. different distribution of results).
Drift	A special cause producing a gradual change in a process performance.
Stable process	A process whose performance is not subject to the effect of any special cause, and whose performance thus lends itself to statistical prediction.
Process control	A process designed to monitor another one and keep it stable. A control system receives information from the other process, processes it (reassesses stability), and sends control instructions as required to correct it.
SPC	Statistical process control. A rigorous control system based on statistics.
Capacity management	A management process whose task it is to control operating processes, in such a way that capacity and demand are continuously matched in the most profitable way possible.

    With a standard deviation of 3.3, temperature appears more constant than humidity, at least in absolute terms. Percentage variation, however, would be much more useful. This is called the variation coefficient and is calculated by dividing the standard deviation by the mean. It shows (Table 8.2) that humidity displays four times the variability of temperature. A more useful measure yet would be to compare the actual variation with what Judy considers acceptable. This is illustrated in Figure 8.1 and Figure 8.2. The comfort zone reflects the voice of the customer, that is, the translation of the intangible and subjective feeling of comfort (CTS) into specific values of two measurable variables (technical characteristics, or critical to quality [CTQ]). The connected dots reflect the voice of the process, that is, the actual values produced by the underlying processes. Comparing the voice of the process to the voice of the customer shows (as a time series in Figure 8.1 and a

Table 8.2   Temperature and humidity data for 30 days in Judy's home, compared to comfort levels.

Day	Humidity	Temperature	68°-72° Temperature OK	35%-45% Humidity OK	Both OK
1	37.9	68.6	X	X	X
2	40.4	64.3		X	
3	49.2	69.7	X		
4	19.9	69.0	X		
5	46.3	66.2			
6	32.4	67.4			
7	36.6	70.7	X	X	X
8	29.9	78.8			
9	38.3	68.1	X	X	X
10	39.1	73.6		X	
11	47.6	74.7			
12	42.0	75.4		X	
13	35.0	69.2	X	X	X
14	49.5	73.5			
15	45.1	65.9			
16	30.0	68.4	X		
17	51.2	67.3			
18	36.3	69.3	X	X	X
19	37.9	75.0		X	
20	30.0	67.2			
21	33.6	73.8			
22	40.7	73.4		X	
23	30.1	68.3	X		
24	44.3	72.2		X	
25	34.1	69.0	X		
26	30.9	71.2	X		
27	49.2	72.3			
28	39.2	72.5		X	
29	51.4	73.7			
30	34.2	69.1	X		
Total			12	12	5
Mean	38.7	70.6			
SD (σ)	7.6	3.3			
VC	20%	5%			
%			40%	40%	17%

SD: Standard deviation
VC: Variation coefficient

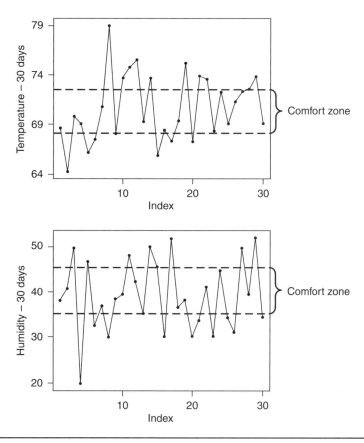

Figure 8.1 Temperature and humidity in Judy's house: Plot of the voice of process against the voice of the customer.

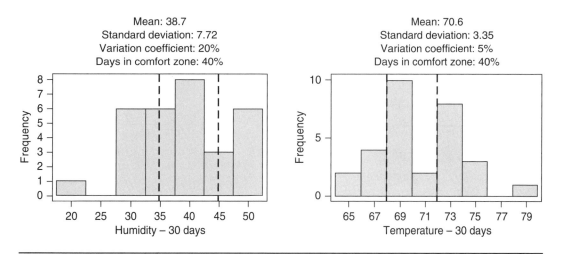

Figure 8.2 Temperature and humidity data in Judy's house: histogram with basic statistics: 30-day sample.

histogram in Figure 8.2) the capability of the process to meet customers' requirements. A tentative quantitative value could be given to this capability, by calculating (see Table 8.2) the proportion of the sample that lies within the comfort zone. On this count, both CTQs seem comparable (40 percent for temperature, 40 percent for humidity). Indeed, while humidity displays much more variation, the comfort zone is also much broader for humidity than it is for temperature. A common measure of process capability is based on the ratio of the voice of the customer to the voice of the process. The target value here is often set at two.

One problem with the above capability analysis is that the conclusions were based on a sample of 30 observations. Drawing another sample would certainly produce different numbers, and the difference could be very significant. For instance, the *hole* in the distribution of the temperature data (in the 70 to 72 degree range) is most likely not representative of the population.

An obvious solution is to increase the sample size. Assume that Judy goes on gathering data for 500 days. The resulting distributions are shown in Figure 8.3. It turns out that the initial sample resulted in a substantial overestimation of the variability of humidity, resulting in an underestimation of the capability of the process to meet Judy's requirements.

Increasing sample size, however, is not always feasible or economical. In order to improve the estimation resulting from a small sample, statistical techniques are used. Discussion here is limited to the normal distribution. The area under a normal curve sums to one. The area over any range of values thus represents a probability (with a total of one (100 percent) for the entire range (minus infinity, plus infinity)). The normal curve is shown as the curved lines in Figure 8.3. Figure 8.4 shows the probabilities associated with various intervals, defined by the number of standard devia-

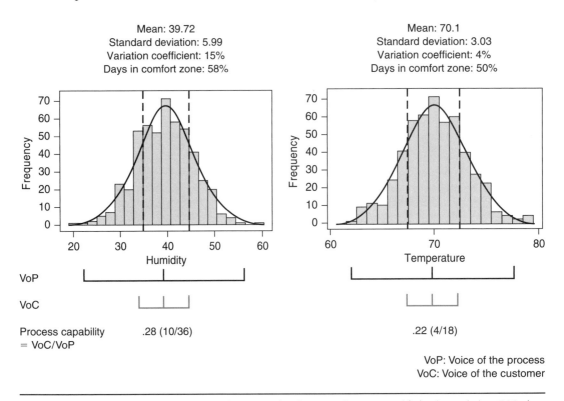

Figure 8.3 Temperature and humidity data in Judy's house. Histogram with basic statistics: 500-day sample.

tions on both sides of the mean. If it can be assumed, for instance, that variations in relative humidity in Judy's house are normally distributed with a mean of 40 and a standard deviation of 6, then it is known that there is a 68.26 percent probability that the temperature falls in the range (34, 46), that is, in the range ((mean − sigma), (mean + sigma)). Hence, the probability to be in the comfort zone (35, 45) can be calculated at any point in time as the probability (found in Table 8.3) that a normal distribution lies within 5/6 sigma on either side of the mean, or about 58 percent[1]. With the relatively bad sample available at first, the estimate would be 49 percent. The improvement in the estimate results from using the additional information now available (or rather that has been assumed in this case) about the shape and the properties of the distribution of the population. Statistical tests are available to verify the normality hypothesis.

The normal distribution nicely describes many naturally occurring phenomena, which are the sum of a host of independent individual actions and events. Other distributions are known and available to approximate other phenomena and thus improve estimation accuracy.

A common way to calculate process capability is by dividing the voice of the customer by the voice of the process. In the case of relative humidity, the voice of the customer is calculated as the range of the comfort zone (45-35 = 10). The voice of the process is taken to be three standard deviations on each side of the mean, that is, an interval spanning six standard deviations (see Figure 8.3), representing 99.74 percent (see Figure 8.4) of the area under the curve. This assumes that the voice of the process is centered on the central value of the voice of customer. While this is the case in this example, it is obviously not always the case. When the process is off center, this calculated capability will not be actualized until it has been centered.

8.2 PROCESS CONTROL—A SYSTEMS VIEW

Judy's actions to maintain and improve her comfort level fall within the realms of process control. This is illustrated in Figure 8.5. Judy is controlling three distinct processes: exchanging air, humidifying the air, and heating the air. The ITO (that is the center part of the *SITOC*, that is, without specifying the supplier and the customer) are shown in the boxes within the inner circle in Figure 8.5.

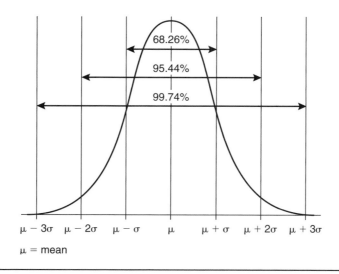

Figure 8.4 Areas under the normal curve.

Table 8.3 Areas under the standard normal curve for various values of x, the number of standard deviations away from the mean (prob (X > μ +xσ)).

X	Probability	X	Probability
0.1	0.46017216	3.1	0.0009676
0.2	0.42074029	3.2	0.00068714
0.3	0.38208858	3.3	0.00048342
0.4	0.34457826	3.4	0.00033693
0.5	0.30853754	3.5	0.00023263
0.6	0.27425312	3.6	0.00015911
0.7	0.24196365	3.7	0.0001078
0.8	0.2118554	3.8	7.2348E-05
0.9	0.18406013	3.9	4.8096E-05
1	0.15865525	4	3.1671E-05
1.1	0.13566606	4.1	2.0658E-05
1.2	0.11506967	4.2	1.3346E-05
1.3	0.09680048	4.3	8.5399E-06
1.4	0.08075666	4.4	5.4125E-06
1.5	0.0668072	4.5	3.3977E-06
1.6	0.05479929	4.6	2.1125E-06
1.7	0.04456546	4.7	1.3008E-06
1.8	0.03593032	4.8	7.9333E-07
1.9	0.02871656	4.9	4.7918E-07
2	0.02275013	5	2.8665E-07
2.1	0.01786442	5.1	1.6983E-07
2.2	0.01390345	5.2	9.9644E-08
2.3	0.01072411	5.3	5.7901E-08
2.4	0.00819754	5.4	3.332E-08
2.5	0.00620967	5.5	1.899E-08
2.6	0.00466119	5.6	1.0718E-08
2.7	0.00346697	5.7	5.9904E-09
2.8	0.00255513	5.8	3.3157E-09
2.9	0.00186581	5.9	1.8175E-09
3	0.0013499	6	9.8659E-10

These three processes are automated. The only human interventions required consist of setting dials. They are shown to function within the internal environment of the house, with all the other human, animal, chemical, and microbiological processes that take place within its confines. The house itself exists within an external environment, influenced by several environmental factors. All these processes interact with each other, either in a synergistic or antagonistic fashion, thereby conditioning the air that Judy feels and breathes. Some of these processes are controllable (taking a hot shower), others are partially controllable (such as the quantity of pollutants introduced into the house environment by the cat), and yet others lie totally beyond her control (such as physical (condensation) or chemical (rust) reactions).

Judy measures two characteristics of that air: temperature and humidity. She has bought a thermometer and a hygroscope at a hardware store. She placed them conveniently on the kitchen counter,

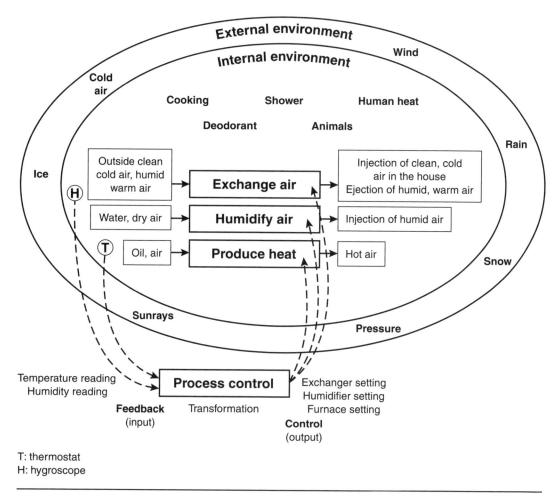

Figure 8.5 A system view of Judy's process control problem.

where she spends much of her time, and glances at them when she feels something is wrong. Thus, this feeling, together with the data she reads on the instruments provide feedback on the joint effect of all these processes on the climate (the input arrows to the control system box in Figure 8.5). Judy processes this information mentally. She first assesses the extent to which her feeling of warmth and dampness has strayed from her comfort zones. Then she tries to understand why this has happened and what she should do to correct the situation. This is the transformation (the T of the *SITOC*) that the control process operates. The outputs are decisions on the settings for the three knobs (or variables) she controls (the output arrows, transmitting operating instructions to the three automated processes). She then goes on with her business, until a feeling of discomfort again interrupts her.

Where there are processes, there is variation, and this system is no exception. In the previous section, the variations Judy observed when looking at her two instruments were discussed. Here is a partial list of other sources of variations:

- Measurement errors and time lags in the two instruments

- Measurement error in the thermostat and the humidity measurement systems of the humidifier and the air exchanger

- Judy's human error in her feeling of warmth and dampness

- Judy's logical error and memory flaws in her decision-making process

- Judy's human error when setting the dials

- Variations in the many uncontrollable external environmental factors (wind, humidity, atmospheric pressure, temperature)

- Variations in internal generation of heat and humidity (more cooking, showers, and so on)

- Special events (such as a party with 30 people)

- Variation in the heat generated by the furnace, at a given setting, and similar variations in the humidifier and heat exchanger

- Slow decline in the humidity generated by the freshly completed plaster wall

Variation falls into two broad categories, random and special cause. Random variations are the result of a host of independent variables that are impossible to identify. This type of variation has a tendency to be distributed normally, as illustrated in Figures 8.3 and 8.4. Special cause variation takes place, as the name suggests, when a potentially identifiable factor is affecting the variable. These events fall in two categories, according to the specific signature they leave on the data. A drift is recognized by an upward, downward, or cyclical trend in the data triggered by a phenomenon that unfolds gradually. Seasonal drifts in outside temperature, for instance, or even global warming, might well display such patterns. A shift, on the other hand, is produced by a discrete event (temporary, recurrent, or permanent) that makes the variable suddenly jump up or down from its normal pattern. The arrival of the meteorological phenomenon known as El Niño, for example, might produce such a shift in temperature. In Table 8.4, the notions of shifts, drifts, and control loop are illustrated further using three examples of simple personal processes: brushing your teeth, making toast, and planning your day. Within cycle controls are actions taken during an instantiation of the process. They are meant to influence the outcome of the process in that instance. Between cycles are actions taken after analyzing the outcome of a cycle and applied to the next one.

Anyone worried about weight has a *specification* in mind, that is, an ideal weight or figure to achieve and maintain. Two major processes are involved here: eating and exercising, that is, energy input and output. When it comes to controlling these two processes, weight is the *Big Y* (see

Table 8.4   Illustration of control loops, process shift, and process drift in three personal processes.

	Brushing your teeth	**Making toast**	**Planning your day**
Control loop (within cycle)	"Ouch!" (Action: reduce pressure)	Burnt toast smell! (Action: get it out)	"You'll never do all this—be realistic (Action: review schedule)
Drift (gradual, between cycles)	Increasing number of cavities (Potential cause: shorter brushing time, brush wear)	Toast increasingly dark (Potential cause: bread increasingly dry because you eat less)	Increasingly falling behind (Potential cause: tired, working more slowly)
Shift (sudden, between cycles)	Gums starts bleeding (Potential cause: gum disease)	Toast is now white! (Potential cause: bread is now kept in refrigerator)	Don't follow your plan anymore (Potential cause: sudden change in work habits)

Chapter 7) and the specification may be set on a continuous scale such as (160 pounds to 165 pounds) or using a so-called *go—no go* gauge: "do I fit in my black pants or not?" The *small y* for the eating process may be the number of calories absorbed in a day and that of the exercising process, the number of calories burned while exercising (which many training machines actually measure). The voice of the customer for each process may then be set as a standard and a tolerance (that is, 1500 calories, +/- 50). Failure to meet the standard on either process has a direct impact on the Big Y. Controlling these processes requires measuring this data, capturing it, analyzing variations, and taking corrective action when required, that is, process control.

An upward drift in the eating process is a frequent phenomenon, leading to stoutness, with the health risks it carries. Upward shifts are also very common, as you suddenly change some eating habit, such as starting to drink a beer or two before dinner or lunching at a fast food restaurant twice a week. A downward drift in the exercising process is also very common, as you start skipping training sessions occasionally, always for a good reason, of course! A common cause, such as excessive workload and the pressure and stress it creates, may be at the root of all these phenomena. Without a good control system, because the positive effect associated with eating more (feeling good) and training less (easier, getting more work done) are immediate and the negative effects on weight and health in general are delayed, many people are easy prey for such phenomena. Unless you are able to detect adverse trends and introduce countermeasures early, correction will have become very hard—often discouragingly so—by the time you feel the need for change.

Thus, variation patterns carry a wealth of valuable information about the underlying phenomena that produce it. To secure the benefits of such information, you must analyze variation carefully, in order to be able to tell apart its various components. This is where statistical analysis comes in. Without it, you are liable to misinterpret the data, seeing a trend where there is none and attributing a significant shift to random variations. This may result in taking actions that will throw off course a stable process or leave a process at the mercy of the forces affecting it. This is discussed further is Section 8.3.5.2.

The temperature and humidity variations discussed in the previous section are overall results of all these variations. To make the matter of controlling variation more complex, these variations are related in complex ways. This makes it harder for Judy to draw the right conclusions from the information she gets. She may still feel excessive humidity an hour after changing the humidifier setting because the sensor is located in a dryer area of the house, because outside temperature (which she does not monitor) went up and sensors have not yet detected the more humid air coming in, or because of the hot coffee pot next to her. If the world would only stand still for a while, she sometimes wished, then she could start changing one variable at a time and find out what happens . . .

Delays between action and response are another factor that often wreaks havoc in process control. Indeed, between the time a discrete event takes place, such as setting the thermostat higher, and its effects on the system unfold and are eventually felt (by Judy) or detected (by her instruments), 30 minutes may go by. If Judy is not aware of that, she will suffer a serious learning disability as a process controller. Most informal control systems (such as controlling your weight or your home environment) do not adequately factor that delay into control decisions. Often, this results in attributing a change in the state of the system to a recent occurrence or corrective action, while it may in fact be the delayed effect of an earlier one. This results in overcorrection (turning the thermostat still higher, even though *the heat is already on its way*) and eventually into overshoot and collapse (also called *boom and bust*) cycles.

Judy's basic problem was her lack of understanding of the factors involved and their interrelations. Not being able to understand causes and effects, she tends to look for immediate, obvious changes that she notices, and thus often draws the wrong conclusion and fails to learn—a common situation for many process owners in organizations.

As you design a process, you must also ensure that it will be controllable. Designing the control system at the same time is the best way to do this. Deciding how to control a process involves making the following decisions:

- What should be measured?

- How will it be measured?

- How often will it be measured?

- How many units will be measured?

- How will the data be analyzed and a decision made if action is warranted?

- Who will decide what action to take, if any?

- Who will carry out the corrective action?

- Who will be responsible to prevent recurrence?

8.3 PROCESS CONTROL IN PROFESSIONAL SERVICES

In this section, an elaborate example of process control in a drugstore, linking strategic, professional, and operational considerations is first presented. Examples started in earlier chapters are then pursued about youth protection services (Midtown CPS, Chapter 5) and consulting services (QKM, Chapter 4), this time from the angle of process control.

8.3.1 Positioning and Operations Strategy at GYD

To transfer the notions discussed above to professional services, the example of a pharmacy specializing in services to an elderly population is used (see Box 8.2). Taking a high-level view of GYD's strategic situation, the drugstore's positioning is illustrated in Figure 8.6, based on the model previously discussed in Figure 5.5. GYD's value proposition is radically different and clearly superior to those of its two competitors for the targeted market segment. The pharmacy services they receive blend seamlessly with their daily routine and integrate well with the clinical services they receive from other professionals.

GYD seduces a targeted professional labor segment of clinically oriented pharmacists by creating a stimulating multidisciplinary service and research environment in geriatrics. Professionals are encouraged to get involved with universities (that is, supervising interns, writing articles) and to spend all the time required with the patients and interacting with other health professionals. Pharmacists are leveraged to the maximum by technicians. They never perform tasks that less-qualified (and less paid) personnel can perform. The pressure for volume, prevalent at competitors, takes second place here to professional excellence and quality of relationship. To prevent boredom, the pharmacists alternate between filling prescriptions, visiting the patients, and preparing sterile products. The job concepts offered to the technicians and clerical workers are not shown.

GYD generates profit leverage in a number of ways. The attraction that the job concept presents for the right pharmacists is such that they are willing to accept a somewhat lower level of remuneration than that offered by the competition. They are also very loyal and the turnover is very low. Using a highly leveraged (that is, high technicians/pharmacist ratio) assembly line to fill prescriptions allows the professional to focus on activities where the most value can be created (for the patient and for self): detecting problems and communicating with the patients and other professionals. Doing so reinforces the loyalty of patients and other health providers, thereby bringing in more business and reducing patient attrition. Since a pharmacist costs three to four times as much as a technician, this is achieved at a lower cost than the competition achieves. This is the operations strategy: it increases patients' benefits and reduces costs at the same time.

A few selected processes are shown in Figure 8.6. Boldface processes are value-adding processes. Shaded processes are enabling processes critical to the delivery of the job concept (value-adding processes also play a very important role here). The quality assurance and scheduling processes are also important enablers, while maintaining a close relationship with the seniors' community is a strategic marketing and defensive process.

Box 8.2: Customer service at Golden Years Drugstore (GYD)

Issue: *Issues in managing a professional service delivery process*

GYD is one of three drugstores in a small community. Shopper's Pharmacy's greatest asset is its convenient location in the community's largest mall. Shoppers typically drop their prescriptions as they arrive at the mall and pick up the drugs as they leave. Customers are willing to pay a little more to avoid waiting. Discount Drug Mart, on the other hand, targets a more price-sensitive market segment. They draw people to their more remote location by offering lower prices on drugs and on a host of dollar items they sell. GYD opened when a large, upper-end seniors' complex was built on the outskirts of town, next to a private long-term care hospital for chronically ill elderly. Ida Smith rents the premises next to the medical clinic, at the entrance of the central service building of the complex. She designed the store with geriatrics in mind from the outset, with plenty of comfortable chairs in which to wait. With an average age of 85, customers are well-off retirees, used to getting first-class personalized service. All employees are trained for general and specialized services to the elderly.

Even though prices are high, very few customers would consider going anywhere else. Indeed, they enjoy the personal relationships they have with the pharmacist and the fact that all the information required is available—because the pharmacist has immediate access to their doctors and nurse—to give them advice that improves their quality of life. Going to the competition would be expensive (taxi), long (they would have to provide much information to a pharmacist who is not familiar with them and their problems), and initially risky (it is so easy to miss a critical interaction between two medications, especially for a generalist pharmacist). Far from giving in to complacency, however, Ida realized that it would be relatively easy for either one of her competitors to open an annex store on the other side of the street and copy many of her practices, should customer discontent to build up.

The basic service process for a new prescription (order fulfillment process) at GYD goes as follows (see Figure 8.6). The customer hands in a prescription to a technician at a reception counter. The technician locates the patient's file in a computer database, checks the identity, enters the new prescription information, prints the vial labels, and places them, together with the prescription itself, in a basket. A second technician takes charge of the basket as soon as available, assembles the required medication, places the medication in appropriate vials, together with the labels and invoice, and then places the basket on another counter. As soon as the pharmacist is available, the basket is picked up and the pharmacist goes to the computer screen to analyze the patient's record. This involves verifying the dosage, medical interactions, and any possible contra-indication. A physical inspection of the medication then takes place (*content-container* inspection) and the pharmacist meets the patient at a consultation counter or in an

Continued

Continued

enclosed office, as required, to give advice on how to take the medication, possible side-effects, and contingency plans. A third technician then takes over from there to process the payment. The processes for renewals and new patients were slightly different.

When the pharmacist detects an interaction or another problem with the prescription, the doctor is called and they resolve the issue together. Other PSDPs at GYD include a roving pharmacist who visits the patients in selected locations, a back-office pharmacist who prepares *sterile* products (such as syringes with palliative drugs for terminally ill patients), and a team of three to five back-office technicians preparing medication organizers for patients, their nurses, or the ward masters, under the supervision of a pharmacist. The pick-up and delivery service is another important non-professional service process.

8.3.2 A Systems View of GYD

Figure 8.7 presents a systems view of the major clinical and service processes, as described summarily in Box 8.1. Figure 8.7 parallels Figure 8.5, with a number of differences. First, the inputs and outputs of the four processes depicted are not shown, for sake of simplicity. For lack of space, the process control box itself is not shown either, but it is very much present, and discussing how it works is a central topic of this section. The reader will also remember that an organization is a system of processes (such as that illustrated by the APQC model in Figure 3.2 or the limited subset shown in Figure 3.4). Processes adjacent to those shown in Figure 8.8, however, are not shown either, to allow focus on feedback and control of a limited subset of processes.

All of the variables shown in Figure 8.7 display variations in one form or another. Pharmacological and medical developments, for instance, may produce shifts and drifts in demand. The sudden withdrawal of a medication (such as Vioxx) from the market, or the publication of the results of an important study (such as that on the relationship between hormone replacement therapy and cardiovascular diseases), either through the effect they have on the patients, the doctors, or both, can produce a sudden jump in affluence. The slow development of an epidemic, on the other hand, or the gradual aging of the customer base, may trigger an upward drift. The introduction of new software may also produce a one-time increase in service time, followed by a downward shift as learning gradually takes place. The arrival of a new employee might have a similar effect. Growing employee fatigue, because of a particularly virulent strain of flu, may produce a steady increase in the number of errors made by technicians. What makes data interpretation even more challenging is that many of these phenomena are liable to occur simultaneously—a situation quite similar to that faced by Judy in the preceding example but much more complex.

8.3.3 Managing the Prescription Fulfillment Process at GYD

So far, various techniques have been used to describe processes: SITOC, FAST diagram, process flow diagrams (PFDs), and process macro-maps. Process mapping is now added to the list. A process map is a detailed description of a process. When you map a process, you are a camera. It requires objectivity and thoroughness. Table 8.5 presents a short description of the various techniques used in this book to represent processes, together with their purpose and use.

Figure 8.8 depicts the basic process for a new prescription at GYD, as described in Box 8.2. Figure 8.9 explains the symbols used for process mapping in Figure 8.8 and for the remainder of the book. Notice that the line of interaction is used to depict face-to-face contact only. Remote contact is depicted as bilateral arrows connecting activities on both sides of the line of visibility.

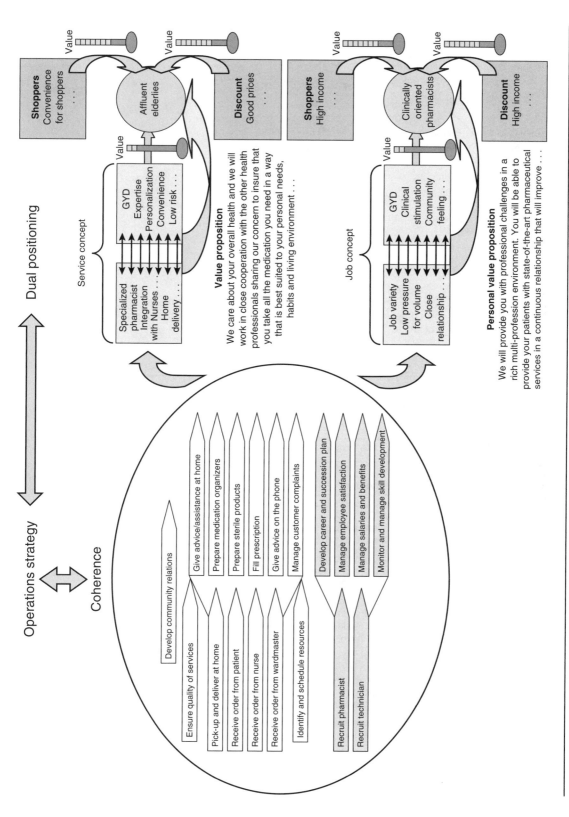

Figure 8.6 The three-way fit between the service concept, the job concept, and processes at GYD.

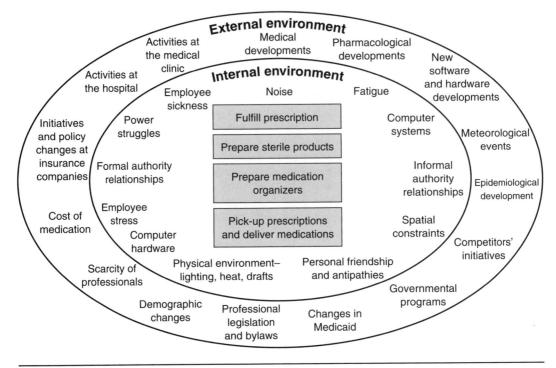

Figure 8.7 A systems view of professional and service delivery processes at GYD.

Table 8.5 Description of major process representation tools, with their purpose and use.

Process tool	Description and use
SITOC	Supplier-Input-Transformation-Output-Customer. A form delimiting the perimeter of a process. The SITOC is generic: it is not a link to a specific way to perform the process. It defines a process and is therefore always the starting point of any discussion regarding a process.
FAST	Functional Analysis System Technique. A functional analysis (generic) identifying the functionalities that the process requires. It is used to analyze an existing process or as a starting point in designing a new one.
PFD	Process Flow Diagram. A generic diagram showing the general flow and sequence of the process, often starting from the functionalities identified in the FAST diagram. It is sometimes used in large processes to get a better understanding of a process than afforded by the FAST diagram.
Process macro-map	A diagram showing at a very high level how an actual (non-generic) process flows. Like a PFD (which is generic) it shows the flow, but adds the swim lanes, i.e. showing how the process actually flows among the various players involved. In complex processes, it helps to have a macro-map to plan the detailed mapping exercise and not lose sight of the forest.
Process map	A detailed representation of an actual process, as is. It is used to document or improve a process.
Process blueprint	A detailed representation of the desired future state of a process (i.e. to be). It is used as a guide in the construction of a new process.

Some comments are required to better understand the diagram. Delays are indicated only when they are likely to affect total cycle time, that is, when they may lie on the critical path. The doctor's and technician one's idle time, for instance, are not specified. The diagram depicts the path of an order and the activities of the customer. The players themselves may be involved in other activities, that is, part of other processes, not shown here. A special symbol is used when customers are waiting in line. A range is included to represent the duration of each element. A mean and standard deviation may be used as well, if the data is available. The *organizational line* separates GYD from its partners and suppliers. Sometimes it is useful to represent the computer, or various computer systems, as players in the process. They are then placed beyond an imaginary *line of automation*. Finally, a layout diagram with dotted arrows may be used to display the flow of things (prescriptions, medications) and the flow of people (employees and customers).

The mission of this process is to conveniently provide targeted patients with the prescribed medication, to give them the advice they need, and to promote compliance with the prescription. Its first priority is avoidance of errors. Building a solid professional relationship, empathy, convenience, and speed (in that order) are its other objectives.

Most of the time, there are two pharmacists on duty (as well as five to seven technicians), and one of them acts as the pharmacist in charge. It is the latter's responsibility to ensure the smooth functioning of all SDPs, in such a way that all service standards are consistently met. The standards set by Ida are as follows (see Figure 8.10):

- Zero defects, insofar as professional errors having a negative health effect (*clinical errors*) were concerned

- No more than three defects per 1000 prescriptions filled, for defects involving time or financial losses (*operational error*)

- An average service time of 20 minutes (prescriptions are fairly complex and some instructions need to be given slowly and repeated several times), but not to exceed 30 minutes for more than 1 percent of all prescriptions

- No more than one defection per month based on dissatisfaction with the service provided

To determine whether the processes are functioning smoothly, the pharmacist in charge gets feedback from a number of indicators (see Figure 8.10):

- The number of people in the waiting room

- The number of baskets waiting for the pharmacist to verify

- The number of red baskets waiting (red baskets are used for patients waiting on site)

- The number of baskets waiting at the cash register

- The number of people waiting at the *in-counter*

- Average service time (as monitored by the computer)

- The stress level among technicians, as manifested by comments made and other observable behavior

- Significant special events, such as discharge from hospital, special requests, and absenteeism

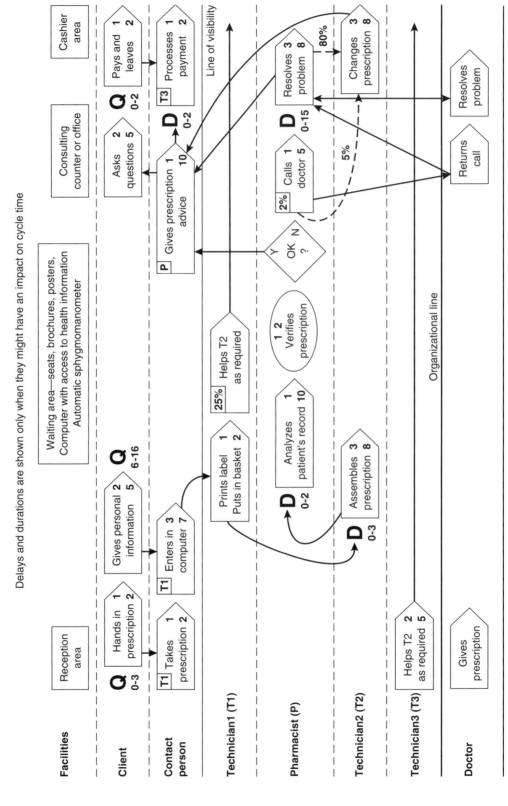

Figure 8.8 Process mapping: Filling a new prescription for an existing customer at Golden Years Drugstore.

 ⟶	One-way flow.
 ⟷	Two-way flows, interaction, back-and-forth.
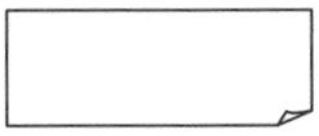 [document symbol]	Document–use sparingly.
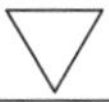 ▽	Storage or filing.
Y / OK ? N / 1 2	Decision. May lead to any number of branching points. The bold numbers indicate a range of duration–i.e. from 1 to 2 minutes. A probability is attached to each outcome.
1 2 ▷	Movement or transportation.
D 0-3	Delay–any time when nothing is happening other than waiting for the next operation. Used only for activities lying (or potentially lying) on the critical path.
T1 Enters in 3 computer 7	Task or activity. When the activity takes place in contact with the customer, the square identifies the player (swim lane) performing the action. A percentage indicates how frequently the task is required.
1 2 Verifies prescription	Inspection, that is, verifying the work done by someone else.
Reception area	Any element of the service delivery system, other than a human being, that comes into contact with the customer.
(A)	Connector. Used to avoid long arrows that would interfere with legibility.
Q 0-3	Customer in queue. This is a special type of delay that has a direct impact on customer satisfaction.

Figure 8.9 *Process mapping symbols used in this book.*

Each pharmacist (professional autonomy) develops trigger points based on various combinations of these indicators. The levers (means to adjust the process) at the disposal of the pharmacist in charge triggered into taking a corrective action include (see Figure 8.10):

- Asking the pharmacist working on sterile products to interrupt work and help bring the process back under control
- Paging Ida herself who is generally available on short notice
- Adding a technician working at some other tasks or trying to reach an off-duty technician
- Starting to use a senior technician to give basic advice to patients, when indicated
- For selected prescriptions, giving the patient what is needed immediately and delivering the rest later

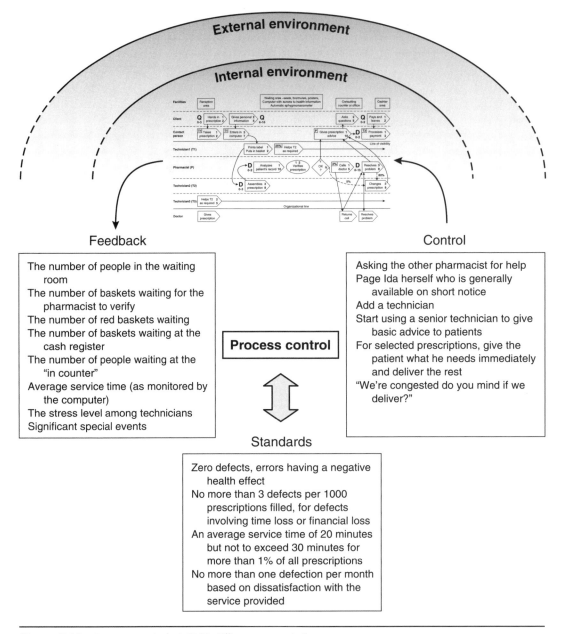

Figure 8.10 Process control at GYD: Filling a prescription.

- Telling technician one to inform incoming patients that wait time is longer than usual and that *we will be happy to deliver*

Figure 8.10 illustrates process control for the *fill prescription* process at GYD, in a fashion similar to Figure 8.5. Contrary to Judy's environment control problem or to simpler service processes, such as that of serving customers in a fast food restaurant, the triggers cannot be programmed (that is, *when there are five customers waiting, open a second cashier position*) and are left to professional judgment. The following questions, for example—all of which affect process control decisions—require professional judgment:

- At what level of pressure or stress does the likelihood of a given pharmacist making a clinical error reach an unacceptable threshold?

- How fast can you really give advice to a patient, without taking the risk of being misunderstood?

- What is the consequence to Mr. Jones if he delays taking his heart medication by two hours (until GYD delivers)?

- How risky is it to ask our senior technician to explain to Mrs. Harper how to take her codeine cough syrup?

- Can I safely give the prescribed medication to Mrs. Stuart, or should I discuss it first with her doctor?

Delays between action and response are omnipresent in this system as well, compounding the challenges involved in process control. Imagine, for instance, that a doctor at the clinic decides to switch from a dermatological ointment available on the shelf to a regulated preparation, and that the practice gradually spreads to other doctors. For each such prescription, a 15-minute mixing time replaces the old serving time of two minutes. As more and more such prescriptions come in, the average service time, and thus customer waiting time, gradually inches upwards. By the time this phenomenon reaches the awareness level of the pharmacists and is traced to the right source, a month or two may have gone by. By the time a solution is found and fully implemented, such as training two technicians to do this and processing these orders in batches every other day, another two to three months (of low service quality and higher tension in the team) may have gone by. A glance at Figure 8.7 should make it clear that such an event would be but one occurrence in a dynamically shifting set of variables.

Your professional judgment is initially formed during training and honed through experience. The employer has little control over it. Even in professions where practices are best codified, professional judgment is subject to considerable variation. This additional source of variations compounds the process control challenges in professional services. As much as Ida tries to standardize the process and decision rules, each pharmacist has a way of doing things, to which the technicians must adjust, as best they can. Ida's professional competence and reputation, more than her organizational status as owner, is her best source of leverage on clinical practices and process control. Thus, she regularly holds clinical meetings to review recent events and explores practice and process improvement.

The process described in Figure 8.8 is a manually-paced assembly line. It has two inventories (excluding customers, who are not *inventoried* as such, but placed in a waiting line—though impatient customers cannot really tell the difference . . .): baskets waiting for inspection by the pharmacist and baskets waiting for payment processing. These inventories fully *uncouple* the pharmacist from the technicians working upstream and downstream. This is important because the former needs to be able to take all the time required to do a professional job. With this setup, when the pharmacist takes more time, inventory builds up upstream. If the pharmacist works fast, inventory builds up downstream. The pharmacist—the scarcest and most expensive resource in the process—is the bottleneck and sets the pace of the line. If it takes the pharmacist three minutes on average to verify a prescription, then the maximum capacity of the line is 20 prescriptions per hour, provided the pharmacist is never idle. Adding more technicians beyond the number required to ensure that the pharmacist is never idle is a waste of resources. An hour gained at the bottleneck has a direct impact on productivity, while an hour gained at a non-bottleneck station only adds to idle time. If the pharmacist detects an imbalance between the two inventories, technicians can be reallocated to correct the situation.

8.3.4 Managing Other Processes at GYD

Controlling the prescription fulfillment process, as described above, is limited to short-term fixes. The *operations planning process* is directed at the mid-term horizon (one to six months, say). Its mission is to determine the resources required to consistently meet service standards and ensure that they are available where and when they are required. Resources include pharmacists, technicians, support personnel, medication, supplies, and so on. It consists of forecasting demand levels and patterns, translating them in resource requirements, exploring resource availability and alternate ways to meet demand, and dispatching resources. The performance of the operations planning process determines the leeway available for short-term control (discussed in the previous section). Through building sufficient safeguards and contingency plans, a good operational plan reduces the risks of imbalances such that short-term process control cannot cope.

Capacity planning is a process taking the long view of capacity needs and solutions. Over the long term (six to 18 months, typically), it is possible to consider capacity strategies that are not available in the short to medium term. This may include changes in computer hardware or software, recruitment and training of new personnel, changes in layout, or the development of new modus operandi with other health professionals (nurses, doctors, dentists, or ward masters) or suppliers. This process is linked upstream to the strategic planning process, which sends it scenarios to explore and test for operational and financial feasibility.

Figure 8.11 presents a hierarchical view of the various layers of process control just described. Higher-level processes in Figure 8.11 span a longer time horizon, and thus have more leeway.

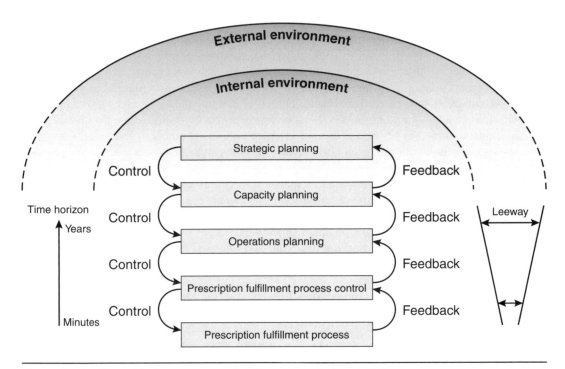

Figure 8.11: Hierarchical process control: Filling a prescription at GYD.

Strategic planning, for instance, may cover a horizon of two to four years. There are very few aspects of the drugstore that Ida cannot consider changing over this period. Once she made her strategic choices, however, these will limit the options remaining for the capacity planning process. Once a long-term lease is signed, for instance, increasing seating capacity in the waiting room may not be an option anymore. In turn, when capacity decisions are made, such as recruiting and training two more technicians, the operations planning process has two more resources to schedule, and so on. Each process in Figure 8.11 feeds useful information about difficulties encountered in functioning within its current operating parameters to the higher-level process, for consideration in the next cycle.

Scheduling pharmacists' vacations and setting store hours belong to the capacity planning process. Preparing pharmacists' weekly work schedules is part of the operations planning process. Yet both of these processes have a strong influence on the pharmacists' job concept. While the customers appreciate long store hours (nights and weekends), they ultimately reduce the pharmacists' quality of life. Pharmacists also like regular schedules, but demand patterns sometimes require shuffling the schedule. GYD's positioning alleviates somewhat this problem, however, compared to the predicament of competitors: elderly people are not stuck with a 9-to-5 work schedule and many of them live in the complex. Thus, evening and weekend hours are not as important to them as they are for other market segments. In managing these trade-offs between the service concept and the job concept, Ida must always bear in mind the risk that a competitor makes to one of her pharmacists *an offer he cannot refuse* to change employers at better conditions. Such a move would greatly facilitate the task of a competitor wanting to take on Ida on her own turf.

This section is continued by discussing various aspects of process management for selected processes within the drugstore.

Feeding the line, that is, ensuring the flow of *things* within the drugstore, is another important process in any assembly line. Any shortage of medication or supplies disrupts the operation and hence has an immediate impact on service time and risks of error. The voice of the customer translates here into standards for the number of shortages, frequency of substitution of medication, or excess inventory. The major challenge involved in that process is that of managing the trade-offs between the cost of shortages and the cost of excess inventory. Indeed, most medications are expensive and have a limited shelf life. They must (imperatively) be discarded past their sell date. Quantity discounts must be factored as well into the reordering policy.

Assuring the quality of pharmaceutical procedures rests primarily with the pharmacist, with a risk of stiff professional sanctions in case of malpractice. The role of the owner in that respect is to create a work environment (including processes, technology, and installations) conducive to clinical quality. In the eye of the customer, however, quality goes beyond that and includes, as previously discussed, such factors as convenience, empathy, and speed. Since many processes have an impact on quality (refer to those shown in Figure 8.6, for instance), the process of assuring quality involves the coordination of the design and operations of these processes so that they perform consistently with GYD's quality standards (such as those shown in Figure 8.10).

Assuring, for instance, that such processes as preparing sterile products, keeping a trace of every procedure to a specific pharmacist, and never exceeding the prescribed maximum ratio of pharmacists to technicians on the premises, are appropriate, understood, implemented, updated, and monitored is part of the quality assurance process. It is particularly challenging for Ida to manage the many interfaces (and the corresponding potential for friction and conflict) between the clinical responsibilities of the pharmacists and her overall responsibility for quality, productivity, and profitability. In the case of over-the-counter (OTC) medication, for instance, (which do not require prescriptions) it is important but difficult for the pharmacist to reach an objective decision to deny a medication to a client because the client is using too much of it. The fact that denying the medication is clearly not in the pharmacy's immediate financial interest may (consciously or not) distort the professional's judgment.

In concluding this section, four more processes are worth mentioning: recruiting, training, posting, and dispatching technicians. Some technical tasks, such as preparing medication, are very repetitive and can be boring for someone who constantly needs new challenges. Boredom leads to lack of focus on the task, which in turn leads to mistakes, disturbances in the assembly line, conflicts, and stress for all involved. Other tasks involve face-to-face contacts, many of them with disabled, sick, or otherwise impaired persons. Unless Ida recruits technicians with the right dispositions, no amount of training or coaching will succeed in avoiding the negative cycle triggered by stress on the part of the technician, generating frustration on the part of the patient, and producing ripple effects all along the assembly line. As much as the pharmacist on duty must be alert and ready to respond to shifts and drifts in the process, the pharmacist (and the general manager) must be alert to the level of stress of the technicians, and ready to respond by bringing in reinforcements, switching technicians around, or taking other appropriate measures. If competitors were indeed on the lookout to win over a pharmacist, they would like nothing better than to bring one or two disgruntled technicians along.

The foregoing discussion illustrates the notion, introduced in Chapter 3, that an organization is a complex web of interconnected and interacting processes. Light but effective feedback and control loops are needed to make these processes, and thus the organization, manageable. Constant awareness of GYD's dual positioning in the market and in the labor market, of GYD's own and competitors' strengths and weaknesses, and of operations strategy, is essential to make the right trade-offs. Without this ability to translate global thinking into coherent local action, operations is at best strategically neutral and can never be the strategic weapon that it should be.

8.3.5 Managing the Intake Process in Youth Protection

At GYD, a single professional controls a process where all other players are technicians. In many PSOs, however, several professionals, often from different disciplines, interact with one another. Midtown CPS, discussed in Chapter 5, is a case in point. The case in general and the intake process in particular are first revisited, and then focus moves to how statistical process control (SPC) could be used in that context.

8.3.5.1 Understanding the Dynamics of the Process

Figure 8.12 shows a high-level representation of the intake process for youth protection, of which Midtown CPS (Box 5.2) assumes the front-end. A macro-map of that process would show that there are many players involved, belonging to several different organizations, including Midtown report reception department (described in Box 5.2), Midtown evaluation department, the police department, reception centers, juvenile court, Midtown legal department, and lawyers for the various parties. The process is similar to that shown in Figure 4.1, presenting a generic professional dispatch process. It consists of a series of filters involving various categories of professionals, making diagnostic, orientation, and therapeutic decisions. A social worker typically receives the call (as described in Box 5.2). After validating, completing, and assessing the information (*receiving* for short), the social worker may send an emergency team (or the police), refer it to colleagues for detailed evaluation the next day, or decide that no further action is required. The emergency team may resolve the immediate crisis and refer the child for further evaluation, or they may have to go to court in the next 48 hours, should they decide to remove the child from the home. Taking the children in charge may be consensual, or may again involve the court.

Whilst receiving involves only two to three hours of work, detailed evaluation requires about five days work (typically spread over a 30-day period). Going to court involves about the same amount of time for the social worker, plus another five days for a lawyer. Children taken in charge

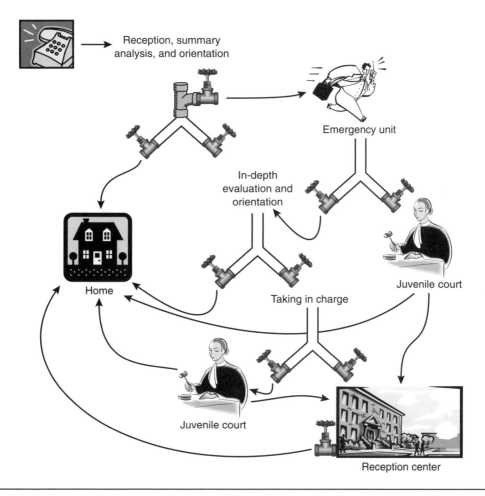

Figure 8.12 Simplified view of intake process (dispatch process) at Midtown CPS.

by the system may require years of assistance and are a huge drain on its resources. Since the number of children the reception center can deal with at any point in time is limited, its *throughput* depends on the rate at which it can reintegrate them in their family or in the community (foster family or relatives). The mission of the intake process at Midtown CPS is to allocate available protection resources between needy children, through its orientation decisions, to ensure that each of them gets the best possible short- and long-term protection possible. Accuracy (sound professional judgment), consistency (always using the same criteria, in the same way), and speed of decision are the priorities of that process. As Sam Alonzo at Midtown CPS is in the process of making a decision about the report he just received, he is mentally comparing available data to process standards (accepted guidelines and standards): "Did I probe enough to get all the information I could from the caller, such as a history of problems, current state of the children, and options available? In such a case, should I try to check with at least another source before making a decision? Have I explored all the possibilities?" What Sam is doing is referred to as *within cycle* process control. It can be performed either by process workers themselves or by a process manager.

Controlling this process is quite a challenge from several perspectives. Even though all players agree that the interest of the child is foremost in all decisions, the specific nature of that interest and of the best decision you can make to promote it, are the subject of much debate. The practitioners can make two basic errors:

> Type 1 error: Intervene in a situation that does not require it, that is, the child is not at risk

> Type 2 error: Decide not to intervene in a situation where the child is really at risk

Understandably, when in doubt, practitioners tend to err on the safe side. This is a major fail point in the process. This type of defensive practice is self-defeating. Because the system is resource-bound, an excessively liberal reception process (a wide-tipped filter) means that the downstream process will become congested, resulting in waiting lines, more cursory interventions, or both. If the receiving practitioner, for instance, does not exert critical professional judgment to the fullest, the reception process fails in its contribution to the mission and becomes redundant. It would be better to do away with the process and replace it with a mere answering service that would pass all the call on directly to an evaluator (*in-depth evaluation and orientation* in Figure 8.12).

The valves in Figure 8.12 represent some of the control points in that process. Tightening or loosening the orientation criteria at various decision points regulates the flows through the process. The pipeline metaphor ends there, however, as this is obviously much more complex than turning a knob, and the personal consequences on the child and family can be dramatic, traumatic, and life changing. Merely sending the signal to receiving professionals that the emergency team is overloaded does not guarantee results. Senior professionals are individually *calibrated* through their training and experience. They are very conscious of the professional and personal risks they are taking by turning down a concerned citizen's request to help a child they believe to be in need of protection. Extensive coaching and support are needed to help practitioners develop risk management strategies, such as asking a relative to take in the child for the night. Adding resources at bottleneck points is an alternative, but even if such resources are available, they may end up merely deferring the problem to the next process (evaluation or taking in charge). Substantial delays may also be involved in implementing any step the manager may select. Thus, by the time the solution comes online, it may be a response to yesterday's problem and only contribute to making today's problem worse.

8.3.5.2 Controlling and Improving the Process

The process manager must use data to assess how well the process is functioning and to decide on control measures. If the social emergency center handles an average of 100 reports a weeks, say, the manager will want to monitor such indicators as how many times children are removed from their homes, how many times police are called in, or how long it takes before any action is taken. The manager will also check with downstream processes, such as those of the reception center or the police department, to see if they have noticed any significant change, trend, or pattern in the inputs that they have been receiving (their inputs, such as a child to take in for the night or instructions to investigate a report, are the output of the social emergency process). However, what constitutes a significant shift or drift in the process? Is an increase from eight to 10 percent of calls necessitating police intervention *significant*? Is the *feeling* of the specialized educator at the reception center that they are increasingly dealing with *heavy* cases significant? A wrong answer to these questions can be very disruptive.

Concluding that practitioners are increasingly turning to police for support may lead the process manager to take action to bring back the drifting process to a stable state, assuming that it was stable in the first place. Such action may include training or the obligation to obtain the approval of a senior practitioner before calling the police. If that conclusion was unwarranted (that is, based on a misinterpretation of the data which really showed only a random increase that did not reflect any fundamental change in the process (then the corrective action taken may create instability in a process that was stable. The Hippocratic precept *first do no harm* applies very well to process controllers. Interpreting variations in the light of their statistical as well as their practical significance thus becomes essential to avoid being unduly swayed by the emotions and the pressure of the moment.

To illustrate how variation data can be used in this context, focus on the time that elapses between the moment a call is received by the receptionist and the moment a practitioner returns the call (henceforth: *response time*). Protecting is about reducing risks. Low risk is critical to customer satisfaction (CTS). Response time is a technical characteristic of the process that correlates directly with risk to the child. Indeed, this initial wait time may be a period of dire vulnerability for a child. Assume that following the reception of several complaints, refuted by the practitioners, the process manager decides to go to the bottom of the issue. The manager first explores the possibility of measuring response time. Since no measurement system is in place, and there is no possibility to automate it in the near future (budget constraints), measurement would have to be manual. Practitioners perceive the request for measurement as an effort on the part of management to control their professional practice, and they resist it. In addition, since they are unionized, they resist the pressure to work harder. A compromise solution is reached whereby one practitioner will randomly (warning bell on the computer) measure the response time to one call a day.

The manager plots the data gathered on a chart (see the first 50 data points in Figure 8.13). Then the mean (light broken line) and the control limits (UCL, LCL—bold broken line) are calculated, drawing them at 3σ on either side of the observed mean (while setting the minimum at zero, however), and plotted on the graph. Since one observation lies beyond the control limits, a conclusion is reached that the process is out of control. A pattern is also noticed in the data: every seven days (on Sundays) the response time jumps markedly, only to fall back the next day. The one point that is out of control is also a Sunday. As it turns out, that was Easter Sunday.

Concluding that the process is out of control means that a special cause (or special causes) is at work, influencing the performance of the process and throwing it off its normal performance.

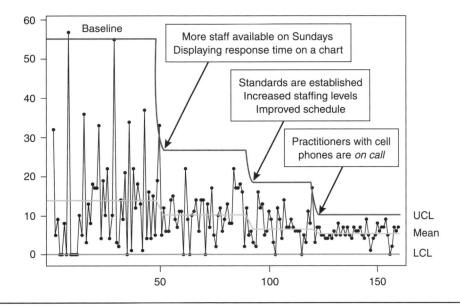

Figure 8.13 Statistical process control chart for response time at Midtown CPS.

Normal process variation is caused by the joint action of a host of random variables (general causes). Concluding that the process is in control (or stable) means that the process is performing normally (not necessarily to your satisfaction, but as well as it normally does), that is, it does not need fixing, and it should be left alone, unless an improvement drive is under consideration (see Chapter 10). Thus, the manager finds objective support for the decision to correct the process. Statistics tells us that the odds of making a type I error is very low (probably less than one in a thousand in this case), having observed two phenomena that would be very unlikely to occur in a process under control.

While a detailed discussion of process improvement is deferred to Chapter 10, assume that the manager concludes that the department is understaffed on Sundays and overstaffed on Mondays. In a staff meeting, new scheduling rules are announced and arrangements are made for the daily response time to be posted on a chart the next day, for everyone to see. You can see the effect of these changes in Figure 8.13 (data points 50 to 90). Variation is reduced considerably, as illustrated by a tighter *voice of the process* (the range between UCL and LCL), and the mean response time reduced by three minutes (see the red line) to ten minutes. At the end of this period, the manager sets (after long discussions with all stakeholders) the following service standards (there were none before): no call should have to wait more than 30 minutes for a response, and the average service time on any day should not exceed 20 minutes. To meet these new standards, staffing levels are increased, and further refinements are made to the scheduling system. Data points 90 to 120 show the effect of these new corrective measures. The last data points (120-150) show what happens when a new system is set up whereby additional practitioners are equipped with cell phones and asked to be *on call* (with compensation) during selected *time buckets* during the week. Appendix 8.1 provides more specific instructions about building and using statistical process control (SPC) charts.

The process manager must finally take into consideration a number of vulnerabilities and fail points of the process:

- The receiving job is very stressful, very much like that of the doctor in the emergency room. Whereas the latter can rely on some objective data, the former is always threading in shades of gray, interpreting words, tones of voices, and silences from an unknown interlocutor. Managers must be very careful in any attempt to manipulate the intake *valve* not to place additional pressure on the practitioners. It is very important to the job concept that they continually feel supported rather than blamed by management when problems occur.

- Like in any profession, there are different philosophies regarding when a withdrawal of children from the home is indicated. One school of thought, for instance, suggest that a family crisis is an opportunity, as long as the intervention is quick thereafter, to understand and resolve problems in dysfunctional families, and that withdrawal at that time may create a chasm that will be very hard, long, and costly to bridge. Social workers try to improve the social dynamics within the family. Special education teachers try to help dysfunctional children (and sometimes families) to structure their lives and relearn basic personal, family, and social skills. While the two aforementioned professions are trained to help people, criminologists are clearly oriented toward crime prevention and protection within a legal context. The intake *assembly line* is quite likely to have a criminologist making a decision to withdraw a child from the home and transferred to a social worker for evaluation, who may transfer the child in turn to a special education teacher in a reception center. Since smooth transitions and continuity of interventions are important determinants of success, managing these interfaces, resolving conflicts, and fostering the emergence of a common intervention philosophy are critical roles of the process manager.

- The legal system responds to a completely different logic than the therapeutic and assistance system described above. Society, the child protection service, the reception center, the parents, and the children are parties, represented by lawyers, with rights and obligations under the law. The social workers, medical doctors, psychiatrists, and psychologists are expert witnesses to be cross-examined by lawyers. The judge is a referee whose decisions are enforceable. The reaction of the helping professional when immersed in that system is rather like that of magnesium in water. The consequences for the children, the parents, and the establishment of a productive relationship with the caregivers are very important. Thus, of all the interfaces and fail points to manage, deciding when to go to court and how to do it is a critical one.

To bridge the gaps between the different steps in the process and between the various professions, team-based approaches are very useful. A multi-stage, multi-profession process team, for instance, including a senior representative from each stage in the process, coordinated by the process manager, can address short- and medium-term process issues and determine the scope of process improvement initiatives. Personalized transfers between process stages, particularly between evaluation and taking in charge, can also be established to ensure a smooth transition. The joint preparation by all involved (during the evaluation stage) of an individualized service plan for the child plays a similar role.

8.3.6 A Job Shop—Capacity Management at QKM

The challenges involved in managing capacity at QKM (refer to Figures 4.2 and 4.3) are quite different, mainly because QKM is a job shop, and not an assembly line like GYD above, or a flow shop (that is, a process involving several paths always flowing in the same direction), like Midtown. A job shop is characterized by jumbled flows. If you were to map the *sell and provide services* process at QKM, using the consultants as players, you would see that depending on the job at hand, consultants may be called upon at different points in the proposal or in the execution phase, and that the extent of their involvement would vary considerably from one job to the next. In addition, different consultants can perform the same work, albeit not necessarily with the same quality or within the same timeframe. Thus, depending on uncontrollable arrivals of request for proposals (RFP) with different scopes and schedules, on the (controllable) way proposals are written, on the (partly controllable) success rate, and on the (partly controllable) rate of progress of the jobs, bottlenecks will appear and move around in complex and unpredictable ways.

Bottlenecks involve delays in the work and quality problems (with the customer complaints that these entail). These create stress on the resources at the bottleneck and slack for the other resources waiting downstream. In other words, bottlenecks are bad for business. The responsibility for managing capacity falls on the managing partner. A FAST diagram of that process would typically include the following functions:

- Determine current capacity utilization and identify bottlenecks

- Forecast future demand (by type of resources)

- Forecast future capacity available (by type of resources)

- Identify imbalances and potential bottlenecks

- Explore options to correct the situation

- Negotiate solutions with all involved (partners, managers, consultants, and clients)

- Implement and follow up

Typical actions that the partner can take include:

- Negotiate with clients to accept a delay or a substitute resource (if available)

- Speed-up some contracts by adding resources

- Change the criteria used to make bidding decisions (go—no go, resources involved, mark-up applied)

- Hire sub-contractors (such as free-lance consultants or selected *cooperators*)

- Slow down the pace of work, even if client objects

- Advertise, contact old customers, organize free seminars, and find new ways to drum-up new business

- Hire additional consultants (longer term) or lay off employees, temporarily or permanently

- Find ways to increase productivity (longer term)

Supplemental Exercise 8.1 discusses how the managing partner could go about using SPC to control the process.

8.4 SUMMARY

Variation is the enemy of value, but the friend of those who want to improve the process. In the measurement and analysis of variation lies the key to decoding the dynamics of a process (the DNA of the process), and thus to identifying its fail points and its leverage points. Variation analysis is the key to process learning, and hence to organizational learning. Whoever wants to control a process must understand it from a strategic perspective and understand the external and internal environments in which it evolves. By making the process visible, detailed process mapping is an important tool that helps in the identification of the underlying variables.

A control system receives feedback on the important performance variables of the process, compares the values obtained to carefully set standards, decides whether corrective action is required, selects appropriate actions, implements them, and monitors results, thus triggering new control cycles as required. In professional services, the professional must be a part of the control system. The process managers must pay particular attention to the autonomy of the professionals and to the interfaces between professionals, between professionals and technicians, and between professionals and management.

SPC bring the science of statistics to bear on the analysis of variation and on the decision to intervene or not. It consists of control charts that make variation visible and decision rules to facilitate and make more objective the decision about whether or not a special cause of variation is at work.

EXERCISES

8.1 Systems view of your business

Refer to the work you did in end-of-chapter exercises in Chapter 6, and particularly to the five projects for which you formulated a mission statement in Exercise 6.5. Prepare a systems view of these processes (similar to that shown in Figure 8.7), specifying the major variables that influence these processes in the internal and external environments.

8.2 Mapping

Prepare a detailed process mapping of one of the processes discussed in Exercise 8.1 above (see Figure 8.8 for an illustration). Use the symbols presented in Figure 8.9. You may select a process for which you have already prepared a PFD and macro-map in earlier exercises. If you select another process, you will find it useful to prepare these diagrams before mapping the process. The best way to do this is to assemble a team of process workers and to use sticky notes on a flip chart. Physically taking a walk along the process path can be a useful preparation for this exercise.

8.3 Control system

a) Identify potential feedback variables, standards, and potential corrective action that you could take to control the process mapped in Exercise 8.2 above. Refer to Figure 8.10 for an example.

b) Interview the manager or managers who act as process manager for that process. Ask them first how they manage the process. Then show them the diagram you prepared in Exercise 8.3a and discuss the differences (a series of directed *why* and *why not* follow-up questions generally yield useful insight into ways to improve process control).

8.4 Statistical process control

a) Review your answers to Exercise 8.3 above and select a metric (pick a continuous variable, such as elapsed time or cost) from the feedback variables which you feel is particularly important and has not been used (at least not systematically) so far. Review the measurement system used for that variable. If it is inappropriate or if none exists, design and implement one. Gather at least 30 data points, either using historical data (if valid data is available), measuring the next 30 units or designing a convenient sampling system.

b) Build a control chart for that process, such as that shown in Figure 8.14 (UCL and LCL, USL and LSL—either one or both, as required), following the procedure described in Supplemental Exercise 8.1 and Figure 8.14.

c) Apply the four decision rules presented in Appendix 8.1 and Figure 8.15. Draw your conclusions. Share the chart and your conclusion with managers involved in the process and, if appropriate considering the work environment and climate, with the employees.

d) Use this control chart to control the process over a significant period (this may vary depending on the cycle time and the volume), marking the dots on the chart, and interpreting the results. Whenever you conclude that the process is out of control, investigate to find the special cause at work. See if you can bring (or keep) the process under control.

e) Set a standard for that metric and draw the line (or lines) in the control chart (such as the yellow dotted line in Figure 8.14. Draw your conclusions on process capability.

8.5 Professional considerations in process control

a) Review your answer to Exercises 8.3 and 8.4, as well as your answer to Exercise 4.7, dealing with fault lines in your PSDPs, and Exercise 2.6, dealing with your job

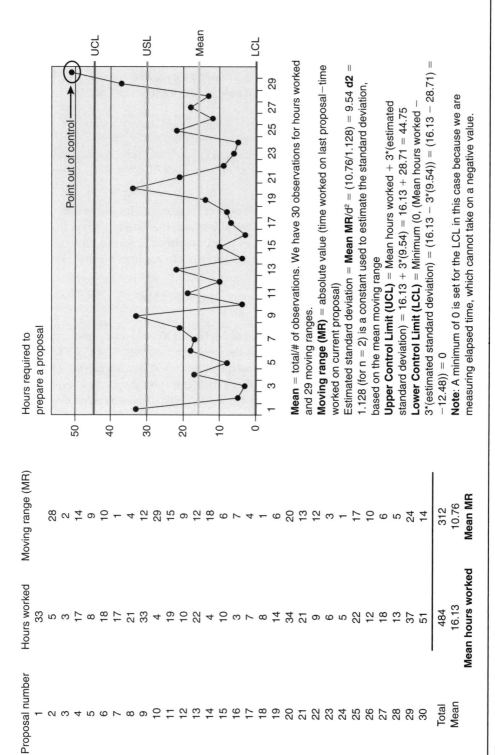

Proposal number	Hours worked	Moving range (MR)
1	33	
2	5	28
3	3	2
4	17	14
5	8	9
6	18	10
7	17	1
8	21	4
9	33	12
10	4	29
11	19	15
12	10	9
13	22	12
14	4	18
15	10	6
16	3	7
17	7	4
18	8	1
19	14	6
20	34	20
21	21	13
22	9	12
23	6	3
24	5	1
25	22	17
26	12	10
27	18	6
28	13	5
29	37	24
30	51	14
Total	484	312
Mean	16.13	10.76
	Mean hours worked	**Mean MR**

Mean = total/# of observations. We have 30 observations for hours worked and 29 moving ranges.

Moving range (MR) = absolute value (time worked on last proposal – time worked on current proposal)

Estimated standard deviation = **Mean MR**/d^2 = (10.76/1.128) = 9.54 **d2** = 1.128 (for n = 2) is a constant used to estimate the standard deviation, based on the mean moving range

Upper Control Limit (UCL) = Mean hours worked + 3*(estimated standard deviation) = 16.13 + 3*(9.54) = 16.13 + 28.71 = 44.75

Lower Control Limit (LCL) = Minimum (0, (Mean hours worked – 3*(estimated standard deviation) = (16.13 – 3*(9.54)) = (16.13 – 28.71) = –12.48)) = 0

Note: A minimum of 0 is set for the LCL in this case because we are measuring elapsed time, which cannot take on a negative value.

Figure 8.14 Statistical process control chart at QKM: Time required to prepare a proposal.

concept. Identify legitimate sources of concern that arise as you try to implement this type of process control in the organization. Make sure you separate the issues that relate to the relationships between various groups of professionals and technicians from those that relate to management-employee relationships.

b) Explore strategies to circumvent these problems, such as team-based approaches, peer groups, and auto control.

SUPPLEMENTAL EXERCISE 8.1: PREPARING AN "I" CHART

To build a control chart, first use an initial dataset as baseline. In Figure 8.13, for instance, 50 data points were used for that purpose. Suppose that QKM decides to start controlling the process of preparing a proposal, and more precisely its productivity. Since all personnel turn in a timesheet every week, the managing partner sets up a procedure whereby an account number is assigned to each proposal and the time spent on a proposal is automatically calculated when the proposal is closed (that is, the client accepts or rejects it). The partner decides to build a control chart to analyze the time required for each proposal. Figure 8.14 illustrates how to go about it.

The chart shown in Figure 8.14 is an *I* chart (I stands for Individual observations), and is normally part of a so-called *I-MR* control chart tandem (the MR control chart will not be discussed here). The hours worked on the last 30 proposals are displayed in Figure 8.14. After calculating the moving ranges, the partner computes the mean for both variables. The mean hours worked becomes the center of the chart. The standard deviation used in setting the control limits is estimated based on the mean moving range, using a correction factor, as shown. The UCL is plotted at three standard deviations above the mean, and the LCL at zero, because the calculated value is negative, and thus meaningless when you are dealing with time.

A number of decision rules can be used to interpret a control chart. It is concluded that the process is out of control, that is, that special causes are at work, if any of the four conditions apply:

- Rule 1—there are points (or a single point) lying outside control limits

- Rule 2—a consecutive series of seven points all lying above or below the mean (process shift is likely), or all moving in the same direction (trend, suggesting process drift)

- Rule 3—any unusual pattern in the data, such as a cyclical pattern or systematic alternation above and below the mean

- Rule 4—the proportion of all points lying within a one standard deviation range above and below the mean differs markedly from 2/3 (suggesting a change in the dispersion of the data)

Figure 8.15 illustrates all four rules, using material prepared by the United Kingdom's National Health Service Institute for Innovation and Improvement. Rule 1 applies to the proposal preparation process, meaning that the process is not under control. Thus, further investigation of the last proposal is likely to yield useful information about the variables that affect the time required to prepare a proposal. Even if the process was in control, it does not mean that its performance is found acceptable. For instance, imagine that the partner feels that spending more than 30 hours on any proposal is unacceptable, then 20 percent of the proposals do not meet this standard (that is, fall above the upper specification limit [USL]) in Figure 8.15.

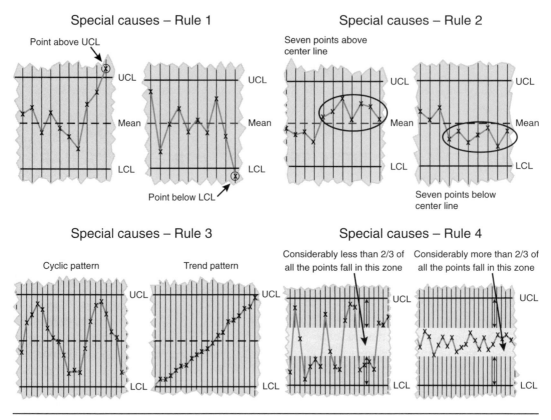

Figure 8.15 Illustration of the use of SPC chart to decide on the presence of *special causes:* four decision rules.

Source: NHS Institute for Innovation and Improvement—Posted on the web February 17, 2005.

If the process was in control (not the case here), the partner would conclude that even though the process is functioning normally, its current performance is unacceptable from a normative standpoint. Then an improvement initiative would be set up (as discussed in Chapter 10) or a new process designed from scratch (as discussed in Chapter 11). Referring to Figure 4.3, which presents a macro-map of the process, a typical improvement would be to include early in the process a *go— no go* decision to avoid wasting time on proposals that do not meet an *a priori* set of criteria, and setting a specific time limit (as opposed to a unique standard) to spend on each proposal.

There are many different types of control charts, including (for variables) mean and range, and mean and standard deviation, as well as control chart for attributes, including charts for proportions (p-chart), number of non-conforming items (np-chart), number of nonconformities (c-chart), and number of nonconformities per unit (u-chart). These are discussed in detail in Mitra (Mitra, 1998), for instance. For a general introduction to analysis of variation and SPC, see Wheeler (Wheeler, 2000). MINITAB is probably the best software available to perform the kind of computations discussed here.

Notes

[1] (45-40)/6=5/6=.83. Reading at 0,8 in Table 8.3, .2118554 or .212 is found. It is concluded that the probability associated with the range (40-45) is .288 (.5-.212), since the curve is symmetrical, and thus that the area associated with the range (35,45) is twice that value, or .576.

9

The Learning Cycle[1]

The learning pump lies at the heart of the learning organization. It is often difficult to decide which methodology, tools, and change vehicle to use to make the most out of every improvement opportunity. The impact of mismatches can be fatal to a fledgling improvement program. A framework is presented to reduce this risk.

As previously mentioned, (Sections 1.3, 3.4, and 5.3) organizational learning is vital to long-term competitiveness. At the core of this capability lies the learning cycle, which is referred to as *the leaning pump* in Figures 1.4 and 5.10. In this chapter, how the cycle works is explained. It requires a good understanding of the nature of processes (Chapters 1, 3, and 8), of the linkages between strategy and processes (Chapters 2, 4, 5, and 6) and of the cycle anchorage point: project scoping (Chapter 7). After giving an overview, each of the four phases of the cycle is presented in turn: process problems, change vehicles, methodologies, and tools. The chapter concludes on the challenges involved in good matchmaking among these elements.

9.1 THE LEARNING CYCLE: MOVING PROCESSES

Processes are at the core of continuous improvement, and improvement is always the result of a process being changed in one way or another. From Kaizen events and just-in-time manufacturing, invented in Japan, to Six Sigma projects and reengineering, invented in the United States, philosophies, methodologies, and tools have been developed to make processes more effective and more efficient. These management innovations have originated mostly from management practice, with academics coming in later to interpret and clarify the recipes such innovations embody (Spear and Bowen, 1999).

Unfortunately, the abundance of great recipes has created confusion. The *chefs* are prone to promoting their own recipes as the panacea. Since these recipes always involve a considerable investment in time and resources by the organization, picking the wrong one may be very costly. Top management's strong endorsement is always a critical factor in the success of these programs because they involve a change of culture, so backing down and recognizing a mistake, when one is made, is very difficult. Thus, failures are merely glossed over and lessons are not learned. This contributes to employee cynicism, which makes it even more difficult to introduce another program at a later date. Yet, failure does not appear to be the exception (Brown, Hitchcock, et al., 1994).

If the history of management thought teaches anything, it is that there is no panacea. Most improvement approaches that have gained a foothold in management practice are valuable in some circumstances and fail miserably in others. The problem lies in the fact that these circumstances are poorly understood. The purpose of this chapter is to propose a framework that organizations can use to guide them in the selection of the right methodology, tools and change vehicle for the problem at hand.

The following analogy illustrates the nature of process improvement: Say that Jack Jones has to move some belongings from his home on the west coast to his condominium on the east coast. To do so effectively, he has to ask himself four specific questions (see Figure 9.1): What is it exactly that has to be moved (the problem)? What are the major steps I will have to take to move the material (the methodology)? What tools will I need (the toolkit)? What type of vehicle will I need (the vehicle)?

Any organization that wants to improve a process must ask itself these same four questions. It needs to identify the type of process improvement problem it is facing. Next, the organization needs to look at available process change methodologies and process improvement tools. It finally needs to take a look at the different process change vehicles available. Only then will it be able to effectively and efficiently undergo process improvement.

9.2 PROCESS PROBLEMS

Process improvement opportunities are as varied as management itself. Most business problems (and opportunities) are bound to be rooted in processes and can only be solved by changing some process or other. Figure 9.2 presents a typology of process problems and opportunities[2], organized along a tree structure (see Table 9.1 for definitions).

A first category of opportunities stems from the introduction of *new products* (1a) and *new services* (1b). While this may involve modifying existing processes, it generally involves the design of processes that do not exist. For example, when McDonald's decided to add pizza to its product offerings, a whole range of new processes had to be designed. Such processes should be designed from the outside in; that is, first define customer requirements, then specify what is expected of the process, and, finally, design a process to meet the specifications. It is very challenging conceptually to start with a customer need—which is often intangible and hard to fathom—and finish with working processes.

Processes that simply do not exist (2) belong to another category. They do not exist in the sense that, even though somehow actions are performed, there is no systematic way of performing them. Take risk management as an example. When asked what they do to manage project risk, many organizations will—after a while—list a number of activities which they perform in this regard, such as listing project risks, discussing risk issues at meetings, and taking action to mitigate a risk as the anxiety level rises. Few, however, will be able to show a systematic process which has been designed with the end in mind, which is in current use, and whose performance is systematically monitored with a view to detecting slippage and identifying opportunities for improvement. The first need here is for the organization to recognize that this is a process and that investing time and resources in doing it right is worthwhile. The process should then be designed using an *outside-in* approach, as suggested above. The conceptual challenge—the ability to handle and correlate abstract notions with practical aspects of organization of work—is just as important for the change process as it is for new products and services.

Many processes are ineffective (3), that is, they do not produce the desired results for the (internal or external) customer. This manifests itself through customer dissatisfaction, defects, low throughput, reworks, and a high cost of quality control. Security inspection processes at airports—

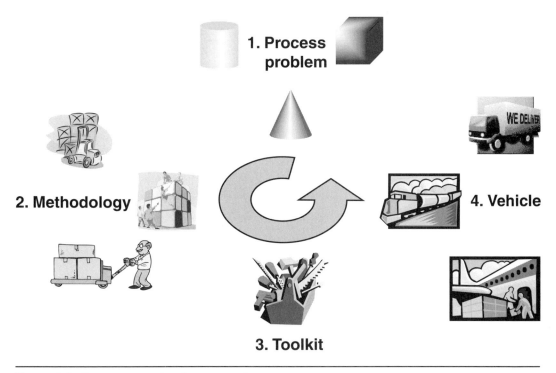

Figure 9.1 Four steps to planning process improvement.

as is now well known—have been ineffective, as was the punch-card voting process in Florida during the 2000 presidential elections mentioned in Chapter 1. Fixing these processes may not be quite as challenging conceptually as categories (1) and (2) above, because a process is already in place. However, using the existing process as a starting point may not lead to the best solution.

Inefficient processes (4) are in a category of their own (see the discussion of process characteristics in Section 5.2.1). They deliver the goods, but long delays and excessively high costs are involved. In other words, these processes generate waste (of time and of money). For example, some organizations have very inefficient processes for controlling office stationery. When you need a writing pad and a couple of pencils, you go to the clerk in charge. If the clerk happens to be absent, then you have to come back later. When they finally connect, the clerk interrupts whatever is being worked on, gets the key to the stationery locker and checks to see whether the items are available. If not, out comes a requisition form . . . "There has to be a better way," is what typically comes to the mind of any outside observer of such a process. Here, the organization has an opportunity to increase profit margins and to free up resources for other tasks. At a deeper level, there is also an opportunity to eliminate employee cynicism about their jobs and about the organization that employs them. The process is easy to fix, through identifying activities that add little or no value and finding ways to eliminate them. Benefits are immediate and easy to measure.

Complex processes (5) are a separate class of the ineffective processes described above. The complexity stems from the number of variables involved and their interaction. Whereas improvement opportunities for inefficient processes are quickly made obvious by a structured process analysis, complex processes will not respond to such an analysis. Many machining processes will fall into that category, with variables such as pressure, heat, feed speed, and thickness of material

Table 9.1 Short definitions of problems, methodologies, tools, and vehicles.

Definitions	
Process problems	
1a. New product	Designing a new car.
1b. New service	Designing a new vacation package.
2. Inexistent process	Disjointed activities performed in a haphazard manner.
3. Ineffective process	Process does not meet customer requirements.
4. Inefficient process	Requirements are met, but process is wasteful.
5. The complex process	Results depend on the simultaneous action of a number of intricately related variables.
6. Black box process	Results are produced, but we really don't know how.
7. Physical flow problems	Flow of people, parts or forms produces congestion, shortages, damage or other waste.
Methodologies	
DFSS	Design for Six Sigma. Start with the end in mind. Know the capabilities of your processes up front. Think statistically. Products.
DMADV	Same as above, adapted for services and processes.
DMAIC	Six Sigma's trademark improvement methodology. Demings' wheel, next generation.
JIT/Lean manufacturing	Simplicity, frugality, and economy in controlling physical flows from raw material to end-use.
Improvement tools	
FMEA	Failure Mode and Effect Analysis. Identifies and prioritizes process risks.
VAA	Value added analysis. Identifies activities that do not contribute to the desired end-result.
Poka-Yoke	Failsafing. Simple devices that avoid defects.
Kanban	Visual card system to control physical flows.
SPC	Statistical process control. Using statistics and charts to interpret variations and keep a process within control parameters.
QFD	Quality functions deployment. Matrix driven correlation technique used to deploy desired results onto metrics and processes.
FAST	Functional analysis system technique. Identifies functions that a product or process must perform.
Change vehicles	
1a. Project	Small part-time assembled around a full-time expert. 2-6 months.
1b. Basic tool project	Same, but does not use advanced statistical tools.
2. Kaizen event	One or more full time teams, fully empowered to transform a process. 1-2 weeks.
3. Workout	Broader and less rigourous effort to bust bureaucracy. 2-3 days.
4. Process management team	Managers assembled around a process owner to design process. Mid-long term.
5. Semi-autonomous work team	Process workers organizing to control a process on a day-to-day basis. Ongoing.
6. Just do it	Team involved in implementing a process change. 2-6 months.

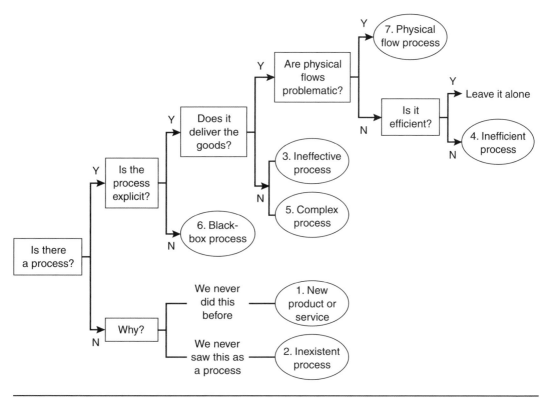

Figure 9.2 Typology of process problems.

interacting in complex ways. There are also complex aspects to professional services processes. A pharmacist evaluating the possible negative interactions in a cocktail of medications prescribed to a specific patient, given the complexities of a human being with a unique medical history, is faced with the same type of problem. Because of this complexity, a very small process must be scoped for improvement—as illustrated by these two examples—lest the number of variables and interactions grows exponentially and the problem becomes intractable. Thus, the involvement of many departments, with the resulting jurisdictional conflicts that this potentially entails, may not be a problem in many cases. Further, the complexity is such that the use of advanced tools (that is, statistical tools such as regression analysis or designed experiments) will be required to solve the problem.

Black-box processes (6) can be effective and efficient—for now—but management would be hard pressed to spell out how and why they work. This situation corresponds to the initial stage (or level 1) in the Capability Maturity Model (Paulk and Chrissis, 1995). Motivated, dedicated employees can make things work in spite of *official* processes. Such organizational know-how, however, usually rests with but a few individuals—none of whom will have a holistic, explicit understanding of the process, and the process can thus be fragile. Further, this know-how cannot evolve to meet changing circumstances, as it is strictly implicit. In the 1980s and 1990s, for instance, many banks created administrative centers to rationalize clerical tasks performed in branches. What the business cases did not consider, however, was the impact centralization would have on critical roles played by senior clerical personnel in branches. They in fact played a vital—but non-documented—role in training and supporting the tellers (an entry position at the time). The loss of know-how was tremendous and was immediately felt by customers. The business case was perfectly accurate, based on what the organization knew at the time. The need here is to make the process *explicit*, find out what is critical to its performance, control it, and ensure that it evolves over time.

Processes where physical flows are the root cause of all the problems (7) have unique vulnerabilities. They are another sub-category of the inefficient processes described above. Processes in that category are mostly found among manufacturing processes, but also in some transactional processes where the flow of a document, a parcel, or a person is central. Moving parts from warehouse to shop floor, producing an insurance policy, delivering a parcel from New York to Hong Kong, or delivering passengers to their respective aircraft might fall into that category. Rethinking quantities, lot sizing, set-up time, division of work, and physical flows can generate significant gains in these processes.

Of course, reality generally defies categorization, and indeed most process problems are mixed. However, careful diagnostic examination of a process will generally permit identification of a major problem or opportunity.

Consider, for instance, the case of a bank trying to improve two processes involving professionals: renewal of credit lines and dealer audits. The problem with the former is that some 30 percent of credit lines have not been reviewed at the pre-established date and are automatically extended, exposing the bank to unknown risks. The current process is very long and bureaucratic, involving several forms and three or four departments. Since there is a process and it does not deliver the goods, Figure 9.2 points toward cases 3 and 5. As the process does not involve complex interactions between variables, it can be classified as an ineffective process.

A division of the bank is involved in financing car dealers' inventories. Since they foresee an imminent economic downturn, they feel that it is urgent to improve their auditing process. There are but a few experienced auditors (all professional accountants) available to audit hundreds of dealers. A first effort at coming to grips with the process results in the process being split into three distinct sub-processes: audit planning (deciding who should be audited), auditing, and follow-up. The team immediately sees that audit planning offers the greatest potential for improvement: Unless you knock at the right door at the right time, the audit dollar is wasted. As they start to map that process, it dawns on them that there is no process (inexistent process), that is, whatever activities take place depend on the evolving best judgment of many managers. While the auditing sub-process is formalized, crucial aspects of the process, such as developing the specific audit plan, are poorly understood, resulting in important non-conformities being missed (complex process). Finally, the audit follow-up process delivers the goods, eventually. Very bureaucratic, the process involves back-and-forth exchanges between several players (auditors, dealer, and head office) that take forever (inefficient process).

9.3 CHANGE VEHICLES

Processes can be changed in a number of ways, ranging from sending a memo to all involved to putting together a fully empowered full-time team. Six such ways are described, referring to them as change *vehicles* because they (figuratively) *load* a process to be designed or improved and *take it to its destination*: a fully implemented new way of doing things. Just as vehicles come in different sizes and with different payloads, and have different traction and speed specifications, each change vehicle has its own individual characteristics that enable it to take specific changes to fruition. Figure 9.3 shows the six most common vehicles used by many organizations in the form of a tree structure. Among the many existing variants, presented here are the most prevalent form of each.

A *project* (1) is a two- to six-month endeavor led by an expert in the methodology and tools. A team of employees intimately familiar with the process is built around the expert, all of whom report to a manager (the *project owner* or *champion*). The expert has been trained extensively for that task,

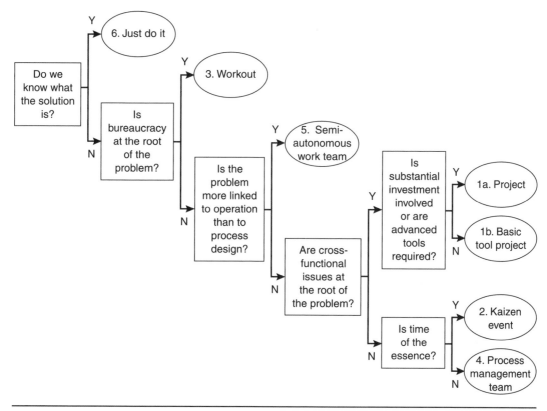

Figure 9.3 Typology of process change vehicles.

and manages two or three projects in parallel on an ongoing basis. Team members typically spend two to four hours a week on the project. The project owner gives the mandate to the team, receives their report at the end of each phase, makes decisions about future directions, and is accountable to senior management for the results. Authority to change anything rests with the project owner. A *basic tool project* (1a) is one that does not involve advanced statistical tools (that is, one that uses tools similar to those presented in Chapter 10), and can thus be led by someone with lesser qualifications, that is, by a *green belt* instead of a *black belt* in Six Sigma terminology.

A *Kaizen event* (2) is a one- to two-week intensive drive to change one or more processes (in parallel). For each process to be transformed during the event, a full-time multifunctional team is organized, composed of key representatives from all departments (typically five to 10, depending on complexity) involved in the process. The mandate of each team is to fix its process by the end of the week (assuming a one-week event). The teams assemble in the morning in a central room to receive their marching orders for the morning. The instructions include training, given by managers acting as coaches on basic process tools. They then retire to their respective *war rooms* to use the tools they have just learned. Later, the teams return briefly to the central room to present their work to one another and to their coaches. This sequence of activities is repeated throughout the week. At critical junctures during the week—completed diagnostics, completed prescription, and final presentation—managers and employees are invited to react to what the teams propose in end-of-day forums. Of course, much preparation is needed before that week and a two- to three-month follow-up is required to tie up loose ends. This is the vehicle that will be used for the examples presented in the next two chapters.

The word *workout* (3) was coined by GE to describe an even more intense—typically lasting two days—vehicle for change. Workouts, which are less rigorous than projects or Kaizen events, involve more people, and are not limited to processes, have spread to many other organizations. For Jack Welch, *busting bureaucracy* (Dumaine, 1991) involves outside experts (consultants or university professors) coming to a site and organizing a broad-based problem identification session, followed by quick-hit solutions. Management, placed on the hot seat, must decide on the spot and justify any negative answers.

A *process management team* (4) is typically assembled around a process owner to design, improve, and monitor a high-level process. The team is always multifunctional and meets for short but intense periods—typically two days at a time—first to design or redesign a process, then to monitor and improve it. The time requirement decreases when the process is implemented and capable. Each team member acts as the unique contact point for that process in their own department. Process problems are channeled through that contact person to the process team. The process owner is accountable to the management committee for process performance. The team may use other vehicles such as projects and Kaizen events to address specific, lower-level process issues.

Semi-autonomous work teams (5) have been around for a long time. Whereas a process management team owns the design of a process that is generally repeated in many parts of the organization, a semi-autonomous work team manages and operates a specific application (or *instance*) of that process. For example, a process management team may design the process for preparing a service proposal and a semi-autonomous work team may prepare proposals for specific systems or for a specific geographic area. As long as they respect the design parameters set forth by the former, the latter, generally a cross-functional team, disposes of much autonomy in the operation of the process. Semi-autonomous work teams may also have a degree of autonomy in some human resource aspects of the work, such as member selection, gain sharing, and interpersonal problem solving, thus the common reference to it as part of a *socio-technical* approach to work.

Sometimes, when process problems arise, the organization knows the cause and the solution. All that is needed then is to *just do it* (6). A project is involved and a team is generally needed to execute it. This, however, is very different from the process improvement and process design teams presented above. The team does not have to clarify the problem and look for a solution, but rather to clarify the solution and look for the best way to implement it. This is no easy task either, however, as the change management challenge can also be daunting. On one occasion, when I was conducting a project definition session (generally referred to as a *scoping session*), a manager suggested that an improvement project be conducted on the following topic: "We don't do design reviews any more." In the discussion that followed, it quickly became clear that many problems could have been avoided if this manager and his colleagues had kept to that practice. This example would be a typical candidate for a just-do-it project. A word of caution is in order here, however: often, managers think that they know what the problem, the causes, and the solution are, but this initial view does not bear detailed analysis for very long.

Adapting these vehicles to suit a particular organizational environment and implementing them are complex undertakings, requiring careful attention to the human and technical aspects as well. Each comes with its own organizational requirements, risks, and success factors. They are complementary and can be used individually or in combination.

9.4 PROCESS CHANGE METHODOLOGIES AND TOOLS

Three process change methodologies will be discussed: the process improvement methodology or DMAIC (presented in Chapter 10), the service and process design methodology or DCDV (presented in Chapter 11), and the product design methodology. Each acronym, however inelegant, consists of the first letter of each phase of that methodology. A short overview of each of these methodologies is given below.

Deming's wheel, or the Plan, Do, Check, Act cycle, is certainly the best-known (high-level) process improvement methodology used in business today. DMAIC, however, goes further and is more rigorous. After an improvement project has been scoped, process is described and measured. The vital few or *critical to process* variables are then identified. Only then is an optimal break-through solution sought, prior to putting in place a control system to ensure that the gains are not lost once the project has been completed.

The DCDV methodology is used for designing or redesigning a new service or a new process based on the customer-in approach. It proceeds from an initial problem statement to identifying what the (internal or external) customer wants. These wants are then translated into metrics and the metrics are deployed onto process functions. This is followed, in sequence, by high-level and detailed design, prototyping, validation, and rollout. The methodology was illustrated summarily in Chapter 1 using the movie selection example.

While the product-design methodology, also known as *design for Six Sigma* or DFSS, is more recent and the subject of more debate, its premises are not: products should be designed with a clear understanding of required process capabilities. These capabilities, and their interactions, need to be understood statistically with a view to meeting customer specifications. Most products will never reach Six Sigma unless they are designed with that goal in mind. DFSS follows the same logical flow as DCDV. However, because product specifications and machine tolerances are being dealt with, the methodologies are quite different in practice.

Other well-known methodologies include those associated with the capability maturity model (CMM), the ISO 9000 standard, and the JIT/lean manufacturing philosophy (these are discussed briefly in Chapter 12). These are different, however, in that they deal with company-wide improvement and are not limited to single improvement projects. Nevertheless, they are quite compatible with the methodologies discussed above.

Process tools fall into six categories: awareness, diagnostic, design, operation, improvement, and measurement and control. Process awareness tools are essential for process workers to gain a holistic view of their process. They include process mapping, process flow diagrams (Chapter 3), procedure writing, and documentation techniques. Ishikawa diagrams, value-added analysis (VAA[3]), and complexity analysis are typical diagnostic tools (Chapter 10). Design tools include quality function deployment (QFD), functional analysis (FAST) and the Pugh design matrix (Chapter 11). Process operations require process-oriented systems such as enterprise resource planning and customer relationship management. Failure mode and effect analysis (FMEA, Chapter 10), fault-tree analysis, poka-yokes, and design of experiment are improvement tools, while defect rate calculations, capability indices (Chapter 8), and statistical process control (SPC, Chapter 8) fall into the measurement and control category. The tools listed are but a few examples of what is available in the process toolkit. Categorization involves some grey areas, as some tools have a broad spectrum of functionality. SPC and FMEA, for instance, can also contribute significantly to process diagnosis.

Choosing the right tools for the job is as important for the process change leader as it was for Jack Jones, when faced with the problem of moving his belongings, in the analogy mentioned earlier. A manufacturing plant was launching its first Kaizen events with the transformation of two different processes: first article inspection (FAI) and non-conformance reports (NCR's). The FAI process was inexistent (category 2 in Figure 9.2) and the NCR was inefficient (category 4)—though the company was unaware of these distinctions. The only methodology available was DMAIC. Starting on Monday, the teams received 30 minutes of instruction on process mapping in the morning and on FMEA after lunch, and came back three hours later to present their findings to one another. By late afternoon that day, the FAI team appeared disgruntled, while the NCR team was all smiles. Just before lunch on Tuesday, the NCR team came back very excited with the results of their VAA analysis. That was enough to trigger a crisis in the FAI team, who could not do anything with it. As the team threatened to quit, an emergency plan was quickly drafted to realign the methodology and select appropriate tools.

Tool selection depends on the type of process problem being addressed, on the methodology that will be used and on the change vehicle selected. Some tools are also especially effective for specific process problems. VAA, for instance, is a great way to reveal opportunities in inefficient processes. Kanbans (JIT methodology) work well in improving cycle time and reducing waste in processes involving physical flows. Complex processes often require designed experiments. Other tools, such as sampling design and process capability calculation, are universal and constitute an essential part of any process design or improvement drive.

Finally, some tools are well adapted to particular change vehicles, but will not work well in others. Advanced statistical tools, for instance, require a good educational background on the part of the user, as well as substantial training, and thus will not work well in a Kaizen event, where the team—not the expert—needs to feel empowered. Designed experiments and Monte Carlo simulations typically do not respond well to either the time pressure or informal environment of the Kaizen event, or the workout where experts do not play an important role.

9.5 THE MATCH

The definition phase of the project is the appropriate moment to match process problem to methodology, toolkit, and change vehicle. Because these notions are not well understood, mismatching is common. In the best of cases, the resulting difficulties are puzzling for everyone, as people seek to understand why QFD, for example, did not work out in one project while it produced fantastic results in another. Such puzzles have been seen repeatedly. It takes its toll on the improvement program, and it may turn out to be the deciding factor when a new program faces its first challenges and unqualified success is required.

Understanding the ways in which process problems, methodologies, and change vehicles are related is essential to avoiding these problems.

Table 9.2 presents a three-way matching of these entities. A single, preferred methodology is proposed for each process problem, and the main body of the table specifies problem-vehicle matches. The *YES* cells represent a good match. The dotted cells indicate that this vehicle can contribute to the solution of that problem. The striped cells are caution beacons and the solid cells indicate a mismatch.

The DFSS methodology is specifically designed for new product introduction projects. However, a process management team can use it just as effectively, with the added benefit that the designers are the same people who will operate and keep on improving the new processes—great for motivation! The same holds true for service design, with the DCDV methodology fitting the job perfectly. The DCDV methodology is also well-suited to design processes where none had existed before. In the case of the audit planning process discussed earlier, since time is of the essence for the bank, a Kaizen event, or a variant involving three three-day sessions spread out over a longer period, can be used to quickly mobilize the organization behind the initiative. An initial workout can also be used to jump-start the exercise, and semi-autonomous work teams can help make the process come alive afterward. A project would take too long in this case.

An ineffective process may be improved using DMAIC if it has potential, or redesigned using DCDV if it does not. Kaizen events may sometimes suffice, as long as advanced statistical tools are

Table 9.2 Three-way match between process problems, methodologies, and change vehicles.

Process problems	Methodology	Vehicle					
		(1) Project	(2) Kaizen event	(3) Workout	(4) Process management	(5) Semi-autonomous work team[1]	(6) Just do it
New product (1a)	DFSS	Yes			Yes		
New service (1b)	DCDV	Yes	Yes		Yes		
Inexistent process (2)	DCDV	Yes	Yes		Yes		
Ineffective process (3)	DMAIC or DCDV	Yes			Yes		
Inefficient process (4)	DMAIC		Yes				
The complex process (5)	DMAIC	Yes					
Black box process (6)	DMAIC		Yes		Yes		
Physical flow problems (7)	JIT	Yes	Yes				

[1]None of the methodologies discussed here apply. This vehicle has to be used in combination with one or more of the others.

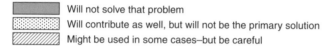

■ Will not solve that problem
▫ Will contribute as well, but will not be the primary solution
▨ Might be used in some cases—but be careful

not needed. If the solution is known, a just-do-it project may be in order—but any time spent making sure that it is the right solution is a wise investment. In the case of the expired credit line above, the bank is exposed to unknown risks. Thus, it would be well advised to start with a workout to identify and address any immediate exposure, and follow it up with a project or process management team, using the DMAIC methodology. It should, however, be ready to switch to a DCDV methodology *on the fly* if the actual process turns out not to have the required potential.

Kaizen events are very well-suited to fixing inefficient processes, because basic tools are generally sufficient, and the multifunctional team dynamics thus created go a long way toward bringing solutions to the surface. Projects may be risky in this context, however, because they often lack such dynamics. The audit follow-up process mentioned above appears to be a good candidate for a Kaizen event, using the DMAIC methodology.

One of the major contributions of Six Sigma[4] lies in the application of DMAIC with advanced statistical tools to the improvement of complex processes. Although all the tools were available already, the methodology puts them together in a highly effective way. The auditing process for example, is a complex process. It involves analyzing many financial and operational variables related in complex ways. The way the dealership is operated impacts the financial results of the business. Understanding these results will provide critical clues as to how best to conduct the audit, focusing on the vital few aspects of the operation and not wasting time and money on trivia. A project will afford the team enough time to perform the rigorous data gathering and analysis required to optimize the process.

By contrast, the job required in connection with a black-box process is much more fundamental: understand and give some basic structure to a process that is unknown. Not only would the rigor of a DMAIC project be wasted here, but such rigor would risk zooming in on some complex aspects of the process at the expense of the overall coherence required. In such a case, Kaizen and process-management teams are much better suited to the job at hand. The best methodology for improving physical flows is just-in-time (JIT). The optimum implementation of JIT is through a combination of projects and Kaizen events, with the other change vehicles potentially contributing to the improvement drive as well.

Further examination of Table 9.1 shows that three change vehicles (workouts, semi-autonomous work teams and *just do it*) are essentially complements to the three major process change vehicles, with *just do it* always being subject to caution.

9.6 CONCLUSION

In considering how he is going to move his belongings, Jack Jones needs to learn quite a bit about the moving business. While he knows his things very well, from the static angle of using them every day, he has never looked at them as objects to be moved. Neither has he ever considered moving as a process, being strictly interested in the results. To see them in this new light, he needs to start thinking like a mover, that is, to adopt the dynamic view of objects being prepared for transport, handled, transported, and reinstalled. Similarly, organizations that want to improve processes must learn to view improvement as a process in its own right, to be designed and improved. They must see processes as objects of improvement, each with its specific requirements (Figure 9.2). They must understand that several methodologies and a host of tools are available, each with unique features. They must finally be acquainted with the complex characteristics of change vehicles (Figure 9.3) and how they best combine with improvement methodologies and tools to solve various types of problems (Table 9.2).

The miseries and risks created by the use of an inappropriate methodology or vehicle can be avoided. In order to do so, the process problem being addressed needs to be accurately characterized during the initial definition phase (Chapter 7) and a proper match must be achieved. Clearly, however, not all methodologies and vehicles are available at the outset of an improvement program, as each requires a substantial investment in learning, training and communication. Thus, some process problems have to be side-tracked initially for lack of an appropriate methodology or change vehicle to address them. It is critical that the reasons for this be explained to all involved and that a timeframe be given within which to address each type of process problem. Failure to do so will result in increasing frustration, as some types of problems are systematically tossed aside or worse, as the organization gives in and uses an inappropriate methodology or vehicle, thereby taking the wind out of the sails of a fledgling program.

9.7 SUMMARY

The learning pump lies at the heart of the learning organization. There is a variety of process problems, ranging form inefficient process to black box. Depending on the nature of the process problem, the ideal methodology to use (among DFSS, DCDV, DMAIC, and JIT/lean manufacturing) will be different. Selection of tools (AVA, FMEA, or Ishikawa, for example) also depends on the nature of the problem and the methodology selected. Change vehicles have different functionalities that make them more effective for specific purposes. Learning to discriminate between the various types of problems, methodologies, tools, and change vehicles is difficult, but essential. Without a good matching capability, the pump will never perform up to its full potential and learning will proceed at a slower pace.

EXERCISES

9.1 Exploring the challenges of matching

Refer to the work you did in end-of-chapter exercises in Chapter 6, and particularly to the five projects for which you formulated a mission statement, in exercise 6.5.

a) Classify the major problem of each process, using the decision tree provided in Figure 9.2.

b) Which methodology would be appropriate for each project (refer to Table 9.2)?

c) Using the tree structure provided in Figure 9.3 and Table 9.2, identify the change vehicle that would be most appropriate for each project.

9.2 Kaizen event

If you are aware of a (non-competing) company that regularly conducts Kaizen events, contact them to explore the possibility of participating in one. Many companies welcome such participation, as the guest is much more than a passive witness: A fresh point of view from someone totally unfamiliar with a process can richly enhance a team's capability. If you do not know any such company, your local ASQ chapter may help in that regard.

Notes

[1] This chapter is largely drawn from: Harvey, J. "Process Improvement: Match the Change Vehicle and Method to the Job", *Quality Progress,* 37, (1), January 2004, pp. 41-48.
[2] The words *problems* and *opportunities* are used interchangeably.
[3] All tools are discussed at length in Chapters 10 and 11.
[4] A methodology developed by Motorola in the 1980s.

10

Doing Things Better: Improving an Existing Process

The DMAIC improvement methodology, adapted to a professional service environment.

O nce important processes have been identified and the appropriate methodology and change vehicle selected, the *trip* begins. In this chapter, the improvement methodology is described, and in the next one, the design methodology. After presenting a bird's-eye view of the methodology and some of the principles that underpin it, it is illustrated with a detailed example (QKM). The chapter is concluded with further thought about how and why the methodology works.

10.1 HIGH-LEVEL VIEW OF THE IMPROVEMENT METHODOLOGY

The improvement methodology includes five stages: define, measure, analyze, improve, and control (DMAIC, for short—see Figure 10.1). Since the reader is now familiar with processes, it is useful to understand that the methodology itself is a process—a process to improve a process. It includes five sequential sub-processes or phases, each defined by its respective action verb, as listed above. The input to the process is an improvement idea, which comes from an idea hopper, such as that discussed in Chapter 6. The output is an improved process that is stable and capable. Each phase or sub-process contributes to that transformation. The Define stage is described in detail in Chapter 7. It starts from the improvement idea and produces a well-scoped project. It uses the tools presented in Chapter 7. The Measure phase describes the process, the flows involved, the variables, and their measurement systems. The Analyze stage takes in these variables and separates the *vital few* from the *trivial many*, to produce a validated diagnosis. The Improve phase proceeds from the diagnosis to formulate and validate a prescription. The Control phase implements the new process and ensures that the improvement will not be lost once the organization's focus moves on to another agenda. Figure 10.1 shows some of the tools available to effect these transformations in their respective toolboxes.

Contrast this with the normal way of *resolving problems* in most organizations. The problems are typically discussed during a meeting, and when time is up, it is considered defined and the boss assigns the job to fix it to an *owner*. Often, no data is available. Sometimes there is bad data, measuring the wrong thing, the wrong way. The organization brainstorms informally for causes,

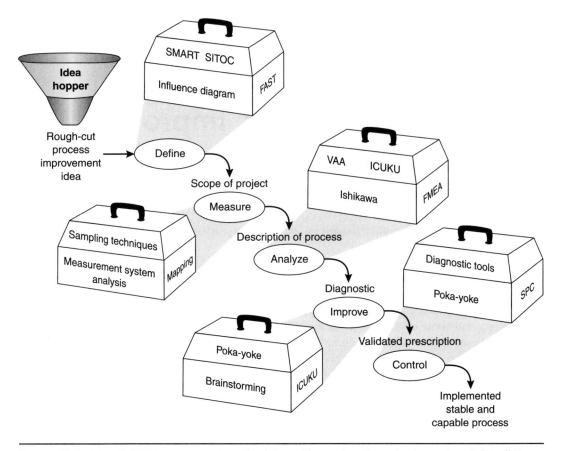

Figure 10.1 The DMAIC improvement methodology: Phases, inputs, outputs, and partial toolkits.

jumps on one that sounds right, labels it a diagnosis, and starts looking for quick fixes. The process is tinkered with a little, until it is felt the that initial symptoms are gone or attenuated, then move on to the next problem without ever looking back. These organizations suffer from *short attention span disorder*, a learning disability that condemns them to repeat the same mistakes and face the same situations repeatedly. As discussed in Chapter 12, in such *firefighting* organizations, the culture is perpetuated by promoting the best firefighters, and no one is ever promoted for preventing a fire.

The DMAIC methodology is about rigor. Listed below are some basic principles that underpin it:

- Any process improvement drive must be based on a well-defined problem statement.

- If you cannot measure it, you do not know much about it, and thus cannot improve it. If you ever do improve it, it will be by chance and you will never know for sure.

- Never trust data unless you know where it comes from and how it was gathered.

- Problem finding before problem solving. Get consensus on an explicit diagnosis before moving on to the prescription.

- Formulate hypotheses that are grounded in facts.

- It is fine to work on the basis of an unproven hypothesis. However, the practice (lack of rigor) of accepting such hypotheses as true, called superstitious learning, is a fatal cultural trait.

- Prove the solution before implementing it.

- Following up is the most difficult part. Confining rigor to the improvement events, and going back to firefighting mode the day after, will only foster cynicism.

A detailed example is now presented.

10.2 BACKGROUND

The reader should first review Box 4.1, glance anew at Figures 4.2 and 4.3 and read Box 10.1 to understand the company's background and the situation. QKM agrees with the client that the CAP has potential and that it can be improved. Hence, they set up a joint Kaizen event. KQM's managing partner is designated as the process owner and the client's chief learning officer accepts to act as process owner within the client organization. They hold the Kaizen as a joint event, on the client's premises. QKM is expected to draw on its experience with the CAP in many organizations since its inception to ensure that the client deploys a world-class process. The co-owners ask a senior person from each organization to help in the scoping exercise.

Box 10.1 Quality Knowledge Management (QKM)—The action course

Issue: A consulting firm wants to improve a hands-on training process

Among its other services, QKM (see Box 4.2) assists organizations embarking on process-based quality initiatives, such as CMM, ISO, TQM, ABC, or Six Sigma. Since competition in this field is fierce, involving several firms much larger and better known than QKM, the firm is a niche player. When it considered entering into this market, it conducted a survey. It indicated that there was much dissatisfaction. Several organizations felt manipulated by consultants repackaging old programs, re-branding them, and marketing them as novel. They also felt that once they had entered the organization, some consultants made themselves indispensable and stuck around, charging as much money as they could. QKM felt that much of the industry managed that particular fault line poorly: exploiting the customers' trust and the consultant's superior knowledge to extract more financial advantage.

Since these perceptions were more widely spread in small to medium-size companies, QKM had targeted companies with 200 to 2000 employees. Its value proposition went as follows: "We will assist you in the creation of durable and profitable know-how in the field of processes and quality—the tried and true as well as the most recent developments. We will not sell you fish, but we will show you how to fish and leave as soon as you have acquired the know-how. We will coach you along as you reach higher levels of capabilities". As part of its offerings in this program, QKM had developed a training process to jump-start the initiative, produce quick results, and build a critical mass of managers and employees, sharing a common understanding and common beliefs in the fundamental notions underpinning the initiative. This was complemented by a parallel offering consisting of coaching top management in the connection of strategy to operation and in the creation of a quality culture. The QKM consultant acting in that capacity also assumes the role of coordinating the process action course (or PAC).

Continued

Continued

The PAC consists of five one-day *in-class* sessions and one day of coaching, spread over a five-month period. Twenty managers or other high-potential employees were selected and asked, before the sessions started, to select an improvement project on which they would work, together with a team (team members did not take the course), throughout the course. They receive the material prior to the course to prepare them and guide them through project selection and initial scoping. Top management is consulted in selecting the trainees and the projects. The PAC typically generates much action in the organization—*teaching it how to fish*—at a relatively low cost for QKM, and thus acts as a major profit lever.

As part of its own continuous improvement efforts, the PAC itself has surfaced as a process that holds substantial improvement potential. The major opportunity lies in improving the success rate of the projects. While the projects are primarily for learning purposes, their success is an important ingredient in the recipe for changing the culture, that is, changing beliefs through a significant personal and organizational experience. Another aspect that needs improvement is the startup or pre-course phase, which many customers feel is long and cumbersome. QKM has recently performed a PAC for a new client: a large national organization that asked them to set it up as a pilot, based on which it would decide whether it should proceed to national deployment. While the client was impressed overall, deployment would only be approved if QKM agreed to work with them on improving the process beforehand.

10.3 DEFINE

The goals of the project are to improve the success rate of training projects undertaken by all participants to the PAC and to streamline the launching of a course. As illustrated in Figure 10.1, the input to the Define phase is a vague idea and the output is a well-scoped project, ready to enter the Measure phase.

The scoping team follows the methodology presented in Chapter 7. The *Big Y* reads as follows: "Training projects currently suffer a failure rate of 30 percent. It should not exceed 10 percent." This is a *SMART* statement. *SMART* (see Chapter 1 and Chapter 7) is an acronym that stands for Specific, Measurable, Ambitious, Realistic, and Timely. *Improving the performance of the process* would not be specific. The goal or goals selected must relate to something important for the organization (meaningful). The target must be ambitious and stimulating, yet achievable. A valid measurement system must be available to allow tracing the progress of the project toward the goal. Finally, a date must be set to achieve the target. They also identify a secondary problem: "It takes 32 days to start a course. It should not exceed 15 days." While the team realizes that inefficiency is also a problem, it feels that the bulk of the waste occurs in the startup phase, and that reducing startup time would simultaneously improve efficiency.

They initially start exploring the process: *deliver the PAC*. They formulate its mission as: "To deliver to participants a process improvement experience that will induce a change of belief, and transform them into positive change agents towards a quality culture." The FAST diagram shows that there are five sub-processes:

- Plan the course

- Set up the course

- Teach the course

- Support the projects

- Follow up on the projects

The team explores the relative importance of each of these functions using an influence diagram, and assesses the current performance of these sub-processes using an efficiency-effectiveness diagram (examples of both are shown in Chapter 7). They then proceed to prepare a macro-map of the process (see Figure 10.2). It shows that nine generic players are involved, all of whom are at play during the pre-course phase, and that the process is large—too large in fact for a single improvement project. The preceding analysis, much of which is not shown here, reveals that the pre-course (or course setup) sub-process holds the greatest potential to achieve (or contribute to) the *Big Y* and other secondary goals. Hence, it is selected for improvement in this project (see the FAST diagram in Figure 10.3). It includes selecting the trainees and their projects, selecting and assembling the material, setting up the logistics, class-preparation (for the instructor), and supporting the trainees in their preparation for class. Depending on the results achieved at the end of the project, the team feels that it might be worthwhile to tackle the *support projects* sub-process next.

The team then proceeds to formalize the new, narrower, scope. It first formulates a SMART problem statement as follows: "the percentage of *trainee-project* couples that do not meet all selection criteria is currently 70 percent. It should not exceed 10 percent." This goal is shown in Figure 10.4. This representation makes it clear and visual, thus focusing the project and the team on the goal. The indicator selected (the *small y*) is directly related to the *Big Y*. Selecting the right trainees and pairing them with a project that has the potential to *induce a change of belief* is the key contribution of the process. Counting the number of such pairs that do not meet all criteria (that is, the criteria for selecting the trainees, and those for the project) is one possible metric for this. Counting the number of criteria not met would be another.

The SITOC is also shown in Figure 10.4. The process delivers outputs to both the client and internal customers. As in most business-to-business (B2B) service delivery, the process interacts with various players within the organization. Internal customers are generally processes, and thus this process supplies inputs to other downstream processes. The inputs to the process are the outputs of other *supplier processes*, namely in this case: *plan training* and *plan project selection*. The SITOC sets the perimeter of the project and delimits it in time as well. Figure 10.5 completes the scope of the project by specifying relevant customer needs, identifying technical characteristics, and spelling out the mission of the process. In this case, the SMART problem statement is a direct measure of the extent to which the process achieves its mission. This only happens when the purpose of the project is to improve effectiveness. When dealing with an inefficient process or one that is too slow, the SMART and mission statement are not directly related.

It is important to see the chain of internal customers (or internal processes) that connects the process to the end customer. One must make every effort to identify end customer needs that the process affects, however remotely. The needs of internal customers are also identified, as the process must meet these as well. We finally identify a number of technical characteristics related to quality, cost, and timeliness. Even though the project normally centers on one or two specific goals, it is useful to consider all three dimensions, if only to make sure that what is gained on one front is not lost on another.

The owners then select eight team members as follows:

- A senior QKM partner, expert in Kaizen events and the DMAIC methodology, but without past involvement in the PAC program and its deployment, to act as team leader

- The coordinator involved in the recently concluded PAC pilot, who is also the person responsible for managing the process on a day-to-day basis, to act as co-leader

- Two QKM instructors and another QKM consultant who often act as coordinator

- Two executives and the person designated to act as logistician for the client

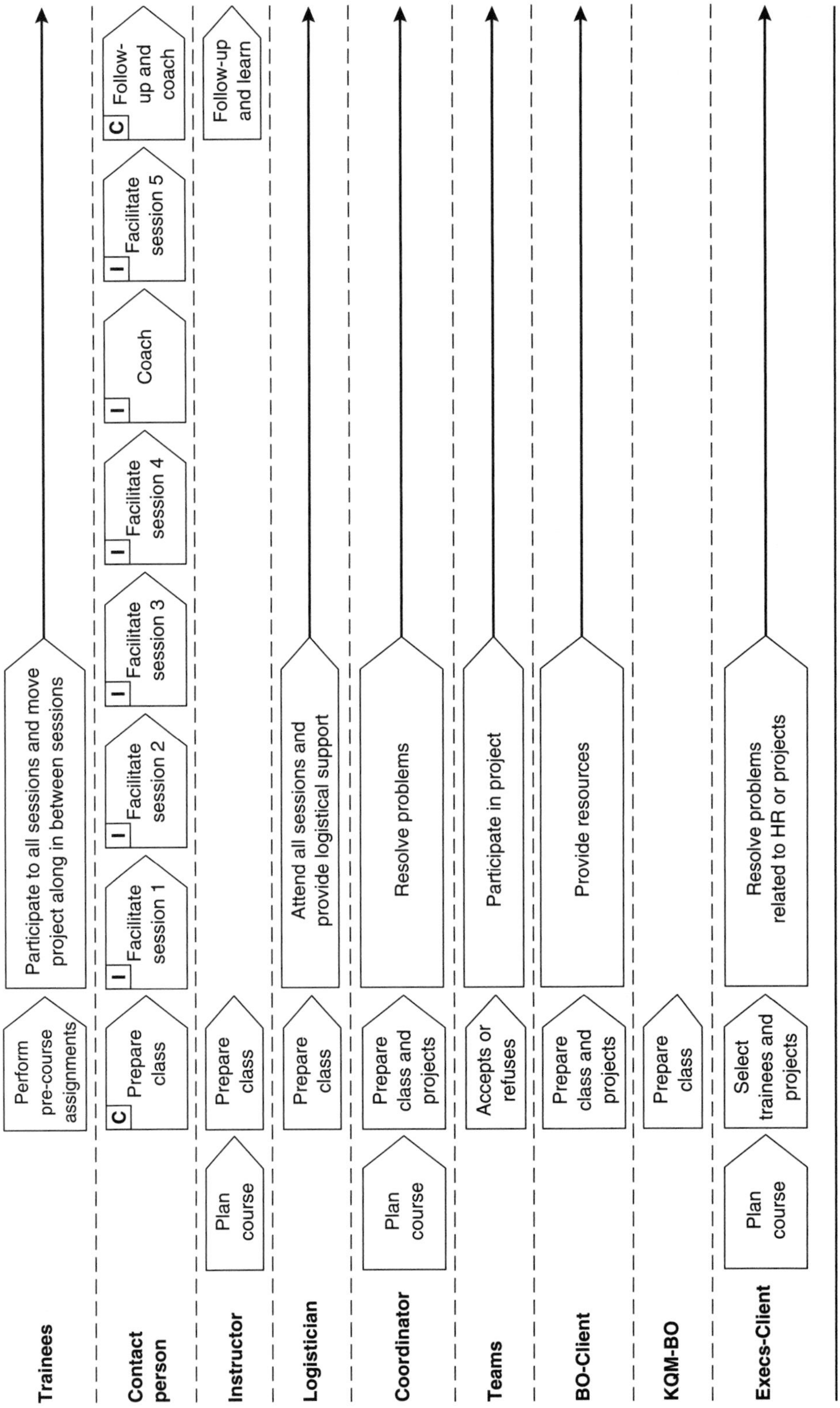

Figure 10.2   Macro-map of the PAC at QKM.

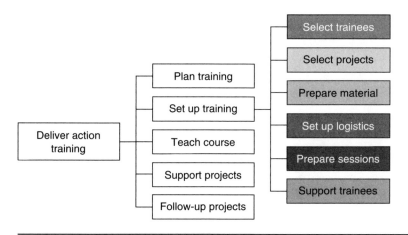

Figure 10.3   FAST diagram of the PAC, with details of the setup phase.

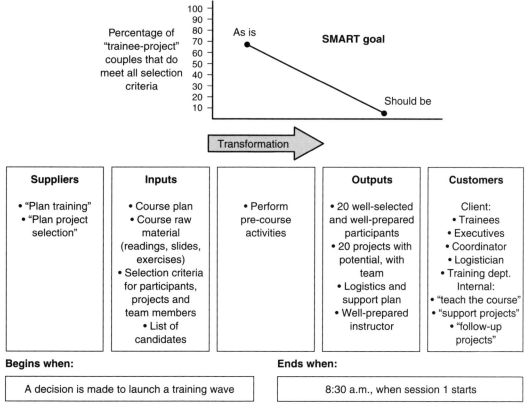

Figure 10.4   Project scope: SMART problem statement, SITOC, boundaries, and comments.

Chain of internal customers connecting the process to the client

> Process is direct to client, and indirect as well to the following processes:
> *teach the course–support projects–follow-up projects*

Relevant client needs

> Trainees: Hands-on knowledge, a value-changing experience, feeling supported

Relevant needs and priorities of internal customers

> Well-selected and well-prepared participants, well-scoped project (*no surprise*)

Technical characteristics

Quality
> Percentage of well-scoped projects
> Number of participants meeting selection criteria

Cost
> Savings per project
> Start-up cost

Time
> Number of participants receiving material
> with sufficient lead-time

Process Mission
> To deliver, when training begins,
> 20 well-prepared participants,
> with the right profile, the right
> mindset and a well-scoped project.

Figure 10.5 Project scope: Customer needs, technical characteristics, and process mission.

They make sure that all team members are experienced and credible within their respective departments to ensure that they are in a position to exert the leadership role that is expected of them. Considering the size of the process to be improved, they decide that a four-day event should be sufficient. They schedule forums (see Chapter 9) to be held at the end of the second day (diagnosis), the third day (prescription), and at the closing (fully developed process, with control system). The owners then call a two-hour kick-off session during which they present and discuss the mandate with the team.

10.4 MEASURE

The output of the measure phase is a detailed description of the process, allowing for identification of all variables, and a validation of relevant measurement systems. At the outset of day one, the team assigns a number of specific roles to be played by various team members: idea manager (to capture ideas that come out, place them in a *parking lot* for future action, and cut short any premature discussion of solutions), a time-keeper, and a *scribe*.

Process mapping is a key deliverable. Without a good visual representation of the process, no analysis is possible. The SITOC and FAST diagrams serve as guidelines in the preparation of the process map (see Figure 10.6). Remember from Chapter 8 that the line of interaction is used to

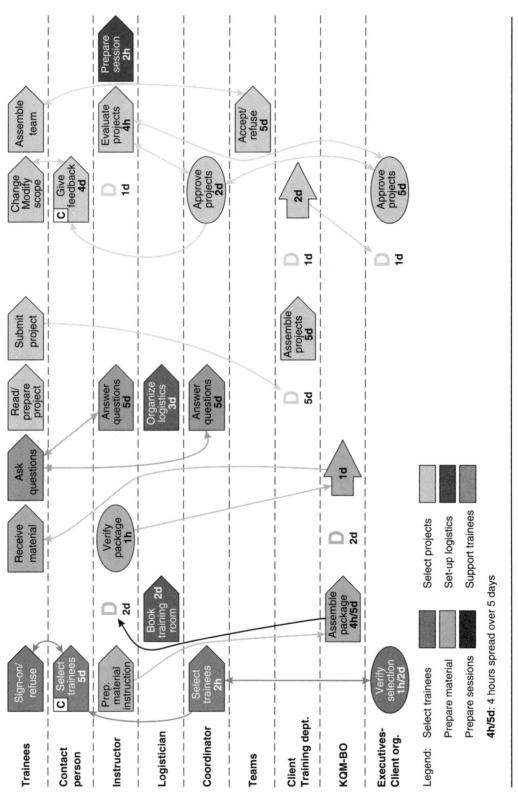

Figure 10.6   Process mapping: Pre-course segment.

depict face-to-face contact only. Remote contact is depicted as bilateral arrows connecting activities on both sides of the line of visibility. The symbols and conventions used are those presented in Chapter 8, with a few exceptions. A first difference is that average durations are used instead of ranges, for simplicity's sake. Notice that some tasks take a few hours while others last days. The latter were mapped, for practical reasons, at a higher level than the former, that is, they are aggregates of many different things. For instance, both the coordinator and instructor spend five days at the task *answer questions*. Obviously, they do not spend five days on the phone. A truly complete mapping of this task would specify, for each call made by a trainee, a decision point (instructor available or not?), a delay (if not available), a call back, another decision point (trainee available or not?), and so on. Since this would be impractical, a single symbol is used. This issue is addressed in more detail in Section 10.5.4 dealing with value-added analysis.

A shading scheme is used to visualize the different functions identified in the FAST diagram (the same scheme is used in Figures 10.3, 10.6, 10.8, and 10.10 to highlight the connection between the FAST diagram and process mapping). The process involves nine players, two organizations, and as many as a hundred people, including the trainees, team members, and executives. It involves 17 *hand-offs*, that is, instances when the flow crosses over from one lane to another. Since several players can act as *contact person* (though, as it turned out, only one does in this case), a letter is placed (each player is identified by a bold letter) in the upper-left corner of the task box to specify. The instructor, the coordinator, and the back office of QKM (QKM-BO in Figure 10.6) are QKM employees, the other players work for the client.

Process mapping is not an exact science. As the team maps it, it makes many choices. The map shown in Figure 10.6 is still at a high level. We could split *Selecting trainees*, for instance, into a much more detailed map, specifying the intricate back and forth that takes place between the coordinator, the executives, and potential trainees. The choice the team makes in representing it as it does, is to *dig* selectively in areas where analysis indicates that it may be worthwhile to do so, thus keeping it simple. Further, only the delays that can potentially lie on the critical path (that is, actually make cycle time longer) are mapped. Thus, the team does not map delays in returning phone calls, or waiting to receive the material, especially since nobody is idle during these periods.

The process map allows for a first round of identification of variables. The notion of variable is discussed in Chapter 8, and illustrated with the example of humidity and temperature control in a house. These are continuous variables, such as cycle time in the case at hand. A discrete variable only takes on a limited number of values, generally positive integer values, such as the number of trainees in this case. A categorical or nominal variable is nonnumeric. A mode of contact, for instance may be face-to-face *tight spec*, face-to-face *loose spec*, and so on. Examining Figure 10.6, the team can see that the process really consists of many variables. Here is a partial list:

- Duration and span time of each task

- Number of trainees

- Number and identity of executives involved

- Extent of involvement of executives

- Selection criteria for trainees

- Selection criteria for projects

- Material selection: which and how much?

- Who is involved in the selection processes? Who recommends? Approves? Vetoes?

- In what sequence are they involved?

- Division of work between instructor, logistician, and coordinator

- Who does the clerical work involved in preparing the initial package?

- Deadlines for the various assignments (select a project, turn it in, select team members)

- Degree of support given to the trainee during project selection

- Degree of leeway given to the trainee in project selection

- How is the information and support given: individually or in group?

- Modes of contact for each contact point

- Criteria for selection of team members

- Number of team members

- Where is training to be conducted? (size of room, breakout rooms, electronic support, meals, and so on)

- Duration of each task, delay, and transport

- How many mistakes are made at each step? How many are caught and corrected in time?

These variables are often referred to as the Xs, or independent variables. The dependent variable (*the small y*) is a function of these variables. This is formalized as:

$$y = f(X_1, X_2, X_3, \ldots X_n)$$

In processes where all variables are numerical, this equation can take on a strictly mathematical form. This is seldom the case in professional services, however, though the dependent variable itself must always be numerical. While *the number of projects not meeting criteria* was selected as the *small y*, other dependent variables include cycle times (global and for each function) and number of criteria not met. Some dependent variables are controllable, some are partly controllable, and others are uncontrollable. Identifying the latter is equally important, though, as you may set the value of controllable variables as a function of uncontrollable variables, that is, while you cannot control these variables, you may consider them in process control.

Once the team has mapped the process and identified its variables, it is ready for data gathering. For numerical variables, the team first evaluates existing measurement systems. In the Define phase, for instance, the scoping team estimated that 70 percent of all trainee-project pairs did not meet all the selection criteria. The project team found out that this was based on a *guestimate*. This is not good enough. Thus, the team decides to go back to past courses, pull the project and trainee selection sheets from the files, and evaluate the quality of that information. It finds that the sheets, showing tick marks on a five-point scale next to each criterion, are quite usable in general. Some sheets, however, are incomplete and the team decides on the minimal requirements for a sheet to be usable. Further, after interviewing the people who filled out these sheets, the team decides to consider a score of three or better on any criteria as a *passing grade* (that is, the project or trainee met the criteria).

The coach then proposes a sampling strategy and a sampling plan. Formulating a sampling strategy involves an evaluation of the amount of data available, the quality of the data, and the cost of retrieving it, in the light of the use for the data and the need for validity, reliability, and precision. The strategy strikes the most advantageous balance between these elements and the sampling plan translates into specific instructions (Who? When? Where? How? How many?) for gathering the data. A detailed discussion of sampling is beyond the scope of this book. A number of simple rules of thumb can be useful, however, for someone who does not have access to competent resources in this field:

- When data gathering is not costly, go for the maximum you can get with the resources at hand and within the time available.

- If measurement is ongoing, add a second person to independently measure (in parallel) the phenomenon of interest. To validate the interpretation of *soft* data, that is, data that requires much judgment, interview more than one person involved in gathering and interpreting the data. Have them independently interpret a number of observations and compare the results. Unless you have a very good match, do not use the data. Better no data than misleading data. Design and validate (using the same approach) a new measurement system and start anew. You will have less data, but you will be able to use it safely.

- A *guestimate* or *ball park figure* can be useful, if you recognize it as such. You can improve such estimates by using variants of the *Delphi method*. In cases when several people are familiar enough with the phenomenon to be assessed (the proportion of trainees that do not meet all criteria, say), the Delphi method consists of asking them independently for their best estimates. These are gathered, plotted on a histogram, and shown to the assessors in a meeting. Those with extreme values explain their reasons to the others and a general discussion ensues, following which a new round of independent assessment is conducted. The mean result of this second assessment is your best estimate.

- Having 30 observations, whenever possible, allows for producing confident estimates for the mean and standard deviation, knowing the margins of error. This holds true for any dimension or category for which an estimate is needed. For instance, if four modes of contact are used and it is of interest how long a task takes in each case, 30 observations are needed for each mode of contact.

- The preceding rule should not prevent you from using whatever number of observations is available, as long as the measurement system is valid. Any valid data point is vastly superior to guesswork. You must always remain vigilant, however, not to forget that the margin of error grows rapidly as simple size goes down.

Data collection includes categorical variables as well, such as modes of contact. The team finds out that course material has been delivered by mail in eight out of the ten last courses, and electronically twice. This is data. It shows variation. This variation will be useful in the Analyze phase as a potential factor in understanding why some trainees come up with better projects, for instance. The same holds true for other categorical variables listed above, such as selection criteria and leeway given to trainees in project selection.

Given the cost and time required, the team only spends time on the variables that have, in its best judgment, a strong probability of being useful in the Analyze phase. If they miss some important variable that shows up later, they have to validate the measurement system and proceed to data collection at that time.

The team is now ready to analyze the data.

10.5 ANALYZE

The output of the Analyze phase is a diagnosis. It is a statement of the exact nature of the problem and its causality, together with a summation of the proof.

A lawyer's process to produce a summation or a doctor's process to produce a diagnosis are quite similar to the Analyze phase. The lawyer uses various techniques (interviews, inquiries, expert assessments, and so on) to understand the facts of the matter and make a convincing case—convincing self first, so that other interested parties can be convinced later. The doctor follows the same logical path, interviewing the patient and proceeding selectively to investigations, such as patient examination, blood analysis, X-ray, and biopsy. When all results are in, a mental process of analysis is performed—that is, using training and professional judgment to formulate a diagnosis based on the evidence. The team uses various analytical techniques (see Table 10.1) to formulate a diagnosis shared by all team members. It must first reach a consensus, and then convince other stakeholders. The chapter now turns to a presentation and discussion of each technique.

10.5.1 CTP Identification

An important step toward formulating a diagnosis is being able to weed out the relatively insignificant variables (*the trivial many*) in order to concentrate on the most important ones (*the vital few*). Pareto's law suggests that 20 percent of the variables should be responsible for 80 percent of the problem. As mentioned in Chapter 3, these variables are referred to as *critical to process* variables, or CTPs (see the *movie selection* illustration in Table 1.3). This technique is the team's first effort to identify these variables. At the outset, as the coach hands out a form similar to Table 10.2, the team is presented with the following instructions:

1. Go back to your process map and identify three to five activities you believe to be critical to the achievement of the SMART goal. Base this selection on available data and be ready to justify your choice. Mark these activities with a blue dot.

2. For each of these activities, specify what, exactly, is critical. Be specific. Several things may be critical within each activity. These are the CTPs of your process.

3. For each CTP, identify the mode of control currently used, if any, and explore other possibilities of control that would potentially be more effective or efficient.

The team's work is shown in Table 10.2 (also see the open circles in Figure 10.8). Considering the goal of the project, *selecting trainees* is obviously critical. Team discussion shows that there is considerable variation in the way this is done. The team also pinpoints *answering the questions of trainees*, as either the coordinator or the instructor does this, depending on who is available, sometimes on the fly, even from a cell phone while driving or climbing a flight of stairs. *Giving feedback to the trainee*, to help change the scope as required, is the last critical activity that the team identifies, as most projects need to be *re-scoped* and this is also done in a cursory fashion. The team identifies (see the second column of Table 10.2) three CTPs within the first activity, two in the second, and one in the third. They do this through exploration and comparison of the last few training waves, trying to pinpoint the factors that made a given wave more or less successful than the others. Through heated discussion, the team gradually succeeds in reaching consensus. At first, they formulate a dozen potential CTPs, but the team succeeds in *disproving* six of these.

Table 10.1 The analyze toolkit: Description, purpose, indication, limitations, and challenges involved with each tool.

Techniques	Description	Purpose	Indication	Limitations/Challenges
Influence diagram	Using a systems approach to identify and connect a *priori* variables to processes.	To assist in scoping the project by projecting the team's original understanding of the set of factors at play.	The more complex the set of problems, the more useful the diagram.	You must be careful to limit the number of variables and processes, lest the tool become unmanageable.
Process map	Detailed description of the sequential flow of the process and the role of each player.	To make the process visible, often for the first time, and provide a starting point for the analysis.	An essential component to any process analysis.	Finding the right level of detail at which to map and maintaining homogeneity.
CTP identification	Singling out three to five activities that play a key role in creating, and thus in solving, the problem.	To isolate the vital few from the trivial many, allowing to dig in areas where we are more likely to find gold.	Always useful. The discussions it generates help the team move toward a consensus.	Finding data or evidence to support his analysis can be challenging in *soft* professional services.
Ishikawa diagram	Identifying causes of the problem and organizing them in generic categories.	An alternate way to identify causal variables, catching some that our analysis of the mapping might have missed.	Generally useful because it is not based on the process map—thus providing validation through a different route.	May be somewhat redundant at times, when the mapping and influence diagram have been very successful.
ICUKU	Classifying causes or improvement ideas following three binary criteria: impact, controllable/uncontrollable known/unknown.	To help the team focus on causes/ideas that hold the greatest potential.	Whenever a large number of causes or ideas have been generated and the team does not know where to start.	The classification is somewhat arbitrary and may generate considerable debate.
Root cause (why)	Probing some causes, through a series of "Why" questions, until the root cause is found.	Some of causes generated in the Ishikawa diagram are only symptoms. Only through addressing the root cause can a durable solution be found.	Specially useful when the analysis has been superficial and when high impact, controllable causes with unknown solutions exist.	Sometimes root causes are so philosophical or vague as to offer no viable angle for improvement, at lease within the framework of a project.
VAA	Calculating the proportion of the cycle time when value is being added.	Identify the potential for improvement and help focus the effort through identification of air bubbles.	Particularly useful when the team is working on a process that is inefficient or that has an unduly long cycle time.	If the main problem is that the process is ineffective, the technique may not be helpful.
FMEA	Identifying/rating risks of defects on the basis of three criteria: severity, probability of occurrence, probability of detection.	Focusing on the most important risks to make the process robust. Promote continuous improvement through follow-up or risks.	One of the most powerful tools in the quality toolbox. Can be used in the Analyze, Improve, and Control phases.	Must be based on a detailed mapping of the process. May require exploding selected activities in more detail.
Diagnostic worksheet	Grouping the major conclusions stemming from each technique used and analyzing to find patterns and formulate diagnostic.	Provide at a glance a summary of all the data points available, thus facilitating analysis and validation.	Whenever more than one diagnostic tool is used.	This does not do away with analytical and synthetic capabilities. The tools facilitates the task but does not by any means provide a recipe.

Table 10.2 Critical activities, CTP variables, current and alternate controls.

Activity	It is critical that . . .	How do we currently ensure that this is done right?	What are other possible ways to control this?
The coordinator selects trainees	The trainees understand what they are getting into	It is explained in a memo	They meet with the graduates of the last course
	We ascertain that the trainees have the right motivation for the course	They are asked why they want to take the course	They are interviewed by two graduates
	The trainees be able to devote the time required by the course	They are asked if they can fit the course in their daily work	Their superiors are asked to sign a form specifying the time requirement
The instructor and the coordinator answer questions about preparing an initial project scope	The trainees understand what a process is	Nothing	A half day session is scheduled for that purpose prior to session 1
	The trainees get a clear answer quickly	The instructor and coordinator do their best	Measure response time and trainee satisfaction (survey)
The coordinator gives feedback to the trainees so that they can adjust the scope of the project	The trainees understand what is wrong with their initial submission and why	The instructor and coordinator do their best	Ask the trainee to reformulate on the spot, face to face

10.5.2 Fishbone Diagram (Ishikawa) and Prioritization Tool (ICUKU)

In the Define phase, the team used an Ishikawa diagram (not shown here) to assist in scoping the project correctly. Use of Ishikawa diagrams in this context is discussed in Chapter 7. The trigger they used then was based on the *Big Y*: "Why is the failure rate of training projects so high?" The team uses the technique again here. However, it uses the *small y* as a trigger this time. The coach thus gives the team the following instructions:

1. Paste together two or three sheets of paper from a flip chart and draw a fishbone diagram on it, with six *bones*. Label each with one of the following categories:

   - Methods—activities performed incorrectly

   - Manpower—any human-resources-related cause

   - Information systems and information technology (IS/IT)

   - Equipment and installations

   - Measures—any measurement issue

Organization and culture—any *soft* cause related to power, formal relationship, and shared values

1. You may create different categories, such as *environment* or *suppliers* if you feel this is warranted.

2. Place the following question at the head of the fishbone: "Why is it that so many trainee-candidate pairs do not meet all selection criteria?"

3. In silence, identify all possible answers to this question, write them down on a sticky note, and stick them in the appropriate category. If you start running out of ideas, explore mentally all the categories of the diagram and look at the causes your colleagues are coming up with: this may trigger other ideas.

4. When everyone has run out of ideas, elect a teammate to facilitate a review and rationalization of the diagram, eliminating duplicates, rewording, and reorganizing as the need arises.

This is a useful tool at this point, because it provides a separate route to identify the variables at play, one that is not based on the process map. Using those categories forces the team members to think differently, thus generally bringing out some variables it had not yet identified. However, since the goal of the Analyze phase is to single out the most important variables, this tool alone is incomplete. The ICUKU classification is a companion tool that serves this purpose. The coach now provides the team with the following additional instructions (see Table 10.3):

1. Split a flip-chart page into three columns, labeling them Major, Medium, and Minor.

2. Remove the sticky notes from the fishbone one at a time and stick them in one of the three columns according to the team's best judgment about its impact on the problem. The decisions must be consensual and supported by data.

3. Now, split each column in two, separating the causes that the team feels are somehow controllable from those over which it has no control at all, in the context of the mandate it was given. If the team believes it could have some control, however partial or limited, it should classify the cause as controllable, even though it does not have a specific idea about how it would go about controlling it.

Table 10.3 ICUKU classification of causes according to impact, controllability, and experience.

	Impact		
	Major	**Medium**	**Minor**
Known	Feedback is mostly a one-way street—it does not allow for interaction Some executives do not understand the criteria for project and trainee selection There is no feedback on the revised version of the project before the course The instructor and the coordinator interpret the criteria differently The instructor is not involved in selecting the trainee The coordinator and the instructor do not coordinate with each other	Nobody pushes or pulls if things do not happen in the back office Feedback on initial project proposals is often late Nothing happens until all the projects have been received Nobody measures response time There is confusion about who is responsible to answer trainees' questions	The logistician is often late in booking the training room, resulting in the use of inferior facilities Follow-up on those who miss the deadline for turning the proposals is sporadic The list of candidates is not updated regularly Some candidates are not consulted before their name is put on the list No reminder of the deadline to turn in the project is sent to the trainees
Controllable	Since it is hard to obtain support, trainees do it on their own	There is not standard response time	
Unknown	Some executives are not involved: long response time and poor quality Some candidates are pressured to participate No validation is made of the information provided by the candidates Trainees do not understand what a process actually is Some candidates are never interviewed (too busy, away on a trip, etc)	Back-office people at QKM assemble the training material in their spare time It often happens that the wrong version of the material is picked for assembly The client's training department is generally a bottleneck Nobody wants to be on those teams: it takes time and there is no recognition	Selection of team members is generally not complete at the outset of training and drags on for days, even weeks The instructor and coordinator are very busy, and often happy to see the course delayed Some trainees do not care and just go through the motions Some trainees do not understand the importance of what they are doing
Uncontrollable	There is no consequence to the executive for failure to deliver	The material is hard to understand and lacks examples	The coordinator works on several projects in parallel Some trainees do not read the material

4. Finally, split the first row created in the previous step (that is, the causes classified as *controllable*) into those causes for which the team can readily think of a solution (classify under *known*) and those for which it cannot (that is, *unknown*). Pulling each cause off the page, the team should ask itself: Do we know how to fix this? While the team should not explore solutions in any depth at this time, the team's idea manager should remain on the lookout and keep on filling the parking lot.

In going through these four steps, the team should use the data collected in the earlier phases and bring its experience to bear, supporting its classification with examples and illustrations. These two tools work well together: The first one generates a large quantity of causes, while the second allows the team to focus on the greatest opportunities or *low-hanging fruits*. Table 10.3 brings out a number of important issues:

- Executive involvement is uneven, both in quality and in timing

- There is a disconnection between the coordinator and the instructor

- Support for trainees takes place through asynchronous and *low bandwidth* modes of contact

- Back offices, both at QKM and at the client's, do not consider this task to be a priority

10.5.3 Root Causes Analysis—*Five Whys*

The next tool is closely related to the ones just presented. This technique is particularly useful in—though not limited to—developing a better understanding of the *controllable-unknown* category in the ICUKU classification. Some of the causes originally identified in the Ishikawa diagram are merely symptoms of a deeper problem. While energy devoted to elimination or mitigation of a symptom may produce some effect, unless you fix the underlying cause, this symptom or other symptoms will soon reappear. Finding and fixing root causes is much more effective. The *five whys* or root-cause analysis is one way to do this.

The technique itself is simple. However, using it may prove very difficult for the team, as it involves soul-searching and may bring out fundamental flaws in the process and the organization. The instructor gives the team the following instructions (see Figure 10.7):

1. Pick a cause from the *major impact-controllable-unknown* pigeonhole in the ICUKU classification. Copy it on a sticky note and put it at the top of a flip-chart page.

2. Ask yourselves the following question: Why is this happening?

3. Each team member writes down answers to that question in silence and sticks it under the first sticky notes.

4. When everyone is done, the team leader proceeds to rationalizing and structuring the sticky notes on the page.

5. The team then decides—again based on the evidence—which one of these causes is the most important determinant of the cause the team originally selected. Mark this cause with an asterisk (bold lined boxes in Figure 10.7)

6. Referring now to the cause marked with an asterisk, the team again asks itself: "Why is this happening?" and proceeds to answer this question as it did the previous one.

7. Repeat step six as many times as you can, until you are incapable of coming up with any meaningful answer. At that time, you have identified the root causes. Pushing until

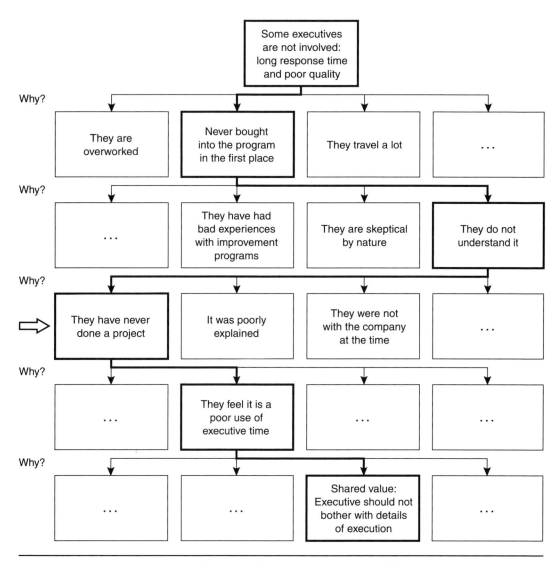

Figure 10.7 Root-cause analysis (*five whys*) for a *major-impact-controllable-unknown* cause from the ICUKU diagram (Table 10.3).

at least five such "Why?" questions have been answered is a useful rule of thumb (hence the name of the technique) to avoid the risk of not *digging* deep enough.

8. Looking at the column of causes marked with asterisks, find one that the team feels it can fix. Mark it with an arrow.

Anyone with young, curious children is implicitly familiar with this technique. They drive to the root cause in their quest to understand, and they sometimes drive you mad in the process . . . When pressed for time, someone facing a problem tends to settle for a symptom instead of taking the time and effort required to understand the origin of the problem. Thus, while the problem appears to be solved, since the bothersome symptom disappears, it surfaces again in one form or other, triggering another short-lived fire-fighting exercise.

When you start to dig, you do not know what lies below the surface. Sometimes the root cause is very philosophical, deeply rooted, and thus impossible to eradicate within the time and resource limitations imposed by the team's mandate. This is why the team is asked (Step 8), when faced with such a situation, to go back up the root until it finds a level of cause at which it can take action. At other times, the team discovers a root cause for which it can find a clear-cut solution that lies outside its mandate. This is what happens with the team with the first cause it picks: *some executives are not involved: long response time and poor quality*. It finds (see Figure 10.7) that training the executives themselves, by having them do a project, would solve several problems observed in the process.

At that point, the team calls in the process owner and asks him if this solution lies outside its terms of reference. The owner tells them that it does, but that it is an action well worth pursuing in the broader context of improving this process (*Big Y*) and that they should bring it up at the forum and share their views with all stakeholders. The team thus moves on to apply the tool to other causes selected from Table 10.3 (this work is not shown here). They reach the following conclusions:

- Many executives do not really understand what a project is, since they have never done one themselves.

- In some departments, the workload of trainees is not lightened and they are overworked.

- The human resource department (at the client's) and the superiors of potential candidates are not consulted in the selection process.

- The current support given to trainees is insufficient.

10.5.4 Value-added Analysis (VAA)

The purpose of a process is to add value to the input as it transforms it in an output (that is, the SITOC logic). Value, as discussed in Chapter 2, is in the eye of the beholder. The market ultimately sets the value of an output. When dealing with an internal process, the internal customer is relied on as a barometer of value creation. The activities within a process can be classified in two categories: those that contribute to value creation and those that do not. Why, might you ask, would any activities other than those that add value be performed? Four major reasons explain why this is done:

- The organization must cater to its two other stakeholders: employees and shareholders.

  —Employees are not all the same—they do things differently. They also need to take a break from time to time (delays).

  —Shareholders want to protect assets and minimize risks. They want to make sure that they will not be sued and that they comply with legal and regulatory requirements of all kinds, from environmental to fiscal.

- The business must be managed. Controls are needed. Records must be kept. Work must be divided up between organizational units and coordinated.

- As discussed in Chapter 3 (Section 3.4.2), processes take on a life of their own, quite independent from customer needs and their evolution. They evolve as individuals and organizational units evolve, as a function of dynamic interactions of all kinds.

- Human beings make mistakes. Sometimes they are caught, sometimes they are also fixed.

The customer is only willing to pay for the tasks that add value, plus a reasonable markup for overhead and profits. While the four families of non-value-added tasks are bound to exist to various degrees, a firm's ability to reduce their relative weight in the process is a clear source of competitive advantage. Indeed, the less NVA there is in a process, the shorter the cycle time, the lower the cost, and the higher the quality. While the first two observations are obvious, the last may be somewhat counterintuitive. You might think that a longer process would leave more time to do a quality job. Remember first that the discussion here is not focused on performing value-added tasks faster, but rather about eliminating NVA tasks. By introducing *air pockets* in the process, NVA tasks interrupt, disconnect, and take the focus away from value-added tasks, just as the output of a water pump that sucks in air through a leak decreases drastically. Thus, it creates opportunities for defects and makes them harder to detect, drowned as they are by NVA tasks, and makes it easier for process workers to unknowingly work at cross-purposes for long periods.

As discussed in Chapter 4, professionals like to protect their autonomy by insulating themselves from managers and other professionals. While this avoids potentially unpleasant discussions, it also deprives the organization of opportunities to expose and resolve issues. A process can be designed either to accommodate problems without too much disruption, or to jam completely when a problem occurs, thereby confronting process workers with it, and forcing them to address the issue. We call the latter a *lean* process, reflecting the fact that value-added activities are not insulated by *layers of fat* (NVA activities).

Now revisit the four reasons why activities that do not add value to the customer are performed. The first reason includes activities that are adding value to two other stakeholders, and thus are necessary. These are *business value-adding* activities. In an ideal world, activities performed for the other three reasons constitute waste to be eliminated or at least minimized. In an ideal world, management would be seamless and effortless, because management systems would be perfect; all employees would be perfectly qualified, be trustworthy, motivated, and have access to the right tools. In such a world, no time would be wasted on control, moving things around (the layout would be optimal), filing or retrieving papers, redoing a task done poorly, or simply waiting. Thus, these activities will be labeled as NVA.

This is not an ideal world. Thus, processes will always include some NVA activities. However, the process with the lowest proportion of NVA is superior. This alone makes it worthwhile to calculate that proportion, benchmark it, and try to reduce it. Telling apart the NVA tasks, however, is also very useful in the identification of zones of opportunity in the process: the team should try to obliterate the parts of the process that add little value. The instructor thus gives the following instructions to the team, specifying how to identify NVA, calculate the value-added ratio, and prepare the corresponding diagram (see Figure 10.8):

1. Go through your process map, task by task, and mark NVA activities with a red dot (in Figure 10.8, solid circles are used instead). Ask yourselves the question: "Is this task essential to meet customers' needs?" Another acid test is: "If the customer was knowledgeable about our business, and was watching as we do this task, would there be comfort in paying for this?" All verifications, controls, rework, delays, and movements are NVA by definition. Leave the customer out of this exercise: This exercise focuses on the value that the customer receives, not the value received from the customer.

2. As discussed above, some activities may be depicted at a higher level (composite or aggregate activities), and the question formulated above cannot be answered in one fell swoop. For these, ask the team to estimate the total value-added time and draw a bicolor (red-green) bar, proportional in length to time span (three days, if considering organize logistics), with a green part proportional to value-added time (see Figure 10.9, where the lighter part of the bar replaces green, and the darker part, red).

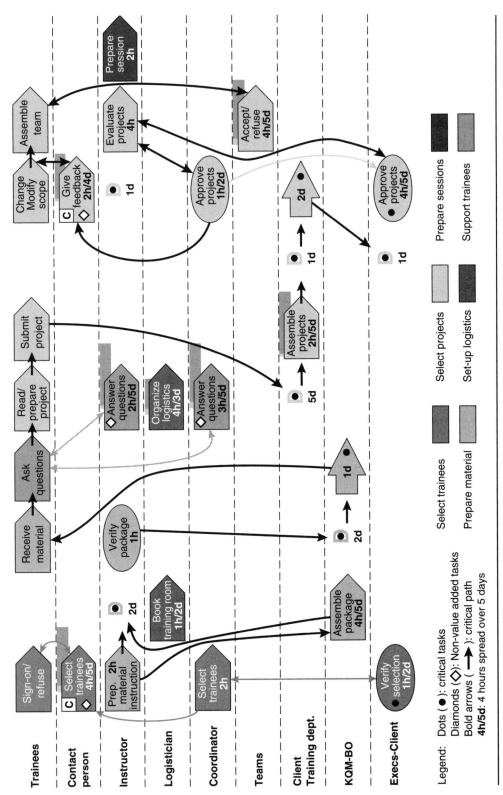

Figure 10.8   Non-value-added activities, CTPs, and critical path.

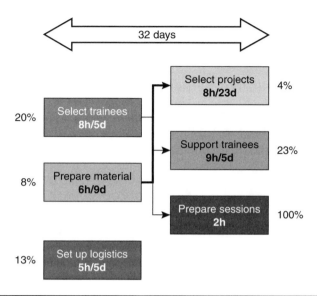

Figure 10.9 Precedence diagram for the six functions, respective value-added ratios, and critical path.

3. Calculate the value-added ratio of the whole process as the sum of all value-added times (assume an eight-hour workday[1]) divided by the total cycle time.

4. Referring to the FAST diagram (Figure 10.3), prepare a precedence diagram, that is, describe visually (see Figure 10.8) the precedence constraints that exist between the functions (project selection, for instance, cannot start until trainees have received the material). Calculate the value-added ratio for each function in the FAST diagram and transfer that information onto the precedence diagram. Identify and mark the longest path in the precedence diagram (the *critical path*). Identify and mark the critical path on the process map (see bold arrows in Figure 10.8).

5. Plot the value-added ratios (global and by function) as shown in Figure 10.9 respecting the precedence relationships as you go.

6. Analyze Figures 10.8, 10.9, and 10.10 and draw your conclusions.

Much of these efforts are meant to make the analysis visual, so that the team can easily relate to it as it tries to formulate an overall diagnosis, and make its case to the rest of the organization. The team draws the following major conclusions from its analysis:

• Executives contribute significantly to cycle time, but do not add any value.

• Back offices are an important source of NVA.

• The back-and-forth between the trainees and support staff for questions and feedback adds much NVA and probably destroys value.

• Moving all the paper-based material is long and NVA.

The team adds many ideas to the parking lot during this exercise.

Two important observations must be made at this time. First, putting a red dot on an activity does not mean that you can simply stop performing it. If you verify whether someone else's work

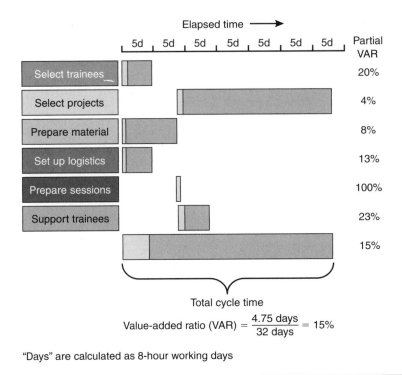

Figure 10.10 Value added: Overall and by function.

was performed correctly, it may be because it is often defective. The solution is not to stop checking, but rather to take action to ensure that inspection is not required any more. Second, sticking an NVA dot on a task that you have been performing for a long time is not an emotionally neutral task. It often triggers a deep awareness that the process is really flawed and has to be changed. Indeed, this tool often helps the team to cross an inner threshold of belief in the necessity and the possibility of change. However, it may also raise a doubt in some team members' minds: "Am I shooting myself in the foot if I put a red not on this task? Am I really sticking a red dot on my forehead?" If this issue is not addressed, it will probably not surface and fester. Thus, the issue must be raised at the outset of the workshop and clear *rules of engagement* must be presented and debated.

10.5.5 Failure Mode and Effect Analysis (FMEA)

Quality is about avoiding defects. In order to do this, defects in the specific process at hand, must be defined. Defects have already been defined at the outset of the project in the SMART diagram (Figure 10.3): Any trainee-project pair that does not meet all the selection criteria is a defect. Counting such defects is a good way to track the evolution of the performance of the process over time, but it does not help us pinpoint improvement opportunities. To that end, identifying specific risks of defects that could occur at various points in the process is more useful. A defect occurs when something is done wrong and thus potentially affects the performance of the process, that is, in the PAC setup, result in missing criteria or increasing cycle time. A risk of defect (also called failure mode) is defined as a combination of variables (circumstances or events) that could occur and result in a defect. Failure mode and effect analysis is a technique that helps in identifying and ranking risks of defects, thereby focusing the team on finding countermeasures for the most critical ones.

To identify risks, concentrate on critical activities identified earlier (see Table 10.2), as important ones are more likely to be found there. The coach gives the team the following instructions regarding how to go about risk identification:

1. Review the critical activities and the list of critical variables identified earlier (see the first two columns of Table 10.2). For each of these activities, go through a silent idea-generation session, thinking about what could go wrong (failure modes) and writing it down on sticky notes. It helps to consider in turn the six categories used in the fishbone diagram (see Section 10.5.2 above): method, manpower, IS/IT, measures, equipment and installation, and organization and culture.

2. Review these ideas as a team, clarifying them as you go, eliminating duplicate entries and brainstorming to generate new ones.

3. Draw a diagram like the one shown in Table 10.4 (consider only the left-hand side of the diagram at this time, as the right-hand side will be discussed later) and paste the result of your work in the first two columns.

The second part of this technique deals with ranking the failure modes just identified in order of importance, that is, in order of priority for the team. A failure mode is more important to the team if its consequences on the customer are severe, if it has a high probability of occurring, and if there is no means of detecting it when it occurs until the damage is done. Hence, FMEA attributes to each risk a risk priority number (RPN) proportional to the importance of the risk based on these three criteria:

• Severity: "How severe are the effects of this defect (should it occur) on the outcome of the process, or more precisely here, on criteria missed and on cycle time?"

• Probability of occurrence: "How likely is it to occur?"

• Probability of non-detection: "How likely is it that we will not detect the defect, once it has occurred, until the damage is done?"

The team answers each of these questions by assigning a relative numerical value, based on a 10-point scale, where a value of one stands for an insignificant risk and a value of 10 for a critical one, thus obtaining three numerical values (digits from one to 10) that are multiplied to obtain the RPN. Hence, the RPN scale ranges from one to 1000, with the latter representing a risk of the highest possible severity, highly likely to occur, and having a high probability of escaping detection. The instructor gives the team the following instruction to complete this technique:

1. Consider all the failure modes you have listed in the FMEA diagram. Which one do you think has the most severe effect? The least severe? Take the time to reach a consensus. Ties are acceptable. Attribute a value of 10 to the most severe and a value of one to the least severe and write it in the appropriate column. Repeat the procedure for the other two criteria.

2. Using a 10-point scale, rate the severity, probability of occurrence, and probability of non-detection of the first five failure modes you have identified, proceeding one risk at a time. Use the ratings you have attributed in step one as boundary values, maintaining comparability as you go. Write the values on small sticky notes and place them in your FMEA diagram. Calculate the RPN by multiplying the three values. Place it in the diagram as well.

3. Review and normalize your ratings. In order to do that, compare, one column at a time, the ratings you have attributed to the risks just rated. Adjust the ratings on each of the three criteria as required.

4. Proceed to rate the other risks.

Table 10.4 Partial failure mode and effect analysis (FMEA).

Critical activity	Failure mode	Severity	Occurrence	Non-detection	RPN	Poka-yoke	Severity	Occurrence	Non-detection	New RPN
Select trainee	Evaluator misinterprets the meaning of a criterion	10	4	9	360	Provide sheet with examples	10	2	8	160
	The evaluator skips a criteria	4	1	4	16	Require the evaluator to calculate a total	4	1	1	4
	The candidate misunderstands a question (wording problem)	1	5	5	25	Provide the candidate with a sheet containing simple, alternate wording	1	3	3	9
	Candidate's answer is less than candid (wants to be rejected)	6	6	9	324	Use more than one evaluator and make joint assessment	6	2	7	84
	...									
Answer trainee's questions about project scoping	Trainee misunderstands the answer (wording problem)	5	5	4	100	Ask the trainee to repeat understanding of the answer	5	5	1	25
	Evaluator misunderstands the issue	7	4	6	168	Ask other trainees to be present and reformulate the issue if needed	5	3	3	45
	Trainee is afraid to ask a question for fear of looking dumb	7	6	10	420	Ask each trainee to write an anonymous question on a piece of paper. Collect, answer, and discuss	5	2	10	100
	Evaluator does not know the client's business well enough to answer the question	9	10	7	630	Have client executives present when questions are asked	9	1	2	18
	...									
Give feedback to trainee on the project	Evaluator does not know the client's business well enough to provide accurate feedback	9	10	7	630	Have client executives present when feedback is prepared and given	9	1	2	18
	Negative feedback is taken as blame	7	7	9	441	Provide evaluator with standard introductory formulas to use	7	4	9	252
	Feedback is not specific enough for trainee to make required changes	8	6	9	432	Provide feedback and *rescope* immediately with the evaluator in attendance	8	1	2	16
	Trainee cannot reach the evaluator	7	7	1	49	Provide an easily reachable in-house coach	2	7	1	14
	...									

Among the failure modes identified, the most severe is that the evaluator does not understand a criterion. If that happens, many projects or trainees will be defective. The most probable is that the evaluator does not know the client's business well enough to answer the question, as the current process does not include any mechanism through which the coordinator and instructor can learn the customer's business. A trainee's fear of asking a question is the risk least likely to be detected. Among the 12 failure modes listed in Table 10.4, *evaluator does not know the client's business well enough to provide accurate feedback* is the most important (RPN = 630).

The full FMEA (not shown) lists 25 failure modes. As the team was working on the diagram, a teammate entered the information on an electronic spreadsheet. Performing a sort operation by RPN allowed reorganizing the risks in the completed Table 10.4.from the most to the least important. The four following failure modes came out on top:

- Evaluators do not know the client's business well enough and their feedback is not specific enough.

- Coordinators, evaluators, and executives do not always see eye to eye on what the criteria mean.

- Trainees hold back for fear of looking dumb and perceive negative feedback as blame.

- Candidates often do not answer evaluators' questions candidly.

Three observations about this technique are in order. First, as the team identifies failure modes and assesses their severity, it thinks about what could happen that would affect the outcome of the process. However, the project is focused on two different outcomes: meeting all criteria and having a short cycle time. The failure modes that affect these two outcomes may not be the same. Whenever this is the case, the team must split the original idea-generation session to consider the two outcomes separately, using sticky notes of a different color to capture the risk they identify. The same goes for assessing severity. Hence, it might be worthwhile to prepare two FMEA tables.

Secondly, sometimes an alternate way to use the 10-point scale is used. Whenever some failure modes may endanger human health or lives, such as may be the case in health services, each value on the scale can be defined in absolute rather than relative terms. A value of seven, for instance could de defined as: *a 10 percent probability of non-fatal injury*. Creating such a scale is an elaborate but essential undertaking when the stakes are so high.

Finally, the level of rigor of the exercise can be raised considerably, whenever possible, by using numerical data. Severity data can be assessed through discussion with the customer. Probability of occurrence/detection can be assessed through calculation of past frequencies.

10.5.6 Formulating a Diagnosis—Diagnostic Worksheet

The team must now formulate a diagnosis. To do so, it must first collate all the partial conclusions it has reached (independently) using eight different techniques. It must then analyze this information (comparing, correlating, and cross-validating the elements), synthesize it into an incisive diagnosis, and present it forcefully to convince all the stakeholders (see Figure 10.11).

The coach gives the team the following instructions:

1. Draw a diagnostic worksheet such as that shown in Table 10.5.

2. Revisit each technique used so far in the Analyze phase. Write down what the team has learned from that technique, which it should consider in the formulation of a diagnosis. In other words, ask yourselves the following question: "What do we know about the causes of the problem that we did not know before using this technique?"

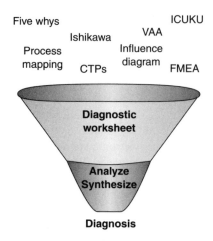

Figure 10.11 Collating and analyzing partial conclusions from eight techniques; synthesizing a diagnosis.

Try to summarize your answers into three or four major points and insert them in Table 10.5. If you end up with five, that is all right. If you end up empty-handed with some techniques, that is all right as well.

3. Compare and explore relationships between the various elements posted on the worksheet. Some elements are essentially the same. Others are closely related, complementary, or represent different facets of the same underlying issue. Use color coding to visually relate these elements to one another. If you find apparent contradictions, go back to the source and resolve them.

4. For each factor (number coded from 1 to 8) found in Table 10.5, write a one-sentence statement that captures its essence. For instance, the three elements coded as number five could be summarized as: "Even though much information is available, we depend solely on the candidates themselves to assess their capability."

5. Considering all the summary factors produced in the previous step, write a short (three lines) overall diagnosis, and copy it in a form similar to that shown in Table 10.6, completing it with a one or two-line description of each individual factor or problem.

This amounts to distilling the essence of the diagnosis from a loose collection of disjointed elements, gathered through a host of different means. This again is quite similar to the critical diagnostic task performed by doctors and the court strategy and summation performed by lawyers. It is professional work at its most complex and most value-added. It requires the judgment, intuition, rigor, and synthetic capability that distinguish professional work from any other type of work.

Making the diagnostic so short may result in leaving out some details, but these can be revisited as the team wraps up the Improve phase later on. However, it also makes it concise, dense, and rich enough for the team to be able to present a vivid image of the situation, and focus the discussion with other stakeholders on the fundamentals. By eliminating the *noise* that relatively trivial issues may create at this time, the *signal* is made all the clearer. In complex situations, it is sometimes worthwhile at this point to prepare a new influence diagram, to illustrate the dynamics of causes, effects relationships, and make the diagnosis visual.

Table 10.5 Diagnostic worksheet.

Mapping	CTPs	Ishikawa-ICUKU	Five why's	VAA	FMEA
Many players are involved and much back-and-forth goes on (1)	We do not validate the information used for trainee selection (5)	Executives involvement is very uneven, in both quality and timing (6)	Many executives do not really understand what a project is, since they have never done one themselves (6)	Executives contribute significantly to cycle time, but do not add any value (6)	Evaluators do not know the client's business well enough and their feedback is not specific enough (6)
There are six long delays, for a total of 12 days (2)	We do not ensure that trainees understand what a process is (1)	There is a disconnect between the coordinator and the instructor (4)	In some departments the workload of trainees is not lightened and they are overworked (1)	Back offices are an important source of delay (7)	Coordinators, evaluators, and executives do not always see eye to eye on what the criteria mean (4)
Little face-to-face contact takes place with the trainees (3)	Support and feedback in general are deficient (3)	Support for trainee takes place through asynchronous and *low bandwidth* modes of contact (3)	HR and bosses are not consulted in the selection process (5)	The back-and-forth between the trainees and support staff for questions and feedback adds much delay probably destroys value (2)	Trainees hold back for fear of looking dumb and perceive negative feedback as blame (8)
There are few contact points between the coordinator and the instructor (4)		Back offices, both at QKM and at the client's do not consider this task to be a priority (4)	The current support given to trainees is insufficient (3)	Moving all the paper-based material is long and non-value-added (7)	Candidates often do not answer evaluator's questions candidly (5)

Table 10.6 Process diagnosis.

Global	
Summary diagnosis	The process involves too many players acting independently, involving delays and interference at each hand-off. Contacts are remote and asynchronous, and lack the richness and *bandwidth* that the nature of the task requires. Too much paper is processed.
Details	
Problem 1	There is confusion between the roles of the instructor and coordinator throughout the process.
Problem 2	Executives add much delay and little value, yet much of the knowledge of the business and the candidates that exists is not brought to bear on trainee and project selection.
Problem 3	Assembling and transporting course *kits* in back offices is long and fraught with errors.
Problem 4	There is much noise and delay in feedback given to trainees on their projects. Not enough knowledge of the business goes into this and there is little interaction between those who know and those who want to learn.

That night (end of day two), the team presents its diagnosis to all stakeholders, walking the group through a guided tour of the evidence that supports it. This creates a rich environment, conducive to discussions, in a level playing field, focused on issues and evidence rather than personalities, and thus to consensus.

10.6 IMPROVE

The output of this phase is a validated *prescription*, that is, a new process that meets the goals of the project, ready to rollout.

The general flow of this phase is to first generate more improvement ideas—remember that many ideas generated throughout the Analyze phase are waiting in the *parking lot*—by revisiting each diagnostic tool, selecting the best ones, and designing a new process on that basis. The coach gives the team the following instructions:

1. Go back again to each diagnostic tool in turn. Looking at the problems (causes, defect, CTP, NVA), ask yourselves: "How could we fix this?" Answer the question as a team, using the idea generation and brainstorming technique described earlier. The idea *parking lot* should be filled to capacity by the time you are done.

2. Look for simple solutions. Keep the sweeping, costly, and risky solutions (such as automation) as a last resort. If executives had wanted to do that, they would not have called this event.

3. Clean up the parking lot: eliminate duplicates, dump the ideas you cannot understand, and combine similar ideas. *Here is a sample of the ideas left in the team's parking lot at that stage:*

   • Include an initial screening of the list of the candidates.

   • Only involve executives who have gone through the training.

- Conduct post-course debriefing with executives, showing the savings involved with well-scoped projects.

- Perform selection of candidate live, in a half-day session. The core team would act as selection committee.

- Perform project selection live in a half-day session. The core team would act as selection committee. Each trainee brings and passes around copies of their project to each participant. Trainees who miss the session would be barred from the course

- Organize a *trainee-instructor-coordinator Q&A* session in a web-conference. Set the time at the end of the trainee selection session.

- Eliminate approval of trainees and project by all executives.

- Criteria: give the limited number of places to the most willing and facilitate opting-out for the others.

- Invite all executives who want to attend the selection committees.

- Leave it to each trainee to decide whom to consult with.

- Make the last assignment of the course the sponsoring and coaching of a new trainee.

- Feedback session: all together—live *re-scoping*.

- E-material only. Hard-copies: in-class as needed.

- Make it a part of every employee's goal to participate in two project teams every year.

- Let the instructor assemble an electronic package and upload it to the client's intranet.

- Accept that there may be fewer trainees per wave because of the new process—focus on quality. Success will create its own momentum.

- Create a core team at the outset consisting of the instructor, the coordinator, and selected executives.

- Training room must be booked before a date is formally set to launch the session.

- Updating the list of trainees is another process (upstream) delegated to HR.

- Hold a full-day session to do all of this.

- Add an assistant from the client to work with the coordinator.

- Standardize and freeze the training package—always have an inventory ready that would be sufficient for any training wave.

4. For each remaining idea, fill out an idea evaluation card (this is the job of the idea manager) such as the one shown in Table 10.7. The questions are self-explanatory. The first purpose is to help the team build a shared understanding of each idea and to clarify them. Cost estimates can initially be rough, such as high, medium, or low, so that no time is wasted evaluating the cost of an idea that will be quickly discarded, or

Table 10.7 Idea evaluation card.

Name:	Number:
Description:	
What problem (refer to diagnosis) does it address:	
What proportion of the problem would it eliminate (%):	
What does it require (constraints, equipment, software, HR changes . . .):	
Is it linked (complementary, substitute, antagonistic) with any other idea:	
What will it cost?	
How long will it take to implement?	
Pros	**Cons**
Adopted	**Rejected**
For future consideration (out of scope)–Who should follow up on this idea?	

for which cost is not a deciding consideration. Do not decide right away whether the idea should be accepted or rejected. You should consider together or group ideas that are strongly linked. Ideas that are mutually exclusive should be tied and considered together.

5. Sort the remaining ideas using the ICUKU classification scheme presented earlier. Use the original sticky notes, cross-referenced to the idea cards. The controllable-uncontrollable dimension is now interpreted as: "Is this idea within scope—that is, would it be infringing on some constraints or instructions given to the team with its marching orders?" The known-unknown dimension now means: "Do we have experience with whatever is proposed (known) or is this totally new—and thus risky (unknown)?"

6. Create a new working area on a flip-chart page. Label it *Adopted Ideas*. Go through the ideas pasted in the ICUKU classification, starting with the *major impact-controllable-known* category and working your way toward the opposite corner. Discuss the idea and decide whether to accept or reject it. Paste the ideas you accept on the new page. Place a red dot on ideas you reject and leave them in the ICUKU classification. When the team cannot agree after a reasonable amount of time, place a yellow dot on the idea, and leave it there as well.

Table 10.8 Prescription: High-level description of the solution and explanation of the major elements.

Global		
Summary prescription		
Much of the interaction that now takes place remotely will be reintegrated in a limited number of face-to-face forums, involving all the required players. Only executives capable of contributing will be involved. The role of mentor/coach will be created. Paper kits will replace the binders.		
Details	**Justification**	**Responsible, constraints, timing**
Element 1		
Selection will be done face to face in real time, in a half-day session involving a core team including the instructor, the coordinator, and selected executives	A core team will have more ownership and cohesion. Face to face is required to better assess the candidates.	See Gantt chart (*not included*)
Element 2		
A question and answer web-meeting will be held by the core team with all trainees attending	It is important that the trainees listen to the questions of their colleagues and to the answers. This eliminates repetition and avoids confusion.	See Gantt chart (*not included*)
Element 3		
A face-to-face half-day feedback session will be held (core team + trainees) and *rescoping* will be done on the spot	This is a crucial point both for learning and scoping the project right. It is worthwhile to provide the richest forum possible to do this and to maximize interaction and cross-learning among trainees.	See Gantt chart (*not included*)
Element 4		
Before being certified, each trainee will have to act as mentor/coach to a new trainee	This is a win-win-win solution for the trainees, the client organization, and QKM. It solves an important process problem and is effective and rewarding for all involved.	See Gantt chart (*not included*)
Element 5		
The instructor will prepare and send all material electronically	This avoids many non-value-added intermediaries, sources of delays, and defects. Hard copies can be printed selectively by the trainees as required	See Gantt chart (*not included*)

7. When you are done, revisit the yellow dotted ideas, considering them this time in the light of what they would add to the joint effect of all the ideas you have already accepted. The decision is normally much easier at this time.

8. Fill out a prescription form similar to that shown in Table 10.8. The summary has to be short: present the essence in such a way that the reader (or listener) will be able to see how each element fits in the global vision. There may be more than the five elements than you can fit in Table 10.8. Bring these up in the question and answer session that follows the presentation at the prescription forum.

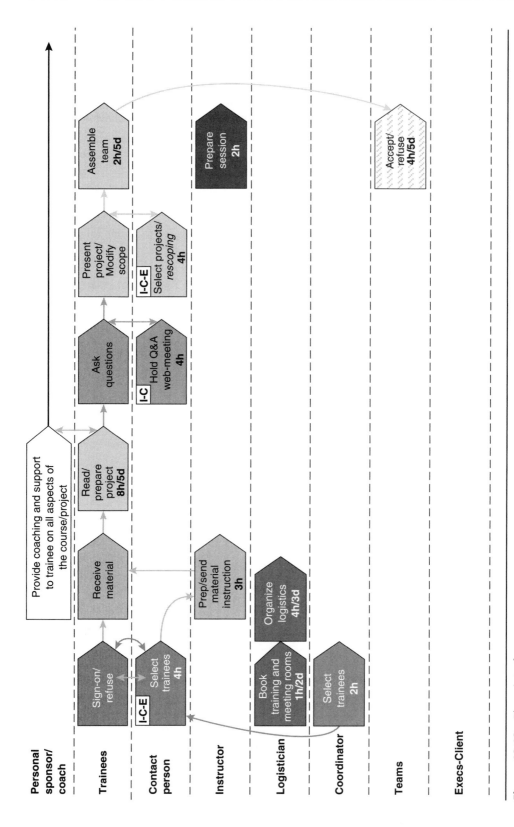

Figure 10.12 Blueprint of new process.

9. Prepare a blueprint (See Figure 10.11—it looks like a mapping, except that it does not represent the process as it is, but rather what it will look like once implemented), trying to include all the ideas you have accepted. Incoherencies and gaps may appear as you go, since you are creating a new process based on an old one and a set of relatively disjointed ideas. You may have to reformulate or clarify some of the ideas, reconsider earlier decisions, and generate new ideas to fill the gaps and insure global coherence.

10. Calculate the value-added ratio of the new process, using the technique described earlier. Explore ways to improve it further.

11. Consider in turn each element of the blueprint of the new process as well as the ideas you have accepted. Identify actions of all kinds that will have to take place to make the new process become a reality. These will fall in categories similar to those used in the Ishikawa diagram. Write these actions on sticky notes and paste them in a table similar to that shown in Table 10.9. Notice that it includes a section labeled implementation plan. Since this is preliminary and subject to review following step 12, you only need to give a general idea of what the implementation stage will involve in terms of resources and timing. It may be included on a Gantt chart (a bar diagram with a time line).

12. Present your work to the prescription forum (end of day three). Do not be dogmatic or defensive. There is not a unique solution to a problem. Listen to alternatives that may come up and debate them with an open mind. Considering the work that the team has done, however, and the make-up of the team, it will take considerable evidence to prove that something is fundamentally flawed with your solution. Any comment involving a reconsideration of the diagnosis is not receivable at this point. This debate was closed with the end of the Analyze phase. Absents are in the wrong.

Process improvement can take many different forms:

- Reintegration of work: eliminating a step in the process, *disintermediation*, that is, avoiding going through an intermediary, combining steps

- Outright elimination of a player from the process

- Changing modes of contact

- Involving the customer

- Changing accountability and incentives

- Training

- Changing or improving tools

- Automating a step or a part of the process

- Changing the flow of information

- Adding *poka-yokes*

Poka-yoke is the Japanese word for a failsafe device, that is, a simple mechanism to prevent a defect. When you create a password on a computer, you are asked to enter it again to validate. Since the likelihood of making the same mistake twice is much less than that of making it only once, the risk of defect is reduced considerably—at a negligible cost. This is a poka-yoke. A checklist to use

Table 10.9 Elements of the new process: Choices already made and decisions to be taken (partial).

Equipment	Installations	Materials	Suppliers
• Make sure all trainees have easy access to a computer	• Appropriate meeting rooms for the new live sessions will have to be found	• Prepare a new criteria scoring sheet, including a user guide with examples	• Make sure HR can deliver on their promise to keep up-to-date list of candidates
		• Review course outline to reflect the new process . . .	• Review training plan to take into account the fact that some trainees will drop out before the course starts
HR aspects	**IS/IT**	**Procedures**	**Implementation plan**
• Communicate the new roles to executive	• Make sure all trainees have access to Netmeeting and the latest version of Acrobat reader	• Prepare legal procedure to insure a binding commitment to confidentiality of material	• See Gantt chart attached (*not included*)
• Change evaluation procedures to recognize membership in a team	• Evaluate new group-ware	• Organize scheduling so that the coordinator and instructor can be available at the same time	
• Mediate the disagreement between coordinators and instructors	• Develop security procedure for the uploaded material	• Document new process	
• Valorize the role of executives on the core team	• Create a standardized electronic repository for all training material		
. . .	. . .	. . .	

in performing a task is a poka-yoke. To identify a poka-yoke, you must have a clear and detailed idea of the genesis of that defect. In the password example, for instance, the risk arises from the interaction of two variables: 1. When you type your password, it does not appear on the screen and 2. Widespread clumsiness in using a keyboard. Understanding this, it can be seen that making the keyword visible onscreen would solve the problem, but it would also create a potentially worse security risk. Repeating it is the best solution since, even though it requires some time and is not absolutely failsafe, it does not create any other risk. This is the type of analysis that you must perform in evaluating alternate solutions. For a more elaborate discussion on failsafing, see Chase and Stewart (1994) and Nakajo and Kume (1996).

The right-hand side of Table 10.4 presents a number of poka-yokes for the failure modes appearing on the left-hand side. Providing the evaluators with specific examples of good and bad applications of the criteria is a way to reduce the probability of occurrence of the failure: *Evaluator misinterprets the meaning of a criterion*. The team thinks that it would reduce it from a *four* to a *two* on the 10-point scale. It would also reduce the probability of non-detection, as the evaluator could refer to the examples to check its work. Thus, the RPN would be reduced from 360 to 160. In searching for a fix, prevention, that is, reducing the probability of occurrence is always best. Failing that, one should look for a *detection* poka-yoke and a *mitigation* poka-yoke (that is, reducing severity), in that order. The team should first sort the risks (in decreasing order) based on the left-hand-side RPN and start from the top.

10.7 CONTROL

The output of this phase is an implemented, stable, and capable process, together with the *owner manual* necessary to keep it that way. A process is stable or *in control*—see discussion in Chapter 8) if it is functioning within its usual operating parameters, that is, it is not affected by shifts or drifts, and its performance is thus predictable. It is capable if the voice of the process falls well within the voice of the customer, that is, if the number of *defective* trainee-project pairs stays clear of the desired 10 pecent maximum and the time required to start a training wave never exceeds 15 days.

This is the phase where the team follows up on implementation until it is ready to pass the baton, that is, turn the process over to the process owner and process workers. Minor adjustments to the process and fine tuning are often necessary to stabilize the process. The team often does this through a pilot project. It develops a control plan (see Table 10.10) specifying what to measure, how, where, and when. The plan also assigns, after consultations with the process owner, responsibilities for taking corrective actions and for drawing improvement lessons from defects. In this specific case, forms are to be filled out at the end of the selection and the *rescoping* sessions by the coordinator, the instructor, and the executives in attendance. The instructor will later fill out a form, at the end of the course, which will be compared with those filled out at the beginning. This way, the criteria and the way to apply them can be honed through every occurrence of the process.

At this time, the team also documents the process, completing the write-up of the essentials of the process (a procedure is complete when you cannot make it any simpler without losing important content) for future reference and training of new players. The owner will also use the FMEA table (Table 10.4) as a continuous improvement tool. As defects are identified using the tracking system proposed in Table 10.10, the owner will use the FMEA chart to reassess probabilities of occurrence and probabilities of non-detection for various failure modes, update the chart (calculating new RPNs and re-sort), and look for new poka-yokes for emerging risks. SPC charts will also be developed (see Chapter 8) as sufficient numerical data becomes available.

10.8 UNDERSTANDING THE DMAIC METHODOLOGY

The *idea hopper* (see Figure 10.1), the Analyze, and the Improve phases share a common principle: first generate a quantity of elements, then distill quality out of the mass of elements generated. In any contest, the higher the number of candidates, the more likely you are to find

---

Table 10.10   Control plan.

> **What must be measured?** Number of projects not respecting all criteria. Number of trainees not respecting criteria. Cycle time, from launch decision to the beginning of session 1.
>
> *How (measurement system)?* Criteria: Two forms have been designed: one for projects, one for trainees. Cycle time will be calculated based on the date of the initial email from the logistician to QKM requesting a new session.
>
> **Who must measure and when (sampling plan)?** Evaluators will fill out a form together at the end of the trainees selection session, and another one at the end of the rescoping session. The instructor must decide on the number of trainee projects not meeting all criteria at the end of the course. The logistician will measure cycle time. SPC charts will be gradually built up.
>
> **Who is responsible for corrective action and what rules must he/she apply?** Coordinator and instructor–jointly.
>
> **Who is responsible for learning and disseminating the lessons learned?** The process owner, through the dynamic use of FMEA and poka-yokes.

high-quality ones. The higher the number of project ideas entered into the hopper, the more likely you are to find a high-potential one. The more detailed the mapping, the more likely you are to identify with precision the vital few variables. While the elements generated (activities, causes, and risks), the methods used to generate them (brainstorming, process description, and risk identification), and the filtering technique used (search for critical elements, ICUKU classification, and risk evaluation) vary, this logic is repeated for all the other techniques: VAA, Ishikawa, FMEA, and improvement ideas.

Rigor is about logical validity and severe accuracy. The inherent logic of each tool presented above is obvious, even though they all approach the problem from a different perspective. The result of logical reasoning, however, is only as good as the data to which you apply it—garbage in, garbage out. It is in the Measure phase that most of the data is gathered. Data are individual facts or items of information—numerical or qualitative. Statistics is the science that helps you deal rigorously with numerical facts. The statistical tools presented in this book are basic. A host of more advanced tools, lying beyond the scope of this book, are available when the situation warrants it. In professional services, qualitative facts are legion. They are described with words and sentences, such as those used to describe CTPs, causes, activities, risks, and ideas. Accuracy of wording is therefore of the utmost importance. Seeing eye-to-eye on the facts is always a challenge, especially when various professions are involved. Indeed, a simple word such as *fact* can give rise to semantic confusion if lawyers, doctors, and engineers are around the table. Thus, for quantitative data, rigor lies in establishing and describing concisely the phenomena that take place and their prevalence. Tight wording avoids semantic confusion.

Much thought has been devoted to managing change, in the way the DMAIC methodology has been deployed in the Kaizen event (the change vehicle). Consider the factors required to succeed in a change initiative, as discussed in Chapter 9. Calculating the value-added ratio and identifying failure modes, for instance, typically brings out dissatisfaction with the current situation and shows that there is room for improvement. The team does all the work on sticky notes and flip charts, using colored markers and dots. This makes the process and the analysis visual and readily accessible by the team throughout the event, as they leave all the work they do on the wall. This facilitates the emergence of a shared diagnosis and of a vision of the future process. It also facilitates the sharing of these visions to the rest of the organization—a central element in the change leadership role that the team must play.

The simultaneous use of many diagnostic tools serves three purposes:

- Reducing the probability of missing an important causal factor.

- Helping the team isolate the most important factors. Obtaining the same result through different tools constitutes validation and increases the team's feeling of confidence, without which they could not be as convincing to others.

- Depending on the problem and the process, some tools are more powerful than others. Unfortunately, there are no set rules for predicting how effective each tool will be in any given situation. Hence, it is better to spread out the limited time available to formulate a diagnosis on many techniques, rather than using a single technique to the fullest.

Finally, two additional success factors for change are addressed with this approach. Since the team is mobilized full-time for the event, and since time pressure is present throughout, there is no lack of a sense of urgency. Further, the anxious team is not at risk of going around in circles: It is guided from beginning to end, by means of detailed instructions and coaching, through a rigorous methodology. Thus, the DMAIC Kaizen event constitutes a rigorous overall game plan for change. It is a vital piece in any corporate change strategy.

10.9 SUMMARY

The DMAIC methodology provides a detailed roadmap for process improvement. It consists of five phases: Define, Measure, Analyze, Improve, and Control. The chapter is built around the example of a consulting process improved using a Kaizen event as change vehicle. The improvement project starts from a rough-cut improvement idea. The Define phase determines the precise scope of the project. The Measure phase describes the process, identifies variables, and validates measurement systems. The Analyze phase takes the data thus produced and formulates a diagnosis, which becomes the basis for the development of a new process in the Improve phase. The Control phase works on incorporating the improved process in the fabric of the organization, in such a way that the gains achieved are sustainable.

Each phase uses a number of techniques that are described and illustrated throughout the chapter, together with the instructions required to use them correctly. Each technique approaches the problem and the process from a different angle, applying a different logical grid to different parts of the dataset. The use of several techniques in parallel allows for more rigor, and helps the team to make their case more compelling, thereby reinforcing its leadership role. Taking place as it does here in the context of a Kaizen event, the methodology has been molded in such a way that it addresses all the major factors required for successful change: exposing dissatisfaction with the current situation; creating, projecting, and building support for a vision of the future state; maintaining a sense of urgency; and providing, through a logical methodology and specific instructions, a solid framework for action.

EXERCISES

10.1 Conducting a DMAIC Kaizen

Your task is to apply the tools and methodology presented in this chapter to the improvement project you scoped in Chapter 7. If your business circumstances make it possible and if you have had the opportunity to witness a Kaizen event, as suggested in Exercise 9.2, use the Kaizen event as change vehicle. Otherwise, plan and execute the project in any way that you see fit, while making sure, however, to respect the critical success factors presented in Chapter 9.

Notes

[1] In some circumstances where real time is what matters, we should use 24-hour days. In the case of a patient waiting for heart surgery, for instance, every minute matters.

11

Doing Things Right the First Time: Designing a Process That Works

The DCDV process design methodology, adapted to a professional service environment.

In this chapter, the design methodology is presented. It is a radical departure from the improvement methodology presented in the previous chapter. It is illustrated using an example that is a direct continuation from the FPA case used in Chapter 6. The mode of presentation parallels that used in Chapter 10. The chapter concludes with a retrospective and insights on the methodology and with a comparison with the DMAIC methodology.

11.1 HIGH-LEVEL VIEW OF THE DESIGN METHODOLOGY AND PROJECT SETUP

"Don't automate, obliterate," advocated Michael Hammer (1990) more than a decade ago. The idea of designing from scratch, starting with the end in mind, gave birth to Business Process Reengineering (BPR). Though the case for reengineering was compelling, there was little nuance and even less methodology behind the advocacy. Many companies added it to their ongoing total quality management (TQM) initiative, and seem to have benefited from it (see, among others, Farzaneh, 2003). Now most experts understand that improving and designing are not two distinct quality initiatives, but rather two essential and complementary methodologies belonging to the same global quality initiative.

In Chapter 1, a bird's eye view of the design methodology was presented, using a personal example (movie selection). The purpose of this chapter is to present it in detail, using a professional service example, and discuss the opportunities and challenges it offers. Figure 11.1 shows, using a format similar to that used in Figure 10.1, the logical flow of the design methodology as presented in this chapter: Define, Characterize, Design, and Verify (or DCDV). Each phase consists of two steps. In Table 11.1, the questions addressed at each step and the design principles that underpin the methodology used to provide an answer are specified. Figure 11.1 presents the inputs and outputs of each phase.

The questions addressed in the Define phase are the same as those asked in an improvement project: What is the problem? What is the process that must be designed? The anchor point of the methodology is very different however: It starts from the customer, not from the process.

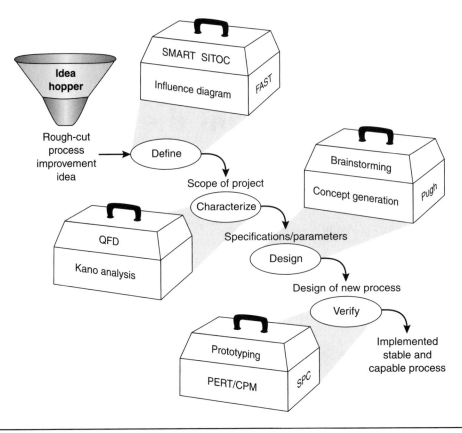

Figure 11.1   The DCDV design methodology: Phases, inputs, outputs, and partial toolkits.

Characterization involves a description of customers' needs, metrics, and process functionalities (or sub-processes) involved. The outputs of this phase are the specifications that the new process must meet. The Design phase turns out a process design that meets these specifications. It involves an alternation between creativity and rigor, and proceeds from a high-level design to a detailed one. Then verify that the process performs in the field as expected before proceeding to full-scale deployment. The underlying design principles are discussed in the corresponding sections of the chapter. Partial toolkits for each phase are shown in Figure 11.1 and the complete toolbox is presented in Table 11.2.

The chapter now turns to a guided tour of the methodology, using an example that is a direct carryover from Chapter 6. FPA concluded that training and educating their clients in finance and investment was a critical process to improve. This is the starting point of this example. Obviously, few organizations go through the project selection methodology presented in Chapter 6. While doing so greatly increases the odds of selecting *the right thing to do*, it is not a prerequisite for using the design methodology. Thus, besides using the general context presented in Chapter 6 as background to the example used here, none of the results derived in that chapter are used. This will ensure that this example has general applicability and constitutes a valid illustration of stand-alone use of the design methodology. To refresh your memory of the FPA case, you should refer to Section 4.2.3.2, and Box 4.2 in particular, and Section 6.2 that presents a summary of FPA's strategy.

Table 11.1 The DCDV design methodology: questions addressed and design principles at each step.

Phase	Step	Question addressed	Underlying design principle
Define	1. Problem statement	What seems to be the problem? What's the overall goal? Why is this important?	Design outside-in, i.e. start with customers and markets, end with the process.
	2. Process scoping	Where does the process start? Where does it end?	Cycle through the problem statement-process scope loop as often as needed to get it right.
Characterize	3. Needs and metrics	What are the needs of various categories of customers? What should we measure in this process? How should we measure it? What are the target values?	Group customers with similar requirements. Design a standard core process, customize at the end.
	4. Critical sub-processes (or functionalities)	What functionalities or sub-processes must be included in the process? Which ones are the most important?	Identify all required functionalities and focus the design efforts on critical ones, that is, the biggest bang for the buck
Design	5. High level design	How will the new pocess work in general? (30,000 feet view)	Make sure the best high-level design has been found before committing time and money to details. It is a common and costly mistake for a team to settle too quickly for a design without fully exploiting their creative potential.
	6. Detailed design	How will the new process work, in details? (ground level view)	Alternate systematically between creativity and rigor, gradually converging on final design.
Verify	7. Pilot	How will the process perform in a controlled environment?	Perform a pilot project early on, before time and money limitations eliminate any remaining flexibility. Use simulation and prototyping to reduce risks and overall cost.
	8. Implementation and continuous improvement	How will the process perform in the field? How are we going to ensure that it gets better over time?	The project does not end when the roll-out starts. It ends when the process is stable and capable.

FPA's executive committee decides to do the scoping itself. During the scoping session, it puts together a design team consisting of a mixture of senior partners from the three merged entities and two outside experts, one in the field of adult education and training and another in courseware. Considering the complexity of the tools, they hire a freelance consultant to act as coach. The coach's mandate is to explain the tools, give instructions, facilitate discussions, and manage the human dynamics of the projects. The market research firm that conducted the survey agrees to send an expert during the morning of the first session. While an improvement team consists of people who are intimately familiar with the process so that they can perform a detailed analysis of what goes on, such familiarity with any actual process would only result in limiting the team's creativity during a design project. The members of a design team must have a broad understanding of the business, be open to new ideas, and must have a background and a mindset that allows them to generate such ideas. They must not have any interest in preserving the status quo and be very open to radical change. Thus, the presence of outsiders, who have no fear of challenging the organization's *sacred cows*, is a great asset.

Table 11.2   The DCDV design methodology: toolbox.

Techniques (step)	Description	Purpose
QFD (3-4)	A matrix driven technique that takes in a weighted list of items and deploys it onto another one. A connected set of matrices can be used.	To generate a short but complete set of indicators and to identify the most important processes. Also, to verify the adequacy of a service package.
Kano (3)	Not really a technique. Classification of service features according to their effect on the client.	To adjust the service package to create maximum competitive advantage in the target market.
House 0 (not used in this chapter–see Chapter 6)	Input: customer needs. Output: Weighted service package	Verify the adequacy of the service package.
House 1 (3)	Input: customer needs. Output: Weighted metrics. If House 0 was used, the input is the weighted service package.	Identify a short and complete set of metrics. We refer to the most important metrics as CTQs, CTCs, and CTDs. Set target values for the critical metrics. These become specifications for the process to be designed.
Fast (4)	Functional analysis to identify required process functionalities	Identify all functionalities for which processes have to be designed.
House 2 (4)	Input weighted metrics. Output weighted functionalities. If you are looking at a complete business unit, the outputs are weighted value-adding processes.	Identify critical functionalities.
House 3 (not used in this chapter–see Chapter 6)	Input: weighted value-adding processes. Output: weighted upstream processes.	Identify most important value-enabling processes, support processes, partners' processes, and suppliers' processes.
Concept generation (5)	Idea generation and combination into overall process concepts.	To explore different ways to meet the specifications.
Pugh matrix (5)	A matrix, including weighed criteria. All concepts are compared to a standard.	To compare the process concepts generated above and select the best.
Blueprint (6)	A *to be* process map where all players and their respective roles are identified.	Specify the process concept in more details, including *"who does what?"*
Design table (6)	A table that identifies all the elements required to make the blueprinted process a reality.	To give *design mandates* to various individuals and teams, for all aspects of the process.
FMEA/VAA (6)	See Table 10.1	See Table 10.1
SPC (7-8)	See Chapter 8	See Chapter 8

FPA's executive committee chooses a modified Kaizen formula as change vehicle, split into two parts, each consisting of three days. The initial project team is to stay intact until the completion of the first part, that is, when high-level design (Step five) is complete. They schedule three full days, one week apart, each one ending with a forum with executive committee members. The team will use the time in between sessions to verify hypotheses made during the session and gather whatever data they require to proceed with the next session. At the end of the first part, the team will make recommendations for changes in the team composition for the remaining steps. When the organization has agreed on a high-level design, outside experts have served their purpose and it is time to move on to the second part, that is, to think about details and implementation. This is a good time to bring in representatives of the various groups whose daily work will be directly affected by the new process, and who thus care more and can contribute more to the details. Further, the sense of

Table 11.2 *(continued).*

Techniques (step)	Indication	Limitations/Challenges
QFD (3-4)	A must for rigorous product, service and process design.	This is a complex technique, especially when used serially. Beyond a certain size, the matrices become unmanageable. Getting the data is challenging.
Kano (3)	A must for service package design/adjustment	Getting it right requires customer surveys, focus groups, and customer observation.
House 0 (not used in this chapter–see Chapter 6)	More useful when a service package already exists. When it does not, service package design is part of concept generation (see below)	Getting the data is the challenge.
House 1 (3)	Whenever we need to go from intangibles to metrics.	Size limitations.
Fast (4)	Without the FAST, you would not know what it is that must be designed	It is critical to take a broad view so as not to place unnecessary constraints on the design
House 2 (4)	Whenever we want to design anything.	Size limitations.
House 3 (not used in this chapter–see Chapter 6)	When we want to do a complete assessment of an organization's processes, to target processes for improvement and design.	Size limitations.
Concept generation (5)	This is the creative part of the methodology.	Creating an environment conducive to creativity and getting the right people on the team.
Pugh matrix (5)	A superior design requires much creativity.	Getting the right criteria and assigning weights can be a challenge.
Blueprint (6)	Creativity sessions must be combined with reality checks to ensure that the final process is feasible. A must for any new process to be implemented.	Defining the roles of the various players and specifying further the selected concept may be a challenge.
Design table (6)	Essential to *land* the design and implement it without forgetting anything or creating undue delays.	Challenges: Project management and ensuring that the integrity of the design is not loss.
FMEA/VAA (6)	See Table 10.1	See Table 10.1
SPC (7-8)	See Chapter 8	See Chapter 8

having some control over the change greatly reduces resistance. Other original team members whose presence may now be redundant can leave the team as well.

11.2 DEFINE

The input to this phase (see Figure 11.1) is a *rough-cut* project idea. In FPA's case, the idea can be stated as follows: "It is critical for our client base and for the execution of our strategy that we design from scratch a process to train and educate our clients in financial and investment matters. The only thing we did in the past—though we did that very well—is to develop public seminars to recruit new clients. Whatever else we did does not constitute a valid starting point for the process we need." This project idea could be the result of a structured approach such as that presented in Chapter 6, of a strategic planning process, or from simple brainstorming by top management.

The output of this phase is a well-scoped project, that is, a SMART problem (or opportunity) statement (this is Step one in Table 11.1) and the perimeter of the project to design (this is Step two), as presented in a SITOC (refer to the discussion of these tools in Chapters 3, 7, and 9). The executive committee itself performs the initial scoping using the methodology described in Chapter 7. The result is shown in Figure 11.2. The high-level metric that will allow tracking the performance of the new process is the percentage of the customer base involved in the training and education program. A successful training and education process (henceforth *training process* for short) will attract and keep new and existing clients as they embark on a training trajectory, stay the course, and get increasingly involved in managing their own portfolios. Analysis of the composition of the client base, coupled with that of data from the market study, leads the executive committee to think that a 70 percent goal is achievable over a two-year horizon.

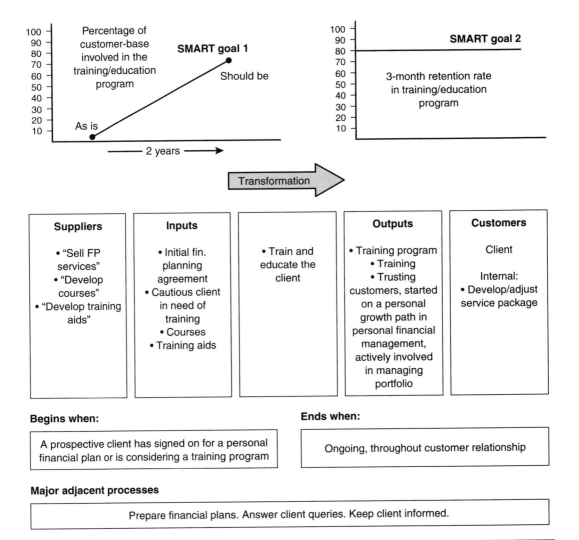

Figure 11.2 Project scope: SMART problem statement, SITOC, boundaries, and comments.

The executive committee, however, feels that this goal is insufficient. Indeed, if the program succeeded in attracting many new clients, only to see them drop out of it within a few months, FPA might be misled in thinking that it is on the right track. Hence, they decide to set a target retention rate of 80 percent, based on data obtained from a training and education-benchmarking center. The two metrics complement each other well in allowing the executive committee to monitor process performance at a high level.

Turning now to the perimeter of the process (SITOC in Figure 11.2), it is shown that, beside the client, the *develop/adjust service package* process is also an (internal) customer of the process to be developed. Recall that one facet of FPA's strategy is to take advantage of a *fault line* in the services offered by competitors: They have a stake in keeping their clients dependent on their knowledge and services. FPA believes that, given the right pricing structure, making clients as autonomous as they want to be can be a win-win proposition. As clients progress through the training program, they gradually acquire new abilities, allowing them to become more involved in managing their financial affairs. Consequently, FPA must adjust its service package to allow this to take place in a timely fashion.

Sell financial planning (FP) services is a supplier process. It delivers a new client of FPA that could potentially embark on the training program. Signing on this new client is part of the process to be designed. Developing courses and training aids are considered to be supplier processes as well. This is a scoping decision. The processes exist and are performing well. *Train and educate clients* will give specifications to these processes and use courses and training aids as inputs or building blocks to design personalized training programs.

The mission of the process is a short statement of why the process exists, that is, what is its expected (direct or indirect) contribution to value creation and to strategy (this is discussed in Section 6.8). The mission of the process, as formulated in Section 6.8, is: "to create for each client a learning environment conducive to personal growth in financial management, and to the parallel evolution (upgrading) of the client's portfolio management system, with FPA as trusted adviser and service provider." This is the role this process plays in the execution of FPA's strategy. FPA's executive committee formulated the SMART goals for high-level monitoring of the new process, to make sure it is on the path to actualizing this mission.

Note finally in the SITOC that the process has no ending point. It is meant to be an on-going process, with training and education goals continuously evolving with the client's knowledge and know-how, as well as with the evolving financial and investment environment.

11.3 CHARACTERIZE

Starting with the process scope as just defined, the outputs of this phase are the specifications the new process will have to meet as well as the identification of its critical functionalities. This output is produced in two steps. In Step one, needs and metrics are identified. In Step two, key functionalities of the new process are identified. Customers' needs will guide FTA to important metrics and these, in turn, will allow pinpointing of important functionalities. Clients' needs are first identified based on market research and then prioritized. QFD is used to first deploy these needs onto technical characteristics (metrics) and then deploy the latter onto functionalities (sub-processes). This is quite similar to the methodology presented in the first part of Chapter 6, with an important difference, however.

In Chapter 6, FPA's objective was not to design a new process (or a new service, which amounts to the same thing—see discussion in Section 3.2.6), but to identify the processes on which it should focus in priority. This requires a broad-brush scanning of the complete business. A new service

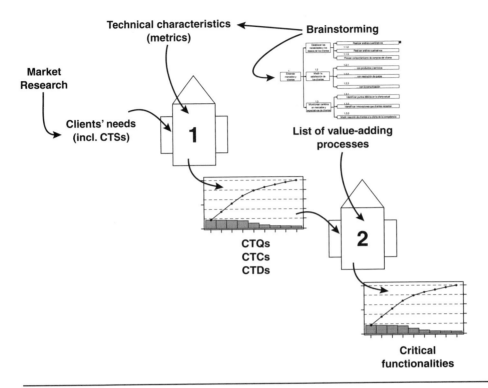

Figure 11.3 Flow of the characterization phase.

delivery process is now being designed, and thus a new service. Because of this, three houses of quality (or QFD matrices) will not be used, but only two: a modified House 1, and House 2 (see Figure 11.3). Indeed, the service package (offerings) must be designed at the same time as the process is designed. Thus, this is left to the Design phase and House zero is skipped altogether. The House 1 used here deploys weighted customer needs directly onto technical characteristics. The coach gives the following instructions to the team:

1. Synthesize market data to produce a weighted list of client needs, such as the one shown in Table 6.1. Use the customer activity cycle and affinity diagrams such as the one used in Chapter 2.

2. For each need, specify whether it holds the potential to develop *basic*, *performance*, or *delight* service features (refer to Kano model, Section 6.4.1). Draw the customer activity cycle and use an affinity diagram (see Exercise 2.2).

3. Considering each need in turn, generate through brainstorming possible metrics, or measurable technical characteristics (refer to Section 6.5, remembering that the inputs are now clients' needs and not service offerings), that correlate closely with it. Look first for indicators that already exist, that are as objective as possible, that can provide quick feedback, and promote early detection of shift or drift (see Chapter 8). Failing that, look for ordinal scales that could be developed or a metric associated to an upstream process that ultimately affects this need. Follow the procedure set forth in Section 6.5 and illustrated in Figure 11.3 to build House 1 and rationalize it, that is, adding and deleting metrics to obtain the smallest possible complete set.

4. Prepare an importance chart of the resulting weighted metrics (this completes Step three, in Table 11.1).

5. Prepare a FAST diagram for the process to be designed. Starting with the transformation shown in Figure 11.2, identify the functionalities that the process requires, that is, break it down logically into sub-processes, as illustrated in previous chapters. Outsiders can play an important role in this task. Insiders, even executives, are often so close to any existing process that they lose their way in details and fail to recognize the functionalities that individual tasks perform. To prepare a good FAST diagram, one does need to understand the current process. Only logic and general familiarity with the industry is required. Outsiders should go at it first, asking clarification questions to insiders as required.

6. Build House 2, using the weighted metrics generated in House 1 and the sub-processes identified in the FAST diagram.

7. Prepare a Pareto chart diagram of the resulting weighted sub-processes. This completes Step four.

Table 11.3 shows the result of the first two tasks. There are 14 needs, grouped under eight headings. With 24 percent of total weight, *insight* represents the client's desire for assistance in better understanding needs, preferences, and evolving emotions vis-à-vis investments, yield, risks, and retirement needs. Market research shows that competitors are doing a very poor job in that regard and thus that expectations are low. No offerings would be considered basic. Offerings that deliver on this need would be meeting a key customer need head on (performance), with much opportunity for seduction. The situation for trust (18 percent) and knowledge (12 percent) is quite similar. As for treatment (14 percent), convenience (13 percent), and intelligence (12 percent), some offerings would be basic, as this segment is used to receiving much from the competition, but focus groups show that when it comes to consideration, ease, and information, for example, more is better (performance), and there still exist ways to surprise them (delight). The only proactivity (9 percent) to be found at competitors is sales effort. Hence, being proactive in helping the client grow and become more autonomous holds much seductive potential.

Technical characteristics are translations of these needs into measurable process (or service offering) attributes. These are not direct measures of satisfaction, such as those you obtain from customer surveys, which are also needed, but do not provide the quick and specific feedback needed to keep processes in control (see Chapter 8). After generating a list of metrics (see Table 11.4), the team groups them into natural categories to check for balance. They then develop a seven-point scale, based on the study of the existing client base, to evaluate the gaps between the client's goal and actual market performance. They have to develop and test several other scales for characteristics that require professional judgment, such as assessing the number of radical shifts in investment strategy and the quality of the client's self-initiated tactical moves.

They then enter the list into House 1 (see Figure 11.4) and correlate it with clients' needs. Analysis of House 1 shows that indicators seven and eight are *co-linear*, that is, they correlate in exactly the same way to clients needs. Indeed, the number of clients giving up on training and the number progressing to higher levels are but two facets of the same question: Is the training program working? While they are not redundant, simplicity requires that only one is used as a guide in the development of the process. The same goes for indicators 11 and 12, both related to response time. To keep House 2 to a workable dimension, the team decides to keep only the metrics that rate 6 percent or better in the bottom row of Figure 11.4. This leaves the seven metrics highlighted in House 1. The performance gap comes out as the most important indicator, with number of contact points and number of FP suggestions accepted by the client coming close behind.

Table 11.3 Weighted client needs, with the potential they hold for various categories (Kano) of service features.

Need–high level (importance)	Needs–details	%	Basic	Performance	Delighter
				Potential for service features (Kano model)	
Insight (24)	Help me understand my true needs and attitude towards risk taking	12		X	X
	Help me manage my emotions (greed, fear, panic...) and make rational decisions	12		X	X
Knowledge (12)	Facilitate my understanding of the major choices I am facing and their implications	12		X	X
Intelligence (10)	Give me all the information I need to make enlightened choices, while ensuring that I do not suffer from information overflow	6	X	X	X
	Help me assess the implications of events in the environment on my risk/yield levels, and eventually on my financial security.	4		X	X
Treatment (14)	Communicate in a language that I can understand and don't make me feel dumb	4		X	X
	Treat me like a VIP	10	X	X	X
Convenience (13)	Help me with the IS/IT required to access the information sources and systems required to be autonomous in the complex world of finance	5		X	
	Make the process simple and painless	5	X	X	X
	Be reachable at all times through my medium of choice	3	X	X	X
Trust (18)	Assign me a top-notch personable professional whom I can trust and who will remain my single contact over the long term	12		X	X
	Don't hold anything back and be candid about your own business interest (make me as autonomous as I can and want to be)	6		X	X
Proactivity (9)	Back me up proactively in areas where you feel I'm not ready to take ownership	5			X
	Monitor my progress and coach me along	4			X

The team then refines the scale for each of these metrics and obtains some comparative data from an industry benchmarking association, setting aggressive but realistic targets for each, that would leave them in the top 1 percent to 10 percent, depending on the indicator. Some of the indicators they develop, however, are so personalized as to preclude any valid comparison. In those cases, they use data on the existing client base, digging back in historical data and performing retroactive calculations of new indicators to establish valid baselines and set targets accordingly. If you cannot compare with other organizations, you should at least compare with your own past performance. These indicators, together with the target values, are the specifications for the new process.

The team thus sets out to identify required process functionalities. This is Step four in Table 11.1. They performed the functional analysis (FAST diagram, see Figure 11.5) and identified seven

Table 11.4 Generating technical characteristics (metrics) and isolating them.

Category	Technical characteristics
Customer Results	Performance vs. goals (gap)
Skill levels	Number of radical shifts in strategy
	Frequency of access to online portfolio (bull's eye)
	Assessment of client's tactical moves
Learning	Score in finance test
	Number of training programs changes within a month
	Number of clients giving up on training
	Number of clients progressing to higher level
	Number of unnecessary calls to FPs
Support	Time to respond to clients' financial queries
	Time to respond to clients' IT queries
	Time to fix IS/IT problem at the clients'
	Number of calls for technical support
Relationship	Attendance at FPA events
	Percentage of FP's suggestions that are accepted by client
	Number of people in direct contact with client

major functionalities or sub-processes. The process is triggered when a new client has signed on to obtain a financial plan or when an existing client (for other services) is willing to consider embarking in FPA's new program. Someone then has to assess needs, develop a personalized program, and get the customer to sign on. Someone else must then set up the customer in the required IS/IT configuration, deliver the training and support program, monitor results, adjust the program as required, and adjust other investment services to match the client's evolving level of ability. Upon reviewing its work, the team finds that *deliver training and support program* contains a much larger chunk of the process than the other functions, that is, the sub-processes they identified are not at the same level. Consequently, they explode this functionality further, by asking the question: How? Five additional functionalities are thus added to the diagram. The team feels comfortable to carry on its design work with these functionalities, the original six, plus the five additional sub-processes replacing the seventh one that they just *cracked open*.

House 2 is used to identify the most important of those sub-processes and help formulate a mission statement for each of these. Figure 11.3 shows where the inputs come from. House 2 (see Figure 11.6) correlates the sub-processes identified in the FAST diagram with the critical metrics coming out of House 1. The use of numbers (ones, threes, and nines) is equivalent to the use of triangles, circles, and bull's eyes used in earlier houses. Correlations are obtained by asking of each process appearing at the top of the matrix and for each critical technical characteristic appearing on the left-hand side: What is the impact of this process on that metric? Importance ratings are obtained in the usual fashion. The ratings for each metric appear in the (highlighted) third column. They are obtained by taking the respective ratings in the last row of House 1 (shown in column two of House 2) and rescaling them so that they sum up to 100 (for example: the rescaled weight of *performance vs. goal (gap)* is (14/65) X 100 = 21 (rounded)).

The team singles out the five most important sub-processes (see highlighted numbers in the bottom row of House 2) as the critical ones, as there is a natural cut-off point between the values

Technical characteristics

Technical characteristics (columns 1–16):

1. Performance vs. goals (gap)
2. Number of radical shifts in strategy
3. Frequency of access to on-line portfolio
4. Assessment of client's tactical moves
5. Score in finance test
6. Number of client's tactical moves
7. Number of training program changes/month
8. Number of clients giving up on training
9. Number of training program changes giving up on training
10. Number of unnecessary calls to FP
11. Time to respond to queries
12. Time to respond to clients' calls to higher level
13. Time to fix IS/IT problem
14. Number of calls for technical support
15. Attendance at FPA events
16. Percentage of FP's suggestions accepted / Number of people in contact with client

Clients' Needs (high-level)	Clients' Needs (detail)	Weight
Insight–24	Help me understand my true needs and attitude towards risk taking.	12
	Help me manage my emotions (greed, fear, panic . . .) and make rational decisions.	12
Knowledge–12	Facilitate my understanding of the major choices I am facing and their implications.	12
	Give me all the information I need to make enlightened choices, while ensuring that I do not suffer from information overflow.	6
Intelligence–10	Help me assess the implications of events in the environment on my risk/yield levels, and eventually on my financial security.	4
	Communicate in a language that I can understand and don't make me feel dumb.	4
Treatment–14	Treat me like a VIP.	10
	Help me with the IS/IT required to access the information sources and systems required to be autonomous in the complex world of finance.	5
Convenience–13	Make the process simple and painless.	5
	Be reachable at all times through my medium of choice.	3
Trust–18	Assign me a top-notch personable professional whom I can trust and who will remain my single contact over the long term.	12
	Don't hold anything back and be candid about your own business interest (make me as autonomous as I can and want to be).	6
Proactivity–9	Back me up proactively in areas where you feel I'm not ready to take ownership.	5
	Monitor my progress and coach me along.	4

Importance ratings (by column 1–16): 14, 8, 1, 5, 6, 3, 9, 9, 6, 3, 4, 4, 1, 10, 12, 5

Figure 11.4 Train/educate client: House 1.

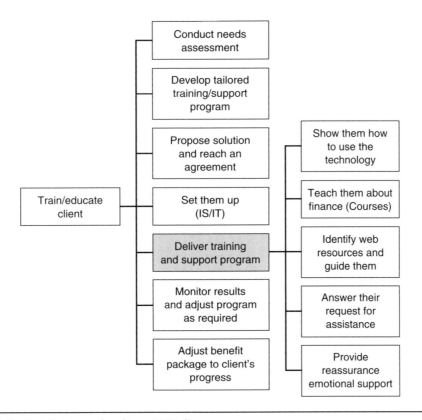

Figure 11.5 Train/educate the client: FAST diagram.

nine and six. These sub-processes are listed in Figure 11.7, together with their ratings. Referring to the mission of the process it is designing (see Section 11.2) and to House 1 and House 2, the team is now in a position to deploy it onto specific mission statements for each functionality (or sub-process). *Conduct needs assessment*, for instance, has a direct impact (see House 2, Figure 11.6) on the number of clients progressing to a higher level in the training program. Following that trail in House 1, this technical characteristic is seen to correlate strongly (bull's-eye) with:

- "Help me understand my true needs and attitude towards risk taking"

- "Facilitate my understanding of the major choices I am facing and their implications"

- "Help me assess the implications of events in the environment on my risk/yield levels, and eventually on my financial security"

- "Make the process simple and painless"

The team is also aware (see the FAST diagram in Figure 11.5) that this is an upstream func-tionality that will have an impact on all the others. Armed with the knowledge of the role that this sub-process plays, the team formulates its mission as follows: "To understand and capture the true needs and preferences of the client in a painless way to ensure that everyone involved in the design and delivery of the training package will be focused on a unique, accurate target." Applying this approach to the other four critical processes, the team writes the mission statements shown in Figure 11.7. These statements will be very useful in the design phase, when the team has to explore and compare different ways to achieve these missions, and select the best one.

Key metrics—from House 1	Original weights in House 1	Rescaled weights (sum = 100)	Conduct needs assessment	Develop tailored training/support program	Propose solution and close agreement	Set them up	Show them how to use the technology	Teach them about finance (Courses)	Identify web resources and guide them	Answer their request for assistance	Provide reassurance and emotional support	Monitor results and adjust service bundle to client's program	Adjust service bundle to client's progress
Performance vs. goals (gap)	14	21	3	3	1	1	9	3	3	9	9		9
Number of radical shifts in strategy	7,7	12	1	3		1	9	3	9	9	1		
Score in finance test	6,2	10	3	9	1	3	9	3	1	9	3	3	
Number of clients progressing to higher level	9,4	14	9	9	1	1	9	1	3	9	1	3	
Number of unnecessary calls to FP	5,7	9	3	3	3	3	9	3	9	9	3	3	3
Attendance at FPA events	10	15	0			3	1	9	9	3		9	
Percentage of FPs suggestions accepted by client	12	19	3	9		9	9	1	9	1	9	1	3
Importance ratings			9	14	2	2	3	22	7	7	17	11	6

Figure 11.6 Train/educate client: House 2.

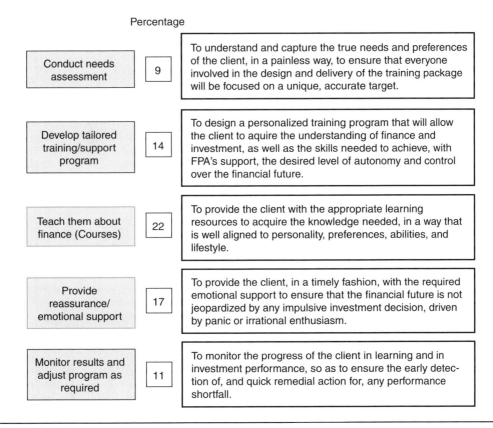

Percentage

Conduct needs assessment	9	To understand and capture the true needs and preferences of the client, in a painless way, to ensure that everyone involved in the design and delivery of the training package will be focused on a unique, accurate target.
Develop tailored training/support program	14	To design a personalized training program that will allow the client to aquire the understanding of finance and investment, as well as the skills needed to achieve, with FPA's support, the desired level of autonomy and control over the financial future.
Teach them about finance (Courses)	22	To provide the client with the appropriate learning resources to acquire the knowledge needed, in a way that is well aligned to personality, preferences, abilities, and lifestyle.
Provide reassurance/ emotional support	17	To provide the client, in a timely fashion, with the required emotional support to ensure that the financial future is not jeopardized by any impulsive investment decision, driven by panic or irrational enthusiasm.
Monitor results and adjust program as required	11	To monitor the progress of the client in learning and in investment performance, so as to ensure the early detection of, and quick remedial action for, any performance shortfall.

Figure 11.7 The mission of the most important functions identified in House 2.

Having identified critical metrics (and targets to reach) and characterized the critical processes that affects them, the team is now ready to proceed to the design phase.

11.4 DESIGN

The output of this phase is a process design capable of meeting the specifications formulated in the Characterize phase. It is produced in two steps: high-level design, followed by detailed design.

11.4.1 High-level Design

In High-level Design (Step five in Table 11.1) the team produces a broad-brush description of the new process. In Detailed Design (Step six), the team *lands it*, producing a detailed process design, specifying every aspect necessary to proceed with a pilot project. Having rigorously zeroed in on the critical functionalities to design, it is now time to be creative! High-level design proceeds iteratively from the generation of alternate ways to perform each sub-process (see the *movie selection* illustration in Figure 1.3) to the selection of the best one, assuring that the process improves with each iteration, eventually converging on a final concept.

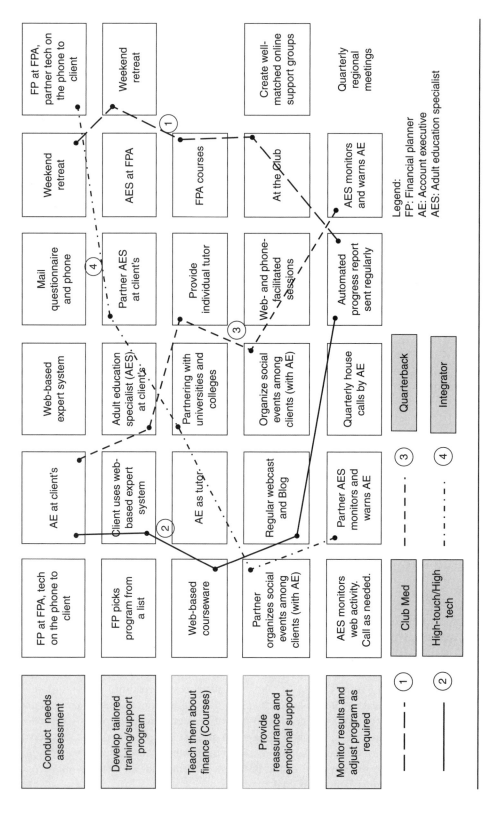

Figure 11.8 Initial generation of ideas for key functions and combination into process concepts.

The coach gives the following instructions to the team for initial concept generation:

1. Generating ideas. Write down on sticky notes the names of the critical sub-processes identified in the Characterize phase and place them as a column on the right-hand side of a page (see Figure 11.8). Start with the first one: *conduct needs assessment*. Review the mission of that sub-process as spelled out in Figure 11.7. Sitting silently around a table, try to generate as many individual answers as possible to the following question: How could we go about assessing client's training needs? Each team member writes down the ideas that come to mind on sticky notes that are placed in the center of the table. When a member runs out of ideas, it is useful to walk around the table, looking at what the others have written. This often triggers new ideas. They do this for each of the five critical functions. When they run out of ideas, they analyze their collective work, eliminate duplication, combine similar ideas, and stick the final lineup as shown in Figure 11.8.

2. Combining ideas into process concepts. You must now combine these ideas. A process concept is a high-level description of a possible way to perform the complete process. It is a logical grouping of the ideas generated around a theme. There are 6480 possible combinations of the ideas presented in Figure 11.8 (6X5X6X6X6), assuming that the ideas formulated for each sub-process are mutually exclusive, which is not always the case. It is impossible to explore each of these, and most do not make sense anyway. Thus, you must now analyze Figure 11.8 and use your intuition and creativity to think of possible themes around which you can organize individual ideas in a cohesive and meaningful way. You should then give each concept a name, the more colorful the better, to make it vivid and allow the team to visualize it and *manipulate it* in the next technique.

3. Describe each process concept in a few short sentences capturing its essence.

Process concepts are alternate visions of what the future process could be. To proceed with the comparative evaluation that follows, the team must share a common (high-resolution) mental image of that process. Much discussion is required to achieve the crispness for this analysis to be meaningful.

The team generates many different types of ideas. For the first sub-process, for instance, the person performing the work may be either an FP (alone or with the help of a technician), a dedicated account executive, or the client using an expert system. The technician could be an FPA employee or work for a supplier (or partner) to whom FPA would outsource such work. Whoever does the work could do it on the phone, travel to the client's home, or receive the client at FPA's offices.

In looking for logical combinations, the team first selects a number of ideas involving group activities. They label this concept *Club Med*, a name that, in their minds, is associated with group fun and mutual value creation, and conveys well the spirit of the concept. The team spends some time exchanging views about how the process would work and is soon comfortable enough with it to write the short description presented in Figure 11.9. The team soon generates three more concepts (depicted in Figure 11.8) and repeats the process, ending with the summary descriptions presented in Figure 11.9. In *high-touch/high-tech*, a strong relationship is centered on the account executive (AE) and technology is used wherever possible. In *quarterback*, the AE coordinates a team of FPA specialists. *Integrator* is similar, except that the specialist roles are outsourced. *Cafeteria* involves letting the client choose from a menu of options, with different prices. For the sub-process *teach them about finance*, for example, the client could choose between web-based courseware, using a personal tutor, or attending a course at FPA. This option could not be depicted like the other four in Figure 11.8.

This a good place for a slight digression. Compare two notions: service concept and process concept. You should first review the short discussion of service and customer contact in Section 3.2.6 and Figure 8.6, presenting an integrated view of the strategy to operation connection in the case of a drugstore (GYD). In Chapter 2 (Section 2.3.3.2), a service concept is defined as the features-benefits pair. In the case of GYD, benefits include, among others, expertise, personalization, convenience, and low risk. Giving advice to elderly clients at home is one of the service features (or service offerings) that contributes to the *convenience* benefit. Since *giving advice* includes an action verb, it is obviously a process as well. Since it is impossible to separate the *advice* from the *giving*, it is impossible to separate the offering from the process. More precisely, it is impossible to separate the customer-contact part of the process from the service offerings.

Figure 11.10 illustrates the foregoing discussion. Since the customer-contact part of the process is so intimately linked to service features, designing a service concept has direct implications for the part of the process where the organization comes into contact with the customer. This is sometimes referred to as the *co-production* zone, since both the employee (or system) and the customer

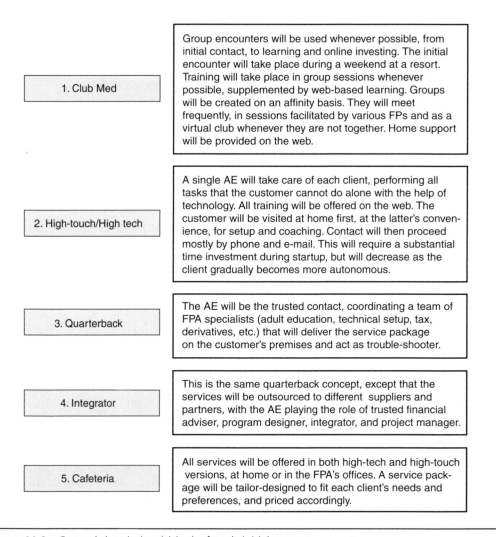

Figure 11.9 General description (vision) of each initial process concept.

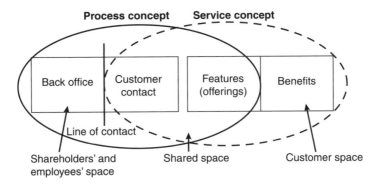

Figure 11.10 Relationship between service concept and process concept: division and sharing of the service space between the three stakeholders.

work together to produce the desired result. While the client cares much about the work the former performs with the contact-person (see Section 2.1.2 dealing with the service experience), they do not care about the way work is divided up in the back office, as long as it *works*.

On the other hand, for the same reason, designing a service delivery process necessarily affects the service concept. Just as a close connection is needed between the front office and service features, coherence is also needed between what goes on in the back office and in the front office (see the dotted circle in Figure 11.10). Since the general path of the methodology goes *from the customer-in*, start with the customer space in House 1, pinpoint the important processes in House 2, and then move on to generating process concepts that present a global coherence and internal integrity between the back office, the front office, and service features. Comparing the description of the five initial concepts in Figure 11.9, it is shown that they imply differences in all three.

Back to our team, now. The process concepts the team developed include only the five most important sub-processes. To get a more complete picture, the team must now *connect the dots*. The coach thus gives team members the following instructions:

1. Expand Figure 11.8 to include all the functions in FAST diagram.

2. For each concept, *fill in the blanks* by specifying a way to perform each remaining function that is coherent with the theme of the concept while maintaining its integrity.

Figure 11.11 shows the work of the team for concepts one to four. *Cafeteria* is an open concept, since it would leave the client to choose, and pay for, what is wanted. The theme of three of the concepts is reinforced by this exercise. *Quarterback* and *Integrator*, for instance, push further their respective themes of coordination of specialists and partners by an account executive. The *Club Med* is not reinforced by the exercise, merely completed by a series of ideas the team selects the best way it can.

Thus ends the first truly creative exercise of the methodology. The originality and superiority of the final design depend on the creativity of the team. There are many approaches and techniques available to promote creativity. These approaches are not discussed here. Refer to the extensive literature dealing on this topic. De Bono (1985), for instance, has many worthwhile suggestions in that regard.

The coach's instructions have not placed any limitations on what ideas team members can come up with. Consequently, it is quite possible that some of the resulting concepts lie beyond the realm of the possible, breaching some implicit or explicit constraints that the team or the organization face. Are

	1. Club Med	2. High-touch/High tech	3. Quarterback	4. Integrator
Conduct needs assessment	Weekend retreat	FP at FPA, tech on the phone to client	AE at client's	FP at FPA, partner tech on the phone to client
Develop tailored training/support program	Weekend retreat	Client use web-based expert system	Adult education specialist (AES) at client's	Partner AES at client's
Propose solution and close agreement	Weekend retreat	Account exec (AE) at client's	Account exec (AE) at client's	Weekend retreat set up by partner club
Set them up	Sell/install/support/upgrade IS/IT kit	The client does it with web and phone support	FPA technician	Local technician (partner)
Show them how to use the technology	Central courses (FPA) with access to Club	Web-based courseware	FPA technical trainer	Local groups (partner)
Teach them about finance (Courses)	FPA courses	Web-based courseware	Provide individual tutor	Partnering with universities and colleges
Identify web resources and guide them	Net-meetings	Create *resource page* in portal	Provide private coach	Partnering with on-line financial info provider
Answer their request for assistance	Web-meetings	800-line	FP and tech make home calls	800-line
Provide reassurance and emotional support	At the Club	Regular webcast and Blog	Organize social events among clients (with AE)	Partner organizes social events among clients (with AE)
Monitor results and adjust program as required	Automated progress report sent regularly	Automated progress report sent regularly	AES monitors and warns AE	Partner AES monitors and warns AE
Adjust benefit package to client's progress	AE sets it up with client-care rep. (CCR)	AE does it for the client on the portal	AE sets it up with client-care rep. (CCR)	AE sets it up with partner client-care rep. (CCR)

Figure 11.11   Completed descriptions for four of the five initial process concepts.

Process Concepts

Stakeholders	Stakeholder weight	Weight in House 1	Criteria	Weight	Club Med	High touch/High tech	Quarterback	Integrator	Cafeteria
Clients	40	21	Performance vs. goals (gap)	10	+	S	+	+	S
		14	Number of clients progressing to higher level	5	+	S	+	+	S
		15	Attendance at FPA events	6	+	S	S	S	S
		19	Percentage of FPs suggestions accepted	9	−	S	−	−	−
Employees	20	21¹	Perceived value	10	−	S	+	−	+
			Acceptance by FPs	20	−	S	−	−	−
Shareholders	40		Overall risk for FPA	20	+	S	−	+	−
			ROI	9	+	S	−	S	−
			Startup time	5	+	S	−	−	−
			Need to hire	6	S	S	−	+	−
			Weighted sum of "+"		55		25	41	10
			Weighted sum of "S"		6	6	15	21	
			Weighted sum of "−"		39		69	44	69

Legend:
+: superior
−: inferior
S: Standard or Same

¹This weight does not come from House 1. It was assigned by the team, relative to the weights of the four technical characteristics drawn from House 1

Figure 11.12 Comparison of the four initial process concepts, using the Pugh design matrix.

the concepts all acceptable from the perspective of clients, employees, and shareholders? Which one is the best? The team now needs to get back to reality, evaluate the feasibility of the concepts, and select the best one. The team is now out of the realms of creativity and back in rigorous analysis mode.

The Pugh design matrix is the tool that will be used for selecting the best concept. Its inputs are the process concepts just generated and a set of weighted criteria to be used for comparing them. Its output is the best concept. Its general operating principle consists in selecting one of the concepts as baseline or standard and comparing the others to it, on each criterion. Thus, the coach gives the team the following instructions:

1. Draw a matrix such as the one shown in Figure 11.12. Insert the initial process concepts on top and select one as the baseline, against which you will compare the others. Select a concept that does not appear, at first glance, to be either the best or the worst (nothing dramatic will ensue if you end up selecting the best or the worse—only a slight delay). Make sure the concept you select is crisp in the minds of everyone.

2. Select the most important metrics in House 2 (that is, among the most important metrics already selected from House 1), and copy them on the left-hand side of Figure 11.12, together with their ratings in House 2, under the *client* heading.

3. Since this is a professional service, customer perception of what they are getting may be very different from technical quality of the service (see Section 2.1). Clients will assess the value of the service based on their own value equation (see Section 2.2). Even if FPA delivers a service with high technical quality, clients will not buy or stay for long unless they perceive the value. Hence, add a criteria (such as perceived value), also under the client heading, and assign a rating to it, relative to the other client-related criteria drawn from House 2.

4. Add one or more criteria to take into account the differential effect that the concepts under consideration will have on employees, particularly on the professionals.

5. Add other criteria to reflect the interests of the shareholders.

6. If management has imposed specific constraints on the project (not the case here), such as a deadline for implementation, a budget limit, or a physical (*we do not want to rent more space*) or technological (*this has to fit in our integrated operating software*) constraint, add these under the heading *management*.

7. Consult with management and spread 100 points between the four stakeholders (clients, employees, shareholders, and management) according to how heavily you want each group of criteria to weigh on the decision. Spread the rating attributed to each customer among the criteria in each category. For those criteria taken from House 2, rescale the House 2 ratings to sum up to the total allocated to the category. *Performance versus goal*, for instance, is rated as $((21/(21+14+115+19+21))$ X 40 = 10 (rounded)).

8. Compare each concept on each criterion, line by line, to the standard. First, fill the column under the standard with *Ss*, standing for standard. Use a + to reflect a given concept's superiority to the standard, on that criterion, a - to reflect inferiority, and an *S* to reflect equality (*same*). Superior here means preferable. A lower risk, for example, is preferable to a higher one, and thus rates a +.

9. If the team cannot agree on a given rating, this means that further work needs to be done to further clarify the concepts or their implications. Identify the specific issues impeding consensus and design an experiment, a benchmarking exercise, a focus group, or some other analysis to resolve the issue convincingly. Do not reach an artificial consensus or take a majority vote.

10. Calculate the weighted sum of plusses, minuses, and *sames* as shown in Figure 11.12.

11. The concept, if any, with the greatest positive difference between the sum of weighted plusses and the sum of weighted minuses is the best concept of the four. If the weighted sum of minuses is always superior to the weighted sum of plusses, then the standard is the best concept. Review any tie to refine the analysis and break the tie. If you end up with columns full of plusses, it means that the standard is the absolute worst concept. Drop it from consideration, pick a standard amongst the other three concepts, and start over.

The team picks the four most important technical characteristics from House 2 and adds *perceived value* as a fifth client-related criterion. This reflects a special concern that management had raised with the new strategy. They wanted to make sure that as FPA made substantial investments in raising their clients' autonomy, thus making them less dependant on professional assistance, they would still perceive the value of FPA's services and remain loyal.

Thus, the team assigns this criterion the same weight as *performance vsersus goal*, the most important metric from House 2. They also identify acceptance of the new process by FPs as an important comparison criterion. Shareholders criteria include risk, return on investment, time required to start up the new process, and need to hire. In a professional service firm where professionals are soon part of a profit-sharing plan, hiring and firing are always strategic decisions. Since the new culture arising from the merger has not yet fully consolidated, the firm would rather avoid getting into this at this critical moment in its young life.

The team is looking for the process concept that best meets all these criteria. Clearly, however, they will have to make some trade-offs. Hence, during the first end-of-day forum, after presenting what they have done thus far to the executive committee, the team asks them for guidelines in that respect. The executive committee assigns a 40 percent weight to client criteria, 20 percent to employee criteria, and spreads the remaining 40 percent among the four shareholders criteria. The ten criteria, together with their final ratings, are shown in Figure 11.12.

Team members then pick *high-tech/high-touch* as the standard and proceed with the criteria-by-criteria comparison. After several rounds of discussion and further data gathering and analysis, the team finalizes its evaluation. Quarterback, Integrator, and Cafeteria are inferior to the standard, presenting more (weighted) drawbacks than advantages. Club Med, however, is superior to *High touch/High tech*, and is thus the best concept of the five under consideration. Market research had indeed identified a certain sense of isolation and a clear preference for social and group activities in the target segment. The team concludes that group events are more likely to provide the stimulation and motivation clients needs to keep up their learning efforts, progress to higher levels of knowledge, and make better investment decisions. Further, it is cheaper to train people in groups than in individual tutorial sessions. Thus, the concept would create profit leverage (see Section 5.1.2) through the operations strategy formulated by FPA (review Section 6.2).

The Club Med concept has its drawbacks, however. The team assesses that while the process, in its current form, will forge strong bonds between clients, it may fail to create a strong enough relationship with the FP. Without trust, the required synergism between client and FP may not happen. Since close professional relationships with clients is critical to FPs satisfaction (refer to Section 2.4, and to the personal value equation in particular), this concept may generate much resistance to change, from quarters which hold much power, enough to kill the initiative (refer to Section 4.2.3.3). Further, the concept would also require FPs to facilitate (real or virtual) group sessions, a role with which many are unfamiliar, and that some may find uncomfortable.

A related drawback of that concept is that clients may fail to perceive the full value they receive from FPA. Indeed, they may come to attribute the results they are getting solely to their own efforts and to their interaction with new personal relationships that they have created with other investors met at the various FPA forums and events. Without the strong bond with an FP that is part of FPA's operations strategy (see Section 6.2), FPA may create much value with little profit to show for it.

During the second forum with the executive committee, the team presents its work. This generates much feedback and many other ideas. The executive committee then decides to hold a similar forum for all the FPs available that night, again generating much useful feedback and material.

Club Med may be the best among the initial concepts the team has generated, but it is far from perfect and must be improved. Thus, the team must go back to the drawing board for a second creativity session, this time starting with the Club Med concept as the standard. The coach gives the team the following instructions about how to go about this:

1. Go back to the work done so far in the Pugh matrix and start a new column on the right-hand side. Put the Club Med concept as the heading for that column and fill the column with *Ss*. This is your new standard and the starting point for the second iteration, as this task is called.

2. Use creativity techniques to modify and improve on the Club Med concepts. Do not generate new process concepts from scratch. Rather, explore ways to eliminate, minimize, or compensate for the weaknesses of the concept (as pointed out by the three minus signs it rated in the first iteration). You can *borrow* ideas from the other concepts that rated a + on those same criteria. You can generate new ideas altogether for these weak aspects of the concept or use the ideas that arose during the forums. As you try to make up for the deficiencies of the concept, avoid weakening its strong point and try to maintain its integrity, that is, the glue or theme that gives it meaning and makes it coherent. Feel free as well to improve on other aspects of the process that rated a + in the first iteration. A + simply means that it is better than the standard against which you are comparing it, not that it is perfect. As you enter into a creativity session and as the team understands the concept with increasing clarity, such ideas are bound to occur as well. While you must not reinvent the process from scratch, neither should you discard any good idea.

3. Give each new process concept you generate a name that makes it vivid. The name should start with CM, followed by its defining character. Place these names at the top of subsequent columns in the Pugh matrix. When the creativity session concludes, compare these concepts to the original CM concept and rate them as you have in the first iteration. The differences between the concepts will not be as marked as they were in the first iteration. Hence, your analysis will have to be finer. The concept that comes out on top is your new benchmark.

4. Repeat this procedure several times, until you reach a point when the team cannot enhance the process further. Call a forum at that point, to validate the results and see if ideas injected by participants cannot launch a new wave of creativity.

The team thus generates four variants around the CM team. Their work is shown in Figure 11.13. At the center of the figure lies the original CM concept, copied from Figure 11.11 and described in Figure 11.9. The boxes under each of the four concepts describe the additions or modifications the team has made to this concept. When the idea(s) in the box relate to a specific functionality, an arrow is used to show it. Sometimes the idea or ideas have general applicability throughout the process and no arrow is required. The result of the team's evaluation of the four variants is shown in Figure 11.14.

The main idea in *CM GO team*[1] is to create teams of three FPs that would share the professional tasks to be performed in the new concept. These tasks include organizing and leading group sessions, one-on-one counseling and coaching, electronic monitoring of individual results, answering phone queries, and developing personalized training programs. Some of these tasks are new and may not be to the liking of every FP. A team approach, where each team has total latitude to allocate the tasks and spread the workload among members, gives FPs some control over what they do and is likely to reduce the stress that the new concept can create and attenuate resistance to change. While relationships with three professionals may not be as convenient to some clients, it is better than constantly changing contact persons, and some clients may appreciate hearing different views, or hearing them in different words and personal styles. This relationship is likely to improve performance and perceived value as well. The only drawback, the team thinks (see Figure 11.14), is that since this is a new approach that touches on culture, work habits, and financial incentives, it is riskier than the original CM concept.

The *CM High-tech* concept borrows some of the ideas from the *High-tech/High-touch* concept, as additions to the CM concept rather than as substitutes. This would improve the performance of

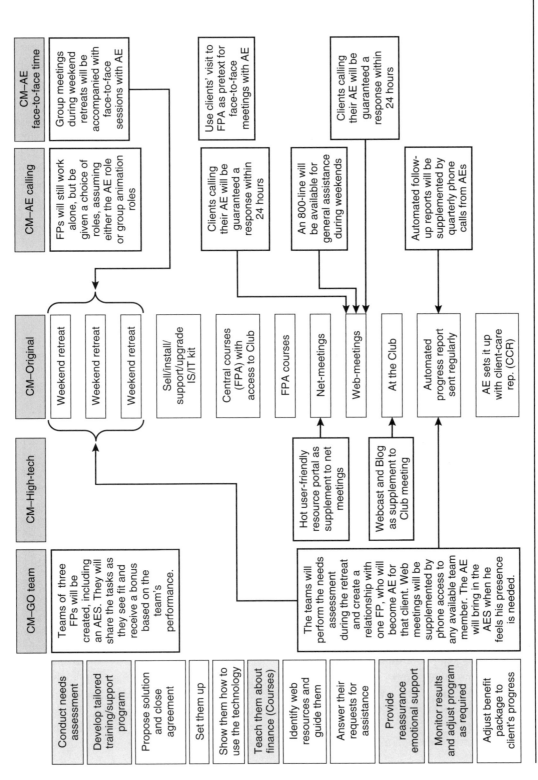

Figure 11.13   Comparison of the four initial process concepts, using the Pugh design matrix.

Criteria	Weight	Club Med	High touch/High tech	Quarterback	Integrator	Cafeteria	Club Med	CM-GO team	CM-High-tech	CM-AE calling	CM-AE face-to-face
			First iteration					Second iteration			
Performance vs. goals (gap)	10	+	S	+	+	S	S	+	+	S	S
Number of clients progressing to higher level	5	+	S	+	+	S	S	+	+	S	+
Attendance at FPA events	6	+	S	S	S	S	S	+	S	S	+
Percentage of FPs suggestions accepted	9	–	S	–	–	–	S	+	S	S	+
Perceived value	10	–	S	+	–	+	S	+	+	+	+
Acceptance by FPs	20	–	S	–	–	–	S	+	S	–	+
Overall risk for FPA	20	+	S	–	+	–	S	–	–	S	–
ROI	9	+	S	–	S	–	S	S	–	–	–
Startup time	5	+	S	–	–	–	S	S	–	S	+
Need to hire	6	S	S	–	+	–	S	S	S	–	S
Weighted sum of "+"		55		25	41	10		60	25	10	55
Weighted sum of "S"		6		6	15	21		20	41	55	16
Weighted sum of "–"		39		69	44	69		20	34	35	29

Figure 11.14   Comparison of the four initial process concepts, using the Pugh design matrix.

the clients and increase perceived value. It would, however, be costly and involve a technological risk, as well as a delay in launching the concept. The main idea behind *CM AE calling* is to add phone support throughout the process, thus increasing perceived value. However, it is costly to do so and would require FPA to hire more personnel. Further, since this is a task that good FPs typically do not like, it would create more resistance to change and would probably not increase performance. The *CM AE face-to-face time* involves adding more face-to-face contact with an AE throughout the process. This would largely eliminate the drawbacks of the original CM concept. It would come at a cost, however, and thus produce inferior financial results and put FPA at risk.

Examination of the second iteration in the Pugh matrix (Figure 11.14) shows that the original CM concept is preferable to *High-tech* and *AE calling*, both of which involve more drawbacks than advantages. *GO team* and *AE face-to-face time* are superior concepts, but the balance of benefits favors the former. This is the conclusion of the second iteration. The team could pursue its work by entering a third creativity wave to try to reduce the risk involved with the latest concept. For the purpose of this chapter, however, we will take the *GO team* to be the final concept. Thus ends the high-level design step (Step 5 in Figure 11.1).

Having gone through this exercise, it is now possible to better understand the rationale behind the Pugh matrix. The *optimization algorithm* proceeds in steps (or iterations) from one solution to another, making sure at every turn that the next solution is better than the previous one. This is illustrated in Figure 11.15. The four initial concepts generated in the first iteration (A-B-C-D) are vastly different from one another, as illustrated by the distance between them. The process moves from

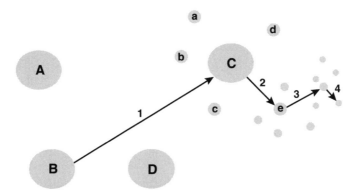

Figure 11.15 Illustration of the optimization algorithm behind the Pugh matrix.

the initial standard (B) to the best of the four concepts (C) (as illustrated by the numbered arrow). The other three concepts are discarded, consider C as the new standards, and generate *variants* around it (a-b-c-d-e). The variants are much more similar to each other than A-B-C-D were in the first iteration, since they only involve minor modifications of the C concept. Concept *e* now comes out on top, but the gains made in this iteration (arrow number two) are typically smaller than in the previous one. Variants of *e* are then generated, producing an even smaller gain in the third iteration, and so on. While the gains are increasingly small as the process converges, they still represent a huge rate of return on the time invested.

The discussion now turns to Detailed design (Step 6 in Table 11.1).

11.4.2 Detailed Design

The input to this step is the final high-level concept obtained in the previous step (CM-GO team). The output is a complete process design, ready for field-testing. High-level design started from 30,000 feet (from a clear view of the complete business and its competitive environment) and took us down to 10,000 feet, that is, a broad vision of how the new process will flow. Now to land it, that is, specify the many operational details that are not visible from the bird's eye view taken in the previous step. All means available have to be used to make sure that the process is as good as it can be before it is released for field-testing. This step marks the start of the second part of the Kaizen event, and team composition is thus modified as discussed above.

The two major tools used to specify the design are the blueprint and design table (see Table 11.2). On the face of it, a process blueprint looks just like a process map. There is a fundamental difference, however. A process map describes the process *as is*. A blueprint describes the process *to be*. Just as you use a blueprint to build a house, a blueprint is used to build a process. Starting from the high-level design, the team must first add the organizational layer, which it has not addressed so far, and specify how it will proceed as a series of detailed tasks flowing from one player to another. As it does so, many design issues will arise. The team will capture these and classify them in a design table. Thus, the coach gives the team the following instructions:

1. Study the high-level design in details and identify the organizational players who will have a role to play. Write their names on sticky notes and place them on the left-hand side of a flip chart, just as you would if you were building a process map.

2. You will now view the process as a play for which the team is writing the script. Your task is to visualize the customer's experience by simulating it. Since there must be a

representative for each player (department) on the design team, assign roles to each team member in such a way that all players, including the client, are represented. The player that initiates the process should then start (speaking in the first person) describing what the person does, what inputs are needed to do it, what outputs are produced, and what other players are triggered into action. As each player is talking in turn, capture the unfolding action using sticky notes and arrows. Stay at a high level for the first take and avoid getting lost in details. Come back to the beginning when you are done and go through it a second time, adding details and clarifications to improve resolution. Refine the blueprint as much as you can, identifying areas that need further investigation.

3. Walk through the process again, this time asking yourselves at every step: What does the organization need to make this happen? The answers you provide will fall in the following categories: equipment, installations, materials, suppliers, human resources, information systems/information technology (IS/IT), procedures, and implementation plan. Draw a table such as the one shown in Table 11.5. Capture each required design element in the appropriate category.

4. When the table is complete, revisit each element, specifying in *design mandates* decisions or choices to make, additional data to obtain, analyses to perform, or experiments to conduct. Assign all design mandates to team members based on expertise, contacts, affinity, or availability.

5. Prepare a detailed design plan encompassing all design mandates. Specify the support and resources required to make it happen and present it to the executive forum.

Figure 11.16 presents an extract from the macro-blueprint the team first prepared. Since the process is large, the team first had to stick to a broad-brush depiction of it (the macro-blueprint is to the blueprint what the macro-map is to the process map). The diagram is largely self-explanatory. As the team pushes deeper it will have to provide much more detail, captured in a detailed blueprint, about how such tasks as *set up technological support for weekend* or *analyze customer data and plan weekend*, for example, will be performed.

Table 11.5 gives a partial list of the design elements that will be the object of design mandates. The tasks require a variety of expertise and skills, ranging from human resources to information technology, including procurement, layout, logistics, and ergonomics. Some mandates, such as organizing for catering, are straightforward. Others, such as adapting web-meeting technology to fit FPA's needs are quite challenging. The human resources category generally includes some of the most difficult challenges, especially in professional services. Creating FP teams, reorganizing the tasks of FPs, and developing team incentives all touch on the job concept of a very powerful group of employees, and thus on FPA's positioning in the labor market. These mandates have clear strategic implications for the organization and must involve the executive committee.

The forum at which the team presents its detailed design plan requires more time. Executives make decisions on the spot about support and resource requirements to produce the detailed design, while all key players are present and the analysis and past deliverables of the team are fresh in everyone's mind. The forum is a level playing field, rich in facts and data, to be used to the fullest.

When the plan is adopted, the team does not have to work together all the time any more. Since team members share a vision of the new process, and have agreed on a game plan to make it happen, they can each go their own way to perform their own bits of the detailed design plan. They keep in touch virtually and come together regularly to check progress, identify and resolve interfacing issues between design elements, and make sure that when the parts come together, the end-process will function as well a whole.

Table 11.5 Elements of the new training process to be designed (partial).

Equipment	Installations	Materials	Suppliers
• Equipment to support off-site training • Equipment to upgrade client's installations • Upgrade call centre • Furnishing for Club room • Upgrade car fleet	• Revamp training room • Build Club room • Refit the entrance hall	• Review all brochures and forms with advertising agency • Develop training needs assessment forms.	• Resort • Social events • Caterer • Sports events • Club room designer
HR aspects	**IS/IT**	**Procedures**	**Implementation plan**
• Design and validate approach to create FP teams and team-based incentive system • Develop team management system and train FP's • Select and train FP's with the right skill set to become facilitators • Review renumeration policy for off-site work.	• Develop net meeting technology • Develop web-meeting technology • Develop automated progress report • Organize to support off-site training • Develop automated client monitoring • Computer setup for Club room • Review online forms	• Procedures to assess and upgrade clients' home installations • Team management procedures • Expense reports procedure • Procedures to calculate all the indicators appearing in House 2 (Figure 11.6), monitor results and use the information for correction and learning purpose.	• See Gantt chart *(not included)*

To improve on the design whose final contours are now taking shape, as the nature of the task suggests, a tool is borrowed from the improvement methodology toolkit. The coach instructs the team to perform a process design FMEA (refer to Section 10.5.5). Again, the technique looks very much like the FMEA used in the process improvement methodology. The difference lies in that the team is not trying to fix a broken process, but to identify risk and prevent defects before they occur. While it is relatively easy to identify defects in an existing process, fixing the process can be costly. When the process is still on the design table, it requires more effort to identify the defects that might occur (risks). However, fixing them is much, much cheaper. By filtering the process through a rigorous FMEA, the team is able to introduce many *poka-yokes* as well as risk reduction and risk management features.

Simulation tools of various kinds, including demos, mock-ups, enactments, or computer simulation software, may be used at this point to obtain previews of the *voice of the process* (see Chapter 8) and test it against the specifications (that is, the *voice of the customer*) that came out of the Characterize phase.

The team brings the final design to an executive forum, together with House 1, House 2, and the Pugh matrix that led to it. All participants are then encouraged to probe the design and challenge its capability. This ends the Design phase. The team is now ready to see how it performs in real life.

11.5 VERIFY

This phase starts with the detailed blueprint of the process developed in the previous phase. Its output is a process—fully deployed, stable, and capable. It evolves around a pilot project that lies at its core. It is followed by standardization and deployment.

A pilot project is used to create a low-risk, yet representative environment that will allow the process to be put to the test. Selection of the test site is critical. At this point, the riskiest features

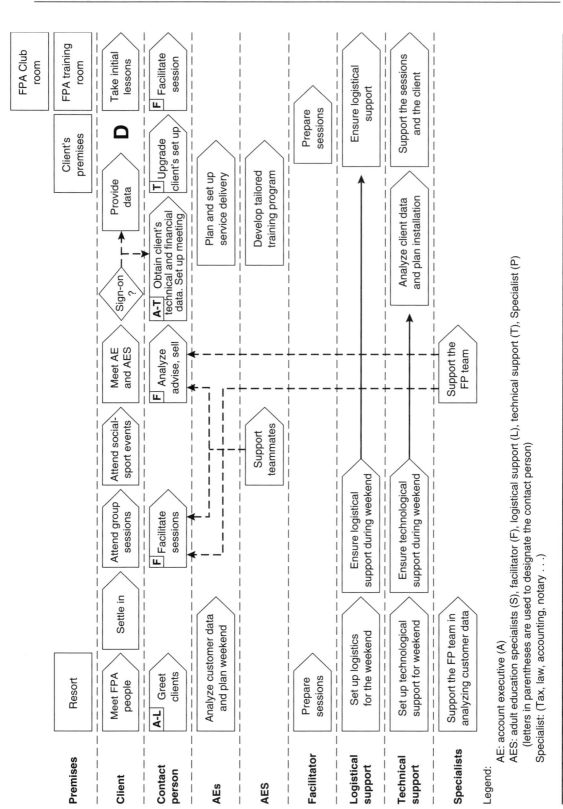

Figure 11.16 Macro-blueprint (partial).

of the process are well known. In terms of change management, test results must be, and fence-sitters must see that they are, valid guides to planning full-scale deployment. On the other hand, it would be unduly risky to select the site that provides the harshest testing ground for the project.

The development tools the team used provide useful information about the process's vulnerability. The minus signs in the Pugh matrix provide clues about weak areas. The various iterations through the matrix show the aspect of the process that the team was trying to correct. The FMEA table rates all the risks identified by the team, before and after the fix or *poka-yoke* the team has found. These elements allow the team to develop a risk management plan for the pilot project.

No matter how rigorous the design methodology, the reality test will yield a wealth of useful information. Thus, the team has to set up a learning system to capture this information and use it to improve its design. Client's agenda, mystery shopping, observation, focus groups, and surveys of all kinds are but a few of the tools available to the team. A dollar invested at this point of the project will yield huge dividends later in terms of field results. The team holds regular progress meetings throughout the pilot projects to translate its findings into process improvements.

An essential output that the team must provide is a *user-manual*. This involves documenting the process, developing a control plan, and providing the process owner with the tools needed, such as FMEA and SPC, to keep the process at peak performance level. You should review Section 10.7, discussing the Control phase of the improvement methodology. The major difference with the improvement methodology, of course, is that the process is completely new and thus that everyone who will be involved in it has to be trained from scratch. Thus, having a well-documented and well-instrumented process is critical to a successful deployment.

To deploy the process, the team uses the best process management techniques. The team develops a training program that is respectful of the people's ability to learn. A support team is built to help those who will be affected by the new process and a help desk is created. The team also builds contingency plans and puts together a strategic team to monitor the deployment phase.

A major mistake is very common at this point. Time gets its revenge on what is done without it. Unrealistic deadlines are always disruptive and often destructive. It may be a great opportunity and time may well be of the essence. Even more reason to do it well. Launching the new process in a panic, with poorly trained employees, goes directly against the rigor of the approach used thus far, and thus denies its benefits. Further, when a project goes over budget, this is generally the point in the project cycle when the team is more likely to run out of money. The temptation to cut on training, resulting in the project meeting its scheduled launch date and budget, may be strong. Resist it. It will only result in incurring huge costs trying to fix it after deployment, and an uphill battle to restore a reputation among customers and employees that has been tarnished.

11.6 UNDERSTANDING THE DESIGN METHODOLOGY

The design principles underlying each step of the methodology are presented in Table 11.1. They are self-explanatory. However, a recurring principle of the methodology might have escaped the reader, as it is difficult to understand the logic and the connection when you are focused on the details of each technique. Just as in the improved methodology (see discussion in Section 10.8), each technique proceeds by first generating quantity, then distilling quality from the elements generated (see Figure 11.17). A number of different approaches are used to generate elements, such as customer needs, technical characteristics, process functionalities, process concepts, process variants, or failure modes. Different filtering techniques (various types of rating schemes and matrices) and different criteria are then used to identify the best or the most important elements, which should be the focus.

The sequence of generators and filters is shown in Figure 11.18. A quantity of customers' needs and wants are generated by walking in their shoes through the customer activity cycle. An affinity diagram is then used and 100 points are spread to identify the critical needs. Brainstorming is used

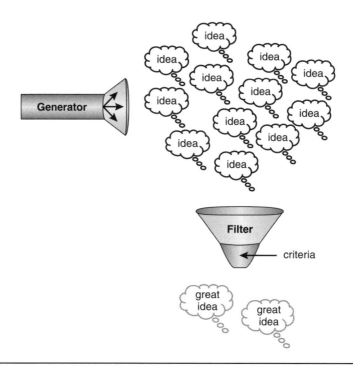

Figure 11.17 An underlying principle of the design methodology: From quantity to quality.

to generate an initial list of possible metrics and a matrix (House 1) is used to filter them through the weighted needs, to distill the most important metrics (CTQs, CTCs, CTDs). The FAST diagram is then used to identify process functionalities and the most important ones are identified by filtering them through the critical metrics in House 2.

Concept generation proceeds from these critical functionalities, through brainstorming and combination of ideas, to generating process concepts. These are in turn filtered through the Pugh matrix, using criteria reflecting clients' (from House 1), employees', and shareholders' needs to distill the best concept. This concept is then run through several iterations of the cycle of generating variants and selecting the best one. The blueprint of the final process is then screened through an FMEA, allowing designers to isolate and manage the most important risks.

Figure 11.19 provides yet another view of the methodology, closely outlining how the flow is cut up into four phases, following the customer-in pattern first depicted in Figure 5.5. The Define phase shows the role of strategy (see Chapter 6) and analysis of existing processes (see Chapter 7) in scoping the process. The arrows between the SMART statement and the SITOC illustrate the iterations and adjustments involved in scoping a project. The Characterize phase proceeds from two different points of the SITOC. Analysis of the clients leads to identifying CTSs and then to CTQs, CTCs, and CTDs. Analysis of the transformation, using the FAST diagram, leads to isolating the most important functionalities, as the two prongs meet in House 2. Analysis of any existing sub-processes in the organization is also useful at this point. Some critical sub-processes identified in House 2 may already exist and perform well somewhere in the organization (or may be accessible through process benchmarking). If that is the case, it is best to focus the design effort on other sub-processes.

It is seen as well in Figure 11.19 that the Design phase involves cycling through the *concept generation—Pugh matrix* cycle until it converges on a high-level view of the best process. It is indeed a common mistake when designing a new process to settle too quickly on high-level design

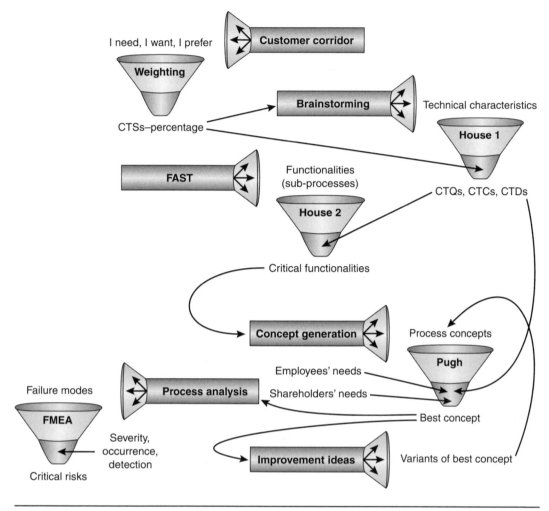

Figure 11.18 The design methodology: A series of generators and filters.

decisions, before fully exploring alternatives. Iterating through this cycle is fast and cheap, whereas detailed design is costly and time-consuming. By forcing such iterations and involving executives and other players in the forums, you create much value and make change management much easier in the implementation phase.

11.7 COMPARING DCDV AND DMAIC

The design methodology presents a stark contrast with the improve methodology. Its anchor points are the clients and strategy, whereas the improve methodology is anchored on an existing process, as described by the process map. Remember from Chapter 7 that the improve methodology is used when there is a belief that the process, while currently unsatisfactory, has potential. Thus, there is no need to question whether the process is *the right thing to do*. Efforts proceed directly to trying to understand the causes of its poor performance (diagnosis), and from there to fixing it. The

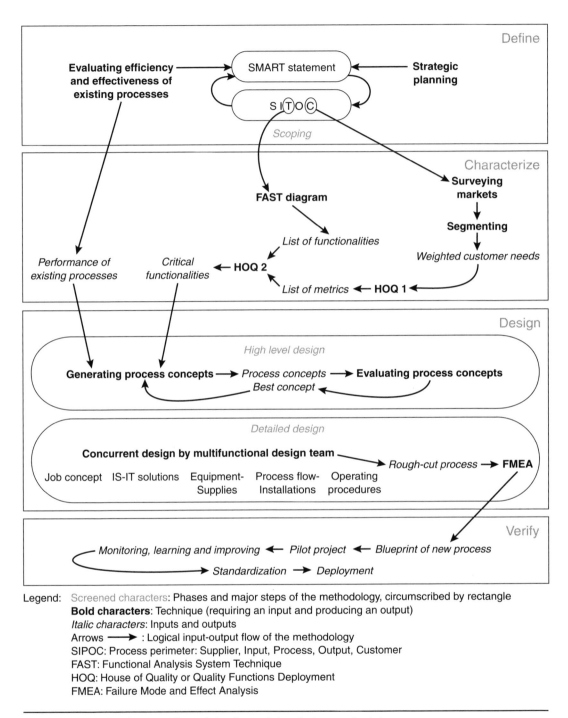

Figure 11.19 An alternate view of the flow of the design methodology.

approach used for reaching a diagnosis involves several techniques used in parallel, culminating in a synthesis (see Table 10.5). There lies the biggest intellectual challenge of the methodology.

If one technique in the DMAIC methodology is used poorly and does not yield results, the odds are that the other techniques applied in parallel will make up for it and that the right diagnosis will be reached. This is not the case for the DCDV methodology. Since the techniques are used serially, the output of one becoming the input of the next one, a major mistake at any point is not likely to be corrected downstream by other techniques. The need for rigor is therefore even more important when designing a new process than it is when improving one. This may explain why the latter is much more widespread than the former.

Even an organization that has successfully implemented DMAIC—and thus successfully faced the challenge of rigor in process improvement—is likely to find this new challenge daunting. As previously discussed, considering the nature of the task and its starting point, the composition of a design team has to be very different from that of an improvement team. Designers and improvement experts share a number of attitudes and aptitudes, such as a passion for rigor and leadership and a mastery of statistical tools. They are, however, two different breeds. Designers are very good at dealing with broad, abstract concepts such as (internal or external) customer needs and market segments. Typically, improvement experts are at their best when disentangling intricate interactions between concrete process variables. The best designers tend to have strong conceptual abilities—together with the corresponding tolerance for ambiguity—which allow them to view the global picture. The best improvement experts have a more analytical mind. The former are very good at zooming out, while the latter's comfort zone is limited to zooming in. While these attitudes are not totally incompatible, it is difficult to find them in the same individuals, together with the leadership skills required to participate and lead change.

Further, intimate knowledge of the process is an important asset for members of improvement teams, whereas it is a liability for members of design teams, inhibiting their creativity. The latter must be able to take their distance from any existing process or organizational practice. People who have been exposed to different ways of doing things are best. Finally, process workers are likely to feel threatened by radical change and its implications for their job and those of their friends and co-workers and thus less likely come up with or support such changes.

As process improvement skills become more widespread, the battleground to become the best learning organization may well move to excellence in process design. No matter how good an organization is at repairing broken processes, it will not be able to compete with organizations capable of designing a high-performance process on the first attempt.

11.8 SUMMARY

The flow of the design methodology is very different from that of the improve methodology. The latter starts with what already exists, that is, using the actual process as anchor for the analysis, and will not work if there is no process. The former starts with the customer and proceeds inward to selecting the appropriate metrics, setting standards, and developing a process from scratch. The anchor point are the customers and their needs—a much more abstract notion than an existing process. The example used is a direct carry-over from Chapter 6, as FPA now develops a process to train and educate clients belonging to a specific market segment.

The methodology involves the development of a set of metrics using quality functions deployment. The same technique is used to identify the most important functionalities of the process. These rigorous activities are interspersed with creative ones, as the team explores and compares alternate ways of performing the process. The latter steps involve detailed design, field verification, and implementation.

Importance (percentage)

Type of metric

Technical characteristics	↑ ↓ ⊕ Target values	Measurement system explanation/justification

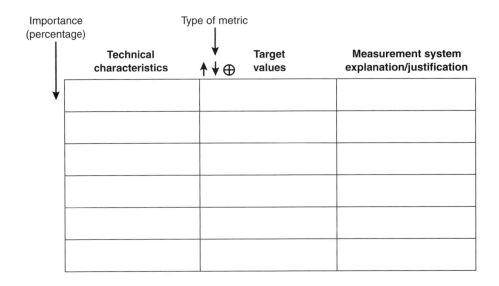

Figure 11.20 Voice of customer for key metrics and validation of measurement system.

The methodology presents the organization with the challenge of introducing rigor into an area still believed by many to be the sole preserve of intuition and improvisation.

EXERCISES

11.1 Conducting a design project

Your task is to apply the tools and methodology presented in this chapter to the design project scoped in Chapter 7. You might find the two additional forms included as Figures 11.20 and 11.21 useful. After you have completed House 1, use Figure 11.20 to set the target values (the voice of the

Functions	Technical characteristics impacted (1-3)	Priorities to consider during design

Figure 11.21 Key functions, metrics impacted, and priorities to consider in design.

customer) for the critical metrics and evaluate the respective measurement systems. After House 2, use Figure 11.21 to specify the metrics impacted by the key functions and the priorities to consider during design.

Since the methodology is more complex, and thus riskier than the previous one, you should manage this additional risk by using an outside resource to help you or perform the project first in a *simulated* setting. The latter involves sharing the book with three or four colleagues, and performing the project *off-line*, that is, without involving anyone in the organization. This might give you the added confidence you need to be able to guide an actual team through the methodology.

Notes

[1] *GO* is short for "Gentil Organisateur" (literally, kind facilitator), the term used by the French resort to refer to the young people it uses to animate the *village* and make the customers' vacations an enjoyable experience. They refer to the customers as *Gentil Membre* (kind member). The team wanted to pursue the CM analogy further and include this aspect of the club/brotherhood spirit to capture the distinctive feature of this variant of the CM concept.

12

The Learning Organization

An organizational learning maturity framework can help the organization identify learning bottle-necks and plan an improvement path.

In this chapter, a global portrait is painted of the learning organization and a tool is proposed to evaluate where your organization stands in terms of its *learning maturity*. Possible actions the company could undertake to progress on the maturity scale are then suggested. After a discussion of change management, the chapter concludes by illustrating how this material applies to personal and single-person professional processes as well.

12.1 ONE SIZE NEVER FITS ALL

Box 12.1 shows (tongue in cheek) that when you copy, you are always one step behind. Mindless adoption of other company's practices (*they are so much better than we are, we can't go wrong copying them*) is just as bad as trying to reinvent everything, including the four-hole button, yourself. It is much like taking medication that was prescribed for your neighbor, because he is a human being, just like you are. This has nothing to do with the quality of the medication. It is just that organizations are different, each with a history, a culture, and challenges that are its own. Conducting a design Kaizen event is a great initiative, if you are ready for it. If you are not, it may meet with such a negative reception that you will have a hard time introducing any new initiative for a long time.

Box 12.1: Learning from the best

Issue: *Mindless benchmarking is risky*

Six executives from two competing companies are about to embark on a train taking them to an industry fair. Three executives work for ADD, which suffers from an attention deficit disorder. The three others work for LO, a learning organization. The three ADD executives purchase

---

Continued

Continued

their tickets and, as they wait for their competitors, they watch dumbfounded as they purchase only one ticket for the three of them.

"What are you doing?" asked one of the ADD executives.

"Oh, this is standard practice in this organization," replie the LO executive.

"But, what are you going to do?" the ADD executive asks again.

"Just watch us, you might learn a thing or two," replied the competitor.

As the three ADD executives take a seat, they are shocked to see the three competitors enter the bathroom: the three of them in the same one! The train starts. The conductor soon enters the car: "Tickets, please!" As he is about to leave the car, he suddenly halts, turns around, and come back to the bath room, knocking: "Tickets, please!" Under the watchful eyes of ADD executives, a ticket suddenly materializes from under the door. The controller bends down, picks it up, and resumes his rounds with a resounding: "Thank you!" The ADD executives are impressed: "so this is why their costs are so low" they think to themselves.

Three days later, the same six executives are on their way back from the convention, again about to embark on the train. One of the three ADD executives stops at the counter to buy a ticket, as his two colleagues exchange knowing glances with the competitors.

"Benchmarking!" says one ADD executive to a competitor with a wink, "we are into that too at ADD, you know." As he is saying that, however, he notices that none of the LO executives bought a ticket.

"Hey guys," he says, "you forgot to buy a ticket."

"Oh, this is standard practice at LO on the way back from a trip," says the LO executive.

"But, what are you going to do when the conductor knocks at the bathroom door?" asks the ADD executive.

"Watch us," replies the competitor mysteriously, without further explanation.

The three ADD executives enter the car's bathroom, giggling. The three LO executives enter the bathroom on the other side of the corridor, deadpan. The train takes off. A few seconds later, a bathroom door opens slowly and an LO executive peeks out carefully. He walks out, steps right across the hallway, and knocks gently on the door of the other bathroom: "Tickets, please!"

To pursue the prescription analogy, you should use this book as a doctor uses the pharmacopeia available: Do not prescribe anything until you have a diagnosis. This falls under this broader maxim of the medical profession: first, do no harm. There was once a consultant to an organization that, after years of neglect of continuous improvement, suddenly awakened and decided that they wanted *the best program*. They had gone to an organization they admired, asked them the name of their program, and went shopping around for a consultant that would help them become just like their model organization. The change projects and the methodology they used were so inappropriate that they soon had a revolution on their hands. I came on board with the undertow of that first wave of change, assessing the needs and the damage done by that initiative, and introducing a more appropriate change vehicle, a simplified methodology, and more basic tools. While the strategy worked and the program was salvaged, the initiative never achieved its full potential. The backlash that

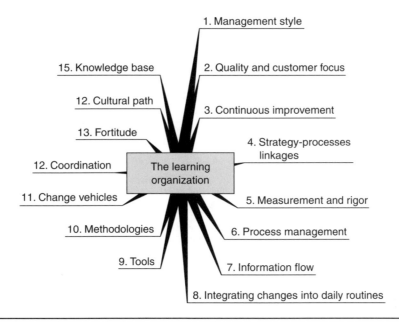

Figure 12.1 The 15 dimensions of the learning organization.

followed the initial approach left scars and created opponents so staunch that they could never be fully brought back on board.

In the next section, you are presented with some of the elements you will need to prepare a diagnosis that will help you avoid that company's fate.

12.2 THE DIMENSIONS OF THE LEARNING ORGANIZATION

Learning organizations share fifteen characteristics (see Figure 12.1 and Table 12.1) of various natures. These are discussed in turn in this section, correlating with various chapters of the book as it goes. You can make a quick assessment of where your organization stands on these dimensions using the five-point scales presented in Figure 12.2. This is not a statistically validated measurement instrument. It strictly reflects my opinion.

12.2.1 Management Style

As discussed in Chapter 1, as well as parts of Chapters 3, 5, and 9, learning is not the sole preserve of the strategic apex of the organization. Unless the organization is managed in such a way that every individual has the motivation to learn and is given the means and opportunities to do so, the organization learning rate will remain sub par. It lies beyond the scope of this book to explain how to transform a *command and control* type of organization into a participative one. However, you should be aware that much of the potential of the material presented in this book will remain bottled up unless a participative management style permeates the organization. Rate your organization at five in Figure 12.2 if this is the case. If an authoritarian and repressive management style is the rule or predominates (one or two), or even if the management gives equal place to both styles of management (three), this is a clear hurdle that you have to overcome before embarking on the journey proposed here. Professionals do not grow in such an environment and given their power, a tug of war often ensues with management.

Table 12.1   Defining the dimensions of the learning organization.

1	Management style	Is the business managed with an authoritarian and repressive approach, or in a participative fashion conducive to sharing and learning?
2	Quality and customer focus	Are customers' needs explicit and do we have systems in place to assure that we deliver quality services?
3	Continuous improvement	Do we share a philosophy of continuous improvement?
4	Strategy-processes linkages	Do we have a process vision of value-creation in this business and can we connect processes to customer and strategy?
5	Information flow	Does our information flow along process lines, or does information flow essentially within functional groups?
6	Process management	Are business processes actively managed?
7	Measurement and rigor	How rigorous are we in measurement and decision making? Is the scientific method (by any name) the accepted way to move forward?
8	Integrating change into daily routine	Are process changes systematically integrated into daily operations?
9	Tools	Do we use all the tools available to improve and design processes? Is a critical mass of management and employees acquainted with these tools?
10	Methodologies	Do we use formal methodologies to improve and design processes?
11	Change vehicle	Do we have a *fleet* of systematic change vehicles and do we use them judiciously?
12	Coordination	Is the learning cycle well understood? Are all change projects the object of global coordination? Are we geared up to evaluate and improve the cycle?
13	Fortitude	Do we stick to our learning drives no matter what, or do we forget everything and change paths when we experience growing pains (internal or external)?
14	Cultural path	Do we manage the evolution of our organizational culture, ensuring that each new initiative is coherent with the culture and contributes to its evolution?
15	Knowledge base	Does the organization's knowledge base rest with a few individuals, or is it explicit, shared, and evolutive?

The author has worked with an organization whose management style rated something between three and four. The official line professed participative management, but the body language often denied this. Despite punctual successes in deploying some of the tools and vehicles presented here, in the end, a bottleneck was encountered. As with any bottle, it lay at the top of the bottle—in this case, at the very top. It was never really circumvented. Much cynicism on the part of the employees existed at the outset of the initiative, and rightly so. The level of sarcasm had ramped up one notch by the time the initiative was dropped. Better not start what you will not be able to finish. Better keep the aircraft on the ground, than take off without a good probability of having a landing strip available when you reach your destination.

12.2.2 Quality and customer focus

Understanding evolving customer needs and understanding how you can create more value than competitors for targeted customers are the topic of Chapter 2. Without an explicit understanding of this, the alignment of processes to value-creation is impossible. In the professional world (Chapter

		1	2	3	4	5
1	**Management style**	Universal belief in command and control	Command and control dominates	Coexistence of various beliefs	Participative management dominates	Shared belief in participative
2	**Quality and customer focus**	We rely on professional's diplomas or license	Some quality procedures exist	Most quality procedures exist	Quality certification obtained	Quality system used as learning engine
3	**Continuous improvement**	Not a clue what you are talking about	Only in crisis mode	Sporadically	Systematically	Shared belief
4	**Strategy-processes linkages**	None	Within functional silos	Limited to one or two business processes	Some efforts are made, with limited results	Central aspect of governance
5	**Measurement and rigor**	Fireman culture, shoot from the hip	Some rigor in accounting and financial data	Some high-level indicators taken seriously	Systematic use of rigorous measures	Generalized use of statistics
6	**Process management**	Nothing	A committee resolves cross-functional issues	Through service-level agreements	Systematic measurement of all processes	This is the way we manage the company
7	**Information flow**	Antiquated functional systems	Modern functional systems	Some patches and bridges	Several *integrated* systems	Seamless horizontal flows
8	**Integrating changes into daily routine**	No follow through	Gains last about one month	Gains last about six months	Some changes stick	Perfect integration achieved
9	**Tools**	No tools	Some basic tools	Some statistical tools as well	More advanced statistical tools	Full toolbox regularly updated
10	**Methodologies**	None	Deming wheel (P-D-C-A) used sometimes	DMAIC used	Some elements of DCDV	Judicious use of complete gamut
11	**Change vehicles**	None	One vehicle, used intuitively	One formal vehicle	Two vehicles	Full fleet–used judiciously
12	**Coordination**	Projects are totally unrelated	Some projects are linked	Global management of a project portfolio	Regular evaluation of lessons learned	Continuous improvement of the learning pump
13	**Fortitude**	No initiatives are ever introduced	Flavor of the month	We let go at the first hurdle	We hold as long as we can, then we let go	Resolve grows during crisis periods
14	**Cultural path**	No systematic initiative	Disconnected sporadic initiatives	Adoption of every new program	Recognition and learning from failures	Culture kept on a controlled evolutive path
15	**Knowledge base**	In the head of the boss	In the head of the top management team	Some efforts to capture knowledge	Base exists, but use and update are sporadic	Universal and evolutive
	Legend	Attention deficit disorder	Functional intelligence	Sporadic learning	Sporadic memory blanks	Learning organization

Figure 12.2 Five levels of learning maturity.

4), regulating bodies also specify individual standards required to obtain and maintain certification. Learning organizations not only maintain certification at both an individual and organizational level (level four in Figure 12.2), but also use their quality system, be it based on ISO 9000 or some other industry standard, as a learning lever (level five). All organizations (such as health organizations) that require certification to operate must minimally perform at level four on this scale (assuming that the certification process itself is capable).

12.2.3 Continuous Improvement

The philosophy of continuous improvement is discussed at length throughout the book, specifying its dynamic in the discussion of the learning cycle in Chapter 9. The philosophy rests on the belief that it is worthwhile to constantly strive to be the best at what you do, dedicating time and resources to the task. Many organizations never start on that path (level one and two in Figure 12.2). When they want to increase output (either quality or quantity), they put more pressure on their professionals. They see the result immediately: output increases. Thus, their belief is reinforced that this is the way to go. What they do not see, however, is that when people simply work harder, they eventually become tired, and when they do, they start cutting corners. Professionals are smart enough to cut where the cutting will not show up, at least not in ways that are traceable to them. Process improvement, learning, and growth activities fit the bill. The effects of a cut there are diffuse and delayed. When the lost capabilities eventually start to show and output decreases, management believes, incorrectly, that it is because the effect of the original pressure they put has waned. Consequently, they go back to putting pressure on professionals, never waking up to the vicious cycle in which they are stuck.

Indeed, when an organization initially invests in improvement, the short-term result is a decrease in output, as an immediate consequence of resource reallocation (that is, from production to improvement). Thus, getting started on the virtuous cycle of continuous improvement is difficult, because it requires patience and the fortitude to maintain course in spite of naysayers. Some organizations make many false starts (level three) until they get it right (level four and eventually level five). In organizations operating at level one and two, you would often hear the command: "I want results, no matter how." In level five organizations, *how* matters even more than results, for if you do not know it (that is, the process), you cannot repeat it.

12.2.4 Strategy-processes Linkage

Much of Chapter 5 and the whole of Chapter 6 are dedicated to the conceptual and technical exploration of the linkage between strategy and processes. The methodology presented in Chapter 6 amounts to deploying customer needs and strategic priorities onto processes, using metrics as a bridge. This is critical to avoiding the execution gap discussed in Chapter 1. At levels one and two, such connection is absent. From level three to level five, the linkage grows from being an experiment to being a central aspect of governance.

12.2.5 Measurement and Rigor

The importance of measurement and rigor permeates this book. It may be an overused expression, but many managers are at their best when they fight fires. They love the pressure. They feel that it allows them to show their mettle. They enjoy the feeling of accomplishment when the crisis is resolved. Firefighting organizations value such achievements, reward them, and promote the best firefighters. For these people, the crisis mode is a way of life. It is the only thing that they know. They soon occupy the higher echelons of such organizations and would feel lost if there were no fires to fight. Thus, these organizations do not place much emphasis on prevention and do not reward people for promoting logical validity, precision, and accuracy in measurement and compliance discipline that is, promoting rigor.

Such organizations would rate a one or two in Figure 12.1. Organizations at level three try to be rigorous when dealing with aggregate data, a pursuit that is much more beneficial if rigor exists at the operating level. Reaching a point (level five) where statistics become the shared language to talk about variation and uncertainty (see Chapter 8) requires a quantum leap that only the best-run organizations are able to make.

12.2.6 Process Management

In medieval times, an artisan walks from village to village, selling services along the way. Nearing a large city, a worker cutting stones with a chisel is noticed. The worker is seen to not be putting much heart into the work and the workmanship was shoddy. The artisan asks:

> "What are you doing?"

> "I'm cutting stones," the worker answers.

> "Why?" asked the artisan.

> "Because my boss told me to do so. When I have cut a hundred stones, I'll be paid five crowns," the worker replied.

Nearing the town, the artisan saw many more workers, all producing the same shoddy output. Finally, the artisan notices a stack of stones, only half as big as the others, but consisting of impeccably cut stones. Curious, the artisan approaches the worker responsible for this feat and asks:

> "What are you doing?"

> "I'm building a cathedral."

Maybe a more contemporary example will drive the point home better. First-year students arriving on the campus of a large university are greeted every year by a huge sign: "Room control welcomes you to campus". Fortunately, the poor students are probably too worried about the initiation ritual that awaits them to think much of it. No more than the unmotivated workers of the preceding story, do the employees involved in *room control* understand or identify with the finality of their work. However, they have control of many resources (including poster boards) and use it fully to display their *we* feeling.

As essential as it is to productivity and to the growth of specialized expertise in the organization, division and departmentalization of work can produce what Karl Marx called alienation of the worker. Just as the four American runners (Section 3.3.4) could not win the 400-m women's relay race in the 2000 Sydney Olympics, without a clear understanding of their collective task and careful management of the interfaces between them, the output of any process will be sub-standard unless all workers share a common vision of the process.

As discussed in Chapter 3, a business process is a logical chain of commitments, from input to output, linking professional, technical, and clerical workers spread in several organizational units. A mechanism is required to bridge the gaps between these units, making the process seamless and agile.

In some organizations, inter-departmental issues are never resolved (level one). Others set up a committee (ad hoc or standing) to address such issues as they arise (level two). Yet others have internal customers and suppliers sit together and negotiate service-level agreements, which they may or may not enforce seriously (level three). Adding systematic measurement of end-to-end processes reinforces this approach (level four). However, making someone accountable for the performance of the process (level five) is the only way to make it come alive.

Just like in a relay race, where each runner has a personal coach, process workers have their functional bosses (sales, accounting, legal, credit, and so on), whose role it is to foster excellence and coherence in their respective fields. The process owner's job, like that of the coach, is to ensure alignment and cohesion. In the 1960s, the U.S. armed forces greatly improved inter-arm coordination by adding a provision that promotions to the rank of major and beyond would require the concurrence of the other arms. As long as evaluation and incentives are strictly vertical (that is, functional), efforts exerted to align horizontal flows with processes will go against the grain and remain ineffective.

12.2.7 Information Flow

So-called *legacy* systems were built around functions. They allowed a group of specialists (be it in finance, marketing, credit, human resources, or other) to share information. These systems were designed to fit well within functional boundaries. Unfortunately, they fall apart when it comes to making people from various functions work together, that is, when it comes to processes. Many organizations (levels one and two) are still stuck in that old paradigm. This creates a bottleneck. It limits any progress the company can make on the other dimensions of the learning organization. Some organizations, understanding their predicament, improve matters (level three) by patching together or building bridges between old systems. Others (level four) go for the *integrated system*, which is never integrated enough, so that they have to keep some of the older ones. They end up with a complex web of systems and are still in search of integration. The best organizations have resolved the issue, building a new system from the ground up, mostly through using purchased infrastructure systems (called enterprise resource planning, (ERPs) or enterprise systems). Workflow automation systems can also be very useful for any organization.

12.2.8 Integrating Changes Into Daily Routines

Several years ago, I was hired to help a service organization getting started on the path to continuous improvement. I conducted three Kaizen events, successfully fixing six broken processes. As is my practice, I trained the organization to be able to conduct the event without my assistance. About six months later, the company, invoking growing pains, asked me to come back to help them conduct the next Kaizen event. Puzzled, I accepted. As I was kicking off the event, explaining that the payoffs the organization would get from this initiative were well worth their time, one of the participants raised a hand to ask a question:

"Yes," I said.

"Remember when you were here last fall to fix the planning process?" asked someone from one of the two teams.

"Yes, I do. What about it?" I replied.

"Well, I was there on that Friday afternoon when the team made a demonstration of the new process. I was amazed that a team of our people could come up with so many great ideas, and make them work."

"Thank you for pointing that out," I said, turning away from the participant to carry on with the kick-off.

"There's a problem, however," continued the participant.

"Oh! And what might that be?" I asked, beginning to worry.

"Well, it's just that we don't do any of this anymore. We gradually dropped most of these ideas, and we are now essentially back where we started. So what's the point of sweating it out for a week if we're going to revert back to our old ways soon thereafter anyway?"

This organization was willing to make a one-week investment but was unable to follow through. The Kaizen event bypasses regular management and control procedures, and breaks barriers between departments for one process, one team, one week. The Monday after, it is back to business as usual. Thus, unless *business as usual* is changed so that it is able to accept, adjust to, and take care of a new process, there is no point to designing and improving processes. This requires follow-through and good process controls. Rate your organization one to five, from *no follow-through* to *perfect integration achieved*. For most organizations, this requires as well a cultural shift toward information flow (characteristic seven), continuous improvement (characteristic three), and rigor (characteristic five).

12.2.9 Tools

The book is loaded with process tools. From SITOC to Pugh matrix, they range from the simple (FAST, SMART) to the more complex (QFD, Diagnostic worksheet). Proven and honed over the years, they are indispensable companions on the continuous improvement journey. The larger the user-base of a tool in an organization is, the more potent the tool. While experts in advanced statistics will never be legion in any organization, statistical thinking and use of basic statistical tools must become widespread.

Some organizations (level one) are tool-less. Others use only the simplest tools (such as Ishikawa diagrams) sporadically (level two). Others yet (level three) use more tools, including the basic statistical ones (such as statistical process control), while at level four, organizations toy with regression analysis, analysis of variance, and even designed experiments. At level five, an organization explicitly manages its techniques as a master artisan does a toolbox, dynamically retiring and adding new tools as the organizational challenges evolve.

12.2.10 Methodologies

In chapters 10 and 11, the improvement and design methodologies are presented as two alternate ways to proceed. In fact, they are not as radically opposed to one another as they have been made to appear. A number of linkages offer potential bridges between them. As well, many tools of one methodology can come in handy to resolve specific issues that arise in the course of a project:

- The improvement methodology assumes that the process has potential and that if a few vital variables are set right, the process will perform up to expectations. It often turns out, however, that it is realized early on that customers' needs are poorly understood and the metrics used are inappropriate. Building a House 1 in the Measure phase can resolve this problem in a structured manner.

- When the process to be improved turns out to be very large, House 2 can help direct the team to the most important sub-processes. It can also give the team the option to design some sub-processes from scratch (using idea generation and the Pugh matrix presented in Chapter 11) and improve the others.

- FMEA (an improvement tool) is already involved in the design methodology presented in Chapter 11. Value-added analysis can also be useful in the detailed design phase, to minimize non-value-added activities.

- It often happens in the early stages of an improvement project that the team realizes that there is no process to speak of. The team may come back from the mapping exercise realizing that there is no set flow to the process, and that an infinite number of combinations exist. Under these conditions, switching to the design methodology, without missing a beat, may be the best way to salvage an initiative that could turn sour, and leave the team with a bad taste that may constitute a threat to the survival of the whole initiative.

- In the course of a design project, the team may find that the best way to design some sub-processes is to benchmark other (non-competing) organizations. The improvement methodology (or any combination of tools from it) then, is helpful in adapting the *borrowed* process to the organization.

Other methodologies, such as JIT/lean manufacturing and DFSS, are mentioned in Chapter 9. Many other variants of these methodologies exist. Prior to the emergence of DMAIC improvement methodology as the dominant methodology, by far the most widespread one was the more basic Deming Wheel, or PDCA (plan-do-check-act). Many organizations still use it (level 2), while others have *graduated* to DMAIC. The beliefs of many organizations (level one) are never strong enough to induce them to make the investment required to learn and deploy a methodology. Businesses at level four and five have separated from the pack by investing in a design methodology (DCDV or equivalent), while level five organizations are actively engaged in improving the way they use their methodologies.

12.2.11 Change Vehicles

Managing organizational change is a complex and delicate undertaking. When an organization decides to use the learning cycle to create strategic advantage, it must set up to negotiate each turn of the wheel carefully. In Chapter 9, a number of improvement vehicles are presented, focusing on the Kaizen event. It is presented in its standard five-day format. In Chapter 11, FPA modified the format to include two three-day sessions, with a modification of team composition in between the sessions. Further, they held the three days of the first session one week apart, to allow for data gathering and validation.

When you are learning to play piano, you must first learn and practice scales, until they become second nature. At that point, you can start introducing variations and combinations into your play. When you start along the path of process management, you should also first experiment with the standard approaches until you reach a comfort zone; that is, you understand how and why they work. When you feel in control, it is safe to start creating your own variants. This will give you more flexibility in tailoring change vehicles suited to any special need that may arise. A three-day Kaizen event, for instance, or a four-person improvement team are not anathema and may well be the right way to go in some circumstances.

Organizations that use a change vehicle implicitly (level two) have an edge over those who improvise every time they face change (level one). Those who are explicit about it (level three) have a marked advantage: they waste less energy (efficiency), make fewer mistakes (effectiveness), and can learn with every turn of the wheel, improving the vehicle as they go on improving processes. At level four, the business has become more sophisticated, and uses two vehicles—projects and Kaizen events are a common combination. Level five organizations have reached a point where they manage a complete *fleet* and are capable of *moving* any process, under any circumstance.

Change management is revisited in more detail in the latter part of the chapter.

12.2.12 Coordination

At every iteration of the learning cycle, new know-how is created. The learning cycle is a repetitive learning process. The organization that manages it best can become the fastest learner: a sustainable source of competitive advantage. We call this *double-loop* learning; that is, learning to be better learners. This is best achieved by treating it as a process—maybe the organization's most critical one—and putting all of the process knowledge to work to make it better. Thus, the process needs an owner, who could be called the chief learning officer (level five). This job, as discussed earlier, is to lead the learning drive (vision, strategy, and communication), ensure alignment and cohesion, set targets, monitor progress, and make the learning process better and faster. This involves, among other things, measuring results, coordinating training (much is required, as this book makes obvious), benchmarking with the best organizations, and ensuring feedback and communication.

At level one and two, the organization performs improvement or design projects without having a global view of the improvement path, or of the global effect it is having on the business. At a level three, it is managing a portfolio of projects, ensuring that the brunt of the effect is felt in areas where the business needs it most. At level four, the organization takes the time to debrief each project to see if anything unusual happened (that is, process variation) that could hide an important lesson to be shared with the rest of the organization.

12.2.13 Fortitude

As discussed earlier, crises put the organization's learning mettle to the test. They manifest themselves as severe market or profitability setbacks, and may be triggered by internal or external occurrences, sudden or gradual. The 9/11 events, technological breakthroughs of all kinds, market shifts, growth crisis, arrival of new competitors, and currency fluctuations, to name but a few, are potential sources of crises. When the organization finds itself under urgent and intense pressure to increase profits, it takes a hard look at its practices and looks for solutions. That is the time when all of the wolves come out of their dens to attack the learning initiatives. Unless its roots run deep when the crisis strikes, it stands a good chance of being uprooted.

Because the initiative initially runs on faith, due to the immediacy of the costs and the delayed nature of the benefits, it is vulnerable. In fact, whoever kills it may look like a hero for a while, as the fresh influx of resources is felt. Many organizations (level one and two) appear to follow a *me, too* strategy, adopting the latest fad, and dropping it at the faintest hint of a crisis. Level three and four differ in terms of the magnitude of the crisis required for them to drop the ball. Level five organizations may put the initiative on a survival regime for a while, that is, put on hold the design of a new fire engine to call all hands to the hoses, they may modify and adapt the initiative to better fit the new reality, but they stay the course (see the discussion below on the cultural path below).

12.2.14 Cultural Path

Some organizations (level one) do not have a culture to speak of. Different parts of the organization, often delimited by functional silos, share different values. Professionals do not really have to share much with their colleagues, since they work in the professional bubble they create and manage. Other organizations have a culture that has evolved randomly (level two). Yet other companies (level three) adopt all new programs that become fashionable (see discussion in Section 12.4.2), sending messages with one that are soon denied by the following one. Organizations at level four draw the lessons to be learned from any program they decide to stop or phase out. They use these lessons in the selection of the next initiative (see discussion in Section 12.4.1). Level five organizations nurture their culture as a precious asset. They cater to it. They assess what the organization requires. They investigate any new program that shows up on their watchful radar, and only adopt what they find to be of value to them. They never adopt a program wholesale. They always make sure that employees understand the addition and the motivation behind it. Upon entering the premises of such organizations, consultants are typically warned: "Do not mess with my culture."

12.2.15 Knowledge Base

Know-how cannot evolve alone. Knowledge must evolve as well (see discussion in Section 3.4.2). Financial institutions need to understand the state-of-art in credit algorithms. Drugstores need to know about drug interactions and new ways to administer medications. Law firms must have access to the latest jurisprudence. Consulting and engineering firms must have access to their *recipes* to resolve various professional challenges they face. Clearly, knowledge bases and processes have a symbiotic relationship. Knowledge bases are created and *nourished* (updated and upgraded) by processes, and many processes *feed on* (that is, need input from) them as well.

Knowledge base skills (and associated technologies) are complementary to process skills in the learning organization. When critical knowledge is in the head of the boss (level one) or the executive teams (level two) they always have to be *in the loop* for processes to work. They are bottlenecks that limit the output. This role monopolizes executives' time. It is an impediment to their involvement in the learning cycle. Levels three to five represent three different stages of evolution in an organization's abilities in capturing, upgrading, and disseminating knowledge throughout the organization.

12.3 LEVELS OF LEARNING MATURITY

Learning organizations require many capabilities, ranging from the soft (culture) to the hard (tools). While there is not a unique sequence to their acquisition, you have to stand before you can run. These capabilities are related in complex ways and imbalances create learning bottlenecks.

In this section, the fifteen dimensions presented above are used to create a typology of organizations according to the *learning maturity* level they have achieved. Figure 12.2 presents the capabilities associated with each of five maturity levels. To find out how mature your organization is with respect to its learning capabilities, mark with an X in Figure 12.2 the ratings you established in the previous section and see at what maturity level the majority of marks lie.

At Maturity level one, which is labeled attention deficit disorder or ADD, organizations do not learn. They repeat the same mistakes, and most steps forward that they take are followed by two steps backwards. This is not to say that they are not profitable. Markets are imperfect and often slow to react to inefficiencies. Thus, companies can survive for some time, vegetating in such local pockets or niches of inefficiency. However, eventually, if there is profit to be made, better companies will be attracted and soon come knocking at the door. Since any competitive asset that they might hold is not sustainable, in time they are condemned.

These organizations need shock therapy. The best source for the shock is internal, that is, administered by a new or a *born again* (so to speak) CEO. The most likely source, however, is external, and may turn out to be fatal. Adopting an industry quality standard (such as ISO-9000) if appropriate, and setting a (realistic) timeline for certification may be a way to jump-start the change initiative.

At maturity level two, which is labeled functional intelligence, some learning takes place, mostly in isolated pockets. The good news is that the organization has flirted with continuous improvement. It has used a basic methodology and has an intuitive feel for a change vehicle. However, since learning is not process-wide, since there is no knowledge base, and initiatives come and go, there is no synergism. The seeds are there, however, for a learning-friendly environment to emerge. Of course, any dimension for which the organization is rated in the ADD category points out where the bottleneck to its progress lies (this holds true for the *sporadic learning* and *sporadic memory blanks* maturity levels as well). Addressing these dimensions is the best place to start.

Since most of what the organization does is intuitive, what these companies need is to make explicit what is implicit, thus making clear the value of current improvement approaches, their potential, and their limitations. Only then will the organization be in a position to leverage what it does, to put the company in motion, clarifying the vision, charting the course, mobilizing the resources, and strengthening its resolve to stay the course. DMAIC Kaizen events may provide the impetus to move ahead, and start investing more efforts in horizontal management and strategy-process connection.

Balanced scorecards are worth looking into as well at this point. Kaplan and Norton (1992) made a great contribution to rigorous and logical measurement of performance by proposing a *balanced* scorecard for the company. Growing and learning employees drive processes and market share, which in turn drives financial results. Selecting a consistent set of metrics from each of these areas allows the organization to build a dashboard to manage the organization.

Members of organizations that have reached maturity level three share strong beliefs about participative management and continuous improvement. They are rigorous and make efforts to connect strategy to operations. They experience problems with horizontal management and follow-through, and they are only using a part of the fleet and arsenal of the learning organization, thus making their learning sporadic, as this maturity level is labeled.

These organizations should move on to the design methodology and start exploring other change vehicles. The methodology proposed in Chapter 6 would be timely, to reinforce the connection between processes and strategy. As well as improving its knowledge base, the company must become more sophisticated about its understanding and management of its culture. The assessment of the impact of past programs, as suggested in Section 12.4.1 below, would be a good place to start.

The only thing missing for companies that have reached level four on the maturity scale is putting it all together. If they could connect all the dots, completing horizontal management, seeing how the mechanisms of the learning pump, knowledge base, and follow-through work together, then everything they still perceive as separate initiatives would blend in seamlessly with the way they manage the business, and they would become a mature learning organization (level five). For these organizations, benchmarking[1] with the best-run companies may be the best way to understand the global vision, complete the journey they have started, and reap its full benefits.

If you are at level five, you belong to the select category of learning organizations. You should first see if there is any dimension rated less than five: This is what you should address next. If you are a *straight-five organization*, you may want to pass this book along to a supplier or partner from whose improvement you would stand to gain.

12.4 IMPROVING LEARNING CAPABILITIES

12.4.1 Special Hurdles and Opportunities: Past Initiatives

For many organizations about to embark on a learning initiative, the greatest risk they face is typically hidden in plain sight. It is the muted cynicism accumulated from past initiatives that have resulted in a failure, never acknowledged, never understood, merely erased from the *official* company history. They never happened. Thus, they are present in everyone's mind whenever the rumor of a forthcoming initiative surfaces. As mentioned earlier, a mistake from which you do not learn is one that you are condemned to repeat. A success has many fathers. A failure is an orphan. The higher up the true father stands in the organization, the more likely it is to remain an orphan forever.

Therefore, the first demonstration of leadership required for the organization to notice that something serious is afoot is an open diagnosis of past initiatives. This should not be a witch-hunt, though humble pie may be on the menu for some people. Not only will this clear a major obstacle lying on the path to learning, it will also provide essential clues about the culture, identify pitfalls to avoid, and pinpoint areas of opportunity

12.4.2 Improvement Programs: What To Do About Them

An improvement program generally comes as a package that includes a complete instruction set. They are developed and honed through their use by many organizations. Consultants, who propose their services as guides, generally promote these programs. Management theorists call them management fads, because they typically go through a life cycle. They are generally born in a large corporation, which uses its success (real or imagined) for self-promotion. Consultants take it from there. The program goes through an introduction phase, followed by growth, maturity, and eventually, decline and extinction. A number of factors trigger the latter two phases. As some flaws in the program show up over time, fixes are eventually found, spinning off *new programs* on the one hand, and being *added on* haphazardly to the old one. After some time, the program loses its integrity and becomes a hodgepodge. Further, the image is typically tarnished by some high-profile failure, or by the bankruptcy of a company whose name was linked to the initiative.

These programs are never as new as consultants claim they are. They often incorporate all the best features of previous programs, now in decline. However, they generally add new elements that were missing in the previous waves, which make them more effective. Unfortunately, they often drop some great features of past programs as well.

Some programs eventually develop into standards, as industry associations, whole industrial sectors, or countries adopt them. As such, they often become a prerequisite to stay in business, or at least to get contracts from specific customers. Since standards spell out minimal requirements, they act strictly as qualifiers and not as differentiators or order-winners, except maybe in the initial stages.

If you are just starting on this journey, and thus are not openly associated with a *brand name* program, I suggest that you create a name of your own for the initiative. It could refer to the learning organization or to continuous improvement, both generic terms. Whatever name you choose, it should be generic and fit well with your culture. On the other hand, if you have had some initial successes with an initiative such as TQM or Six Sigma and the organization buys into it, do build on that success and expand it to include new features you need to progress in your journey towards becoming a learning organization.

12.4.3 Change Management

Most people associate change with loss, and thus tend to resist it. They fear that they will not be able to perform as well in the new environment, that they will lose control, that they will not like it, or that it will hurt them in some other way. Four factors can act as counterweight to overcome this resistance:

- Dissatisfaction (Why change?). This is the stimulus for change. It may stem from immediate poor performance or from an understanding that current ways will not be sufficient in the future. It can stem from a positive mindset (hope to achieve more) or a negative one (fear of what will happen if we do not change). Dissatisfaction pushes people away from the existing process.

- Leadership (Change for what?). As defined in Chapter 2, leadership is the ability to form in your mind a crisp image (a vision) of a reality that does not yet exist, to make that same image—equally crisp—appear in the mind of others, to make it believable and desirable, and to show the path to take to make it become real. The vision pulls people towards another process.

- Sense of urgency (When to change?). As the toaster analogy (Section 1.3.5) shows, there is always something more urgent to do than fixing broken processes. This includes apologizing to customers and making up for the poor quality of the service provided to them because of the broken process. Hence, the responsibility to create a sense of urgency even greater than this one rests on management. The Kaizen event does that wonderfully. A sense of urgency pushes people toward action.

- Action plan (How to change?). Motivated people who share the vision and feel a sense of urgency need to know what to do, otherwise confusion, chaos, and panic ensues. That is why a methodology, tools, and a plan of action are needed. They guide people and keep them on the trail.

Change happens when these four forces of change combine to reach a threshold that outweighs inertia. They work together, in synergism. If one is missing, change is unlikely to take place, and if ever it does, it may not be in the desired direction.

Since process change involves many players, the forces of change must prevail for all categories of players: executive, management, professionals, technical, and clerical workers. Failing that, one group of players will be applying the brakes, working at cross-purpose with the rest of the organization. Therefore, these forces must be managed.

Notice how the Kaizen event manages these forces. The scoping effort (Chapter 7) exposes dissatisfaction among executives and management. Several tools used in the diagnosis phase (Chapter 10), such as failure mode and effect analysis (FMEA) and value-added analysis (VAA), bring out the weakness of the process, thereby convincing the team that it can and must be changed. During the diagnosis forum, the team shares this conviction with the rest of the organization, making a compelling case with their analysis. In the Improve phase (or in the Design phase, for a design project), the team develops a common vision of the new process, and leads the rest of the organization, as it presents it in a forum, together with the underlying analysis. Freeing up the team completely for a full week, and setting milestones and deadlines creates the sense of urgency. The action plan is specific and spelled out in details in Chapters 10 and 11.

The Kaizen event (and other change vehicles as well) structure and manage the forces of change locally, that is, within the learning cycle. However, to get the wheel turning, that is, to embark the organization on a learning initiative, the forces of change must be managed globally.

Comparing the development approaches used by Africa and Korea (see Box 12.2) provides interesting insights into what works and what does not, when it comes to cultural change.

Box 12.2: Comparing the Korean and African approaches

Issue: *The risk of losing touch with the masses*

African countries picked the best and the brightest among their people and sent them abroad to get higher education, to France, England, and the United States, mostly. In general, they excelled, and often obtained doctorates, in a host of different fields. Unfortunately, they grew to be different people in the process and felt that they simply would not fit anymore in their home

Continued

Continued

environment. Many of them never returned. Those who did were not understood: To local people they sounded like Martians, or worse, like colonizers. They were confined to ivory towers and could never cross the chasm that now separated them from the masses. Many chose exile. Others stayed, creating a disconnected elite that was all too often contemptuous of the masses. They were paid well, and did not contribute much. Not only did they not contribute to development, they became an impediment to it.

Korea, on the contrary, invested massively in basic education, on-the-job, technical, scientific, and engineering training. They initially brought experts and scientists from abroad to assist in the education task. In a very short period (in development terms) they produced masses of well-trained workers sharing a common language, thus setting a new standard to which every Korean youth aspired. In parallel, they created a demand for the services of these workers, promoting the creation of large conglomerates (Chaebols, such as Hyunday, Daewoo, Samsung, and LG group). Korean universities then developed their own Ph.D. programs. They now had a reception structure for the best and brightest that they sent abroad to get doctorates.

Building an elite group is risky business. Training the masses to ensure that a critical mass of people is quickly brought on board in the organization, is essential to the survival of a change initiative. This means intensive training[2] starting on day one. For instance, the president of an organization that successfully launched such an initiative decreed that 90 percent of employees, all levels included, would go through a five-day project-based training. Half-hearted measures will not allow the program to take off. When you need technical experts, hire consultants, just like the Koreans brought professors from abroad. Just like them however, do not use them to *catch fish for you*, but rather to *teach you how to fish*. Make sure that their incentives (fees) are well aligned to this task.

While a good business case, communication, and planning may convince people to give the initiative a chance, quick demonstrations of its effectiveness are required to keep them mobilized. Fortunately, this is no feat: This book provides you with all you need to create quick-win situations. These successes, best achieved through improvement Kaizen events, afford the organization time to address the areas where a more profound change and a long-term investment is required, such as horizontal management and strategy to process connection.

12.5 USING THE PROCESS APPROACH TO IMPROVE SINGLE-PERSON PROFESSIONAL PROCESSES

As illustrated in Box 12.3, the process approach can be useful at a personal level as well, if you are so inclined. It is only a matter of reaching a threshold of dissatisfaction, understanding and buying into the vision of the process approach presented in this book, having the discipline to create for yourself a sense of urgency, and following the instructions presented in this book. Of course, you do not have to be as formal in terms of presentation standards, since you do not have anyone to convince but yourself (unless you select a family process), but rigor is just as important.

Personal attitudes toward change vary considerably. Some people resist change to the bitter end. Others, a minority, embrace it and find it fun and stimulating. If you study your own attitude toward change (Spencer Johnson's *Who moved my cheese* (1998) is an easy read and can be very useful in that regard), you will see that it too can change, making many things easier, and life in general more fun.

Box 12.3: Managing my ideas, working out . . . and a great cup of coffee!

Issue: *Benefits of a process approach, at a professional and personal level*

Following the events narrated in Box 1.2, I decided to act at a personal level congruent with my professional beliefs. Since picking a good movie to watch is not my most important goal in life, I decided to pick processes that were more important to me personally. I picked two *strategic* personal processes that badly needed change: *work out* and *manage my ideas*. I felt that I stood to benefit hugely from any improvement I could make to either process. I also picked a tactical process that had been an ongoing source of irritation: *drinking caffeinated beverages*.

While the three projects were challenging in many ways, managing my ideas turned out to be the most difficult (see Table 12.2). Following up on a great idea is very seldom urgent, and it competes with a host of *urgent* matters that require immediate attention. The FAST diagram identified three functionalities: capture my ideas, prioritize them, and follow-up implementation. The process I first designed succeeded in the first, but failed miserably in the latter two. It involved capturing ideas on sticky notes and pasting them on a steno pad that occupied one of the corners of my desk. The yellow notes became almost white through months (if not years) of exposure to the sun . . . The breakthrough came when I succeeded in building a database to classify the ideas, established a clean desk policy (clean my desk every night before I leave), and used automated reminders.

I find that working out brings me all kinds of benefits, from relaxation to good health. Again, working out is never urgent, while one more hour of work gets more *urgent* things done. Besides the challenges involved in creating the time for it in my agenda, maximizing the benefits and minimizing the risks of injuries requires much thinking. Jogging was the mainstay of the process for many years. It is flexible, feels great, and provides great cardiovascular benefits. At some point however, new research data brought out the risks for the knees. As John Maynard Keynes once said: "When the facts change, I change my mind." I gradually moved to cross-training, including triathlon. As my family and work environment evolved over the years, I had to adjust the process, which now includes biking and speed walking. Writing down my training time on the calendar, however, has stayed on over the years as the key metric, though I added a heartbeat monitor when the technology became reliable, convenient, and affordable.

Caffeine is a drug, albeit a mild one. However, it is addictive, more so for some people than for others. I love coffee for its taste and for the immediate energy burst it provides. I hate it when the effect fades away after a while. My wife hates it when I come home without any energy left. I hate it when I cannot fall asleep because of it. Therefore, I decided that for me, it was an important process. I tried to drink fewer cups of coffee, smaller cups of coffee, weaker coffee . . . but I could not bring the process under control, and found the energy I had to put into it was excessive. I eventually decided that the process did not have any potential and I designed a new one. It involves drinking very weak green tea from a thermos when I am working. It initially required raw discipline. My energy level remains constant throughout the day. Research tells me that this has health benefits as well. Green tea is an acquired taste. I now love it. I have coffee during weekends, with friends and family. It still beats green tea any day!

Sometimes I slip (see the defect rates in Table 12.2). As I am finishing this book (an idea that originated on a yellow sticky note), with my green tea thermos lying just about empty on my desk, I have skipped the last two automated reminders to follow up on my ideas. I do feel a little guilty about it ... nothing that a nice ride on my mountain bike cannot cure, however.

Table 12.2 Three examples of personal process improvement: Processes, metrics, standards, CTPs, and case history.

Big Y	Process	Small y	Major interface	Standard	CTPs	Before	Current history	Process
Number of great ideas never implemented	Manage my ideas	Percentage of progression on best ideas	Manage my time	Monthly-Progress rated on all ideas. Progress made on at least five ideas	Always have a sticky note around. Enter in Excel sheet within 24 hours	Many	25 percent failure rate	This took a long time and several waves of improvement. Designing the database and the prioritizing scheme was the challenge.
Major wellness indicators (injuries, weight, blood pressure, cholesterol,...)	Work out	Calendar	Manage my time	Weekly-7 hours 6 hours minimum	Crosstrain and always have a variety of training options available.	1 to 2 hours a week	5 percent failure rate	The process is regularly reviewed as new research changes best practices and my personal environment evolves.
Number of energy drops	Consume caffeinated beverages	mg caffeine absorbed	Work	Daily 60 mg of caffeine	Always have something hot to drink when I work.	600 mg	1 percent failure rate	I tried to improve my coffee-drinking process. I found it did not have potential. I designed a new process based on very weak green tea.

Single person (Section 3.2.1) professional processes present great opportunities as well. Some processes can be scoped in such a way that they lie essentially under the control of the professional, for example:

- Lawyer: making a summation

- Doctor: examining a patient

- Pharmacist: verifying content-container

- Engineer: Elaborating a concept

- Real estate agent: Closing a contract

- Social worker: Conducting an on-site interview with a family

The methodologies and tools can be used to make these processes evolve over time and integrate the evolving know-how of the professional. Groups of professionals can use them as well to share best practices, harmonize their practices, and learn together.

*****

Management is not a science, it is an art. It is the art of leading emotional human beings, with limited rationality, in working together toward the achievement of organizational goals. The concepts, methodologies, and tools of this book show how rigor in general, and the scientific method in particular, can assist the manager in this task, by continually improving the way people work together, thus creating more value for all stakeholders.

12.6 SUMMARY

There are many dimensions to the learning organization, ranging from management style to rigor, flow of information, and methodologies. There is no one path to becoming a learning organization. The organization must first assess where it is, and then chart its own course. A fifteen-point assessment grid is provided that will help the company in identifying the bottlenecks that impede its progression and see what it needs to do next. Some existing programs, such as ISO-9000 and the balanced scorecards, can be useful if used in a timely and judicious manner. Ignoring your organization's culture and blind adoption of *the best program* has more to do with forgetting than with learning. It is important to manage the positive forces of change at every level of the organization. The process approach can be useful at a professional and even a personal level.

EXERCISES

12.1 Drawing lessons from past initiatives

At a session of your executive committee or management group, list all the major operational initiatives dealing with quality, productivity, or performance launched in your organization during the last five years.

- a) For each initiative,

  1. Paste three blank flip chart pages on the wall, labeling them: Successes, Failures, and Lessons.

2. Ask each member of the group to write on sticky notes which aspects of the initiative were successes, which aspect were failures, and what lessons can be drawn from that. This should be conducted in silence.

3. Paste all sticky notes on the appropriate page.

4. Debate and reach consensus.

5. Were the lessons of each initiative learned and used to plan and manage the next one?

b) Paste three blank flip chart pages on the wall, labeling them: Strengths, Weaknesses, Needs. Using the same procedure as above, analyze the lessons derived from each initiative (and from your answer to Exercise 12.1a.5) and conclude the strengths and weaknesses of your organizational culture. Avoid superficialities, and reach deep for shared values and beliefs. Under needs, specify what changes are needed to make the organization learn better.

12.2 Establishing your organization's learning maturity

With the same group of people as above, discuss the 15 dimensions of Figure 12.2. Reproduce the figure on a flip chart, leaving the body of the table blank.

a) Hand out a copy of Figure 12.2 to each member of the group. Ask them to rate (silently) the organization on each dimension. Initially, you can use the five-point scales as if they were a continuous scale from zero to five.

b) When everyone is done (not before!) have each member mark the evaluation on the flip chart in such a way that every persons' evaluation is recognizable. You can achieve this with X's of different colors, colored dots, small sticky notes, or any other technique.

c) Debate the differences. Ask the two members with the minimum and maximum values to explain the reasons behind their assessment. Try to come to a consensus. Do not force consensus or cut the debate short. This is an important discussion. If major differences remain, decide on a course of action to dig deeper into the issue and resolve it.

12.3 Plot a course

Again with the same group of people as above, analyze the result of the two preceding exercises: organizational needs and maturity level.

a) Identify bottleneck issues and prioritize them.

b) Explore ongoing and planned initiatives: Will they, or can they be made to, contribute to the resolution of bottleneck issues?

c) Review the strategic plan of the organization and decide on the course of action to take.

12.4 Single-person professional processes

a) Identify the single-person professional processes that are in need of improvement and prioritize them.

b) Organize an improvement Kaizen event around the most important of these processes. Choose the path of least resistance: Ask for volunteers and set as ground rule that the process that will be designed will not be imposed on anyone, but rather be used by those willing to join a *learning community*. Let that community pick a process owner, whose major role will be to *own* the design, perform benchmarking, monitor results, facilitate the sharing of best-practices and lessons learned, and set up future improvement initiatives as required.

Notes

[1]APQC, at www.apqc.org, is a good place to start.

[2]If you do not know where to start with training, the best place to start is the American Society for Quality at www.asq.org.

Bibliography

CHAPTER 2

Berry, L. L., A. Parasuraman, et al. 1988. The Service-Quality Puzzle. *Business Horizons* 31(5): 33-43.

Harvey, J. 1998. Service Quality: A Tutorial. *Journal of Operations Management* 16: 583-597.

Pine, B. J. and J. H. Gilmore. 1999. *The Experience Economy: Work is Theatre & Every Business a Stage.* Cambridge, MA: Harvard Business School Press.

Schneider, B. and D. E. Bowen. 1995. *Winning the Service Game.* Boston: Harvard Business School Press.

Stewart, G. Bennett. 1999. *The Quest for Value.* New York: HarperBusiness.

CHAPTER 3

Hanks, P. and T. H. Long, eds. 1981. *Collins Dictionary of the English Language.* London: Rand McNally.

Mintzberg, H. 1996. Managing Government—Governing Management. *Harvard Business Review* 74 (May-June): 75-83.

Nonaka, I. and H. Takeuchi. 1995. *The Knowledge-Creating Company.* New York: Oxford University Press.

Pall, G. A. 1999. *The Process Centered Enterprise.* Boca Raton, FL: St. Lucie Press.

CHAPTER 4

Chase, R. B. and D. A. Tansyk. 1983. The Customer Contact Model of Organization Design. *Management Science* 29(9): 1037-1050.

Huete, L. M. and A. V. Roth. 1988. The Industrialization and Span of Retail Banks' Delivery Systems. *International Journal of Operations & Production Management* 8(3): 46-66.

CHAPTER 5

Garvin, D. A. 2000. *Learning in Action.* Boston: Harvard Business School Press.

Heskett, J. L., W. E. Sasser, et al. 1997. *The Service Profit Chain.* New York: The Free Press.

CHAPTER 6

Brown, M. G., D. E. Hitchcock, et al. 1994. *Why TQM Fails and What To Do About It.* Burr Ridge, IL: Irwin.
Fisher, C. and J. T. Schutta. 2003. *Developing New Services.* Milwaukee: ASQ Quality Press.
Gardner, R. A. 2001. Resolving the Process Paradox. ASQ *Quality Progress* March 2001: pp. 51–59.
Hammer, M. 2001. Process Management and the Future of Six Sigma. *Sloan Management Review* Winter 2002: pp. 26–32.
Hayes, B. E. 1992. *Measuring Customer Satisfaction: Development and Use of Questionnaires.* Milwaukee, WI: ASQC Quality Press.
Keen, P. G. W., ed. 1997. *The Process Edge.* Boston: Harvard Business School Press.
Tenner, A. R. and I. J. DeToro. 1997. *Process Redesign: The Implementation Guide for Managers.* Reading, MA: Addison-Wesley.

CHAPTER 7

DeToro, I., T. McCabe. 1997. How To Stay Flexible and Elude Fads. ASQ *Quality Progress* March 1997: pp. 55-60.
Forrester, J. W. 1969. *Urban Dynamics.* Cambridge, MA: MIT Press.
Lynch, D. P., S. Bertolino, E. Cloutier, 2003. How to Scope DMAIC Projects. ASQ *Quality Progress* January 2003: pp. 37-41.
Senge, P. M. 1990. *The Fifth Discipline: The Art and Practice of the Learning Organization.* New York: Doubleday.

CHAPTER 8

Mitra, A. 1998. *Fundamentals of quality control and improvement.* Upper Saddle River, NJ: Prentice Hall.
Wheeler, D. J. 2000. *Understanding Variation.* Knoxvillle, TN: SPC Press.

CHAPTER 9

Brown, M. G., D. E. Hitchcock, et al. 1994. *Why TQM Fails and What To Do About It.* Burr Ridge, IL: Irwin.
Dumaine, B. 1991. The Bureaucracy Busters. *Fortune* 123(13): 36-42.
Paulk, M. C., Weber, C., Curtis, B., & M. B. Chrissis. 1995. *The Capability Maturity Model.* Reading, PA: Addison Wesley.
Spear, S. and H. K. Bowen. 1999. Decoding the DNA of the Toyota Production System. *Harvard Business Review* 77(5): 97-106.

CHAPTER 10

Chase, R. B. and D. M. Stewart. 1994. Make Your Service Fail-Safe. *Sloan Management Review* 36(Spring): 35-44.

CHAPTER 11

de Bono, E. 1985. *Six Thinking Hats*. Boston: Little, Brown, and Co.

Farzaneh, F. 2003. TQM vs BPR. ASQ *Quality Progress* 36(10): pp. 59-62.

Hammer, M. 1990. Reengineering Work: Don't Automate, Obliterate. *Harvard Business Review* 68 (July-August): pp. 104-112.

CHAPTER 12

Hammer, M. and J. Champy. 1993. *Reengineering the Corporation*. New York: Harper Business.

Johnson, S. 1998. *Who Moved My Cheese?* New York: Putnam.

Kaplan, R. S. and D. P. Norton. 1992. The Balanced Scorecard - Measures That Drive Performance. *Harvard Business Review* Jan.-Feb.: pp. 71-79.

Paulk, M. C., C. V. W. B. C., M. B. Chrissis. 1995. *The Capability Maturity Model*. Reading, PA: Addison Wesley.

Index

Define, Measure, Analyze, Improve, Control methodology. *See* DMAIC methodology
delayed effects, 203
delighter elements of service package, 147, 148–149, 150
delivery system dysfunctions, 122
delocation, xv
Delphi method, 252
Deming's wheel, 235, 328
democratic systems, 66–67
demos, 309
dependent variables, 251
derivatives, 172
Design for Six Sigma (DFSS), 230, 235, 236, 328
design methodology. *See* DCDV methodology; movie selection example
Design of Experiments (DoE), 235, 236
design table technique, 284
design tools, 235
detection poka-yokes, 276
developmental processes, 77
DFSS (Design for Six Sigma), 230, 235, 236, 328
diagnosis, 84, 235, 254, 267–270, 332. *See also specific tools* (e.g. Ishikawa diagrams, VAA)
diagrams
  affinity, 311
  c-charts, 226
  control charts, 225–226
  correlation (influence), 176, 177, 254
  Ishikawa (fishbone or cause and effect), 182, 187, 235, 254, 256, 265
  np-charts, 226
  p-charts, 226
  precedence, 263
  process flow, 56, 62–63, 88, 235
  u-charts, 226
digitization of information, 131
digitized systems, 131
dinner guest example, 71–72
disasters, communication in, 2
discipline, 14–15, 91–92
discrete variables, 250
disillusion, 243, 322, 331
disintermediation, 275
dispatch, 83–84, 85–87
distribution types, 200
DMADV (Define, Measure, Analyze, Design, Validate), 230
DMAIC (Define, Measure, Analyze, Improve, Control) methodology
  compared to DCDV, 313, 315–316
  example, 87–88, 93, 221–222, 224, 225
  overview, 230, 234–235, 241–243, 278–279
  phase 1: Define. *See* scoping projects
  phase 2: Measure, 241, 248–252, 278, 327
  phase 3: Analyze, 241, 253–254, 278. *See also* analysis tools
  phase 4: Improve, 241, 270–276, 278
  phase 5: Control, 241, 277

uses, 236, 237
documentation, 235
DoE (Design of Experiments), 235, 236
"doing the right thing right", 141
"doing the right thing wrong", 78
"doing the wrong thing right", 78
"doing things right", 78, 135, 141
double-loop learning, 329
drift, 195, 202
drilling down, 57, 63
drugstore example, 204–216

e-mail communication, 95, 100. *See also* electronic contact modes
economic value added (EVA), 47–48
Edison, Thomas, 4
effectiveness, process, 125, 163
efficiency, process, 126–127, 129, 163
elections, 1, 2, 67
electronic contact modes, 95, 96, 100
emergency communication, 2
emotions
  contact modes and, 95
  in customer-worker relationships, 92–93
  process improvement and, 264, 315. *See also* cynicism
  of professionals, 105
  of workers, 325
empathy, service, 24
employees, 42, 44–47, 260. *See also* positioning, labor market
enabling processes, 77, 78
enactments, 309
enforcement, process, 14
engagement, rules of, 264
engrained beliefs, 4
enterprise resource planning (ERPs), 235, 326
entropy, process, 135
ERPs (enterprise resource planning), 235, 326
errors, human, 70, 260
ethics, 27, 28, 123
EVA (economic value added), 47–48
ex-ante value, 31, 36–39
ex-post value, 31
examples
  accounting firm, 174, 177–178, 180–182, 185, 188
  African/Korean education, 333–334
  BMI, 110–112, 113, 114, 117, 122
  cafeterias, 128–129, 130
  caffeine, 335–336
  campus room control, 325
  consultant feedback, 4–5
  cooking, 3–4
  dinner guest, 71–72
  drugstore, 204–216
  exercise, 335–336
  FPA, 103–104, 144–147, 149–153, 155–162, 164–167, 282–309
  idea management, 335–336

process management teams, 230, 234, 237–238
process mapping, 93, 206, 208, 210–211, 235. *See also* macro-maps
process model, APQC, 58–63, 157
process operations, 235
process owners, 75, 168
process variables, 8, 9–11, 58
processes
  automation of, 70
  changing, 131
  characteristics, 67–68, 110, 125–130, 161–163
  commitment to, 93, 102–105, 108, 131. *See also* chain of commitments
  commonality of apparently unrelated, 15
  in contact, 61
  criteria for identification as, 63–65
  cycle time, 68
  defined, xiii, 55–56
  improvement of. *See* improvement, process
  inputs/outputs of, 69–70, 115, 117
  management of, 135
  problems with, 228–232
  reference systems, 66–67
  selecting for improvement. *See* processes, selecting for improvement
  types, 65–70, 77–78, 128–130, 133, 221
processes, selecting for improvement
  about, 142, 143, 167–169
  characterizing, 77–79
  quick method, 168
  step 1: review strategy, 142, 144
  step 2: establish customer needs/wants, 144–146
  step 3: define service package, 146–153
  step 4: identify key metrics, 152–157
  step 5: identify processes and evaluate impact on key metrics, 157–159
  step 6: assess strategic impact/performance, 159–161, 163–164
  step 7: select based on salience/performance, 165–167
product design methodology. *See* DCDV methodology
productivity, process, 127
professional service delivery processes. *See* PSDPs
professional service organizations (PSOs), flow in, 131
professionals
  characteristics of, xiii–xiv, xv, 45–46
  combining, 131–134
  contacts with, 102–105
  ethics of, 27, 93, 123
  finding correct, 83–84, 85–88, 123
  judgment of, 92, 212–213
  regulation of, 27
  responsibilities of, 27, 84, 88, 91, 93, 105
  support for, 92
profitability, global model of, 112
project definition sessions, 234
project owners, 232–233
projects
  defined, 67

initial, 169
overview, 15, 230, 232–233
scoping. *See* scoping projects
uses, 237
promise to clients, 23, 40, 114–115
promise to the market, 23, 40, 114–115
PSDPs (professional service delivery processes)
  APQC process model and, 85
  commitments to, 93, 102–105, 108, 131. *See also* chain of commitments
  customer contacts. *See* contact modes
  emotions and, 92–93
  evaluation of, 94
  participants in, 91–92, 102–103
  stages of, 27, 83–88, 91, 123
  vulnerabilities, 105–106
PSOs (professional service organizations), flow in, 131
Pugh design matrix, 11, 235
push-pull behavior, 70

QFD (Quality Function Deployment). *See* Houses of Quality
QKM (Quality Knowledge Management) example, 87–88, 93, 221–222, 224, 225
quality
  Houses of. *See* Houses of Quality
  service, 21, 29, 215
  technical, 23, 25, 27–29, 91
Quality Function Deployment (QFD). *See* Houses of Quality
Quality Knowledge Management (QKM) example, 87–88, 93, 221–222, 224, 225

random variations, 202
ratchet effect, 149
real estate example, 33–38, 40–41, 53, 64, 76, 96–98, 106, 113, 121–122
real estate market, 114
receptionists, roles of, 86
redeployment, resource, 15
reengineering, 141, 227
reference systems, 66–67
regulation of professional services, 27
reinforcement loops, 176
relationships
  B2B, 42, 56, 245
  B2C, 42
  customer, 235
  customer-worker, 92–93
  value and, 31
reliability, process, 127, 128, 129
remote contact modes, 95
repetitiveness, process, 67–68
requests for proposal (RFPs), 83–84, 87–88
requirements, weighted, 33, 35
resources, redeployment of, 15
responsiveness, service, 24